ANCIENT AND MEDIEVAL

A HISTORY OF THE WESTERN WORLD

A HISTORY OF

SHEPARD B. CLOUGH
Columbia University, GENERAL EDITOR

NINA G. GARSOIAN
Columbia University

DAVID L. HICKS
New York University

THE WESTERN WORLD

Ancient
and
Medieval

D. C. HEATH AND COMPANY

Boston/Englewood/San Francisco
Indianapolis/Atlanta/Dallas

LIBRARY OF CONGRESS CATALOG CARD NUMBER: 65–11699

PREFACE

This volume is part of a larger work which treats all of European history from the earliest time for which we have written records to the present. So that students may be able to obtain only that part of the text which fits their current needs, the larger work is available in three editions—a one-volume edition, *A History of the Western World;* a two-volume edition, *Ancient Times to 1715,* and *1715 to the Present;* and a three-volume edition, *Ancient and Medieval, Early Modern Times,* and *Modern Times.*

The aim of the authors of these works has been to explain the process by which our civilization came into being. In the execution of their task they have endeavored to show how social values have changed, how political institutions have developed, how relationships among people have evolved, how ways of meeting material wants have been improved, how scientific knowledge of the world has been acquired, and how religions have influenced the lives of men. To make the account of this greatest of all dramas more understandable, the story has been divided into chapters and sections which may be easily arranged into assignments to fit almost any conceivable time schedule and the varied interests of individual teachers and students.

Furthermore, these texts can be used for both beginning and advanced courses, for extensive and up-to-date bibliographies are provided, for the general reader at the ends of chapters and for the more advanced student at the end of the volume. A certain number of the works cited are in foreign languages, for the authors believe that students as they progress in the field should be encouraged to use books in languages other than English; and many are paperbacks which the student can easily acquire.

The planning has from the outset envisaged making the book economical in price to the student. Although nothing which pertains to scholarship, clarity of presentation, or teachability has been sacrificed, expensive frills have been avoided. In place of a few colored maps, there are many useful line maps, especially prepared by the cartographer, Donald G. Pitcher.

The authors who have collaborated in the writing of *A History of the Western World* are specialists in their respective fields with broad experience not only in research and writing, but also in teaching. It seems appropriate to list here all authors of the complete work even though they may not have contributed to this particular volume: Nina G. Garsoian, Associate Professor of Armenian Studies, Columbia University (Chaps. I,I–IV,3 and V,3); David L. Hicks, Associate Professor of Medieval History, New York University (Chaps. V,1–VIII,4); David J. Brandenburg, Professor of European History, The American University (Chaps. IX,1–4; X,1–3; XI,2–3; and XII,1–6); Peter Gay, Professor of European History, Columbia University (Chaps. IX,5; X,4; and XI,1); Shepard B. Clough, Professor of European History, Columbia University (The introduction, "The Nature of History"; and Chap. XI,4); Otto Pflanze, Professor of European History, University of Minnesota (Chaps. XIII,1–8; and XIV,5); Stanley G. Payne, Assistant Professor of European History, University of California, Los Angeles (Chaps. XIV,1–4; and XIV,6–XVI,3).

In any endeavor like this one, a great number of persons become involved to whom thanks for their generous help are due. To them the authors are sincerely grateful. David Hicks wishes to have mentioned particularly that the late Garrett Mattingly, a great historian and a wonderful professor, colleague, and friend, read and commented upon the chapters concerning the Renaissance. David Brandenburg wishes to thank Miriam Haskett of Hood College for having generously made available her special knowledge of seventeenth-century Europe for the chapters on the Thirty Years' War and on the rise of Russia and Prussia, to Albert Mott of American University and to Robert Shipkey for their assistance in preparing the chapter on seventeenth-century England, and to his wife Millicent H. Brandenburg, who interrupted her own career to give his prose those qualities which the reader can easily ascertain for himself. Otto Pflanze gratefully acknowledges the critical assistance of Josef L. Altholz and Theophanis G. Stavrou, his colleagues at the University of Minnesota, who read his early chapters on Great Britain, Russia, and the Middle East. Stanley G. Payne wishes to thank Hans Rogger of the University of California, Los Angeles, for his helpful commentary on the later Russian chapters, and Eugen Weber, also of the University of California, Los Angeles, who read the second half of the volume.

Personally I should like to express my gratitude for the cooperation and good will which have been shown by the authors and publisher. No one who has not been involved in an undertaking of this nature can fully appreciate the trials and tribulations which are encountered, nor realize the number of hours spent in planning, in research, and in writing. The sacrifices have been great, but they are fully compensated for if this work can make the past come alive for students.

Shepard B. Clough, *Columbia University*

CONTENTS

MAPS

By Donald Pitcher

ANCIENT AND MEDIEVAL

The Nature of History

At the beginning of every scientific investigation and, indeed, at the beginning of every attempt to increase our knowledge and understanding, it is essential to state as precisely as possible what the object of the investigation is, what steps will be taken in the process of analysis and synthesis, and what methods will be employed in furthering the undertaking. Such a statement is particularly necessary in the study of history, for this subject is used to encompass so much and so wide a variety of concepts that the uninitiated frequently become confused and then lost in its labyrinthian twists and turns.

THE STUDY OF HISTORY

In essence history is the total recorded past of humankind on this earth—the totality of human experience. Inasmuch as all aspects of this great experience are not of equal importance either to an understanding of how the world of the present got the way it is, or in comprehending how men lived in the past, or in learning how changes were made which got us from primitive society to the present complex societies, the historian has to make selections from the total record for special study. These selections, based upon the major categories of man's behavior in society, provide the historian with his orienting themes. Thus the historian endeavors to explain how man has provided for his material wants at various times in the past and how our present economic system came into being (economic history); he tries to describe how men have organized their social relationships for continuing the society, for procreation, for training the youth, and for establishing rules of conduct (social history); he makes an effort to analyze the way people in society create a government to bring together all members for collective action, to effect compliance with common rules, and to determine policies to be followed (political history); and he aspires to ascertain what the basic values of the society are—what people strive for, be it a place in the hereafter or some goal on this earth, and by what means they hope to achieve their ends, whether through the intercession of a divine being or beings or reliance on their own resources (intellectual history).

This division of man's activities through time for study provides one essential means for making sense out of the vast record of the past, but it is obvious that all mankind in all parts of the world cannot be treated at once.

Consequently, the historian selects segments of mankind for study. On the largest scale, mankind is divided into *cultures* or *civilizations,* each with distinctive ways of making a living, of organizing socially, of governing, of thinking, of creating esthetic works, and of establishing basic values. Thus historians and other social scientists recognize such cultures as the Greek, the ancient Egyptian, Western European, the Eskimo, the Chinese, and the Russian Communist. Parts of these cultures may, in turn, be set apart for study in order to get further understanding of some particular phase of life, such as the city of recent times, the philosophy of the Greeks, or the art of the Egyptians. And, by the same token, the historian may legitimately study relations among cultures or their parts and how one culture has been influenced by others. Indeed, in recent times one of the great developments in the world has been the way in which nearly every culture has attempted to take on some aspects of Western European civilization, especially the economic.

Once the historian has selected his segment of human society for study, he then has to make a decision regarding the time-span over which he intends to trace and analyze behavior. Indeed, the historian must not only select periods for study, but he must also divide his period into sections of time for purposes of clarity and effect, much as the dramatist separates his play into acts and scenes. To some extent such divisions will be determined by major changes in development, but sometimes they may be arbitrary and mere literary conveniences. Thus the student, as well as the historian himself, should never forget that changes in the stream of human experience are seldom so abrupt as represented in history books and that always some parts of former ways of doing things and formerly held values continue to be held by some members of a society when other ways and values have been adopted by a majority.

Finally, the historian needs some criterion for deciding what are the important things which he should isolate for study and which are the unimportant and the insignificant which he may ignore. Obviously the Battle of Waterloo was more important in the Napoleonic period than the head cold of Josephine in 1799; the invention of the steam engine was more important than the curling iron; and World War II was more important than the Spanish-American War. To handle this problem of what is important the historian should, although he not always does, select for study those things and those men who have affected *most* men *most* profoundly for the *most* time. He should observe the rule of the *three mosts*—he should eschew the ephemeral.

THE CHARACTER OF EUROPEAN CULTURE

In the economic phase of man's activity, Western Europe developed a system of production based upon the use of composite mechanisms which stretch all the way from the fulcrum and lever and the bow and arrow down to the most complex computing machines and giant metal presses of the present, and based also upon intricate processes that reach from fire to, let us say, the catalytic method of refining petroleum. This system of production made increasing use of inorganic materials which were stored over millions of years in the earth's crust, and which were infinitely more abundant than organic materials produced in relatively short periods of time. Furthermore, the processes of production were moved by power or energy largely from inorganic resources and sometimes transformed by power mechanisms, like the water-wheel, the steam engine, the internal combustion engine, the electrical dynamo, and the atomic pile. Again, Western man had at his disposal power sources which had never been equalled in any culture. Then, too, man was able to conquer space by rapid means of transportation and thereby bring large quantities of materials together from very distant parts for the use of men in the West. Lastly, Western man made enormous improvements in strains of growing things and in the breeds of animals, as well as in soil fertility, so that what he grew yielded many times more per acre and per unit of human input than what his ancestors of ancient times obtained.

The great productive systems of the present depend in large part upon the ability of individuals to specialize in some aspect of economic activity—in what economists usually refer to as the division of labor. Individuals nowadays seldom endeavor to be economically self-sufficient in the sense of themselves producing everything which they may need for consumption, but they rely upon the exchange of goods and services with others. This reliance upon the market has been made possible, in part, by cheap and rapid transportation and by communication of information about goods and their supplies, and also, in part, by the institution of money, which is a medium of exchange, a measure of value, and a store of wealth. Indeed, money is one of the most important inventions of man, ranking with fire and the wheel, because of its role in establishing a division of labor.

On the social side of European culture the great characteristic of our present day is the enormous complexity of groupings compared with the rather simple family and tribal organizations among primitive peoples. Peoples now fall into groups determined by their families, fortunes, professions, religions, political affiliations, education, and even physical characteristics. Human relations are regulated in large part by the standards set by the groups to which people belong and relations become anarchic when individuals are torn from their groups by some disturbance like war. Nevertheless, within European culture a basic ethic persists—an ethic which comes from the Christian-Jewish tradition—based upon the Golden Rule of doing unto others as you would have others do unto you, and upon the Ten Commandments. In time this ethic became written into law codes and the laws came to be more nearly the same for all groups in society. In the past, the family was a central institution for regulating procreation, for educating the youth in the fundamentals of the culture, and in caring for the aged and the infirm. More recently, as the task of training has come to be more technical and as relations among men have become more impersonal, because of the division of labor, the schools have taken on more of the training task and state organizations have assumed many of the responsibilities for the aged and the infirm (the welfare state).

Other important characteristics of present-day social existence pertain primarily to the increase in population, the lengthening life span of man, and to ever greater concentrations of population in cities and their suburbs. In the last three and a half centuries the population of Europe has grown sevenfold, which has been made possible, in part, by access to the resources of overseas areas. The average length of life of individuals, technically called "expectation of life at birth," has gone up from the 25 or 30 years, that it was from Roman times to the middle of the eighteenth century, to nearly 70 years in the majority of European countries. This has meant that more people can make use of technical training over long periods, and put that training to greater use, but it also means that a larger percentage of the population lives beyond the productive ages and becomes dependent upon society.

Today in the more economically advanced countries of Europe, some 65 per cent of the population lives in cities of 2,500 or over, whereas at the end of the eighteenth century only some 15 per cent of the population lived in such agglomerations. This means that the lives of more and more people are regulated by city customs and values. Among such values are a desire for higher standards of living, which has led to the curtailment of size of families, a demand for more man-made works of art and spectator entertainment, and a drive for more popular participation in the affairs of government.

In the political realm of human activity, the trend in European history has been toward the establishment of larger states, to endow these states with a sovereignty that implied no other power existed over them, to extend their functions until they invaded every phase of life, and to have these states coterminous with "nationalities," or subcultures of Western culture, to which individuals came to attach great emotional loyalties. Many of the traditional histories of Europe have, indeed, concentrated their attention primarily on these issues and upon relations among states, which is an indication of how important they loom in the public life of European peoples. In the present work emphasis will be placed upon them, but always with the end in view of making clear the long and arduous process by which our present-day political system came into being. Furthermore, an effort will be made to show what social groupings controlled political organizations, which ones wanted change, and how those in power used the machinery of the state for advancing the policies which they favored. Lastly, considerable attention will be given to the tensions which arose among states in the process of state-building and to the strife which developed among national states—a strife that in the twentieth century seriously threatened the very continuation of European culture and which greatly lessened the position of Europe in the world.

In intellectual life the outstanding achievement of Western culture has been the development of science, for it has permitted man to extend his control so dramatically over the physical universe. The basic principle of scientific thought has been the ascertainment of the various factors, including their quality and their magnitudes, and the manner and timing in which they came together, which were necessary to produce event "x" and which invariably did produce event "x". The more accurate and precise the data resulting from the application of this principle were and the more thoroughly the explanation for event "x" could be established through repetitive experimentation or observed experience, the more "scientific" the knowledge was considered to be.

Even though in some fields of activity, as in the social sciences, it is recognized that the investigator cannot control all the forces at work, is largely an observer, and cannot know even all of the factors involved, as for example the functioning of Napoleon's endocrine glands during the Battle of Waterloo or what Brutus had for breakfast before he turned sourly against Julius Caesar, the theory of knowledge employed in the name of science in all fields is essentially the same. How this epistemology, or theory of knowledge, came into being over millennia of time will be a recurring theme in the pages ahead. So, too, will be the uses to which scientific knowledge has been put in conquering the physical world. It has made possible the practical elimination of famine; it has freed man from many of the scourges of pestilence and disease; and it has given him so much confidence in himself and his methods that he believes he can accomplish almost any physical task which he may set for himself. Western man has from this confidence developed a firm conviction in "progress" toward a more ample fulfillment of his goals. This confidence has, in turn, led to a great optimism regarding the future, albeit that this optimism is mitigated from time to time by man's realization that he has not been able yet to control relations among men according to the culture's values.

On the esthetic side of man's life the West has tended to glorify the arts. By his oft-repeated use of the expression—"the finer things of life"—Western man indicates how high he esteems works of art. Moreover, in spite of the fact that he places the appreciation of esthetic productions high in his scale of values, he rates creativity in the arts above passive enjoyment. In fact, he invariably places the activist above the passivist in all efforts in conformity with the culture's values.

About the respective merits of the various arts and of the multitudes of artistic styles Western men differ very widely. Esthetic judgment seems to be a highly individualistic thing and esthetes have been at a loss to establish an objective measure for determining excellence. This is embarrassing for the historian who has to rely so heavily upon specialists for forming his own conclusions. He knows, to be sure, that men learned in the arts do set standards which establish some criteria for judging craftsmanship and accomplishment. In the final analysis he is forced to acknowledge that he must accept as esthetically great what most competent judges have most consistently and most universally considered great.

Finally, students of history should have before them one other major consideration—that is, a general conception of the goals of our culture, for it is in terms of these goals that judgments about various historical trends or events are made; and contrary to what is often contended, historians are forever making judgments, and in the opinion of many quite properly so. Be that as it may, however, the values which the West attaches to achievements in various categories of human existence constitute our present-day conception of levels of civilization. These levels are determined, so far as those in Western European culture are concerned, by the degree to which men establish control over their physical universe, are able to regulate human relations among all mankind according to the Golden Rule, and succeed in producing generally recognized masterpieces in architecture, painting, literature, sculpture, music, philosophy, and science. The more a people realizes both qualitatively and quantitatively these tenets of civilization without exception, the more civilized it is. And conversely, the less it realizes them, the less civilized it is.

SOME PROBLEMS IN HISTORICAL STUDY:
EVIDENCE, CAUSATION, AND CHANGE

The historian, much like the lawyer, proceeds to describe human behavior through time by collecting evidence. Sometimes this evidence is scanty, as in the case of population statistics when no censuses were taken. In such instances, the historian has to rely upon subsidiary data like baptismal and death records, or he has to infer size by the walls of cities, the height of buildings, and the number of persons using dwelling units. At other times, evidence may be overwhelming, as for example, the records of World War II. In such cases, selection and condensation are necessary and the historian has to guard against falsifying the story by choosing what is most representative and what is the most relevant to the immediate issue he is investigating.

Both in the amassing of evidence, as well as in the selection of segments of history for study, in the subsequent analysis of why events took place, and in passing judgment as to the desirability of certain behavior, the historian is confronted with the danger of being influenced by his personal likes and dislikes, or his own subjective set of values. The Parisian writing about the Franco-Prussian War of 1870 may produce a very different account of the war than the German; the anti-Catholic may regard the seizure of the Papal States in the nineteenth century in another manner from the members of the Vatican; and the social reformer may look upon the industrial revolution in quite another way from the economist interested in economic growth. The historian acts, like all the rest of us, on the basis of the set of values which he has acquired in his maturing, and what he writes is related to these values. This is the problem of relativity. Its dangers can be minimized by keeping judgments about the desirability of an event or of a development relevant to the values of the culture rather than to the values of the individual and by making whatever values are brought into play clearly explicit.

Once the historian has managed to keep his own prejudices and hopes from coloring his work (or makes clear what his prejudices and hopes are), and has amassed evidence regarding the character of events, he is then concerned with an explanation of how and why these events took place. Here he comes face to face with the knotty question of causation. What were the causes of the event—the war, the invention, the style of art, or the way of thought. In trying to ascertain the "causes" for any event a temptation exists to seek a simple explanation, a single cause. In fact, some historians have tried to explain all of the past on the basis of geography, or of climate, or of economic forces, or of patterns of thought, or of the action of a supernatural power. Unfortunately, monocausal explanations are *ipso facto* inadequate for explaining what is very complex.

The task of the historian is, then, to establish what are the multiple and necessary factors involved in any development or in the background of any event. This is not an easy affair, for so many and such varied kinds of forces come into play that the historian has to exercise his own judgment and has to have very broad competences. He has to know something of psychology, something of economics, and something about sociology, politics, law, art, philosophy, and the physical sciences. And in addition, he must know the languages of the area he is treating, and the techniques for measuring quantities of evidence (statistics), and he must be able to present his materials and his conclusions in effective speech or writing. His task is, indeed, formidable, but not impossible, especially if he has begun early enough in his life to acquire proper training. At all events, the historian finds immense satisfaction in trying to understand human behavior so that man may adopt those policies which will help establish more readily than would otherwise be the case the kind of a world which is in conformity with the basic values of our culture. And there is a great sense of achievement in attempting to provide a synthesis of various aspects of human activity which go to explain the world in which we live.

In the process of attempting to explain how humans have developed the kind of cultures which exist today or have existed at various times in the past, the historian inevitably becomes involved in the phenomena of *change*. This is a subject of such great importance in historical study that a few words about it here may prove useful to the student, for the historian, *perforce,* is primarily concerned with periods of change rather than with periods in which things remain static.

Change is always the result of something new being introduced into a given situation—a platitude which has been raised to what might seem to some a great height of erudition by an elaborate theory of innovation. Contrary to what many observers have said, change may come from any one of the aspects of human existence. It may be initiated by an increase in population, or, for that matter, by a decrease. It may come about from the invention of a new machine, like the steam engine. It may be started by a new pattern of thought, like that of science or Christianity. It may get its original impetus from the appearance of a great leader, like Alexander the Great or Napoleon. It may begin with an alteration in climate, like a long period of drought or flood. Or it may result from a change in the alignment of groups in society and a consequent shift in the locus of power, as in the French Revolution. It may come from within a society (autonomous change), or it may come from without the society (adaptive change). In any case, change is always impending, if for no other reason than the actors on the stage of life are always being renewed. The more gradual change is, the more easily societies seem to be able to adjust to it.

The facility with which change is effected in any society depends in large part upon the range of opportunities for alternative decisions open to the members of the society in question. The greater the range, the more extensive change may be; and the less the range, the less the change which is to be expected.

The extent of the range of opportunities for alternative decisions will depend in turn upon the degree of rigidity in the case under analysis. If a society's culture, institutions, groups, ideologies, and leadership are rigidly fixed in traditional patterns, change will occur more slowly and with greater travail than in a society characterized by flexibility in values and institutions and by mobility of people up and down the social scale.

Rigidity will depend to a considerable degree on the extent to which a proposed change affects favorably the status of those segments of society which possess influence, authority, and power. This proposition represents a drastic modification of the traditional belief that underprivileged classes are the breeding ground of change. It seems clear that the upper groups of society are responsible for a large measure of change, especially that which does not at once threaten their positions, for they have the means of initiating new undertakings and their positions of power give them some immunity from social sanctions when breaking with tradition.

Secondly, rigidity will depend on the extent to which there is a fear of change in society and conversely will be weakened when *progress,* which implies change, is glorified. Thirdly, rigidity is increased if a society has little surplus energy or resources for experimentation—if it lives from hand to mouth and can run no risks. And fourthly, rigidities in society depend in part on physical environment and in part on the biological characteristics of members of the group. Thus change in desert cultures has been less than in the rich valleys of navigable rivers; and it has been less among bodily weak and inactive peoples, like the Pygmies, than among the physically strong and active, like the Western Europeans.

Finally, attention should be drawn to the fact that change will vary in rate, size, and direction according to the nature of the innovation, to the nature of the environment in which it is introduced, and to the leadership that is given it. It will almost certainly affect some phase of life more rapidly than others, so that some phases will seem to be *leading* in the process of change while others will be *lagging.* Among those who favor change criticism will be directed toward the *lags;* and among the reactionaries who oppose change, criticism will be directed toward the *leads.* Rate of change will depend in large part upon the urgency which the society feels the need for what is new and upon its ability to adopt it. And the magnitude and direction of change will likewise be determined primarily by social need, awareness of that need, and ability to do something about it.

In the vast panorama of the past, change as effected by men is of fundamental importance. Only by understanding it in relation to goals toward which society should strive can men form public and private policies which will give us more nearly the kind of a world we want. The study of the past has a very practical side—it is at the bottom of most human decisions, whether it be the purchase of an automobile or the defense of one's religious beliefs. From this it should follow that the better the understanding of the past, the better will be everyday decisions.

FURTHER READING

A great many introductions to the study of history exist for the use of students. See especially Homer C. Hockett, *The Critical Method in Historical Research and Writing* (1955); Jacques Barzun and Henry F. Graff, *The Modern Researcher* (1957); and Marc Bloch, *The Historian's Craft* (1953).

The study of history involves a number of philosophical problems, particularly those having to do with a theory of knowledge (epistemology), the selection of issues for study, the choosing of data relevant to these issues, and the personal preferences and prejudices of the historian. These matters are discussed in W. H. Walsh, *An Introduction to Philosophy of History* (1951); by Herbert Butterfield, *Man on His Past. The Study of the History of Historical Scholarship* (1955); Pieter Geyl, *Use and Abuse of History* (1955); and Ernst Cassirer, *The Problem of Knowledge: Philosophy, Science, and History since Hegel* (1950). Excerpts from many of the recent writers on the philosophy of history are to be found in Hans Meyerhoff, *The Philosophy of History of Our Time* (1959).

For an understanding of the philosophy of history represented in the present work, see *Theory and Practice in Historical Study,* Bulletin 54 of the Social Science Research Council (1946) and *The Social Sciences in Historical Study,* Bulletin 64 of the Social Science Research Council (1954).

Various historians of the relatively recent past, their methods, and their points of view have been discussed by G. P. Gooch, *History and Historians of the Nineteenth Century* (1913), and Bernadotte Schmitt, *Some Historians of Modern Europe* (1942). Different interpretations of certain periods and different types of history are found in collections of passages from well-known historians. Shepard B. Clough, Peter Gay, and Charles K. Warner, *The European Past,* 2 vols. (1964); Fritz Stern, *The Varieties of History* (1956); and in the series, *Problems in European Civilization,* edited by Ralph W. Greenlaw and Dwight E. Lee.

Every student of history should have a good English dictionary and an encyclopedia, at least of desk size, *The Columbia Encyclopedia* (3rd edition, 1963), or *Le Petit Larousse.* He should also have a guide to names, dates, and events, such as William L. Langer, ed., *An Encyclopedia of World History* (1962); and an historical atlas, such as William R. Shepherd, *Historical Atlas* (1956), or Edward W. Fox, *Atlas of European History* (1957).

I

THE BEGINNING OF
CIVILIZATION

1. The Appearance of Civilization

2. The Creation of Empires

3. The Small Nations and the Mediterranean Empire

The earliest appearance of civilization has not yet been determined by scholars, and it is only in recent years that the historian and particularly the archaeologist has gradually worked his way back of the limit imposed by the existence of written documents into the prehistoric world. But with each generation our knowledge of the era preceding the invention of writing has become more precise.

It is now recognized that the prehistoric period, stretching for millennia across the great ice ages and including within itself the major portion of man's experience on earth, was in no sense a negligible stretch of unrelieved savagery. Prehistory can be divided into identifiable periods which mark the enormous changes through which mankind progressed from the level of the nearly animal to the very threshold of history as we now understand it. The last of these transformations or revolutions, the creation of cities and the invention of writing, took place almost simultaneously some five thousand years ago in several river valleys of which the most important for the later development of western civilization were found in the Near East.

Within a millennium of the discovery of writing, a number of centers in the area of the eastern Mediterranean basin developed cultures of a remarkably high level not only from the point of view of political and economic achievements but also in the sphere of intellectual, artistic, and ethical advances. Many of the problems of a sophisticated society had already been raised and had received tentative solutions, and the foundations of an international society had been laid.

1 · The Appearance of Civilization

The first and most obvious problem facing the student of history is where to begin. Even the most perfunctory answer to this question requires some distinction between what history is and what it is not: we must ask what the subject of history is and by what means it is studied.

In the preceding introduction, history was defined as "the totality of human experience" on earth. This statement may seem all-inclusive at first, but closer investigation shows that it limits drastically the possible subjects of historical study. Even though the earth has been spinning in the universe some billion years, human creatures appeared on it, at most, a million years ago. Hence, more than 90 per cent of the existence of the earth is filled with natural phenomena and not human experience. The alterations of the face of the globe, the creation of the continents and the drying of seas, the successive ice ages, and the appearance of life itself lie within the realm of the natural scientist rather than that of the historian.

BEFORE THE BEGINNING OF HISTORY

From our definition, history should then begin with the appearance of man on earth; and indeed, were we able to determine this event, our problem should largely be solved. At the present stage of knowledge, however, although the bones of man-like creatures clearly differentiated from apes have been discovered in all parts of the world, and more continue to appear, nothing distinguishes them as the bones of the earliest man. On the contrary, the oldest known human bones have been found together with objects which may be crude tools and in circumstances which show a knowledge of the use of fire. So these primitive creatures were already in some degree masters of their environment and of rudimentary skills. Still more significantly, a study of early skulls shows that these creatures were capable of speech. Since speech cannot exist in absolute solitude, and words are the arbitrary and conventional association of certain sounds with certain objects or actions in a given social group, the earliest known "men" already lived in some sort of organized groups whose existence implies an earlier and still more primitive stage of which we have no knowledge as yet. Because of our ignorance, the appearance of man cannot serve as the point at which history is said to begin.

The English historian V. Gordon Childe begins his book, *What Happened in History,* by saying that "written history . . . is at best one hundredth part of the time during which men have been active on our planet." This statement gives both a new limitation to the field of history and a criterion for identifying history when it is finally met. The crucial event by which scholars have traditionally divided history from the period known as prehistory or protohistory is the appearance of written records. Such a division naturally does not imply that we have no knowledge of the human experience before the invention of writing, but rather that our knowledge is obtained by different means and is of a different type from true historical knowledge. It is the result of the study of archaeology rather than that of history.

ARCHAEOLOGY AND HISTORY

Archaeology is still a relatively young science, not much more than a century old, but it has already increased enormously our knowledge of the most distant activities of mankind and is constantly adding new information. Although archaeology and history touch and assist each other, their subjects, methods, and capacities are not identical. To the world of archaeology belong all the non-written records left by a group or community. For its earliest period, the surviving record is scarce, scattered, and consequently difficult to understand, but when men begin to settle into communities, as we shall see, the record rapidly grows more complete. By studying carefully the types of objects found on a particular spot, the changes in these objects and their relations to each other, the archaeologist is able to reconstruct much of the life of the community which once lived on that site.

Sometimes twenty or more different communities settled one after the other in a given place, each building on top of the remains left by its predecessors, so that the site gradually took on the appearance of an artificial hill. An archaeologist working his way down through the various levels is able to tell not only the sequence in which the successive communities followed each other, but also the specific characteristics of each one. The widening of the walls surrounding a settlement points to an increase of population and presumably, therefore, to political or economic prosperity. A layer of ash between two levels suggests destruction, whether conquest and destruction by foreign enemies or internal revolution. A layer of sand or mud above an inhabited level indicates a natural disaster such as a flood or the abandonment of the site by its inhabitants. Archaeological finds may even give considerable information about relations between communities. Identical objects found in several sites may indicate either contact between them or similar civilizations. In some early sites of the Near East amber beads have been discovered, but amber is not indigenous to the neighborhood and can only have been brought from the region of the Baltic Sea. So, incredible as it might seem, some contact between Northern Europe and the Near East must have existed in extreme antiquity. Many of the details of daily life can also be reconstructed through archaeological investigations: the type of houses built, the clothes, jewels, and weapons used, the breeds of animals domesticated, the kinds of food eaten, the crafts practiced—even the gods worshipped and the organization of the community with its richer and poorer inhabitants.

Because of the number of questions it is able to answer, archaeology is indispensable as a tool not only in the prehistorical period but also in early historical times and whenever written documents are either scarce or absent. But it must always be remembered that there are questions which archaeology cannot answer. For example, a layer of burned buildings and ashes covered by a layer of empty earth can suggest to the investigator that the site was sacked and abandoned, but it cannot tell him the reasons for the attack or the abandonment. Were all the inhabitants killed; were they led away into captivity; did they leave of their own accord to seek a better location? Another major problem to which archaeology can give only a partial answer is that of chronology. The archaeologist is able to give a relative date; that is, he can determine whether a given stage in a civilization occurred before or after another. But, despite great recent advances in various scientific methods for dating objects by an analysis of their chemical or radioactive content, precise dating is still very difficult without additional knowledge. Archaeological dates remain approximative and subject to continual revision. Finally, specific details of political events and institutions or of religious and intellectual beliefs cannot be obtained from archaeology. For all such questions the answer must be sought in written documents containing information on beliefs, motives, intentions, and aspirations; information absent from archaeological records. It is only with the appearance of written documents, therefore, that we can hope for a knowledge of all the aspects of the human experience needed for its study. Only with them do we reach the level of history.

The Prehistoric Period

Our knowledge of the prehistoric world must be based entirely on archaeological evidence; it grows progressively dimmer as we move back from the threshold of history and as evidence becomes scarcer. But new discoveries continually add information and change our concept of this period which includes more than 90 per cent of man's existence. Prehistory has roughly been subdivided into three great periods of unequal length. These are the Paleolithic or Old Stone Age, stretching to about 10,000 years before the birth of Christ; the Neolithic, or New Stone Age; and the Age of Metals, beginning about 5,000 years ago. These divisions indicate stages of culture rather than chronological periods, for a few Neolithic societies still survive in the modern world. The passage from one stage to another was accompanied by major revolutions which totally altered man's life, the so-called Neolithic Revolution and subsequently the Urban Revolution.

The Paleolithic period includes the earliest semihuman creatures, such as the Java, Peking, and Heidelberg men; the later and more sophisticated Neanderthal man who lived in the late glacial period; and finally the Cro-Magnon man, homo sapiens, or man in the full sense of the word, who appears suddenly and already differentiated into separate groups some 25,000 to 40,000 years ago. To be sure, considerable differences separate the ape-like early creatures from the Cro-Magnon man, but two important similarities associate all of them: 1. The tools used by these creatures were made of stone ranging from crude, barely recognizable flints to quite sophisticated tools such as axes, hatchets, spears, and knives. 2. All Paleolithic men lived more or less at the mercy of their environment. That is to say, despite their control of fire, they were dependent entirely on food-gathering and hunting for their subsistence. Because he had to follow game, particularly as the animals moved northward with the retreating ice of the last glacial period, and because he needed water and had no vessels for carrying it, Paleolithic man was a wanderer, taking shelter in caves.

For all of their limited capacities, Paleolithic men were not mere animals hunting for food. Evidence shows that some form of primitive group society existed among them. As early as the Neanderthal period the burying of the dead shows some concept of an afterlife. By the late Cro-Magnon period man had great skill in the handling of his stone instruments, which were even decorated with carvings. The great cave paintings of animals found at Lascaux in Southern France and Altamira in Northern Spain show such an incredibly high level, both in the observation and drawing of animals and in the use of color, that they were not accepted at first as the work of primitive men. Finally, these paintings indicate a certain intellectual development, since they were probably magic pictures intended to trap the game represented. The animals were often shown pierced by arrows to increase the luck of the hunter.

The Neolithic Revolution

About 10,000 years ago, perhaps as the result of the scarcity of big game after the ice ages, a major revolution occurred, apparently in the Near East. Neolithic man continued to use stone tools as had his predecessor, refining them to a greater degree by grinding and polishing, but his control of his environment was entirely different. Instead of being a hunter and a gatherer of food he became a producer. For the first time the seeds that men had gathered for food were planted to produce a crop. Animals were not only hunted but also tamed to provide milk, wool, and hides, as well as flesh. As a result of his new activities, Neolithic man was forced to settle down into communities instead of being a perpetual wanderer. He still moved with his flocks or as the soil he cultivated became exhausted, but he normally lived in villages built by himself. The earliest houses found belong to the Neolithic period. Other great inventions freed the Neolithic man still more from his surroundings. The discovery that clay could be molded into pots and baked allowed him to store food and carry water from a distance. Spinning and weaving of wool into clothes gave better protection from the elements.

Farmer, stockbreeder, carpenter, potter, weaver, as well as hunter, the Neolithic man naturally led a more complex life than man had in the previous period. Some of the evidence as to his life derives from archaeology, but for other information we must borrow from the science of anthropology, which studies such primitive societies as still survive in our time. As far as we know, the Neolithic village communities were self-sufficient, producing all they needed, though foreign objects found on Neolithic sites indicate the presence of some barter trade. Complicated tasks necessitated cooperation within the community. No specialists existed, though work was divided between the sexes, the man hunting, caring for the animals, and building dwellings, the woman having the special knowledge of plants, pottery, and weaving, as well as the elementary chemical knowledge needed for baking bread and making fermented beverages. The community was composed of families or clans which worked and owned the land in common, and it was headed by elders or a chieftain who ruled according to custom. Handsome tombs indicate the importance of some of these chieftains.

The spiritual life of Neolithic man also shows a great development. Numerous amulets already found testify to the extension of magic. Various idols show the presence of a fertility cult which was probably similar to later "vegetation cycles" in which the fading and renewal of the plant world was re-enacted by the killing—at first actual and then symbolical—of a victim or leader who was chosen anew the following year. The elaborateness of these religious rituals can still be seen in the immense stone circles found at Stonehenge in England or in the alleys seen at Carnac in France, which indicate a sophisticated and organized society capable of accomplishing tasks impossible for small groups, let alone scattered individuals.

The Age of Metals and the Urban Revolution

In spite of their enormous achievements, Neolithic men were still living in precarious circumstances. The need to move whenever land became exhausted by primitive agricultural methods led to conflicts with neighboring communities. Furthermore, the failure of a crop from natural or human cause could mean the total destruction of the community which had no surplus food to tide it over until a new crop could be raised. A new alteration in the pattern of life was necessary to solve these problems.

About 5,000 years ago men found that they no longer had to make their tools of stone but could use different materials which, if heated until they were soft, might then be molded into various shapes. The first of these materials were gold and copper, which are found pure in nature; but later the metal used was a combination of copper and tin, known as bronze, which became so widely used that it gave its name to an entire period. In themselves the new tools were perhaps no better than good polished stone ones, but the use of metal changed many aspects of the existing civilization. One result of metallurgy was the end of the self-sufficient village. Copper, and especially tin, are not found everywhere and trade became a necessity. From this dependence on trade, new skills had to be developed. Animals had been tamed in the Neolithic period, but now they were yoked or harnessed to drag loads. To increase the load which could be transported, new means of communication appeared. Primitive boats had been built earlier, but the use of the sail now gave a new source of power. Still more important, wagons moving on wheels and dragged by harnessed animals appeared for the first time. The discovery of the wheel, incidentally, affected another aspect of life as well, since clay thrown onto a rapidly spinning horizontal wheel could now be shaped into far more perfect vessels than was possible by hand.

The new inventions brought about a profound change in the social structure. A man cannot both till his field and travel as a merchant; mining, smelting, refining of metals, pottery making, alloying, are special and time-consuming skills. Not every member of the community had the time or capacity to acquire them, and so the Bronze Age brought about the development of specialization. Men became smiths, potters, or merchants. In exchange for the wares of the specialist, the ordinary man had to find some source of barter, and his best means was the growing of extra crops to feed the specialist who could not raise his own. With the appearance of surpluses one of the worst problems of the Neolithic age had been solved. In addition, craftsmen and traders function better in centers where their competitive skill and exchange of goods and ideas are more convenient than in scattered village communities. About 5,000 years ago, just about the time when the invention of writing brings us to the true historical period, we witness another major transformation of society; the appearance of unified centers inhabited by a complex, specialized society. This is known as the Urban Revolution.

River Civilizations

The Urban Revolution and the crossing of the boundary between prehistory and history seem to have taken place almost simultaneously in a number of places and to have followed rapidly upon the beginning of the Bronze Age. As far as we know, this significant advance seems to have been made in regions bordering on great rivers. It has been argued that the rise of these "river valley civilizations" was due in some part to the river's providing water for agriculture and a means of transportation, and at the same time requiring a cooperative effort for damming and irrigation found only in a stable and skilled community. Two of these civilizations are of particular interest to us: the cultures which develop respectively in the valley of the Nile and in the land between the Tigris and Euphrates rivers, to which the Greeks gave the name of Mesopotamia (the land between rivers). These are not the only two important ancient cultures. Equally interesting ones arose in India and China; but we will leave them aside because their relations to western civilization long remained fairly remote.

Historians have argued inconclusively as to the precedence of Mesopotamian or Egyptian civilization. The present state of research, which may be changed at any time, seems to indicate that the two cultures were almost contemporary in their development. This fact must be remembered, as we discuss them successively only for the sake of convenience.

MESOPOTAMIA

The swampy lowland region between the Tigris and the Euphrates is often divided into two regions: one to the southeast called Sumer, running down to the Persian Gulf and composed of half-drowned swamps of clay and reeds; the other to the northwest, Babylonia, which is slightly dryer. Despite

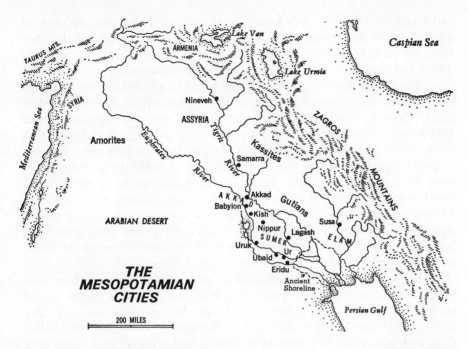

THE MESOPOTAMIAN CITIES

200 MILES

the differentiation, however, boundaries are arbitrary in this region which stretches from the Zagros mountains in the north to the desert in the south, with little protection and few natural frontiers. The main characteristic is the swamp, crossed and flooded by the two great rivers and separated by patches of dryer ground. Both of these natural factors affected the development of Mesopotamian civilization. The swamps were great reservoirs of game and the land was fertile but the flooding rivers, swollen by the snows of the northern Armenian mountains, were a constant danger which had to be controlled through dikes and irrigation canals. The construction and maintenance of these required an organized community. Although such circumstances encouraged the development of efficient and highly developed city-states, the geographical environment interfered with the unification of the land into a single unit. The individual cities were separated by miles of almost impenetrable swamps, while the absence of natural boundaries left the plain open to enemy raids from the mountains as well as the desert.

Mesopotamian Political Instability

Until a century ago, Mesopotamian civilization had been totally forgotten, and Ur of the Chaldees, the home of Abraham, was only a name in the Old Testament. Now archaeology has rediscovered an active and brilliant civilization extending beyond the beginning of history. The brilliance and continuity of the culture was not, however, attended by a similar political continuity, and rival powers succeeded each other rapidly without establishing a lasting rule. The earliest city-states appeared in Sumer about 3,000 years before the birth of Christ. In addition to Ur, the cities of Lagash, Uruk (or Warka), and a number of smaller sites have been discovered. These were the cities of a people called the Sumerians, of whom we know very little except that they seem not to have been natives of Mesopotamia but to have come into the Tigris and Euphrates plain, probably from the mountains.

Despite the similarity of the culture found in all of them, the Sumerian cities did not form a single political unit, but remained separate independent states. About the twenty-fifth century B.C., they fell to conquerors coming from Babylonia and particularly from its great city of Akkad, which gave them the name of Akkadians. These conquerors also seem to have been outsiders to the Mesopotamian valley, but their home was probably the southern desert since the language they spoke was a Semitic dialect similar to those of the desert nomads. Rather than destroying Sumerian culture, the Akkadians adopted and continued it, but they tried at the same time to create a unified state stretching from the Persian Gulf to northern Babylonia. Their great king, Sargon I (ca. 2400 B.C.), styled himself "ruler of the four quarters of the earth" and may be considered the world's first empire builder.

In spite of his efforts and those of his grandson Naram Sin, whose commemorative victory relief has come down to us, the Akkadian empire proved no more secure than the Sumerian city-state. Within three centuries after Sargon, his empire had been destroyed by the invasion of mountaineers called Guti, of whom practically nothing is known, and replaced once more by a series of city-states ruled by governors, or *patesi*. Ur temporarily recovered its dominant position, and Lagash flourished briefly under its great governor Gudea who has left us an admirable series of sculptures of himself and his court. Still, political continuity was not the fate of Mesopotamia, and the independent cities fell almost at once to new Semitic conquerors, the Amorites. By the beginning of the seventeenth century B.C. the Amorites under their great king Hammurabi (ca. 1680 B.C.) were established in Babylon and were extending their rule over all of Mesopotamia.

The Prosperity of the City-States

Political unity was the exception rather than the rule in the Mesopotamian valley, but this does not mean that this region was totally lacking in ordered government. Each one of the Sumerian city-states had its ruler and contained a highly organized society formed of numerous classes: farmers, artisans, merchants, soldiers, and priests. The wealth of these cities seems to have been very great even by our own standards. Mesopotamian buildings have disappeared in great part because in the absence of stone, which does not exist in the valley, they were built of clay and brick that did not survive the dampness of the climate. Excavations have shown, however, that the earliest builders were sufficiently good architects to design such complicated forms as the first arches and vaults. More impressive evidence of wealth comes from the earliest tombs of Ur, which have yielded enormous quantities of gold objects: necklaces, headdresses, earrings, and carved helmets, as well as musical instruments such as harps with gold animal heads inlaid with lapis lazuli, cornelian, and white shells. The active life existing in the city-states is also confirmed by another source of information. Innumerable small cylindrical seals made of stone and adorned with a low ornamental relief often composed of human and fantastic animal figures have been found. In spite of their remarkable artistic qualities, these seals were not mere jewels but had a highly utilitarian purpose. Most citizens possessed such seals to be used as a signature in all business affairs. The seal with its unique design was rolled on soft tablets of clay, leaving its particular imprint. The tablets were then baked to harden them, and one of them was kept in the temple as evidence of the contract or transaction which had taken place. Thousands of such tablets have already come to light in temple archives and new ones are appearing continually. To aid business activities, the Mesopotamians also developed a system of weights and measures, particularly for silver, the weight of which served as a unit of barter in the absence of any real currency.

Religious Life

The activity and brilliance of the Sumerian cities must not blind us to the fact that the dominant force in life was religious and not secular. Each city was thought to be the property of a god in whose name it was ruled, and the king and governor of the city officially called himself only "the tenant farmer of the god." Even as late as the Amorite dynasty in Babylon, the great Hammurabi is represented on a stele receiving laws directly from the sun god and placing his hand before his face to shade his mortal eyes from the blinding glory of the divine presence. Great temple estates were administered by priestly communities and every Mesopotamian city was dominated by its temple raised on a high, stepped platform called *ziggurat,* to bring it closer to the god to whom it was dedicated. It has been argued by certain scholars that these ziggurats, some of which show signs of having been planted with trees, intended to simulate the wooded mountains characteristic of the Sumerians' native home, though not of the Mesopotamian lowlands; others believe that they were utilitarian platforms needed to raise the temple above the recurring danger of flood. In any case, the ziggurat was such a dominant and striking part of every city that the great ziggurat of Babylon (the Tower of Babel) was later considered by foreigners as an attempt to reach up to heaven itself.

The Sumerians worshipped many gods, among whom the heavenly bodies such as the sun, moon, and stars were particularly revered. Much of this worship was based on magic formulas and incantations, but it simultaneously led to great intellectual advance, particularly in the field of science. The observation of heavenly bodies and the need to know the proper time to pay them reverence led to the development of mathematics both in arithmetic —which developed a system based on a unit of 60 that has survived until now in the measurement of time as well as in the 360 degrees which compose a circle—and in geometry. The dissection of animals, to study their entrails as a means of foretelling the future, laid the foundations for the study of anatomy and medicine.

Of all the achievements of the intellectuals gathered around the temples, the most significant and exciting for historians was the invention of writing, which allows a far better insight into Mesopotamian life than into that of any prehistoric culture. The earliest Sumerian period already possessed a system for noting down its language. A blunt reed was used to make groups of wedge-shaped marks on soft clay tablets, each group corresponding to a character in this system which is still called "wedgeshaped," cuneiform (latin *cunus*-wedge). The Cuneiform system was not an alphabet, since each character corresponded to a group of sounds rather than a single one but it was efficient and flexible enough to survive more than 2,000 years and be adopted by many later peoples such as the Akkadians, Assyrians, Hittites, and Persians, whose languages were completely different from the Sumerian one for which it had originally been created.

The invention of writing immediately produced a remarkably extensive and impressive literature, which is particularly rich in epics. Interested as they were in natural phenomena and obsessed by the perpetual danger of flood, the Sumerians produced epics of *The Creation* and of *The Flood* from which only one human being, Utnapishtim, saved himself through the help of the gods by building a boat, embarking with his family and animals, and so achieving eternal life. The similarity of this tale to the story in *Genesis* is striking even in such details as the sending out of a dove by Utnapishtim to learn whether the floodwaters had receded.

Still more interesting is the great *Epic of Gilgamesh* in which the half-divine hero Gilgamesh wanders in search of immortality to bring back his friend Enkidu from the land of the dead. The Mesopotamian concept of the after-life shown by the *Epic* may seem pessimistic and grim, but in Gilgamesh's search is also reflected a society already attempting to break away from materialism and magic and move toward higher and more abstract values. Gilgamesh is warned again and again on his journey, "the life thou seekest thou shalt not find," the magic branch of immortality which he finally obtains is stolen from him by a serpent as he sleeps, and the only human being to achieve true immortality is old Utnapishtim, who has renounced the world at the order of the gods.

Mesopotamian intellectual development was not confined to religious investigations. The same advance is reflected in the creation of law codes; the most famous of these is the *Code of Hammurabi* which the king is represented on his monuments as receiving from the sun god, Shamash. Some of the provisions of this *Code,* such as "an eye for an eye and a tooth for a tooth," seem familiar and merciless, but even they indicate an enormous social evolution. The law of the *Code* is written down; it is carved on public monuments instead of being the secret of the rulers. Hence all may read it, and it can no longer be altered arbitrarily to suit the ruler's purpose. Indeed, even the ruler is subject to the law, of which he is not the source, having received it from above. Men are not yet equal, for the *Code* differentiates its punishment from class to class, but each of these classes, including women or slaves, has its clearly stated rights which may not be infringed upon. Thus Mesopotamian civilization, for all of its failure to develop large-scale political institutions, had

already succeeded in rising to a remarkable intellectual and moral level at an early stage of its existence.

EGYPT

The political stability and continuity which Mesopotamia failed to achieve characterize, on the contrary, the other great river civilization which developed simultaneously in Egypt. Instead of remaining isolated units as did the Sumerian cities, the early Egyptian provinces, or *Nomes,* were already joined in prehistoric times to form the kingdoms of Upper and Lower Egypt. At the beginning of the historic or dynastic period (ca. 3,000 B.C.) these kingdoms were united by a ruler who is known only under the late Greek name of Menes, but the union is recorded in Egyptian art and lasted several millennia. Thereafter Egyptian rulers, or *pharaohs,* invariably wore both the high, white crown of upper Egypt and the low, red crown of Lower Egypt. Dynastic Egyptian history is traditionally subdivided into three great periods: the Old Kingdom or Ist to VIth dynasties (ca. 3000–ca. 2475 B.C.), the Middle Kingdom or XIth and XIIth dynasties (ca. 2100–ca. 1780 B.C.) and the New Kingdom, or Empire, beginning with the XVIIIth dynasty (1580–ca. 1000 B.C.). These periods are separated in the first case by an internal revolt and in the second by the invasion of foreigners called Hyksos or Shepherd Kings. Some changes, as we shall see, occurred during the great span of time and the capital was shifted at the beginning of the New Kingdom from Memphis southward to Thebes, where it remained, except for a brief period. Nevertheless, Egyptian history is characterized far more by immutability in all institutions than by change.

Even when interrupted, the traditional pattern is recreated with unshakable conservatism. The institutions set down in the Old Kingdom were largely re-established in the Middle Kingdom and continued in the Empire. As in Mesopotamia, geographic conditions played an important part in the creation of Egyptian civilization.

The Geographic Environment

The early divisions of Egypt into Upper (Southern) and Lower (Northern) correspond to the two unequal parts of the Nile valley within the country: the valley proper, which stretches some 500 miles below the first cataract at Aswan, and the swampy triangle of the Delta whose length is about 100 miles from Memphis at the apex to the sea. Both of these sections are united by and dependent on the course of the river, as is the whole of Egyptian life. From Aswan to the Delta the Nile runs in a narrow valley never more than 15 miles wide and encased in high parallel limestone cliffs. Beyond the cliffs and around the Delta, deserts isolate the country so that until the invention of the airplane Egypt was almost inaccessible except from the sea both to invaders and to foreign influences. Between the cliffs the river repeats yearly the same pattern. Beginning to rise in June, it floods the entire valley and finally subsides in October, leaving the land covered with fertile mud which allows the cultivation of two and even three yearly crops. The Egyptians, seeing this inexplicable rise at the very time when rivers normally run dry, worshipped the Nile as a god, and it was only with the discovery of the Nile's sources in the distant African mountains during the nineteenth century that a more reasonable explanation of the phenomenon could be given. The yearly flood of the Nile guarantees the possibility of life in Egypt, but it must at all times be controlled and used to the best advantage; an elaborate system of canals and dikes carries the water over the entire land and at the same time prevents the river from drowning the existing communities. The survival of the entire country depends on the proper maintenance of the irrigation system. Channels and dikes must be kept unobstructed and in good repair; no individual or community may interfere with the common welfare if disaster is to be avoided. The need to preserve such a rigid pattern can be met only by a centralized and absolute administration. The Egyptian pharaoh, son of the sun god Ra, was a god incarnate, and his will was law. All land belonged to him, and all of the classes of society, whether farmers, soldiers, priests, or the civil servants known as scribes, were subject to his authority. Indeed, in the Old Kingdom, he alone was thought capable of true immortality.

The Cult of Immortality

The concern with immortality and life after death was another dominant feature of Egyptian life which increased its conservatism. One of the apparent causes of the revolt which marked the end of the Old Kingdom was the desire of the nobles to share in the immortality of the ruler. Even before the revolt they had tried to be buried as close as possible to the pharaoh. After it their tombs also contained all the attributes which eventually provided the safe return of the soul or *Ka* to its proper body. It is interesting to see that where almost all royal palaces have long vanished, the tombs even of the Old Kingdom still survive. The house of the dead was built with greater care than the house of the living. Within the tomb the dead body was carefully embalmed, wrapped in linen bands, and laid in several elaborate coffins. Every precaution was taken to preserve it from injury so that the *Ka* should find it ready when it returned at the end of its journey. The door of the tomb was sealed and hidden. Numerous statues faithfully reproduced the body to provide alternate homes for the wandering *Ka*. The walls of the tomb were covered with paintings showing all aspects of the daily life and wealth of the dead man to ensure that the soul would be able to pursue its usual occupations and be suitably served. Incidentally, these paintings provide us with the most detailed account of everyday life. Finally, the earliest Egyptian literature consists of a collection of advice, magic formulas, prayers and incantations called the *Book of the Dead,* the purpose of which was to provide guidance for the soul in the other world.

The Pyramids

The best index of the importance of the Egyptian concern with the afterlife as well as of the wealth and power of the Pharaohs is provided by their most striking monuments, the royal tombs known as the pyramids. The most important and most famous pyramids were erected at Gizeh near Memphis by pharaohs of the IVth dynasty (ca. 2700 B.C.) and show the culmination of a long development in funeral architecture. The Great Pyramid, built for the pharaoh Cheops, rises 481 feet above a square base 755 feet on a side and covering 13 acres. It is composed of some 2,300,000 blocks of stone averaging two and a half tons each, intended to protect the tiny burial chamber hidden within the structure, and it was originally covered with smooth polished stone slabs which reflected the sun's rays like a mirror. The fact that each block of stone of the covering surface had to be quarried far to the south, floated several hundred miles down river and dragged up earthen ramps into final position by hand gives us some idea of the authority held by the god on earth. It has been estimated that several hundred thousand workmen, working for twenty years, were needed for the completion of each pyramid.

Art

The religious preoccupation of the Egyptians is reflected in all of their art, which was planned to endure for eternity and therefore conformed to certain regulations or canons set as early as the Old Kingdom. Some variation was possible, but identity of plan, material, shape, and technique can be seen in all periods of Egyptian civilization. The numerous temples built to the many Egyptian gods—Amon-Ra, the sun god of Thebes, Anubis, Hathor, Seth, and many others—are built of the hardest stone available and follow a simple plan. Ponderous and rigidly symmetrical, they progress from the glaring sunshine of a forecourt, entered through an enormous gate or *pylon,* through the growing dimness of the pillared *hypostyle* hall, to the almost total darkness of the shrine.

The gradually lowering ceiling increases the sense of mystery and awe as the worshipper approaches the divine abode. Similarly, sculpture shows a remarkable realism in the rendering of the human body and talent in the handling of the massive stone medium allied to unalterable patterns and a very limited number of poses. The realism itself is the idealized realism of a perfect human figure given in all its details rather than the discerning observation of individual peculiarities needed for real portraits. The subject is always shown at the height of his youth, vigor, and beauty rather than marked by characteristic blemishes or the signs of advancing years. Even painting obeyed the same regulations, with set subjects and conventions in the use of color, such as red for male skin and white for female.

Science and Literature
The overwhelming influence of religion does not seem, however, to have prevented the Egyptians from admirable achievements in this world. The successful functioning of the intricate system of irrigation for almost three thousand years bears witness to the efficiency of the administrative machinery maintained by the pharaohs, as do the numerous records giving detailed accounts of the government of provinces and the management of estates. The fact that the base of the great pyramid is a perfect square with a negligible variation and that its four corners are precisely oriented to the points of the compass shows the precision of Egyptian measurements in the third millennium, and their knowledge of mathematics. Through anatomical studies probably carried on in connection with the embalming of the dead, Egyptian medicine especially flourished. The observation of the rise of Sirius (the Dog Star), announcing the yearly rise of the Nile, permitted the establishment of an almost perfect 365-day solar calendar far superior to the lunar one used in Mesopotamia.

Like Mesopotamia, Egypt was a literate society from its earliest period, and every important household had a secretary or scribe to keep its records and accounts, but instead of using the wedgeshaped cuneiform suited to soft clay, it put down its language on stone or rolls made of the fibers of the papyrus plant by means of stylized pictures called *hieroglyphics*. The hieroglyphic system also was not a real alphabet, though it came very close to developing one. The literature of the Old Kingdom is almost entirely lost, and, in general, early Egyptian literature is not as impressive as its art but consists mainly of the religious texts found in *The Book of the Dead*. Beginning with the Middle Kingdom, however, though we find no great epics similar to that of Gilgamesh, many tales make their appearance. Stories such as the *Tale of Sinhue* or the *Journey of Wen Amon* to the Syrian coast show both the existence of contacts between Egypt and foreign lands and the Egyptian's love of his homeland in the desperate homesickness of Sinhue, and his longing to return to die and be buried in Egypt in spite of his success in Syria. We also find the *Tale of Two Brothers* with its striking similarity to the story of Joseph in the Bible.

Philosophic preoccupations transcending magic formulae appear in prayers and in such literary pieces as the *Dialogue Between A Man Weary of Life and His Soul*. Particularly significant as an indication of moral preoccupation with right and wrong and human responsibility are the innumerable artistic representations of the judgment of Osiris: The dead man stands answering for his actions before the tribunal of the dead, presided over by Osiris, while his soul is weighed on the scales against a feather, and crocodiles lie in wait to devour the soul found wanting. The appearance of the judgment scene in the royal tombs of the Middle Kingdoms indicates the success of the nobles' revolt. A limitation has been placed on the absolutism of the pharaoh, who is now answerable to the gods for his earthly rule. We have here the example of an important change which occurred in Egyptian society and the beginning of the growing influence of the priests attached to the temples of the gods such as Ra and Amon.

Despite the upheaval of the revolt and the changes which it brought about, the pharaohs of the XIth and XIIth dynasties succeeded in achieving almost the same power as was wielded by their predecessors, the pyramid builders. Nor was the invasion of the mysterious Hyksos with their new weapon of war, the horsedrawn chariot, which was still unknown to the Egyptian, able to break the pattern of Egyptian life or weaken the country. On the contrary, as soon as the pharaohs of the XVIIIth dynasty had succeeded in re-establishing the traditional Egyptian administration, they found themselves powerful enough to begin extending it into foreign lands.

FURTHER READING

The transformations in our knowledge of early history continually introduced by new archaeological discoveries make most general treatments of the subject rapidly obsolete. A useful recent attempt is the first section of T. Jones, *Ancient Civilization* (1960), and a general survey of ancient civilizations can be found in L. Cottrell, *The Anvil of Civilization* (1957). Interesting accounts of the methods and development of archaeology can be found in Leonard Woolley, *History Unearthed* (1958), and Mortimer Wheeler, *Archaeology from the Earth* (1954).

For the prehistoric period and the neolithic revolution see particularly V. Gordon Childe, *What Happened in History* (rev. ed., 1942), also J. G. Clark, *World Prehistory: An Outline* (1961), and E. O. James, *A Study of Prehistoric Archaeology* (1961). The beginnings of civilization in the East are studied in H. Frankfurt, *The Birth of Civilization in the Near East* (1956), and the best collection of texts illustrating the entire history of the Ancient Orient is to be found in J. B. Pritchard, *Ancient Near Eastern Texts Relating to the Old Testament* (1950).

An excellent survey of the archaeological discoveries in Mesopotamia can be found in Seton Lloyd, *Foundations in the Dust* (1955), and L. Woolley, *Ur of the Chaldees* (rev. ed., 1950). The many achievements of Sumerian civilization have been studied by S. N. Kraemer, *History Begins at Sumer* (1959), and E. Chiera, *They Wrote on Clay* (1938). For a study of Mesopotamian beliefs see S. N. Kraemer, *Sumerian Mythology* (rev. ed., 1961); the religious and literary texts are published by Th. Gaster, *The Oldest Stories in the World* (1952), and I. Mendelsohn, *Religions of the Ancient Near East* (1955).

For Egypt, J. H. Breasted, *A History of Egypt* (1909), is still very useful, but see also W. B. Emery, *Archaic Egypt* (1961). Ancient Egyptian civilization is studied in John A. Wilson, *The Culture of Ancient Egypt* (1956), and H. Frankfort, *Ancient Egyptian Religion* (1961), as well as S. R. K. Glanville, *Daily Life in Ancient Egypt* (1930) and *The Legacy of Egypt* (1942). I. E. S. Edwards, *The Pyramids of Egypt* (1947), is an interesting account of the building of the various pyramids and of the beliefs which led to such a formidable undertaking.

* Books existing in paperback editions will be indicated with an asterisk.

2 · The Creation of Empires

During the third millennium B.C. we have seen the establishment and growth of centers of civilization in the eastern basin of the Mediterranean. Beginning with the middle of the second millennium these units, dominated by semi-divine monarchs, began to transcend local boundaries, to expand into adjoining territories on which they imposed their culture, and to create large empires. As a result of this expansion, the originally isolated cultures came into contact with each other. Much of this contact was violent and took the form of wars, but peaceful relations also occurred through trade and through intermarriages of the ruling houses. The centers of the new empires generally still remained in the same regions as had witnessed the development of the earliest civilizations, or in adjoining territories: Egypt at first, then the Asia Minor of the Hittites and the Babylonia of the Assyrians. Finally, by the middle of the first millennium B.C. the Persians attempted for the first time to create a world empire, uniting most of the civilized regions of that time under a single rule.

THE EGYPTIAN EMPIRE

By the middle of the second millennium B.C., the Egyptians had learned the new technique of the war chariot with which the Hyksos had succeeded in conquering their land. Starting from Upper Egypt, where the power of the foreigners seems to have been weaker, the prince of Thebes, Ahmose I (ca. 1580–1557 B.C.), succeeded in driving out the Hyksos and extending his rule over the whole of Egypt. With the re-establishment of native Egyptian rule in the Nile Valley by the XVIIIth dynasty, the new pharaohs found themselves strong enough to embark on a policy of expansion. We have already seen that even before this period Egypt had not been totally isolated from the outside world. As far back as the IIIrd dynasty, the Egyptians had built sea-going ships, and by the Middle Kingdom ships such as the one of Sinhue went regularly up the Syrian coast to the Phoenician seaports, seeking particularly the wood of the great cedars of Lebanon, for trees did not grow in the valley of the Nile. Some expeditions had also been made by the pharaohs of the XIIth dynasty in Nubia and Palestine, but with Ahmose I and his successors, particularly the pharaoh Thutmose I (ca. 1530–1515 B.C.), these undertakings took on a far

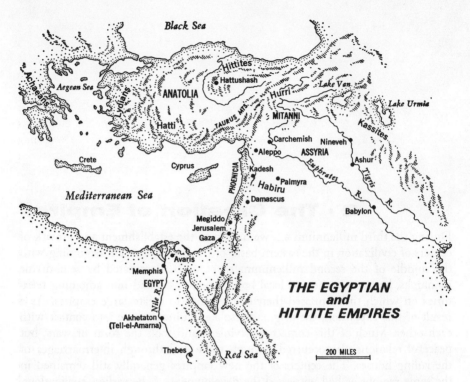

**THE EGYPTIAN
and
HITTITE EMPIRES**

more extensive character. The raiding armies of Thutmose I crossed Syria, reached the Upper Euphrates, and attacked the Northern Kingdom of Mitanni.

The attacks of Thutmose I were only raids, however, and his successors appear to have preferred the consolidation of their power at home. His daughter, Queen Hatshepsut (1505–1483 B.C.) was the only woman to rule Egypt as pharaoh. Not only did this queen apparently possess all the powers of the sun king, but she is represented on her official statues with the body of a woman, yet wearing the ceremonial loin cloth, crown, and beard of a king. With the help of her architect and prime minister, Senmut, Hatshepsut reigned peacefully, sending expeditions to the land of Punt, or Nubia, south of the second cataract of the Nile, to bring back exotic woods, incense, gold, and ivory for adorning her court. The prestige of the queen-pharaoh seems to have extended into distant lands, since in tomb paintings of the period and particularly in the one of Senmut, strangers wearing curious clothes and bearing gifts are represented with the explanatory inscription "the great ones of Keftiu come in peace."

With the next reign, however, the period of conquest begins once more. Thutmose III (1483–1450 B.C.), Hatshepsut's nephew, seems to have taken a savage pleasure in reversing the queen's policy. Almost all of Hatshepsut's statues were destroyed or mutilated, and her name was obliterated on all official inscriptions. Thutmose III has been called the "Napoleon of Egypt" and was unquestionably a brilliant general. Beginning with his defeat of the coalition of local Syrian princes with the Mitanni at Megiddo in Palestine in 1483, Thutmose III went on to conquer all of Syria, Palestine, and the Phoenician coast.

At the same time, his navy controlled the eastern shore of the Mediterranean.

The victories of Thutmose III made Egypt the dominant power of its day. It reached its heyday under his grandson Amenhotep or Amenophis III (1411–1375 B.C.). The pharaoh now ruled not only over the valley of the Nile but over an Empire which stretched from Nubia to Northern Syria. Local princes acknowledged themselves his subjects and sent him yearly tribute. Some of the power and wealth of Amenhotep III are still reflected in the enormous temples he built at Luxor near Thebes, while the prosperity of his court may be seen in the endless banquets and entertainments with dancers and musicians, as well as the innumerable herds of cattle and storehouses, depicted on the walls of aristocratic tombs. Nevertheless, new powers such as the Hittites were beginning to appear in the north and threaten the might of Egypt. To meet this danger the pharaohs added diplomacy to their military might. To secure the alliance of their former enemies, the Mitanni, against the Hittites, the pharaohs sent embassies with presents to their "brother" of Mitanni, and several Mitanni princesses came to marry in Egypt, including perhaps the beautiful Nefertiti, the bride of Amenhotep III's son, the future Amenhotep IV. A great empire had been created: a new political unit which had not yet existed in the world now united under the power of the god king not only Egyptians, but many civilizations, and ranged from the Negroes of Nubia to the princes of Syria. Despite the greatness of the achievement, it is not surprising that this first attempt at supra-national government was not entirely successful, especially in view of the rigidity and conservatism of the Egyptian tradition, which could hardly be adapted to new situations. The very creation of an empire presented problems within the country for which no solution existed and was accompanied by internal difficulties.

The Revolution of Akhenaten

The pharaoh was still a god and his authority presumably absolute, but the reign of a god was not without troubles. Under the XVIIIth dynasty, as the capital, Thebes, grew and flourished, the power of the priests of Amon-Ra, the local sun god, grew progressively greater. The magnificence of the temples of Amon and his great estates shows the wealth his servants had acquired. Amenhotep III and his predecessors proclaimed their allegiance to Amon in their very name. For the first time the temple became more important than the tomb in Egyptian art. The Old Kingdom pharaohs had erected enormous pyramids. The Middle Kingdom rulers and even Hatshepsut had built elaborate funerary temples before their tombs. But the later pharaohs of the XVIIIth dynasty, obsessed with the safeguarding of their souls, abandoned all earthly pomp to hide their tombs so deeply in the cliffs of the Valley of Kings near Thebes that the burial chamber of the last pharaoh of the dynasty, Tutankhamon, remained sealed until it was discovered by archaeologists in 1922.

The growing power of the priests of Amon, threatening both the authority of the pharaoh and the economy of the country, posed a critical problem and at last brought about a violent revolution. This occurred at the very height of the empire under one of the most curious and enigmatic figures of history, the pharaoh Amenhotep IV, or as he is better known, Akhenaten (1370–1350 B.C.), who for a period of twenty years altered radically some of the major characteristics of Egyptian civilization. In the religious atmosphere of Egyptian life it is not surprising that this revolution took on primarily a religious aspect, but the intentions of Akhenaten still remain unknown, and his reform has been interpreted in a number of ways.

In a sudden and startling break with the worship of Amon, the divine father of the pharaohs of the XVIIIth dynasty, and with all the other gods dear to the tradition of Egyptian polytheism, Akhenaten gave his entire allegiance to a single, all-powerful, and merciful creator, the sun disk or Aten whose rays brought blessings to the earth. The pharaoh abandoned the capital of Thebes, home of the now-hated Amon and his priests, to found a new city in the desert north of Thebes on the east bank of the Nile at the place now called Tell-el-Amarna. There he settled with his entire court and administration and built temples dedicated to the Aten. To demonstrate his new allegiance, the king even abandoned the name of his father Amenhotep (Amon is satisfied) which he had borne at his accession, to take that of Akhenaten (it is well with the Aten) while the new capital of Tell-el-Amarna received the name of Akhetaten (the horizon of the disk).

Interpretations of the Tell-el-Amarna Period

There seems to be little reason to doubt the honesty of the pharaoh's attachment to the new god whose praise he celebrated in a famous and moving *Hymn* which managed to survive the attempts to destroy it by its enemies.

> ... Thy dawning is beautiful in the horizon of the sky,
> O living Aten, beginner of life!
> When thou restest in the eastern horizon
> Thou fillest every land with thy beauty.
> Thou art beautiful, great, glittering, high above every land,
> Thy rays, they encompass the lands, even all that thou hast made.
> How manifold are thy works!
> They are hidden from before us,
> O sole god, whose powers no other possesseth.
> Thou did'st create the earth according to thy heart
> While thou wast alone ...

Akhenaten has often been called the first monotheist, leading humanity from the multiple cults of polytheism to the worship of a single omnipotent God. More extravagantly, he has been called a precursor of Christianity, though no historical link has been found to join the two religions, separated by more than thirteen centuries. In addition to the purely religious theory, however, other explanations have been suggested for Akhenaten's reform. Scholars have pointed out that the only way to break the increasing power of the priests of Amon, which was constantly encroaching on the authority of the king, was to destroy the god who was the source of their power. The cause of the reform would then be fundamentally political rather than religious and have as its aim the reaffirmation of the royal power. Indeed, it has been pointed out that the entire revolution was the direct result of the pharaonic will, which had always been the source of Egyptian law. In this sense, Akhenaten was acting entirely according to the Egyptian tradition of royal absolutism, and despite his overt devotion to the Aten, he was more autocratic than his predecessors who had shared some of their power with the priests.

One more explanation has been suggested as well. The gods of Egypt, as indeed of most of ancient paganism, were local gods attached to a specific geographic locality where they were worshipped and from which they might not be moved. Amon, for example, was the god of Thebes, and his greatness was tied to the growth of the capital. Such local gods could be exported only with difficulty and therefore would hardly appeal to the varied population composing the new Empire. Hence, the insistence of the *Hymn* that the Aten's power extended over "every land" has been interpreted at times as evidence that Akhenaten intended to create a new, supra-national, imperial religion more suited to the new political empire than the old, provincial Egyptian gods.

The Art of Tell-el-Amarna

Perhaps the best and most attractive evidence for the extent of Akhenaten's revolution is his capital at Tell-el-Amarna, which has been uncovered in successive excavations. Most of the canons regulating Egyptian art for centuries were now broken, and the new art appears filled with a new freshness and spontaneity. Instead of the darkness and mystery of the traditional temples, the new roofless temple of the Aten was open to his rays. The detailed but rigorously stylized tomb paintings gave way, on the pavement of the royal palace, to gay and unconstrained scenes of flying birds and little calves frolicking among flowering shrubs and bushes. For the first time real portraits, showing even the defects of the sitter took the place of the usual idealized sculptures. Clay masks taken directly from human faces have been recovered from the ruins of Tell-el-Amarna. Not even the divine royal family was spared by the new realism. Intimate scenes replaced the representations of the glories of the pharaoh. One of the most beautiful pieces of Egyptian sculpture is the delicate bust of the queen which fully justifies her name of Nefertiti ("the beautiful one comes"), but another statue reveals the queen aged and deformed by numerous childbirths. Even in his official portraits, Akhenaten is not represented in the usual manner as an erect, beautiful, and ever-youthful god, but rather as a slumped, weary, and aging human being. Neither the long jaw, nor the thin legs, nor the pot belly of the pharaoh were spared by the honesty of his court sculptors and painters.

The Return to Tradition and the End of the Empire

Despite its ultimate significance, the immediate political result of Akhenaten's reform was the drastic weakening of the Empire. The revolution was perhaps too sudden and profound to be acceptable to Egyptian conservatism, and the priests of Amon naturally concentrated all their efforts on opposing the policy of the pharaoh. At the same time the princes of Syria, seeing Akhenaten's attention concentrated on internal affairs, took advantage of the situation and promptly stopped sending their tribute to the pharaoh and revolted against the Egyptian governors. In 1887 an old Arab woman digging at the site of the capital inadvertently found the official correspondence of the Tell-el-Amarna Period recorded on small clay tablets written in Babylonian cuneiform characters. These are the famous *Tell-el-Amarna Letters* which give a vivid picture of the disintegration of the Empire. The subject princes are rising, new enemies are appearing everywhere, and the local governor writing to the pharaoh can only implore again and again, seemingly in vain, "Let my lord send troops— let them come!"

Caught between external and internal enemies, the Tell-el-Amarna period did not survive its creator. The new capital was abandoned at Akhenaten's death and disappeared under the sand of the desert. The immediate successor of the reformer, Tutankhamon, whose very name testifies to the triumph of the priests of Amon, returned to Thebes, where he was to die at the age of eighteen. Egyptian life and art returned to their traditional pattern. The shaken prestige of the Empire in Syria was partially restored by wars of the pharaohs in the succeeding XIXth dynasty, particularly by the greatest of them, Ramses II (ca. 1298–1235 B.C.) and Ramses III (1198–1167 B.C.). Ramses II prided himself on his monuments of the great victory he won over the Hittites at Kadesh in northern Syria in 1286 B.C. But the great victory of which he boasted now seems to have been an inconclusive battle in which the pharaoh's personal bravery succeeded in saving the Egyptian army from defeat and Syria was only partially reconquered. Ramses III, following his predecessors of the XVIIIth dynasty, allied himself with his former enemies, the Hittites, against the new power of Assyria, and married a Hittite princess. Despite all of these efforts the Empire no longer had the strength to face both old and new enemies. The native pharaohs were succeeded first by African, Nubian, and Ethiopian dynasties which ruled in the Egyptian tradition from 1100 to 671 B.C., then by the great foreign powers: Assyria, Persia, and finally Greece. Egypt, which had created the first great empire of history, was rarely to be ruled again by native leaders, though the foreign conquerors long continued to recognize the superiority of Egyptian culture and to maintain its traditions.

THE APPEARANCE OF NEW ELEMENTS IN THE SECOND MILLENNIUM

The Egyptian Empire had been created by the strength and ability of its native rulers, but the great rival powers of Asia Minor grew out of a concentration of new forces which made their appearance in the course of the second millennium. The massive and continuous migration of new peoples into the area of the Near East altered the existing situation and repeatedly counteracted the Empire-building activity of the period. The powerful enemies whom the Egyptian Empire was forced to fight in the north were not Mesopotamians, for the continuous problem of political instability remained unsolved in the Tigris and the Euphrates valley. The kingdom of Hammurabi had collapsed soon after his death, under the attack of a new Semitic people, the Kassites, whose state proved no greater than the one they had just destroyed. The real opposition to Egyptian imperialism came from a region northwest of the great Mesopotamian centers and was due in part at least to the newcomers, now called Indo-Europeans, who were to play an important part in the Near East and to dominate the future history of Europe.

The Coming of the Indo-Europeans

Even before the coming of the Indo-Europeans, the population which had created the civilizations of the fourth millennium was by no means homogeneous. It is generally divided into large groups differentiated on the basis of language. In Africa the so-called Hamitic tribes were the ancestors of the Egyptians. In Syria and Mesopotamia were located the various nomad tribes who are grouped together under the name of Semites because all of them spoke variations of the language classified as Semitic. Among these Semites were to be found most of the contributors to Mesopotamian culture: the Akkadians, the Amorites, the Kassites, as well as the creators of the future empire of the Assyrians. Finally a third group, to whom the Sumerians may have belonged, consisted of the Asianics. This name indicates that they were widely spread in Western Asia, but they can be defined only in negative terms at present. Until further evidence is obtained, all that can be said is that the Asianic Sumerians were neither Semites nor the new Indo-Europeans who were entering into their territory.

Just like the Semites, the Indo-Europeans were not a single race but a collection of nomad tribes associated together on the basis of the similarity of their languages. At the moment of their entrance into history, the Indo-Europeans were already separated into a number of groups whose common language had disappeared and can only be tentatively reconstituted by scholars. Even their original home in Asia cannot be given with certainty. About 2500 B.C. they were settled in the area north of the Black and Caspian Seas, and soon thereafter they began to move in successive waves of migration in different directions. Some pushed eastward toward Persia and India, while others travelled westward into Asia Minor and ultimately into Europe. The date of the arrival of the Indo-Europeans into Asia Minor probably follows closely upon the beginning of the second millennium B.C.

The newcomers were excellent soldiers, armed with characteristic battle axes which allow archaeologists to trace the path of their advance; their horse-drawn chariots gave them a considerable superiority in battle through their rapidity of movement and their ability to ride down enemies on foot. Consequently, the advent of the Indo-Europeans, despite their relatively limited numbers, was soon followed by the creation of predominantly military states, contrasting with the relatively more pacific civilizations which had flourished in the Orient. It is probably among these Indo-Europeans that the source of opposition met by the Egyptians in the kingdoms of the Mitanni and of the Hittites may be found.

The Iron Age

The beginning of the Indo-European migrations marked the early part of the second millennium. The latter half was transformed by a further development in the technique of civilization. Somewhere in Asia Minor, probably in the highlands of Armenia, though no particular locality can be indicated, the working of iron ore replaced that of bronze around 1300 B.C. The new technique could not be kept a local secret in the international society of the time, and before long the use of iron was common in the entire basin of the eastern Mediterranean. The new metal produced far better tools and, in particular, better weapons than bronze; hence it was suited to a militaristic society. Its abundance made it far cheaper than bronze and therefore available to many people instead of being the possession of a small ruling class. Consequently, the use of iron often brought with it a tendency toward the militarization and greater equalization of society. From the transformations of the Near East arose the two great empires of the North, that of the Hittites and Mitanni, and subsequently that of the Assyrians.

The Proto-Hittite Empire

Knowledge of the Hittite Empire is one of the most recent gifts of archaeology; until the present century all that remained of it was an occasional puzzling reference in the Old Testament, and it had even been possible to argue that the Hittites had never existed at all. Extensive excavations in northern Syria and particularly in central Asia-Minor on the site of the Hittite capital of Hattushash, now Bogaz-Keui, have demonstrated the error of such theories. The Hittite state archives, consisting of tens of thousands of clay tablets, have come to light. Nevertheless, much that is doubtful and unclear in Hittite history remains to be explained through further excavations.

Insofar as we now know, the rise of the Hittite Empire was divided into at least two periods separated by a time of temporary eclipse. The first waves of Indo-Europeans conquered a number of Asianic principalities in Asia Minor at the beginning of the second millennium B.C. The newcomers were never more than a ruling minority in the new state then created, a state whose population remained largely Asianic. Nevertheless, by the seventeenth century B.C. a first Hittite Empire had been established with a capital at Hattushash.

The new state differed greatly from its predecessors in the area. The center of the empire was located on the high plateau of Anatolia instead of in the river lowlands of earlier cultures. The heavy fortifications of the cities remaining testify to their military character, as does the art of the Hittites, which is powerful, though by no means as refined as that of their contemporaries. The Indo-European rulers were aggressive toward their neighbors, the Hittite king was not a god but a war chieftain advised by a council of his leading warriors, and by ca. 1600 B.C. a Hittite king had taken and sacked Babylon. Nevertheless, the Hittites could not escape the influence of the more developed Mesopotamian culture. The gods worshipped by them were largely Babylonian and, most important, though Hittite is an Indo-European language, the official records of Hattushash were kept in Mesopotamian cuneiform characters.

The Hurrites of Mitanni and the Hittite Empire

For reasons still unknown, the first Hittite unification was broken into a number of small principalities and briefly replaced by the Hurrite Kingdom of Mitanni, located in the great bend of the Euphrates. Like the first Hittite state, Mitanni was composed of an Asianic population long established in the region, the Hurrites, and a small Indo-European aristocracy, the Mitanni, who appeared around 1800–1700 B.C. and whose relationship to other Indo-European tribes was still clear. The gods worshipped by the Mitanni: Mithrasil, Harunasil, and Indra, were clearly the same as the Mithra, Varuna, and Indra of their eastern cousins in Persia and India. Profitting from the temporary eclipse of the Hittites at the beginning of the sixteenth century, the Mitanni made their bid for power, conquering the small principalities of Northern Syria and so coming into conflict with the advancing Egyptians. But their period of greatness was brief. After their defeat at Megiddo, ca. 1483 B.C., the kings of Mitanni ruled another century with the support of their Egyptian alliance, but they were no match for the recreated power of the Hittites.

The restoration of the Hittites was relatively rapid despite the attacks of powerful neighbors who in ca. 1400 B.C. penetrated far enough to sack the city of Hattushash itself. After the recreation of their power, the great Hittite kings established their domination over their neighbors and rivaled the prestige of Egypt in the East. Mitanni soon gave way before Shuppiluliumash I (ca. 1385 B.C.), who went on to invade Syria. His great successor Murshilish II (ca. 1334–1306 B.C.) came close to breaking the power of the Egyptians at Kadesh, and soon after, Ramses II was forced to sign a treaty of peace with the Hittite king in 1269 B.C. The peace and balance of power created by the treaty, however, was not to be of long duration. Once again new peoples struggling to power attacked the settled empires. The Hittites, less durably established and less protected than Egypt, were the first to be submerged and their Empire disappeared by 1200 B.C., although Hittite successor states lingered in northern Syria for a considerable time.

THE ASSYRIANS

The militarization of the Near East, already begun by the XVIIIth dynasty in Egypt, and particularly under the Hittites, reached its apogee in the Assyrian Empire which dominated the whole of the region in the first millennium. The reputation of the Assyrians has always been that of formidable soldiers distinguished by their cruelty. Their rulers have become legendary figures of ruthless conquerors. Yet for over a thousand years no sign foretold that the scattered Semitic tribes living in the mountains to the northwest of Babylonia would be numbered among the great conquerors of the world. Even the disintegration of the Hittite Empire, which they had helped destroy, did not bring the Assyrians to immediate power. A partial expansion was followed by a setback of about two centuries, as had been the case with the

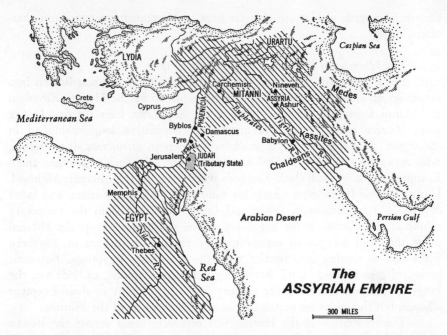

The
ASSYRIAN EMPIRE

300 MILES

Hittites. It was only with the beginning of the ninth century B.C. that Assyria inaugurated its true imperial expansion by reaching to the shore of the Mediterranean sea. Once launched, however, the Assyrian advance received only minor checks. Babylonia and Syria bore the brunt of the early attacks, but by 722 B.C. King Sargon II controlled most of Palestine as well as Syria. Within a century the last great power of the East crumbled as Egypt collapsed under the repeated attacks of Assyrian armies. From his new capital of Nineveh on the Upper Tigris, the great Assurbanipal (669–626 B.C.) could legitimately believe that he had no equal left in the world.

The Sources of Assyrian Power

Much of the Assyrians' fearful reputation was undoubtedly deserved; the success of their expeditions was largely due to a perfected technique of warfare based on a preliminary heavy barrage of arrows followed by a sweeping attack with war chariots, and the use of siege machinery for the capture of walled cities. Also, it cannot be denied that great cruelty attended their victorious campaigns. Cities were razed and burned, populations slaughtered or moved forcibly to be resettled far from their homelands at the will of the new masters. This violence should not, however, be put down to mere thoughtless brutality. The fearful reputation of the Assyrians was cultivated and exaggerated by themselves, not out of mere vanity, but as part of a deliberate policy of intimidation.

The royal *Annals* of Assyria reiterated monotonously the victories and merciless repressions of any opposition. Horrifying statistics drove home the hopelessness of withstanding the conquerors. The same intention guided much of Assyrian official art. The gates of the royal palace, guarded on either side by monstrous figures of winged bulls with human faces, were designed to instill fear into strangers entering them. On the walls of Nineveh and of Sargon II's earlier palace at Khorsabad, endless reliefs depict the king's victorious campaigns and the long, submissive lines of subject peoples bringing tribute to his majesty. Everywhere the military might of the Assyrians was supplemented by a skillful terroristic propaganda.

Assyrian Culture

To see Assyria merely as a brutal if effective war machine would, however, be a mistake. The very use of psychological warfare indicates a considerable intellectual advance. Similarly, the technique of transferring population was a means both of reducing the ever-present danger of revolt and of spreading civilization throughout the empire. Most of the Assyrians' culture was borrowed from the earlier Mesopotamian tradition but their political sense was far superior. The Assyrian administration could rival that of the Egyptians, and a system of roads and messengers kept the king in constant touch with the various parts of his realm. Even more interestingly for our study, the Assyrian adoption of Mesopotamian culture was not something unconscious but rather the result of the first sense of history found in antiquity. The name of Sargon II was an evocation of the memory of the first creator of an empire, Sargon I of Akkad, who had ruled almost two thousand years before. In his palace at Nineveh Assurbanipal collected more than 20,000 tablets to create the first great library in the world. Most of Mesopotamian literature, including the *Epic of Gilgamesh,* has been preserved thanks only to the culture and antiquarian taste of the Assyrian king. Even a certain sensibility cannot be denied to the great conquerors. The hunting reliefs of Nineveh, particularly the magnificent lions and lionesses, in addition to an admirable study of anatomy and movement show a very real sense of sympathy and compassion for the trapped and wounded creatures represented.

The Downfall of Assyria

All of the achievements of Assurbanipal were not sufficient, however, to create an enduring empire. Like their predecessors, the Assyrians failed to find a satisfactory formula for stable government. The power which had developed at the expense of older cultures and maintained itself through fear was not sufficient to withstand for long the double pressure of internal discontent and new peoples who were still pouring into the Near East. After a few abortive attempts, a coalition of Semitic Chaldean princes from Babylon and Indo-European Medes succeeded in storming Nineveh in 612 B.C., putting an end to the Assyrian dominion.

The Neo-Babylonian Revival

The destruction of Nineveh left the Orient in confusion. The Medes and their subjects, the Persians, were not yet ready to take a lead, and local princelings established themselves everywhere. In this temporary political vacuum, Mesopotamian civilization was granted a brief Indian summer. All of the arts and sciences of the past tradition were gathered in the Chaldean capital of Babylon, dominated by its great ziggurat. From the mathematical and astronomical schools of the capital, science was to travel both east and west to create the future learning of India and Greece. The resplendent streets and gates of the city lined with blue glazed tiles and adorned with white and yellow reliefs of lions, bulls, and more fantastic animals give us a glimpse of the magnificence of vanished Mesopotamian architecture. The so-called "Hanging Gardens" planted on the palace roofs were counted as one of the seven wonders of the ancient world.

Following the example of their former Assyrian masters, the Chaldean armies under Nebuchadrezzar II (604–562 B.C.) even marched victoriously into Palestine and transported the population of the city of Jerusalem, which they took and destroyed in 586 B.C., to the capital of Babylon. But the sophisticated culture of the Chaldeans could hardly be expected to succeed where the Assyrians had failed. By 539 B.C. the Chaldeans' power had vanished, and Babylon was once again in the possession of foreigners.

THE PERSIAN EMPIRE

The final formulation of the imperial ideal already attempted by the Egyptians, Hittites, and Assyrians was to be achieved by the Persians. The last of the Indo-Europeans to enter the Near East, they had made their entrance modestly as the subjects of the Medes. But the Persians succeeded in developing the institutions of a world government based on neither force nor fear but on a peaceful and regular administration such as the world had not known before.

The first rise of the Persians to power did not differ greatly from that of the earlier empires. Even before the fall of the Chaldeans the Persians had freed themselves from the domination of the Medes, under the leadership of Cyrus the Achaemenid (ca. 550 B.C.), and established an independent state whose capital was Susa, north of the Persian Gulf. After the capture of Babylon, the Persian army of skillful archers moved swiftly along the now familiar routes of conquest. Within less than a century the Achaemenid kings, Darius the Great (521–486 B.C.) and Xerxes (486–465), ruled over an empire stretching from the cataracts of the Nile to the Caucasus and from the Mediterranean and Aegean seas to India. Darius could style himself on his inscriptions "King of Kings" and the new capitals of Susa and later Persepolis rivaled the former splendors of Nineveh and Babylon.

Persian Administration

The Persians' great achievement was not to be found, however, in mere conquests and military might but rather in the establishment of a workable system for world government, a government which was based on the seemingly contradictory terms, absolutism and toleration.

The divine authority of the King of Kings was absolute in all his dominions. In each of the 21 provinces, or satrapies, of the realm a royal governor and royal officials saw to the execution of his will and watched each

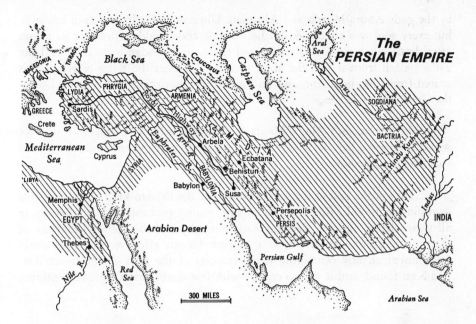

Black Sea

Caucasus

Caspian Sea

Aral Sea

MACEDONIA

THRACE

PHRYGIA

LYDIA

ARMENIA

Sardis

GREECE

Crete

Mediterranean Sea

Cyprus

SYRIA

Euphrates R.

Tigris R.

Halys

BABYLONIA

Arbela

MEDIA

Ecbatana

Behistun

Oxus

SOGDIANA

BACTRIA

Hindu Kush

Jaxartes

LIBYA

Babylon

Susa

Memphis

EGYPT

Arabian Desert

Thebes

Nile R.

Red Sea

Persepolis

PERSIS

Persian Gulf

Indus

INDIA

300 MILES

Arabian Sea

other. An extensive system of roads connected the great cities of the empire. The most famous of these, the "Royal Highway," linking the capital of Susa with the city of Sardis in western Asia Minor, covered some 1,500 miles and was provided throughout with relays for the postal system which carried news and orders in all directions. A corps of special supervisors, or spies called "the eyes and ears of the King," informed the central government of all that went on in the provinces. Each satrapy furnished troops to the royal army when required, and a regular system of taxation provided the finances needed for such an elaborate administration.

For all of its centralization, the Persian government was not a tyranny, and the King of Kings showed a very real preoccupation with the welfare of his subjects. As long as troops were supplied and the taxes paid, the central government interfered very little in provincial affairs. The royal governors were often native princes, and whenever possible, local institutions were maintained. This concern appears clearly in Cyrus' freeing of the Jews from the Babylonian captivity and in such documents as the so-called *Passover Papyrus* which contains directions from the Persian authorities for the proper celebration of the Jewish Passover by the Persian-Jewish garrison stationed in Egypt.

Zoroaster and Persian Religion

The Greek historian Herodotus, who wrote that Persian noblemen were taught two things, "to shoot straight and to tell the truth," specified a crucial aspect of Persian society which was deeply concerned with moral values and the fundamental problem of good and evil. The great Persian prophet Zoroaster, probably born ca. 660 B.C., saw the whole of the world as a constant struggle between the forces of light and the forces of darkness, personified respectively by the gods Ahura-Mazda and Ahriman. Ultimately goodness would triumph, but every soul was concerned in the struggle and would answer for its action after death when the righteous crossed the narrow bridge to heaven, and the evildoers fell from it into the abyss of hell. Not even the King of Kings was spared from the judgment, and on his victory inscription at Behistun, Darius the Great acknowledges,

On this account Ahura Mazda brought me help . . . because I was not wicked, nor was a liar, nor was I a tyrant, neither I or any of my line. I have ruled according to righteousness.

Thus at the end of the sixth century B.C. the Persian king claimed to rule according to moral principles. To be sure, reality probably did not live up to all these claims and the Persians had profited from the accomplishments of their predecessors. Nevertheless, a scheme for an effective and just world government already containing many features of the later divine monarchies had been found, and it was to endure with few disturbances for two centuries.

FURTHER READING

The bibliography of the preceding chapter should be consulted, particularly, J. B. Pritchard, *Ancient Near Eastern Texts* (1950), which contain both the "Tell-el-Amarna Letters" and the "Hymn to the Aton."

On the revolution of Akhenaten, A. Weigall, *The Life and Times of Akhenaten Pharaoh of Egypt* (4th ed., 1922), remains useful though much has been done since its publication. The excavations at Tell-el-Amarna are studied in J. D. S. Pendlebury, *Tell el-Amarna* (1935).

For Anatolia, both Seton Lloyd *Early Anatolia* (1956), which gives a survey of the discoveries in the area, and L. Woolley, *A Forgotten Kingdom* (1953), are of great interest. On the Hittites, the basic works are J. Garstang, *The Hittite Empire* (1929), and O. Gurney, *The Hittites* (1952). The history of the Assyrians is studied in S. Moscati, *Ancient Semitic Civilizations* (1960), and in A. T. Olmstead, *History of Assyria* (1923).

A particularly good study of ancient Iranian civilization has recently been given by R. Fry, *The Heritage of Persia* (1963), but see also the older works: C. Huart, *Ancient Persia and Iranian Civilization* (1927) and A. J. Arberry, *The Legacy of Persia* (1953). A useful survey of Persian civilization is provided by R. Girshman, *Iran* (1954). The history of the Persian Empire is given by G. Cameron, *History of Early Iran* (1936), and A. T. Olmstead, *History of the Persian Empire* (1958), while A. V. W. Jackson, *Zoroaster the Prophet of Ancient Iran* (1938), is a study of the great reformer of Persian religion.

3 · The Small Nations and the Mediterranean Empire

The most spectacular achievement of the second millennium B.C. was the creation of the great political units, which culminated after one thousand years of experimentation in the Persian Empire. Side by side with these enormous territorial agglomerations, however, were smaller nations which could not boast of political might and were sooner or later engulfed in the expansion of their more powerful neighbors. Though they did not succeed in dominating the political scene of their day, these smaller states in many cases achieved a more advanced level of civilization than the contemporary great powers. Their influence stretched farther and more significantly into the future than that of the Hittite and Assyrian armies. Some of these small states were never forgotten by succeeding centuries. Such were the Hebrews and the Phoenicians. Others, the Lydians and the Phrygians, are being rediscovered in our times. Archaeological excavations constantly reveal "lost civilizations," and the uncovering of each of these changes from year to year our picture of the ancient world.

THE HEBREWS

The literary tradition of Hebrew history embodied in the books of the Old Testament was never lost and forms part of the religious background for most of the western world, but it is only recently that archaeology has begun to confirm some of its aspects. The early Hebrew tribes undoubtedly sojourned at some time in the valley of the Tigris and the Euphrates near the territory of the Sumerian cities. Ur of the Chaldees was the traditional home of Abraham, and the similarity between the Sumerian and Hebrew *Epics of Creation and the Flood* cannot be coincidental. At all times the passage of the Hebrews is difficult to trace because, like all Semitic tribes, they were pastoral nomads wandering to and fro after their flocks, living on the edge of the desert and rarely settling in any locality. It has been suggested that these nomads moved southward in the second millennium B.C., perhaps involved in the great advances of the Hyksos or the Hittites. This theory is entirely possible, but such an association is not recorded. Perhaps the Hebrews merely wandered further south in search of grazing for their flocks. In the fourteenth century, among the enemies listed as threatening the Syrian Egyptian gov-

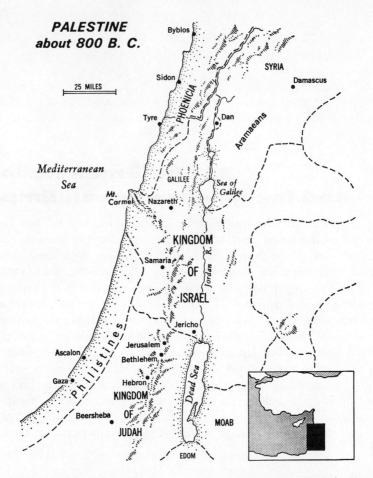

PALESTINE
about 800 B. C.

Byblos

SYRIA

Sidon

Damascus

25 MILES

PHOENICIA

Tyre

Dan

Aramaeans

Mediterranean
Sea

GALILEE

Sea of
Galilee

Mt.
Carmel

Nazareth

KINGDOM

Samaria

OF

Jordan R.

ISRAEL

Jericho

Jerusalem

Ascalon

Bethlehem

Gaza

Dead Sea

Hebron

KINGDOM

Beersheba

OF

MOAB

JUDAH

EDOM

Philistines

ernors in the *Tell-el-Amarna Letters,* are the "princes of the Habiru." Some of
the nomad tribes reached as far south as Egypt, according to both the traditional *Book of Exodus* and local literary sources. The similarity between the
story of Joseph and the Egyptian *Tale of Two Brothers,* dating from the
thirteenth century B.C., must also indicate a point of contact between the two
peoples.

Political Development of the Hebrews

The history of the Hebrews up to this point had been that of separate
wandering tribes. Indeed, political unity does not seem to have been a strong
element in the life of the Hebrews, and the tradition of the desert remained
strong among them. Political unity came relatively late, was forced upon
the Hebrews as the only means of resisting their enemies, and crumbled
rapidly. The wandering Hebrews were naturally the enemies of the settled
population of Palestine, the Canaanites. By the thirteenth century the inscriptions of Egypt complain of attacks by a new people, the Pulestiu or Philistines
in the Delta of the Nile and along the Palestinian shore. This new and serious

threat forced the union of the Jewish tribes, which succeeded in defeating the Pulestiu under their leaders Saul and David (ca. 1000 B.C.). Rather unwillingly, the Hebrews, under David and his son Solomon, settled into a kingdom patterned on the contemporary empires with a capital at Jerusalem. The new state prospered briefly in alliance with the neighboring kingdoms of the coast—Sidon, Byblos, and particularly Tyre. But the union was ephemeral. Under the successors of Solomon, the kingdom split in two: Israel in the north, with its capital at Samaria; Judah in the south, still loyal to the house of David reigning in Jerusalem. The creation of the Hebrew kingdom had been possible only in the breathing spell provided by the decline of both the Hittites and the XIXth dynasty in Egypt. Eternally divided, alienated from their neighbors, Israel and Judah had no hope of surviving the new invasions. Samaria fell to the Assyrians in 722. Jerusalem, temporarily saved from the disaster, was taken by Nebuchadrezzar in 586 and its population deported northward in accordance with the practice learned by the Babylonians from the Assyrians. The end of the Babylonian captivity under the Persian King, Cyrus the Great, did not reestablish Hebrew political independence, which had but a brief revival under the Maccabees in the 2nd century B.C. before the absorption of Judah into the Roman Empire.

Hebrew Monotheism

Political power never characterized the Hebrew nation and the kingdom of Solomon was only a reflection of the greater powers of his time. But the religious advance of the Hebrews was more significant for the western world than the shrines of Amon at Luxor, the Ziggurats at Babylon, or even the magnificence of Solomon's own temple at Jerusalem. Already in the desert the Hebrew tribes had worshipped a single god, Yaweh, who guided them in their wanderings. At the time of their coming into Palestine the Hebrews adopted some of the gods of the sedentary Canaanite population, but this was a departure from the true tradition which condemned as idolatry the worship of the Golden Calf. With the growing enmity between the Hebrews and the other peoples of Palestine, the worship of the one supreme, invisible god was reaffirmed.

The worship of Yaweh gradually came to be celebrated with an elaborate ritual centered in the Temple of Jerusalem, but the essence of the religion was concentrated in a series of moral precepts, presumably handed down by God himself on Mount Sinai. These are the Ten Commandments, which lifted the religion of the Hebrews from the level of ritual to that of ethical teaching. According to this teaching Yaweh was all-powerful and to be found everywhere. In contrast to the other ancient traditions, the Hebrew religion specified that no statue might represent this invisible power and the name of God might not be spoken. The opposition of the religious nomad tradition to the identification of the cult of Yaweh with the city of Jerusalem may be seen in the difficulties encountered by David when he first tried to move the Ark of the Covenant to the new capital. The party favorable to the king won, but Yaweh did not become identified with Jerusalem as Amon had been with Thebes. The one god of the Hebrews developed into an only God, whose authority extended over the universe and next to whom all other presumed deities were powerless idols. He was a jealous God who would punish mercilessly any abandonment of his worship and his exclusiveness expressed itself in his first commandment: "Thou shalt have no other god before me." But he protected his people and would someday send a Messiah who would establish the rule of justice over the entire world.

The power of Yaweh gave great authority to the prophets who spoke in his name. The immediate result of this authority was probably disastrous for the Hebrew kingdoms. Within the realm, authority was divided between the ruler and the prophets, who, as the direct spokesmen of God, allowed themselves to criticize severely and even to oppose openly the actions of the king. In foreign relations, the abhorrence of all contact with infidels, forbidden by divine law, wrecked all hopes for a coalition with the princes of Syria and left the kingdoms of Israel and Judah isolated in the path of their conquerors. Nevertheless, the Hebrews' realization that religion was not attached to a particular political system was far ahead of contemporary concepts. It comforted them during the Babylonian captivity and after the final destruction of the kingdoms. To other nations it suggested new ideas: that divine law transcended that of mankind; that a government, no matter how powerful, was not the institution claiming man's ultimate allegiance; and that the ruler, though God's representative, was not the absolute divine figure of Oriental despotism for he might and even must be disobeyed when he transgressed moral principles that transcended his authority.

THE PHOENICIAN CITIES

From time to time we have already caught a glimpse of the great cities, such as Tyre, Sidon and Byblos, which bordered the eastern shore of the Mediterranean and were inhabited by a people called the Phoenicians. Egyptian ships had come to trade in these cities from the Middle Kingdom. The *Tell-el-Amarna Letters* complained of their turbulent princes, only too ready to revolt. Solomon asked his friend King Hiram of Tyre for cedar wood and skilled craftsmen for his Temple. The Phoenician cities, inhabited by a mixed Semitic population, never formed a single homogeneous state. Alternately ruled by native princelings and passing under the overlordship of the great power of the moment, Tyre, Sidon, Byblos, Berytus show nothing interesting in the way of political development. Their art and religion also were but a patchwork of Egyptian and Mesopotamian traditions.

The position of the coastal cities of Phoenicia forbade them to create an individual state or civilization. Clinging to the narrow strip of shore which separates the mountains of Lebanon from the sea, the coastal cities were barred from expansion by other powers in the hinterland and to the south. The land needed to feed a great state was never available. At the same time, because they stood in the path of all traffic between Egypt and the North, these cities were open to international influences and could develop along their own individual lines. The great prosperity of the Phoenician cities was a direct result of these disadvantages. Barred from the land where communications were difficult and dangerous, the Phoenicians turned to the sea and rapidly became the greatest sailors and merchants of the Mediterranean, surviving a number of political upheavals. Through much of antiquity the word *Phoenician* is taken as meaning "sea-going trader," often with the unflattering additional connotation of pirate.

To support their active trade, the Phoenicians exported a number of articles which were in great demand everywhere. The cedars of Lebanon had always been famous; they are praised equally in the *Epic of Gilgamesh* and the *Journey of Wen Amon*. Two flourishing industries supplemented the export of wood, a busy glass manufacture and the making of magnificent woolen cloths dyed with the purple extracted from Mediterranean shells, by means of a process known to the Phoenicians alone. But native exports were never the only source of Phoenician trade. Almost all the goods which moved in the basin of the Mediterranean at some time travelled on their ships and passed through their hands. This phenomenal activity created a new merchant aristocracy and brought incredible wealth to their cities. Even ill-willing neighbors such as the Hebrew prophet Ezekiel could not keep from being impressed by the memory of Tyre's fabulous wealth (Ezek. XXVII).

The continuous travels of the Phoenicians made them the greatest explorers of antiquity, increasing immeasurably the geographical horizon of the East. The great Oriental empires were landbound, knowing little more than the territories adjoining the valleys in which the earliest civilizations had been born. Phoenician ships were a familiar sight in all the islands of the Mediterranean. By the beginning of the first millennium B.C. they had ventured far to the West. New cities were founded as Phoenician colonies in distant lands: Carthage, the greatest, in northwestern Africa; and Cadiz in southern Spain, made profitable by the exploitation of great tin mines. The explorers sailed through the Straits of Gibraltar into the Atlantic and even down the west coast of Africa to regions which no western man would see again until the first of the great Portuguese navigators of the fifteenth century after Christ.

The Phoenician Alphabet

To facilitate the records needed for the enormous volume of their business transactions, the Phoenicians adopted one of the indispensable tools of civilization, the alphabet. The new system of writing was not invented by the Phoenicians, and they never realized the intellectual possibilities of its use, but the signs used to keep tradesmen's accounts had the flexibility needed to record the most sophisticated and abstract thought. Up to the diffusion of the alphabet, the standard systems of notation were hieroglyphics and cuneiform characters. Babylonian cuneiform was a sort of unofficial world language used for all international relations and read in all the foreign offices of the time. Even the Egyptian governors of the *Tell-el-Amarna Letters* reporting to their king wrote in the Babylonian cuneiform in preference to hieroglyphics. The great defects of these systems were a difficulty in expressing abstract ideas and the enormous number of signs needed, since each one corresponded to an entire word or at least to a group of sounds and could, therefore, not serve again unless the particular group reappeared. The true alphabet, where each sign corresponded to a single sound and could be reused wherever the sound recurred, was of course more flexible. Only very few signs were needed for the entire system, a mere twenty-two in Phoenician. Even more important, these signs had no connection with any picture or word, as in the earlier systems. They were completely neutral in meaning, they corresponded only to sounds, and so they intruded no connotation of their own into the new words they composed. Although the precise location in which the first alphabet was invented is unknown, a crude example dating as far back as the fourteenth century B.C. has been found in the Sinai peninsula. But it was left to Phoenician ships to carry it over the entire breadth of the Mediterranean.

ASIA MINOR

In the hiatus of some six centuries (twelfth to sixth century B.C.) between the Hittite domination and the final reconquest of the Persians, several kingdoms about which we still know very little arose in Asia Minor. South of the Caucasus, the kingdom of Urartu, closely linked to the Mitanni, forced the Assyrians to send armies northward year after year in an attempt to subdue it. In western Asia Minor the Phrygians and Lydians established their rule. The best-known and most important of these minor kingdoms seems to have been that of the Lydians, whose realm had the particular advantage of a natural phenomenon. In antiquity the rivers of Lydia carried gold nuggets, thus providing the king with an income so fabulous that all successive generations have associated his name, Croesus, with untold wealth. These enormous revenues gave considerable power to the Lydians and their capital, Sardis, became one of the great centers of the East. The Lydian kings do not seem to have made any particular innovations in politics or the arts, but they were the first to replace the cumbersome system of payments in weights of silver used up to that time by coining the first real currency. The superiority of the new system was so striking that it was rapidly adopted throughout the Mediterranean.

The legendary reputation of Croesus made Lydia famous even before the study of the ruins of Sardis confirmed its tradition of great wealth. The neighboring states which have not benefited from the same prestige may have been unduly neglected and underestimated. The tradition that King Midas of Phrygia turned all that he touched into gold should be a significant indication of the prosperity of his realm. Recently-begun excavations on the territory of Urartu and at the Phrygian capital of Gordium indicate realms of hitherto unsuspected importance. Similar results have been obtained at the Syrian site of Ras-Shamra, but many tribes and kingdoms, Lycia, Caria, and others, are still little more than mere names to us. Consequently it is to be expected that the history of the entire basin of the eastern Mediterranean will have to be rewritten once more within a few years.

All of our attention so far has been focused on the lands of the Near East in which original civilizations were born and the concept of government developed. Civilization was not, however, restricted to this area. The existence of contemporary civilizations in India and China has already been mentioned. Far more important for us, a great seafaring culture with its own unmistakable characteristics developed on the islands of the eastern Mediterranean and particularly on the greatest of them, Crete. The so-called Minoan civilization of Crete participated in the international world of the East in the Bronze Age, but its greatest significance was for the still barbarous country to the north of Crete on the mainland of Europe, which would be known in the future as Greece. Later Greek tradition remembered its indebtedness to the island civilization. King Minos, who gave his name to its culture, was reputed so wise and just that he became one of the supernatural judges of the underworld. Classic mythology even asserted that Zeus, the king of the gods himself, had been born on Crete. The fusion of Minoan culture with that of northern invaders, related to those coming into the East, laid the foundation for a new nation which would carry civilization beyond the achievements of the oriental empires.

The Source of Cretan History

In spite of its importance, the history of Crete is not known in anything like the detail and accuracy of Egyptian, Assyrian, or even Hittite history. Up to the beginning of the present century, most of what was known of Crete was contained in such legends as that of the great hero Theseus, who came to the island and slew the bull-headed Minotaur which had devoured captive youths and maidens in the maze of the Labyrinth. Minoan culture has now become reasonably familiar, but most of the political history of Crete is still a matter for conjecture. The reason for this situation is to be found in the type of sources available for the study of Minoan life.

Thanks to the intensive excavations begun by Sir Arthur Evans at Knossos in north-central Crete at the end of the nineteenth century and continued throughout the island by international scholars, archaeology has done all it can to acquaint us with Minoan culture. Written documents, however, were not available until very recently, so that many questions remained obscure and Crete had to be treated as a prehistoric civilization. The fault did not lie with the Cretans themselves. Minoan civilization was literate, and numerous inscriptions exist, written first in a system called by scholars "Linear A" and, at the very end of Cretan history (ca. 1400 B.C.), in a new script called "Linear B." But neither system could be read, and Cretan remained one of the mystery languages of the world. In 1953, a young architect named Michael Ventris succeeded in deciphering "Linear B," thus showing that it was an Indo-European language and an archaic form of Greek. The fate of "Linear A" has not yet been settled. Scholars still argue whether it is related to Akkadian, Phoenician, or still another language. In any case, it appears to be a form of Semitic language, clearly unrelated to "Linear B." This difference supports the archaeological evidence which points to Oriental connections for early Minoan culture. Because of the deciphering of the Cretan scripts, the next few years should bring new light to the history of Crete, though the existing documents themselves seem to be composed of inventories rather than political or literary information.

Minoan Thalassocracy

A Neolithic culture had appeared in Crete as long ago as around 8000 B.C., but Minoan civilization does not seem to have preceded those of the Orient. Evans, basing himself on his archaeological finds, imitated the chronology already established for Egypt and divided all of Minoan history into three periods: Early Minoan (ca. 3000–2100), Middle Minoan (ca. 2100–ca. 1750), and Late Minoan (ca. 1750–1400), with an aftermath coming down to 1200 B.C. Both the religion of the Cretans, centered in the cult of a "Great Mother" similar to the Mesopotamian Ishtar and goddesses found in Syria and Asia Minor, and the still tentative indications of "Linear A" point to the Orient as the Cretans' original homeland. Nevertheless, Egypt was the power with which the Cretans established the closest relations from an early date. Egyptian objects appear in the island from the Early Minoan period, while characteristic Minoan pottery is found on Egyptian sites of the Middle Kingdom. The interrelation of the two countries was continued to the very end of Cretan history, for the "Keftiu" found in XVIIIth dynasty tomb-painting of the fifteenth century such as that of Senmut carry Cretan vases and wear Cretan dress. The presence of Cretans on the mainland of the Near East, between about 2100 and 1400 B.C., and the existence of provincial Minoan culture on the islands of the Aegean Sea suggest the formation in this period of an extensive seafaring empire, or Thalassocracy, centered in Crete.

On the island itself, an agricultural society apparently flourished, but the best information about Minoan culture is furnished by the cities and particularly by the elaborate palaces built from the Middle Minoan period at Knossos and a number of other sites. These palaces can only have belonged to a powerful aristocracy. The vastly superior size of the palace of Knossos, with its multitude of rooms clustered around a great center courtyard and its complicated plan, which must be the source of the legend of Theseus, the Minotaur and the inescapable Labyrinth, suggests that it was the home of the Cretan king. An extensive system of paved roads unified the island, and the absence of great fortifications around the palaces built near the seashore point to a sea power depending on a navy and not expecting to be subjected to a regular siege. The indication from Egyptian inscriptions that "the great ones of Keftiu come in peace" and the failure to find any reference to Cretan invasions have led scholars to believe that the Minoan empire was commercial and cultural, rather than military. Nevertheless, life did not always run smoothly on Crete. The great palaces were wrecked and burned several times, although until 1400 B.C. they were immediately reconstructed. Their final destruction apparently coincident with the appearance of the new "Linear B" and the abandonment of most great centers appears to indicate that Minoan

Minoan and Mycenaean GREECE

100 MILES

Mediterranean Sea

civilization had finally succumbed to a foreign attack, though this conclusion is still open to question.

Minoan Civilization

A brilliant and sophisticated culture grew up on Crete during the sixteenth and fifteenth centuries B.C. The palaces, rising several stories high, contained elaborate public and private apartments, as well as extensive store-houses connected by corridors and great circular staircases. They had a sanitation system unequaled in antiquity. The walls of these palaces and even of private houses were covered with frescoes almost always depicting flowery landscapes filled with wild animals and birds, or elegant court scenes of noblemen and court ladies. The subjects of the frescoes suggest that they were painted for decoration and enjoyment rather than for the religious or propaganda purposes of Oriental art. The style of the paintings displays the freedom and imagination of a true artistic tradition which extended even to everyday life. The remarkable decoration of flowers and floating marine creatures, as well as the graceful shapes, turns ordinary household Minoan pots and vases into works of art. Indeed, the revolutionary art of Tell-el-Amarna probably was influenced by the great artistic tradition of Crete since the charming scenes of landscapes and frolicking animals discovered in the ruins of Akhenaten's palace are far more reminiscent of Minoan painting than of the rigid Egyptian tradition. In the Cretan palaces lived a sophisticated if fragile court society whose wasp waists, long curls, fringed loincloths, and tiered bell skirts are still visible on the palace frescoes.

Minoan Religion

For all of its brilliance and the secular themes of its art, Minoan society was profoundly religious. Numerous ivory and faience statuettes and engravings on gold seals represent the Great Mother worshipped in Crete. Dressed in the clothes of a Minoan lady and wearing a high, conical headdress, she often grasps snakes symbolizing her status as the mistress of all life, wild animals as well as mankind. Pictured with her is a male child who is probably to be associated with the Oriental gods of fertility, as is his mother. The worship of the goddess by her priestesses is represented on seals. With the cult of the great mother should probably be associated another characteristic object of Minoan civilization, the bull games. On frescoes, seals, and ivory figurines, are represented men and women somersaulting over galloping bulls in what is believed to be a religious ritual. Archaeological evidence points to the great central courtyard of the palace at Knossos as the site of this ceremony. Hence, archaeology and legend may well agree at this point. The labyrinth palace of Knossos was the home of the bull-like Minotaur whose cult was dangerously celebrated by devotees until it was destroyed by a foreigner from over the sea.

THE MAINLAND

Greek tradition tells us that Theseus of Athens was the killer of the Minotaur; and for an understanding of the people who destroyed the palace of Knossos and of the civilization which they in turn created, it is necessary to rely again on a combination of legendary and archaeological evidence. The great tradition of the Greeks gathered by Homer in the national epics of the *Iliad* and the *Odyssey* preserved the memory of the heroic alliance of their ancestors. The epics tell how these Achaean princes sailed together under the leadership of King Agamemnon of Mycenae to avenge the abduction of his brother's wife Helen by Paris of Troy; how they destroyed the city of Troy after a ten year's siege; how Agamemnon returned to Mycenae only to be murdered at the instigation of his wife Clytemnestra; and how King Odysseus of Ithaca was driven ten years over the sea before reaching his home. Endless controversies have raged over the accuracy, authorship, and date of the Homeric epics. The single authorship of the *Iliad* and *Odyssey* has been denied; their date has been moved from century to century; and even the subject of the epics, the great Trojan war, was at one time rejected as imaginary and with no grounding in historic fact.

The Homeric Epic and the People of the Sea

The precise authorship of the Epics is not of immediate concern here, but their historic content is of the greatest importance. Since 1875 when the German scholar Schliemann identified its site on the northwestern shore of Asia Minor, the existence of Troy has become a historic reality—even though Schliemann misinterpreted the material he had uncovered. We have already seen that the flourishing culture of the Cretan palaces was probably brought to an abrupt end about 1400 B.C. by invaders whose language, found in the inscriptions of "Linear B," was closely related to Homeric Greek. By the end of the fourteenth century B.C. the Hittite king Murshilish II records the presence in Asia Minor of a people called the Ahhiwaya. Through the next century various Oriental sources complain of "the People of the Sea," raiders along the coast of Syria and Asia Minor. On one of his inscriptions the pharaoh Ramses III boasts of a victory won by him around 1200 B.C. over a people attacking the Delta from the sea, whom he in turn calls the Achaiwasha. It seems reasonable to believe that these Ahhiwaya, or Achaiwasha, are to be identified with the Homeric Achaeans. Raiding across the Mediterranean, they destroyed Crete, and at various times reached all the way to the mainland of Asia Minor and the Nile Delta. One of these destructive bands may well have sacked the city of Troy at about the same time. The truthfulness of the Homeric tradition seems to be established by these discoveries, and the Epics consequently may be accepted as historic sources, though certain anachronisms indicate that they were composed long after the period they describe. The problem, however, remains of who these Achaeans were who destroyed Minoan culture, as well as Troy. For an answer to this question it will be necessary to imitate Schliemann and follow Homer to Greece and especially to the city of Mycenae in the Peloponnese.

The Origin of the Achaeans and Their Settlement on the Greek Mainland

In the year following his excavations of Troy, Schliemann began to dig on the unpromising site of the tiny village of Mycenae. There, and at the nearby site of Tiryns, he found flourishing cities. The quantity of gold dug up at Mycenae can be matched only by the spectacular discoveries of the Sumerian tombs at Ur. They fully justify the Homeric characterization of the city as "golden Mycenae." Similar cultures have been found on other Greek sites; among others, one at Pylos on the west coast of the Peloponnese.

Mycenaean civilization, as it is usually called after its greatest center, unquestionably owed a great deal to Crete. Mycenae and Tiryns are cities built around a great palace, as was Knossos, and in the decoration of these palaces reappear many themes of purely Minoan origin. The characteristic octopus and dolphins of Crete decorated the floor of the great hall at Mycenae, and on the frescoes decorating the walls in the Cretan fashion the court ladies still wear Minoan dress.

In spite of their similarities, the Mycenaean cities were not populated by Cretans. The great Minoan goddess is gone, together with her toreador ritual. The language found in the inscriptions of the mainland is "Linear B," which comes to Crete only with the invaders. Some of the figures represented on the frescoes wear a new type of garment; the imaginative freedom of Cretan painting gives way to a new rigid style, and the architecture of the mainland palaces differs from those of Crete. Instead of being relatively unprotected centers set on the plain near the sea, Mycenae and Tiryns are formidable citadels set back from the shore on natural elevations and protected by enormous walls and gates. They are the homes of a military society whose heavily armed soldiers and war chariots appear in artistic representations.

If the Achaeans of Mycenae and Tiryns did not come from Crete, there is also no reason for believing that they had reached the mainland of Greece by sea. As has already been said, their cities are often situated at a distance from the shore, and the gates face away from the sea. Hunting scenes and horse-drawn chariots replace the ships and seascapes of Crete in their paintings. A characteristically military society, resembling in this respect the one already found among the Hittites, confirms the evidence that "Linear B" is an Indo-European language. The newcomers began to infiltrate into Greece around 1900 B.C., the very time when the Hittites first made themselves known in Asia Minor. Consequently, the Achaeans must be one of the many Indo-European tribes moving westward in this period and establishing their military superiority over older populations. They were the forerunners of the many tribes who called themselves the Hellenes, and who are now collectively known as the Greeks.

By about 1600 B.C. the great Mycenaean centers had been established in the Peloponnese, and the Achaeans had come in contact with the superior Minoan culture, the home of which they would soon destroy. The invaders may even have comprised different groups, for Homer speaks of many tribes and with Mycenae, at least, we observe a change in burial customs. The original shaft graves surrounded by a circular enclosure, in which Schliemann found the golden masks of early kings, are replaced by great tombs covered by successive, concentric rings of stone blocks rising to form a dome more than twenty feet above the ground. These so-called beehive tombs are still associated with the names of Agamemnon and Clytemnestra by popular tradition. Toward 1400 B.C., probably as a result of the knowledge that they had acquired from the Cretans, the Achaeans took to the sea. The presence of numerous Mycenaean communities around the Mediterranean shore and the extensive geographical knowledge found in the *Odyssey* have even led scholars to speak of the existence of a loose Mycenaean empire around 1200 B.C.

Mycenaean Civilization (the World of Homer)

The great centers of the Mainland, such as Mycenae, achieved impressive wealth, and their art flourished. Nevertheless, Mycenaean society remained at a relatively simple Bronze-Age level. The Mycenaean empire was never more than a temporary federation of independent princelings united by a similar culture. Most of the cities did not attain the grandeur of Mycenae; and the Homeric ruler is often found seated unpretentiously in front of his palace, or by the hearth inside, surrounded by his warriors and friends who are also his advisers. However, the simplicity of this picture may be the work of a later period no longer able to conceive the true splendor of Mycenae. The clan, based on ties of blood, was the fundamental social institution. Agriculture, supplemented by a commerce difficult to distinguish from piracy, furnished its economic foundation. Homeric religion was relatively primitive, and its gods, ruled by Zeus from Olympus, could not be distinguished from the quarrelsome and vain princes who worshipped them. Nevertheless, Mycenaean society should not be underestimated. Its acquaintance with the Mediterranean world was extensive, and its craftsmanship superior enough to be imitated far and wide. The greatest admiration went to heroic courage, although Odysseus was as wily as he was brave. Respect for the gods, loyalty to one's relatives, and generosity to the unfortunate were the virtues expected of men, and the gods, for all their foibles, saw to it that crime and injustice did not go unavenged. The ruins of "golden Mycenae" were too large to be filled by later inhabitants, but the memory of the legendary brilliance of its civilization lingered after it had been destroyed by a new wave of Indo-European barbarians sweeping down from the North.

FURTHER READING

A history of archaeological discoveries in Palestine has been given by W. F. Albright, *The Archaeology of Palestine* (1949), also G. E. Wright, *Biblical Archaeology* (1957). The discoveries in the southern part of the country are related by one of the main excavators of the area, N. Glueck, *Rivers in the Desert* (1959).

A thorough survey of the history of the Jews is found in W. O. E. Oesterley and T. H. Robinson, *A History of Israel,* 2 vols. (1932), J. Wellhausen, *Prolegomena to the History of Ancient Israel* (1885), is a good introduction; see also H. Orlinsky *Ancient Israel* (1954). The civilization of the Hebrews is studied in S. Moscati, *Ancient Semitic Civilizations* (1960), and E. R. Bevan and Ch. Singer, eds. *The Legacy of Israel* (1927).

Basic works on the Hebrew religion are W. O. E. Oesterley and T. H. Robinson, *Hebrew Religion* (1930), and A. Lods, *The Prophets and the Rise of Judaism* (1937). A good treatment of problems in the Old Testament is found in Oesterley and Robinson, *An Introduction to the Books of the Old Testament* (1934, 1958). Excellent studies on the later history of the Jews are found in E. Bickerman, *From Ezra to the Last of the Maccabees* (1962) and *The Maccabees* (1947).

The best introductions to Minoan civilization are J. D. S. Pendlebury, *The Archaeology of Crete* (1963); R. W. Hutchinson, *Prehistoric Crete* (1962); and G. Glotz, *Aegean Civilization* (1930). J. Chadwick, *The Decipherment of Linear B* (1958), is a fascinating account of the uncovering of the later Minoan script.

For the civilization of the Mainland, see H. R. Hall, *The Civilization of Greece in the Bronze Age* (1928); J. L. Myres, *Who Were the Greeks* (1930); A. Lang, *The World of Homer* (1920); and M. I. Finley, *Ancient Greeks* (1963).

Very good English translations of the Homeric epics have been given by R. Lattimore, *The Iliad of Homer* (1951), and R. Fitzgerald, *The Odyssey of Homer* (1961). Some of the problems of these epics have been studied by D. Page, *History and the Homeric Iliad* (1959). The traditions and beliefs of early Greek society are reflected in *The Greek Myths,* 2 vols. (1955), edited by R. Graves.

II

THE CLASSICAL WORLD

1. Archaic and Classical Greece

2. The Hellenistic World

3. The Roman Revolution and the Principate

Civilization as we know it was born and grew in the Near East, but the next great periods in the development of mankind shifted the focus of history further west: first to Greece, and later to Italy, so that the Mediterranean Sea became the center of the civilized world.

The symbolic institution of the Orient was the great empire ruled by a king who was part god. In the clear light of the Mediterranean, heaven and earth were separated. Religion and politics became divided, and although the world continued to revere the gods, the great achievements of the classical Mediterranean world were found on earth. The human mind began to venture toward the solution of problems earlier left to the supernatural. The intellectual emancipation of mankind went hand in hand with new political patterns. Gradually, first on a small scale, eventually over the entire world, men came to govern themselves. Beset by errors and failures, the man of Greece and Rome was no longer the plaything of his rulers or his gods. He shared in the privileges and the responsibilities of the State. The slave and subject had become a citizen.

1 · Archaic and Classical Greece

Until recently, the study of history began with Greece because of the enormous significance of her achievements for western civilization and because she was considered the creator of an entirely original culture. Now archaeology constantly demonstrates the indebtedness of Greece to earlier Oriental discoveries. Nevertheless, the Greeks, for all their obscure beginnings, moulded all that they had borrowed into a new pattern and added to it startling innovations. Participation in government, the automatic prerogative of every Greek citizen, was unthinkable in even the most tolerant eastern empire. Greek experiments in popular government ultimately ended in failure and tragedy, but they gave to the world a new concept of the rights of mankind. Together with political rights came the right of unhindered intellectual inquiry. The originality and brilliance of the Hellenic world derived from a respect for the human mind that is incompatible with absolutism.

ARCHAIC GREECE

The Coming of the Dorians. The Mediterranean world of the Mycenaean cities came to an end soon after 1100 B.C. as the last groups of Indo-Europeans entered the Greek peninsula. The Dorians, as the new invaders are collectively called, travelled the paths of earlier invasions and were related to the Achaean creators of Mycenaean culture. Later Greek tradition spoke of their advance as "the return of the sons of Herakles" rather than as a new invasion. But in the interval between the two waves of migration, they had developed the new technique of using iron, and their superior military equipment allowed them to subdue the more refined Bronze Age civilization of their Achaean predecessors.

The land into which the Dorians pushed their way was not made to support a large population or to create a great empire. Composed of two unequal parts, the Mainland proper and the Peloponnesian peninsula, joined by the narrowest of land bridges, Greece has the extensive shore line and good harbors suited to navigation—but precious little land for agriculture. Of the actual land area, not a fifth could be cultivated because of the poor quality of the soil and the extremely mountainous nature of a country where valleys are isolated and narrow. To the problem of land must be added the problem of water, for almost all Greek rivers run dry several months of the year, so that even potentially arable land could not bear a crop. The first Greek historian, Herodotus, already acknowledged that "Greece and poverty are stepsisters," and the problem of food is one of the constants in Greek history.

Greek Migration to Asia Minor

The coming of the Dorians upset the precarious balance between land and population, and its effect was to drive many of the older inhabitants out of their homes. Fleeing before the newcomers, numerous Greek tribes such as the Aeolians, Ionians, and eventually even some of the Dorians themselves took the route familiar in Mycenaean times, across the Aegean toward the more fertile coast of Asia Minor, where they settled in successive waves from north to south. In their new home the Greeks came in contact with the more advanced civilizations of the East. From the Phoenicians they learned the use of the alphabet, and from the Lydians that of coinage. Along the routes running across Asia Minor came both trade and acquaintance with the science of Babylonian scholars. Because of their advantageous location, the Asia Minor cities, and particularly those of Ionia, were in the vanguard of Greek political and cultural developments.

"The Dark Ages" (The World of Hesiod)

In Greece itself, the picture was far grimmer than the one in Ionia. The regression of culture following the coming of the Dorians was so great that even the art of writing may have been lost between the eleventh and the ninth centuries B.C. Knowledge of the so-called Greek "Dark Ages" is still extremely sketchy. Archaeological remains are poor and unimpressive, and our best source of information comes from the poems of Hesiod who must have lived about a century after the composition of the Homeric Epics. The difference between the two worlds is shocking. The wide horizon of Mycenaean geography has closed to a narrow local life. The religion and legends of the past are still remembered but as echoes of a golden age contrasting with the sorrows of a present in which scattered princelings quarrel over the insufficient land and a population of farmers struggles on the edge of starvation. In the new Age of Iron the poet laments:

> ... And I wish that I were not any part
> of the fifth generation
> of men, but had died before it came,
> or been born long afterward.
> For here now is the age of iron. Never by daytime
> will there be an end to hard work and pain,
> nor in the night
> to weariness, when the gods will send anxieties
> to trouble us. . . .
>
> ... and all that will be left by them
> to mankind

will be wretched pain. And there shall be no
defense against evil.

The Polis

Local rule in the "Dark Ages" was in the hands of petty chieftains on
whom was lavished the name of kings, and the memory of these "kings" was
to survive in later Greek history, both in the still ruling kings of Sparta and
the elected king-magistrate of Athens. By the end of the ninth century, however, the kingship had practically disappeared and power lay in the hands of
local aristocracies who owned most of the available land and were held
together by family ties. In this period appeared, first in Ionia, the beginnings
of the city-state, or *polis,* which was to become the characteristic institution of
Greek political life. The earliest *poleis* were probably federations of adjoining
villages and later *poleis* grew in size and developed a number of differentiating
local institutions, but the basic concept and structure of the *polis* was uniform
throughout the Greek world.

The *polis* consisted outwardly of an upper city, or *akropolis,* on which
stood the temples of the local gods, and a lower city, in which were located
the houses of the inhabitants and the *agora* or market place with the public
buildings. The settlement was surrounded by walls, but the adjoining lands
which supplied food for the city were always considered part of the *polis.*
Within the city lived a mixed population: slaves, foreigners called *metics,* and
finally the citizens, sometimes a minority, but the only ones who were granted
the name and prerogatives of *politai,* or citizens. In every *polis,* though form
might vary according to local custom, the government consisted of a threefold
system: the magistrates, a relatively small council of elders, and the assembly
of all the citizens.

Citizenship in a *polis* expressed itself in duties rather than rights. Every
male citizen had to serve in the army whenever called, bringing his own
equipment. He was expected to fill any public office to which he was chosen
without pay. Furthermore, all the major expenses of the *polis,* such as the
financing of embassies, festivals, or public buildings had to be undertaken by
the wealthier citizens as an obligation known as a *leiturgy.*

With these duties, however, went a number of compensating privileges
which, together with the limited food supply, restricted the extension of the
citizenship. The *polis* gave to all its citizens a public training and education
which would fit them for its requirements. Only citizens owned land and
shared in the worship of the city gods. Even in the least evolved and reactionary *polis,* every citizen had a say in the government. This participation
might be no more than a vote of "yes" or "no" in the general assembly to an
already formulated policy, but this was more than was enjoyed by the greatest
nobles of the most advanced and enlightened of Oriental states, the Persian
Empire. Consequently, the Greeks came to see themselves as free men and the
Persians as slaves. All of the devotion of the citizen naturally went to his
polis, since outside of it, cut off from religious, political, and property rights,
he was but half alive. Wealthy men competed for *leiturgies* and spent their

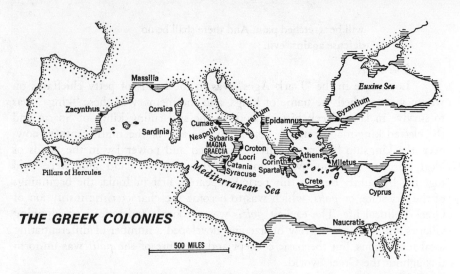

THE GREEK COLONIES

Massilia

Zacynthus

Corsica

Sardinia

Cumae
Neapolis
MAGNA
GRAECIA
Sybaris
Croton
Locri
Catania
Syracuse

Tarentum

Epidamnus

Byzantium

Athens
Corinth
Sparta

Miletus

Crete

Cyprus

Euxine Sea

Pillars of Hercules

Mediterranean Sea

Naucratis

500 MILES

revenues on public buildings and festivals, rather than on embellishing their homes. All citizens fought stubbornly to defend the independence of their city, and Greek history is punctuated by cases of citizens preferring death and the total annihilation of their *polis* to the recognition of any superior authority.

This unlimited devotion to the *polis* helped bring about the creation of remarkable city-cultures, the most brilliant of which was elaborated in fifth-century Athens; but it was also a constant threat to the peace and stability of the country, for it permitted no compromise with the institutions of other cities and pushed the country in the direction of total political fragmentation.

The Panhellenic Institutions

The aggressive individualism of the various *poleis* was partially counter-acted by a number of unifying cultural institutions whose existence allows us to speak of a single Hellenic civilization. The most powerful of these common institutions was religion. Each *polis* gave its first allegiance to its protecting deities whose cult was part of the civic life, but all Greeks recognized the gods of the Olympic pantheon, dominated by Zeus, who had been worshipped since Homeric times. Several famous religious sites enjoyed common respect. The birthplace of the sun god Apollo on the island of Delos and the great shrine of Zeus at Olympia in the western Peloponnese attracted continuous pilgrimages. Later, the mystery cults, whose purpose was to teach the secrets of immortality, brought devotees to Eleusis, near Athens, and the northern island of Samothrace. But the most famous religious center grew around the oracle of Apollo at Delphi. Not only Greeks but foreigners came to consult the oracle. Delphi became an important clearinghouse of international infor-mation, thus giving considerable political influence to the priests of Apollo. Similarly, the great religious, gymnastic, and poetic competitions, such as the one held every four years at Olympia beginning in 776 B.C., provided a peaceful meeting ground where men from every city might exchange ideas. Such Panhellenic institutions, which transcended the provincialism of the *polis*, provided an indispensable minimum of political stability. But the problem of the federation of the jealous *poleis* into a balanced state was one which all the brilliance of the Hellenic mind never succeeded in solving.

Colonization and Tyranny

At the time of their appearance the city-states were little more than agricultural villages, but even the small agglomeration of population formed by them soon exceeded the possibilities of the local food supply. Territorial expansion within Greece was impossible, nor was it available to the Asia Minor cities whose hinterland was held by the more powerful kingdoms of Phrygia and Lydia. The Greeks, consequently, took once more to the sea. The *poleis* periodically sent out groups of young men to settle in distant lands, as had been done before by the Phoenician colonists. The early example of the Ionian city of Miletus was soon followed on the Mainland, and between about 750 and 500 B.C. ceaseless waves of colonization settled the shores of Thrace, the region of the Black Sea, and particularly Sicily and southern Italy. New Greek foundations in this latter area, such as Tarentum, Cumae, Neapolis (Naples) and Syracuse, which became the largest Greek city of its day, were so numerous that the entire region became known as Magna Graecia (Great Greece).

The new colonies were politically independent of the mother-city, but they kept at first a number of religious and economic ties with it. Most importantly, in the early years of its foundation, the colony relied on the mother-city for a supply of manufactured articles such as weapons, tools, and pottery, which it usually repaid in raw materials. As a result of this exchange, the trade and industry of the parent-city grew disproportionately, giving rise to a new class of artisans and merchants who had not existed in the old agricultural scheme of life. With the exception of Sparta, which generally refused to participate in the colonial expansion and preserved unchanged her anachronistic kingship and the rigid social pattern she had presumably received from the legendary lawgiver Lycurgus, the Greek cities underwent a considerable political evolution that followed upon their colonial activity.

The newly-risen classes in the *poleis* had no political power to match the wealth they had acquired, for the government was entirely in the hands of a landed aristocracy which was closed to them. The answer to their demands was provided by the appearance of tyrants in the various cities. Originally the word *tyranny* had no injurious meaning. The tyrant might not be a legally chosen leader, and his rule might often be based on military power, but he appeared primarily as the defender of the poor farmer and new middle class against the oppression of the aristocracy. The tyranny often furthered the growth and embellishment of the *polis* through its patronage of public works, trade, and even the arts. Tyranny as an institution rarely lasted more than one or two generations before being overthrown, often as a result of the abuse of power which has given the word its modern meaning. It served, however, as the means of breaking the stranglehold of the agricultural aristocracy on the life of the *polis* and of giving some political role to the new classes of society.

The political development of the city-states was uneven. Sparta, whose stubborn opposition to commerce and intellectual education and whose constant fear of an uprising of its disproportionately large slave population turned it into a rigid military and reactionary society, never even reached the stage of tyranny. Throughout its history Sparta maintained its political pattern of two kings chosen for life from the same two families and advised by twenty-eight elders who formed with them the council of the *gerousia*. Because of the absence of colonization, the commercial class which had appeared in other cities and brought about their political evolution never developed. All male Spartan citizens were trained for military service alone. They ate at the common mess and the state supervised every aspect of their lives. Five elected officials, the *ephors,* with authority even over the kings, saw to it that no innovation interfered with the maintenance of this rigid tradition.

The Growth of Greek Democracy

Other cities achieved various levels of political advance. But the most complete development of the system of popular participation in the government of the *polis,* which the Greeks called *demokratia,* was gradually achieved in Athens during the sixth and fifth centuries B.C.

Tyranny came relatively late to Athens; an early attempt to establish it was crushed by the nobles. But the growing commercial development of the city made aristocratic absolutism impossible. The first codification of law by the aristocracy under Draco at the end of the seventh century B.C. had much the same effect as that of the *Code of Hammurabi,* since knowledge of the law became public rather than remaining the secret of the ruling class. However, the insufficiencies and the harshness of the Draconian legislation soon made it inadequate, and the attack on the power of the nobles continued. One of the great glories of the Athenian aristocracy is that these attacks were led by members of the nobility rather than by the middle class.

In 594 Solon, a member of one of Athens' oldest families, was formally asked to resolve the quarrels among the various classes. Solon introduced a number of new laws, such as the abolishment of enslavement for debt and the establishment of a uniform system of weights and measures designed to appeal to the poor and commercial classes. But the so-called Solonian Constitution was intended as a compromise. According to it, all Athenian society was divided into four classes on the basis of wealth. From the first two classes were chosen the nine annual magistrates or *archons.* The ruling senate (*boulé*) of four hundred members was drawn from the top three classes, while the poorest class (the *thetes*) attended only the general assembly (*ekklesia*) composed of all citizens, which approved or disapproved of the decisions of the *boulé.* The earlier aristocratic tribunal called the Areopagus was not destroyed, though it lost much of its power, but a new court called the *heliaea* composed of a jury of 5,000 citizens heard cases of appeals and tried impeached magistrates. The Solonian Constitution brought little outward change to the already existing structure of the Athenian *polis.* The aristocracy continued to control

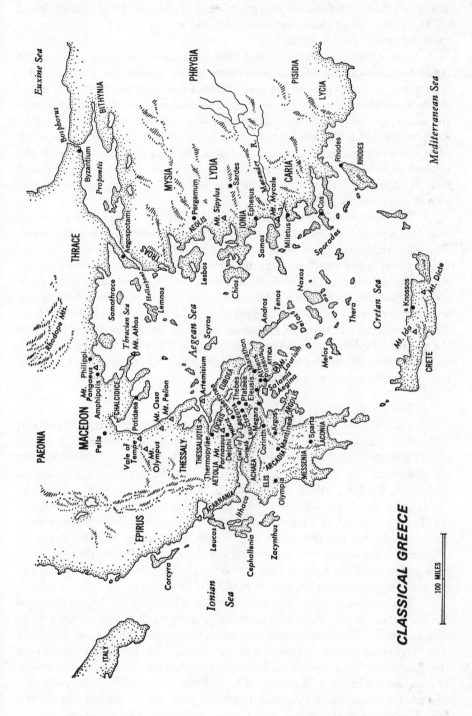

CLASSICAL GREECE

Euxine Sea

Bosphorus

Byzantium

Propontis

BITHYNIA

PHRYGIA

THRACE

Aegospotami

PISIDIA

MYSIA

LYDIA

Pergamum

LYCIA

Mt. Sipylus

Sardes

AEOLIS

IONIA

Ephesus

Meander R.

CARIA

Mt. Mycale

Miletus

Cos

RHODES

Rhodes

TROAS

Hellespont

Samos

Sporades

Mediterranean Sea

Lemnos

Chios

Mt. Dicte

Rhodope Mts.

Samothrace

Thracian Sea

Naxos

Cretan Sea

Mt. Athos

Aegean Sea

Tenos

Andros

Delos

Mt. Ida

Knossos

Scyros

Thera

CRETE

Mt. Philippi.

Pangaeus

MACEDON

Artemisium

Melos

Amphipolis

EUBOEA

CHALCIDICE

Mt. Ossa

Marathon

Potidaea

Mt. Pelion

Chalcis

Athens

ATTICA

Pella

LOCRIS

Thebes

Laurium

PAEONIA

Vale of

Tempe

Mt.

Olympus

THESSALY

THESSALIOTIS

Delphi

BOEOTIA

Plataea

Eleusis

Piraeus

Salamis

AETOLIA

Mt.

Parnassus

Thermopylae

Leuctra

Megara

Aegina

Corinth

ARGOLIS

Gulf of Corinth

ACHAEA

Argos

Mantinea

EPIRUS

ACARNANIA

ELIS

ARCADIA

Sparta

LACONIA

Ithaca

MESSENIA

Olympia

Leucas

Corcyra

Cephallenia

Zacynthus

Ionian

Sea

ITALY

100 MILES

the magistracies and much of the legislative *boulé,* but the composition of this aristocracy had been radically altered. Instead of the old closed nobility based on birth, the ruling class now was accessible to any citizen having the required property qualifications.

The compromise of Solon had the usual fate of satisfying no one, and Athens underwent an interval of tyranny under Peisistratos (560–527 B.C.). The tyrant generally favored the poorer classes who supported him. To assure the food supply of the city he established a number of military colonies near the Bosphorus to control the water route by which the wheat of the region north of the Black Sea was brought to Athens. He also began the great work of ornamenting the city, but he did not alter the laws of Solon. Although the tyranny ended with the sons of Peisistratos, the citizens had to wait almost a century after Solon for a new aristocratic leader, Cleisthenes, to take a new step in the direction of democracy.

The Constitution of Cleisthenes kept the outward forms of the preceding one, but went on to destroy the hold of the aristocracy on the government. The old traditional tribes based on kinship were abolished, and ten new geographical tribes intermingling the classes of society were substituted for them. The membership of the *boulé* was raised to five hundred to make more room within the government. The new law of *ostracism* provided for a ten-year banishment of any leader judged dangerous by a vote of the *ekklesia.* Consequently, every Athenian statesman would henceforth be at the mercy of the people's displeasure. At a later date the new tribes also obtained a say in military affairs by electing ten generals (*strategoi*) whose office was the only one to which re-election was permissible.

The Persian Wars

The cities of Greece had already progressed far in their political and cultural developments when they were faced with a formidable threat to their existence. The conquest of Lydia by the Persians left the Greek cities of Asia Minor face to face with an enemy they did not have the power to withstand. The aid given to the Ionian cities in their revolt against the Persians by the Greek Mainland and particularly by Athens, brought down on Greece the wrath of Darius the Great. The first Persian expeditions were unsuccessful; the initial attempt was wrecked by storm off Mt. Athos in Thrace. In the second, the heavily armed Athenian infantry (the *hoplites*) managed to trap the famous Persian cavalry between the mountain and the sea and destroyed it in the plain of Marathon (490 B. c.).

The next expedition, ten years later, was commanded by the King of Kings, Xerxes in person. It was carefully prepared and supported by a large fleet to protect its communications between Greece and the Asiatic mainland. The beginning of the invasion was successful. The Persian army crossed the Bosphorus on a bridge of boats, swept through Thrace and northern Greece, overwhelmed a predominantly Spartan force holding the mountain pass of Thermopylae, and destroyed Athens, from which the inhabitants had fled. Victory seemed assured, but Greece was saved thanks largely to the ability and foresight of the Athenians. Even before the launching of Xerxes' campaign the Athenian leader Themistocles had realized the importance of the sea in any war with the Persians and persuaded the *ekklesia* to devote part of the city's revenue to the construction of a navy. Now moving from the island base of Salamis to which the Athenians had retired, and repeating in a certain sense the successful tactics of Marathon, the Athenian fleet lured the Persian navy into the narrow space between the island and the mainland of Greece, where it did not have sufficient room to maneuver, and annihilated it. The remains of the Persian fleet that had escaped the rout of Salamis went down in a storm. Cut off from its line of supplies, the Persian army left in Greece was destroyed by the crack Spartan *hoplites* at Plataea. The following year the Greek fleet put an end to all fears of invasion by destroying the remaining Persian navy in a battle off Mt. Mycale on the western coast of Asia Minor (478 B.C.).

The final and unexpected success of the Greeks freed them from the nightmare of foreign domination. The Persian wars had also been the scene of the first Hellenic cooperation. Spartan troops had not come in time to help the Athenians at Marathon, but the second great war had seen the working together of the Greek cities united in the face of the Persian threat. Even after the final victory at Mycale, fear of another Persian attack kept up some cooperation between the cities of the Aegean. Under the sponsorship of Athens the Delian League was created among the maritime cities for their common protection. Each member of the league furnished a battleship or funds sufficient for the maintenance of such a ship for the defense of the Aegean; and the treasury of the league was suitably deposited in the Panhellenic sanctuary on the island of Delos.

The Age of Pericles (461–429)

Athens had been the main instrument in the victory over the Persians, and Athens during most of the following century dominated all of Greece by its cultural prestige. As her historian Thucydides boasted, she was a "School for Hellas." During most of this period the political power was in the hands of one man, Pericles, after whom the most brilliant period of Athens has been named. This designation, though subsequent and arbitrary, need not be considered a distortion, for Pericles successfully epitomized in his person the qualities Athens had come to expect of its statesmen. The family of Pericles came from the great aristocracy, as had most of the great democratic leaders, and like them he increased the political power of the lower classes. In spite of his noble background his authority in politics came not from his inheritance but from an elected office. In other words, under the terms of the law of ostracism of Cleisthenes he remained in power only as long as the popular assembly was willing to support and re-elect him. For more than twenty-five years he successfully walked a political tight-rope and was re-elected to the annual office of *strategos* every year but one. Pericles, though formally holding the office of general, was a skilled diplomat, his friends were scholars and poets, and his house was the meeting place of intellectual Athens.

During the rule of Pericles the last democratic touches were put to the Athenian constitution. The offices which had previously been reserved to certain classes of society were now opened to everyone; even *thetes* might aspire to be *archons*. Every office except that of *strategos* was filled by lot so that no pressure could determine the choice. For the first time citizens were paid to sit on juries and perform their political functions. Scandalized contemporaries called the measure bribery, and indeed it ran counter to the principle that every citizen should serve his city spontaneously and without remuneration. But the innovation of Pericles gave a new reality to democratic forms. The poor, who had never been able to assume those political functions nominally granted them in earlier legislations, might now do so. Trade was encouraged by the protection of *metics,* though citizenship was restricted. Continuing the earlier policy of Peisistratos, Pericles reinforced the northern military colonies, which guarded the wheat route from the Black Sea to Athens. To make sure of sufficient supplies for the population of the city Athens came to dominate the Delian League. The other maritime *poleis* continued to pay their contribution to the common defense, but the ships became solely Athenian. In 454 B.C. the treasury of the league was shifted from Delos to be deposited on the Akropolis of Athens.

The Civilization of the Fifth Century

For later generations the name of Pericles has been attached not so much to his political achievements as to the brilliant intellectual and artistic civilization which flourished in his lifetime and which appears to us as the quintessence of Hellenic culture. It must be admitted now that the Greeks owed much to their predecessors. Architects and sculptors borrowed themes and methods from Egypt, and the early philosophers of the Ionian cities benefited from the accumulated science of Babylon. But their indebtedness in no way lessens the originality of Greek civilization. The themes and materials may be foreign, but their synthesis is purely Greek. The entire focus of the civilization had been shifted from religious to civic life. As in politics, so in the arts, the center of attention was the *polis,* and its glorification.

Both the plastic arts and the drama of Greece have religious background. The greatest masterpieces of fifth century architecture and sculpture, such as the Parthenon of Athens and the great statues of Phidias have religious subjects. The plays of Aeschylus, Sophocles, Euripides, and Aristophanes never separated themselves from the annual festival of Dionysus for which they had been created. Nevertheless, all of the arts transcended their religious origin to find their true theme in human life. The great buildings of the Akropolis and the statues they contained were erected to make Athens the most beautiful city of Greece. They were addressed to mankind rather than the gods. The admirable proportions of the Parthenon are designed to delight rather than dwarf humanity, while the study of the human form in sculpture attains an unequalled perfection. Similarly the drama, born of religious ritual, soon affirmed the dignity of man even before the overwhelming power of the gods. In the defiance voiced by the human chorus of Aeschylus' drama, ordered by Hermes to surrender Prometheus to the wrath of the gods:

> How dare you bid us practice baseness? We
> will bear along with him what we must bear.

rings the defiant answer of the Greek *polis* to the overwhelming might of the Persians on the field of Marathon, where Aeschylus himself had fought. Before the end of the fifth century, the drama had come to concern itself with purely human themes—with the problem of war and of its horrors; and with the problem which was to become immediately critical for Greece as for all mankind, that of the relation of the individual to the state.

The precise observation and record of human life was not the only concern of the artist. Beyond external beauty was an ideal of perfection transcending the immediate, and the search for abstract criteria is as characteristic of Greek culture as is its humanity. This double approach is perhaps best seen in the creation of a literary form which concerns us more closely, that of history. Oriental civilizations had noted the glories of their kings in inscriptions and annals, but these were mere records or in some cases propaganda, rather than intellectual investigation. The father of Greek history, Herodotus, entitled his work *Research (Historia)*, and the research carried him to all aspects of human life. Foreign and Greek, past and present, political, social, economic, religious, or artistic, he was concerned with every particularity of the experiences of mankind. Thucydides, writing less than a century later, did not abandon the research of Herodotus, but he went on to look beyond immediate events to invisible causes that brought them about. The masterpiece he produced remains in its logical perception, accuracy, and impartiality a model for all writers of history. Likewise, Greek scientists and thinkers, such as Thales, Anaximander, Heraclitus, Pythagoras, and Pericles' friend Anaxagoras, beginning with the knowledge transmitted to them from the Orient, proceeded to speculate on the laws of the universe and the first principle of which the world was created. With Socrates and his most brilliant pupil Plato, true philosophy encompassing every intellectual and moral problem of mankind was born. The new Platonic school held the theory that abstract ideas are the true pattern of which visible manifestations are only the multiple and imperfect reflections. Only the ideas have real existence. Their worldly images are illusions of the senses while beyond the ideas themselves and transcending them is the one immutable good. Thus in every aspect of Hellenic culture ran interwoven the double thread of humanity and abstraction which gave it both brilliance and originality and achieved a perfection which remained comprehensible to man.

THE DECLINE OF THE POLIS

The successful synthesis achieved in the arts and intellectual pursuits unfortunately found no counterpart in political life. The jealous *poleis* never succeeded in finding a formula for unification and harried each other to death, at the same time as within them, the very individualism which created the masterpieces of Greek culture undermined the structure of the state. The brilliance of Greek civilization foundered in the conflict opposing city to city and the individual to the state.

The Cities of the Athenian Empire

Thucydides, describing the Peloponnesian war, the great war of his time, attributed its origin to the Greek cities' fear of growing Athenian power. Under Pericles Athens had come to dominate the Delian League originally intended for the common defense of the Aegean, and was turning it into a sort of empire. The other cities might well look askance at the symbolic transfer of the Delian treasury to Athens, but the city itself was caught in a dilemma. The reforms of Pericles which made political life accessible to the poor by paying them for their participation in public activity, and the responsibility of a popular government for the welfare of its citizens made the control of an extensive revenue imperative. Unlimited democracy could survive only as long as it was solvent and as long as the arrival of wheat from the Black Sea assured its existence. In order to achieve this Athens must control the sea and could tolerate no challenge to its supremacy. By 416 the most democratic *polis* in Greece reached the point of destroying the island of Melos and killing its entire male population for having refused to recognize its overlordship.

The Peloponnesian War

In theory, the creation of an Athenian empire might not seem a misfortune since it could have been the instrument for the unification of all the Greek cities into a single state, but the other cities could hardly be expected to share this point of view. As early as 431 the great war of Sparta and her allies against Athens, known as the Peloponnesian war, had broken out; it was to ravage Greece for nearly thirty years and end with the total defeat of Athens.

The first ten years of the war were inconclusive and ended with an equally inconclusive treaty of peace. But Athens had already suffered two severe blows. A frightful epidemic of the plague had ravaged the city, and one of its early victims had been Pericles himself. In the demoralization which followed, Athens was to show every weakness of its democratic institution as each political faction tried to win the favor of the fickle general assembly. War broke out very shortly after the signature of the peace. The brilliant, if unreliable, general Alcibiades persuaded the Athenians to launch an expedition against the Sicilian Greek city of Syracuse, which was allied to Sparta. In itself the plan was not unreasonable, since its success would have separated Sparta from its main source of supplies, but the expedition was doomed from the start. The assembly, presuming too much on the duty of the citizen to serve his city even against his will, elected as co-general a man who had opposed the plan from the start. Hardly had the fleet sailed when the opposition to Alcibiades persuaded the assembly to recall him to face a charge of sacrilege. Rather than face a court controlled by his enemies on what may well have been a trumped-up charge, Alcibiades abandoned his command and fled to the enemy at Sparta. The expedition, deprived of its original instigator, sailed on to total annihilation.

The disaster of the Sicilian expedition spelled the doom of Athens. The cities she had dominated in the Aegean revolted, the fleet which had been her strength since the days of Themistocles was gone, the politicians at home struggled for power with greater and greater violence. Still the city held out for nearly ten years, building new fleets to oppose the one furnished to the Spartans by the Persians, who saw with satisfaction their old enemies at each others' throats, and even recalling Alcibiades to power. But in spite of several notable victories which Athens was too demoralized to exploit, the effort was in vain. The last Athenian fleet was crushed at Aegos-Potami in 405, and the city itself surrendered to the enemy after a siege of several months. The bid made by Athens for the control of the Greek world had ended in total failure.

The End of Greek Independence

The nominal winner of the Peloponnesian war was Athens' oldest enemy, Sparta, but she had little leisure to enjoy her victory. The reactionary militaristic pattern of Spartan life had created a superb army with a reputation that overawed the entire Greek world. But it had never succeeded in producing the leadership capable of exploiting the achievements of this army. Within a few years of the victory of Aegos-Potami, all of Greece was again embroiled in war as various cities attempted to recreate the Athenian empire for their own benefit. The first result of these coalitions and counter-coalitions was an inconclusive peace signed in 386 under the auspices of the King of Persia. The Greeks, who already in 401 had suffered the humiliation of seeing Greek citizens under a Greek general serve as mercenaries for their old enemies the Persians, now had to acknowledge that the King of Kings had become the arbiter of Greek political life and to recognize his suzerainty over the same Greek cities of Asia Minor, the preservation of whose independence had been the cause of the Persian wars.

The "King's Peace" benefited no one but the Persians, and the scramble for power continued. By 371 the city of Thebes had managed to destroy the legendary might of the Spartans on the battlefield of Leuctra, but the Theban control could not succeed where the Athenians and Spartans had failed. The final victor of a century of war was not to be a Greek *polis* but the king of the half-barbarian kingdom of Macedon, which had hardly been considered part of Greece until then. Informed of the situation by his spies and the many friends he had in the Greek cities, King Philip II of Macedon decided to profit by it. In Athens the orator Demosthenes vainly tried to warn the Greeks of their danger. The new Macedonian infantry formation, the *phalanx,* destroyed the remaining Greek armies at the battle of Chaeronea in 338 B.C., and Philip II became the "protector of the Hellenic League." The Macedonian King barely outlived his victory, but the independence of the city-states had come to an end.

The Disintegration of the Polis

The destruction of the *polis* resulted not only from external wars, but also from the internal disintegration of the essential loyalties which bound the *polis* and its citizens. We have already seen how Alcibiades betrayed his city during the Sicilian expedition. We may admire the integrity of the historian Thucydides in blaming Athens for the Melian massacre, but impartial judgment is no more compatible with absolute devotion to the *polis* expected of its citizens than is outright betrayal. In a period of crisis the city could tolerate neither one nor the other if it was to survive the attacks of its enemies.

The clearest illustration of the impasse faced by Athens at the end of the Peloponnesian war is one of the most famous trials in history. In 399 B.C. the philosopher Socrates, accused of corrupting the youth of Athens and of attempting to introduce the worship of new gods, was condemned to death and executed. The execution of one of the greatest minds in the history of the world has never ceased to horrify mankind, but the Athenian jurors who pronounced the sentence were doing their duty, even if unconsciously. The criticism of Socrates and his inquiries into the true nature of justice and good could not be reconciled with the obedience owed to the *polis*. The right of individual judgment was a threat to existing institutions:

> . . . He made me confess that I ought not to live as I do, neglecting the wants
> of my own soul, and busying myself with the concerns of the Athenians.

This famous statement of Alcibiades, which sounds so reasonable and so consistent with modern introspective individualism, could only support the accusation that Socrates had indeed taught dangerous ideas to the young and diverted them from the first duty of the citizen.

Even earlier in the *Antigone* of Sophocles, the conflict between personal and public loyalties had been recognized, and Sophocles had concluded that personal duties had the precedence. But the price set by him on even justified opposition to the state was death. Socrates himself in the *Crito* admitted that the law in his own case must be obeyed even when thought mistaken or injust. Unable to face the challenge of Socrates, Athens was forced to obey the tradition of the *polis* and destroy any deviation from duty by killing its most brilliant citizen. But in doing so it was also destroying the individual inquiry on which the greatness of its genius was based, thus putting an end to all possibility of further growth. After the death of Socrates the *polis* would still find loyal defenders. The special sacred battalion of Thebes died to a man on the battlefield of Chaeronea rather than surrender to the inevitable. But they were defending an ideal which was no longer viable.

FURTHER READING

Studies of Greek history and civilization are far too numerous for any but the most superficial sampling here. For the history of Greece, the following are useful general accounts: G. W. Botsford and C. A. Robinson, *Hellenic History* (4th ed., 1956); E. Bickerman's new edition of M. Rostovtzeff, *Greece* (1963); C. E. Robinson, *Hellas* (1955); A. R. Burns, *Pericles and Athens*.

Among the appreciations of Greek culture, the following introductions are easily available: H. D. F. Kitto, *The Greeks* (1951); E. Hamilton, *The Greek Way to Western Civilization* (1930); and M. Bowra, *The Greek Experiment*.

On Greek life and institutions see A. R. Burn, *The World of Hesiod* (1936), for the so-called "Dark Ages"; T. R. Glover, *Democracy in the Ancient World* (1927); G. Glotz, *The Greek City and its Institutions* (1930); and Johnson and others, *The Greek Political Experiment* (1941). On the setting and economic aspects of Greek life, useful treatments are M. Cary, *The Geographic Background of Greek and Roman History* (1949); J. Hasebroeck, *Trade and Politics in Ancient Greece* (1933); H. Michell, *The Economics of Ancient Greece* (1940); and G. Glotz, *Ancient Greece at Work* (1926).

Excellent introductions to Greek religion are found in J. Hamilton, *Prolegomena to the Study of Greek Religion* (1922), and W. K. Guthrie, *The Greeks and their Gods* (1950).

For the Greek intellectual achievements see: E. Zeller, *Outlines of the History of Greek Philosophy* (1955), and J. Burnett, *Early Greek Philosophy* (1957). B. Farrington, *Greek Science I* (1944), is a particularly good brief survey of the subject. An outline of the literature is given by M. Hadas, *A History of Greek Literature* (1950); a survey of historical writing can be found in J. B. Bury *Ancient Greek Historians* (1957), and H. D. F. Kitto, *Greek Tragedy* (1954), provides a good introduction for a study of the masterpieces of Greek drama. On the various arts see: W. B. Dinsmoor, *The Architecture of Ancient Greece* (1950); G. Richter, *The Sculpture and Sculptors of the Greeks* (1930); and M. H. Swindler, *Ancient Painting* (1929).

Good selections of Greek literary and philosophical writing can be found in M. Hadas, *The Greek Poets* (1937); M. Nahm, *Selections from Early Greek Philosophy* (3rd ed., 1947); W. H. Rouse, *The Great Dialogues of Plato* (1956); and C. A. Robinson, *An Anthology of Greek Drama,* 2 vols. (1959). The best English translation of the Greek tragedies is R. Lattimore and D. Greene, *The Complete Greek Tragedies,* 4 vols. (1953–8). There are also excellent translations of individual authors and works such as, R. Lattimore, *Hesiod* (1959); R. Warner, Thucydides, *The Peloponnesian War* (1954); G. Rawlinson, Herodotus, *The Persian Wars* (1924).

2 The Hellenistic World

The disaster of Chaeronea marked both an end and a beginning in the history of Greek civilization. The city-states had lost their independence, but within a generation Greek culture had covered the Mediterranean, and the name "Greek" was synonymous with civilized man. The brilliant but local culture we have called Hellenic now spread through the world to become Hellenistic, that is, patterned on Greece but transcending its limits. The stage on which this development took place was far wider than any before, reaching from the Indus to the Western Mediterranean, which Odysseus had still seen as peopled with fantastic monsters living beyond the edge of the known world. Now an insignificant little state in Central Italy could no longer remain in isolation but was drawn into the orbit of the great common culture, until it finally came to dominate it. The symbolic *polis* of Hellenic Greece became the *cosmo-polis,* the city of the universe.

THE CREATION OF A NEW WORLD

Philip II of Macedon, the conqueror of Greece, was still a half-civilized barbarian chieftain from the northern border at the time of his victory at Chaeronea. But he had already begun the unification of Greece by his creation of the Hellenic League, for the purpose of fighting the common enemy, the Persian Empire. Philip's son Alexander was only twenty years old when his father was assassinated in 336. Before his own death a little more than a decade later, he had completely altered the face of the existing world. But the figure of Alexander, a god in his own lifetime, has become so completely hidden in legend and romance that it is difficult to distinguish his true intentions.

Alexander the Great (336–323 B.C.)

Approximately a year after his father's murder, Alexander had already reestablished order in Greece and resumed Philip's plan of attacking Persia. His success was as rapid as it was overwhelming. Three years and three main battles were enough to topple the greatest empire in the world. Crossing the Hellespont in 334, he met and overwhelmed the first Persian army at the Granicus river. The following year he trapped the main forces of the Persians, commanded by King Darius III in person, at Issus, near the modern city of

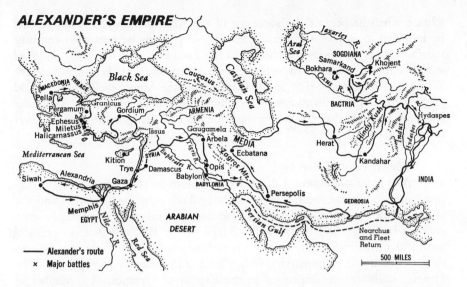

ALEXANDER'S EMPIRE

Black Sea

Caspian Sea

Aral Sea

SOGDIANA
Samarkand
Bokhara Khojent
Oxus R.
Jaxartes R.

MACEDONIA THRACE
Pella
Pergamum Granicus
Ephesus Gordium
Miletus
Halicarnassus Issus

Caucasus

ARMENIA

Gaugamela
Arbela MEDIA
Tigris R.
Euphrates R.
Ecbatana

BACTRIA

Hindu Kush

Herat

Indus R.
Hydaspes

Hydaspes
Hydraotes

Mediterranean Sea
Kition
Trye Damascus
SYRIA
Siwah Alexandria Gaza
Opis
Babylon
BABYLONIA

Kandahar

INDIA

Persepolis

GEDROSIA

Memphis
EGYPT
Nile R.
Red Sea

ARABIAN
DESERT

Persian Gulf

Nearchus
and Fleet
Return

——— Alexander's route
×   Major battles

500 MILES

Alexandretta which still bears witness to the victor's name. As at Marathon, caught between the mountain and the sea and unable to deploy satisfactorily, the Persian cavalry was no match for Alexander's crack Macedonian phalanxes. Darius III saved himself by flight, but his treasure and his entire family fell into Alexander's hands.

Although the victory had been overwhelming, Alexander did not march directly on the Persian capital of Persepolis. Probably because the Persian fleet still ruled the Aegean Sea and so presented a constant danger behind him, Alexander marched southward taking all the port cities of the Syrian coast on the way. In Egypt he was recognized as pharaoh by the oracle of Amon, and founded in the western Delta the first and greatest of the cities which bear his name, Alexandria of Egypt. Then at last he turned eastward, and the final battle took place at Gaugamela near Nineveh in 331 B.C. Darius was murdered by his nobles and effective Persian opposition came to an end.

The battle of Gaugamela, or Arbela as it is also known, marks an important turning point in Alexander's career. He had destroyed the might of the Persians and so more than fulfilled Philip's program. But now he proclaimed himself the successor of Darius III and assumed the title of King of Kings. The Macedonian nobles were greatly affronted at the new Persian ceremonies which they considered humiliating, and some of them revolted, but Alexander pushed on unheeding after having crushed the rebellion. In the trans-Caspian province of Sogdiana he married Roxane, the daughter of a local barbarian prince. At the Indus he reached the furthest eastern limit of the Persian realm.

The question of Alexander's intentions is still open to discussion. Some scholars believe he had always dreamed of a world empire; others say he intended to do no more than continue his father's plan of uniting Greece by a campaign against the Persians. Finally, the intermediate theory holds that Alexander's policy, unclear and limited at first, developed into a universal scheme when he became the successor of the King of Kings. It may be that he intended to stop at the Persian border, or: perhaps he meant to continue indefinitely his victorious march toward the East. Here we are in the realm of speculation, for Alexander's actions were determined by his own soldiers. Weary and fearful of being so far from home, the army rebelled and would go no further. The return journey was long and painful, and before Alexander had time to set out on the new expedition he had planned, he died of fever at Babylon.

The Oriental Monarchy

Alexander's unexpected death left an infant heir and a desperately confused situation in the enormous territory he had conquered. At one and the same time he was hereditary king of Macedon, general of the Hellenic League, pharaoh in Egypt, and the King of Kings in the East. He left no political testament of his intentions, but certain indications make it likely that he was thinking of a mixed monarchy, both Greek and Oriental in character. The Hellenic tradition was implanted in the East by the creation of a number of settlements of Macedonian veterans from the Mediterranean shore to the Indus. Like the greatest of them, Alexandria in Egypt, all of the new settlements were called after the conqueror and were patterned after the classic Greek *polis*. At the same time, Alexander's acceptance of semi-divine honors, both in Egypt and the Orient, show a recognition of the local Eastern tradition of the godking; and wherever he found it he left untouched the old Persian administrative system. The combination of the two traditions was apparently meant to go far beyond government institutions and produce a true mingling of races. Alexander had married a native oriental princess, and he encouraged or forced his officers and men to take Persian wives. Through this fusion, Alexander seems to have hoped that *omonoia* (the meeting of hearts and minds) might truly be achieved.

It is doubtful that even Alexander could have succeeded in holding together the immense territory he had conquered. His death broke the fragile union held together in his person, and his generals fought each other fiercely for pieces of his empire. The son born to him by Roxane did not live to inherit any part of his father's realm. From the merciless struggle which followed Alexander's death, several units finally emerged. In Macedonia an independent kingship developed. Further south two great leagues developed: the Ætolian League joined together the cities of Mainland Greece; the Achaean League confederated those of the northern Peloponnese. Finally Sparta maintained her hold on the southern part of the peninsula. In the Asiatic lands conquered by Alexander, two Macedonian dynasties continued the local institutions of the divine monarchy. Alexander's general, Seleucus, maintained the administration and traditions of the King of Kings in most of the old territory of the Persian Empire, although he soon lost the far eastern territories which had belonged to the Achaemenids, and the capital of the new monarchy was shifted westward to the new city of Antioch on the Orontes river near the coast of Northern Syria. In Egypt, another Macedonian general, Ptolemy, took over the prerogatives of the pharaohs and ruled from the great port city of Alexandria. Macedon, Greece, Egypt, and the Orient formed the main units of Alexander's Empire, but a number of smaller kingdoms, such as Pergamon in western Asia Minor, successfully maintained their independence. The political history of the century following the death of Alexander is one of extreme confusion and constantly shifting alliances among his successors, but the fundamental balance of power between the two great eastern monarchies of the Seleucids and the Ptolemies was not irreparably broken until 200 B.C. By that time a new power had grown in the West and it gradually came to dominate the whole of the Hellenistic world.

HELLENISTIC CIVILIZATION

The political Empire of Alexander could not be held together beyond his lifetime, but a new complex civilization created by the sudden contact of Greece and the Orient outlived the realms of all his successors. Even though the chronological limits of the Hellenistic period are difficult to determine, many of its characteristic innovations—cosmopolitanism, orientalization, exoticism, romanticism, and intellectuality—continued to flourish long after Alexander's death.

The most striking change introduced by the new society was its cosmopolitan nature. After the closed provincial world of the classical *polis,* a common culture filled the entire Hellenistic world. Greek was spoken by all educated men from Sicily to Babylon, and this Greek was no longer divided into innumerable local dialects but was unified into a single homogeneous language known as the *koiné,* or common tongue. Trade carried men from one end of the Mediterranean to the other, and through the new institution of *isopolity* a man could now be the citizen of more than one city. Greek and Macedonian youths came to seek their fortunes in the Seleucid or Ptolemaic administration, and intermarriage with native women continued in all but the royal houses. As the fixed gods of the *polis* no longer suited this mobile civilization, they were gradually identified with other gods having similar powers. Zeus became Amon, the Greek Artemis was seen as a different form of the Egyptian Isis and most other gods were linked in this pattern which is called *syncretism.* Instead of a multiplicity of local gods, the Hellenistic world saw local variations of the same great deities.

Macedonian dynasties with Greek aristocracies ruled the East, and Greek was the administrative and literary language, but the influence of the Orient was profound. The semi-divine monarchy of the East was a more common political institution than the still surviving city-state. The capitals of Antioch, Pergamon, and particularly Alexandria soon matched Athens as artistic and intellectual centers. The great buildings of the Hellenistic age were erected on the Asiatic mainland rather than in Greece. With the orientalization of society came a taste for overwhelming size and elaborate decoration, and particularly for exotic themes which appeared both in the visual arts and in literature for the better part of six centuries.

The great Hellenistic temples of Asia Minor dwarfed the Parthenon in Athens, but despite their size and ornamentation they had neither its perfection of proportion nor delicacy of detail. The sculpture did not aspire to the ideal beauty and detachment of classical works; rather, it was filled with an emotionalism not found before. Works of art were expected to arouse the sympathy or pity of the spectator for the sorrows and pains of the subject who ceased to be a type and became an individual. A taste for the exotic and the unusual widened the range of subjects. Instead of eternally young noble figures, all extremes of society were represented; barbarians as well as Greeks, rich and poor, old and extremely young, beautiful and deformed, commonplace and trivial scenes, even the pet animals of the household became fit subjects for the observation of artists. This interest in the individual rather than the ideal resulted in magnificent portraiture which may be traced through sculptures, coins and particularly the funeral paintings found in the Fayum oasis in Egypt. These strikingly realistic representations of the deceased replaced on the sarcophagi the fixed mask of earlier Egyptian burials.

The emotion found in Hellenistic art and its taste for the exotic was reflected by a new romanticism in literature. An aura of romance gathered around the figure of Alexander, his love match to the exotic princess Roxane, the chivalry with which he spared the captive women of Darius' household after the battle of Issus. The period after Alexander's death saw the first appearance of a new literary form, the novel. Almost every romantic plot of love and hairbreadth escape still in vogue can find its origin some two thousand years ago in one of the many Hellenistic romances. At the same time the so-called "New Comedy" of Menander turned its attention to the same everyday subjects and individual characters that had attracted the interest of sculptors and painters.

Emotional and romantic, Hellenistic society was also enormously learned. Alexander himself had been taught by Aristotle, the greatest philosopher of his day, and he took a number of scientists with him on his Persian expedition to study discoveries made on the way. This emphasis on direct, empirical observation rather than intellectual speculation on abstractions identifies the new philosophic school of Aristotle. Where Plato, one generation earlier, had drawn up the plan of the ideal *Republic,* the *Politics* of Aristotle contained descriptions of the constitutions of as many Greek *poleis* as he could obtain. Still, mere cataloguing of facts was not the end sought by the new Hellenistic school. Starting with an accumulation of material, Aristotle went on to give the rigorous method known as logic for drawing further conclusions.

The new Aristotelian method found its widest development in Alexandria where science was under the direct protection of the state. In 290 B.C. Ptolemy I founded, under the direction of one of Aristotle's pupils, a great library which attracted a number of resident scholars. This institution known as the Museum contained a library which may have held 750,000 volumes. The research carried on there as well as in other Hellenistic centers raised science to a level not equalled until the sixteenth century after Christ. The elements of geometry were laid down by Euclid, and those of Physics by Archimedes. Geography and cartography developed, as did the natural sciences. Less than a century after Alexander's death Eratosthenes of Cyrene had succeeded in calculating the circumference of the earth and Aristarchus of Samos had even gone on to expound the theory that the earth revolved around the sun, a theory still considered revolutionary some two thousand years later.

Social Inequality and Restlessness

The enormous artistic and intellectual activity carried on during the Hellenistic period was made possible by a notable increase in wealth. Alexander had captured the treasury of the Persian kings, and the immense wealth gathered there was suddenly spread through the Orient with the help of a very active commerce. In Egypt, the Ptolemies set up an extremely intricate and profitable system of monopolies through which they controlled most of the lucrative crops and industries of the country. For example, the olive oil monopoly insured that no oil could be pressed, refined, transported, bought or sold for food without direct government supervision and a rigorously set price. Through their multiple monopolies, most of the wealth of the country was channeled into the hands of the rulers. Great accumulation of wealth by the few, however, brought its counterpart, abysmal poverty. The Hellenistic world was one of extremes. The citizen was often released from the more rigorous obligations of his *polis,* but he had also lost the assured place in society which went with these duties, and the city no longer had the same responsibility to feed him as in the age of Pericles. Contemporary literature shows rapid changes in social position; today's master easily became tomorrow's slave and large bands of brigands or pirates seem to have roamed unchecked throughout the Mediterranean. At the same time, the blending of Greek and Oriental culture needed for the *omonoia* dreamt by Alexander did not always progress smoothly. Inscriptions and papyrus documents found in Egypt reveal that Egyptians often took Greek names to make their way in the civil service of the Ptolemies, but the privileges of the ruling Macedonian aristocracy were bitterly resented. In the late third century B.C. violent native rebellions shook the throne of the Ptolemies and gained for Egyptians entry into the army, from which they had previously been barred. The same repressed discontent was felt in the neighboring Seleucid kingdom. In 167 B.C. an attempt by the Seleucid king Antiochus III to impose Greek religious traditions in Palestine provoked an overwhelming revolt of the Jews under the Maccabees and the re-establishment of an independent Jewish kingdom. Hellenistic society was outwardly cosmopolitan, wealthy, and sophisticated, but it was restless and profoundly insecure. Until recently, scholars saw the cultural work of Alexander's conquest as successful, and the Hellenization of the East an accomplished fact. These conclusions have now been questioned because of the many cracks which mar the smooth surface of this society. The degree of contact and interpenetration between the Oriental and Greek societies is one of the most absorbing problems, if also the most difficult to resolve, in Hellenistic studies.

The New Philosophies

The growing complication and insecurity of society raised questions which could no longer be answered by the civic gods of the *polis*. Syncretism and a multiplication of mystery cults provided some of the answers, while several great philosophic schools developed moral teachings suited to the new times. The most important of these were the Epicureans and the Stoics.

Founded in Athens during the lifetime of Alexander, the Epicurean school was based in part on earlier Greek scientific speculation. The Epicureans taught that the gods lived in a distant sphere, unconcerned with human affairs, and that after death the body dissolved into its component atoms so that any afterlife was impossible and man need have no fear of death or the vengeance of the gods. The central problem of Epicureanism was that of human happiness and pleasure. The pleasure contemplated by Epicurus was intellectual and moral, rising above any material satisfaction. But this austerity and detachment had little popular appeal, and his teachings were rapidly perverted into the popular doctrine of "eat, drink, and be merry for tomorrow we die," which came to pass for Epicureanism.

More influential than the widely misunderstood teaching of Epicurus was that of his contemporary, Zeno of Kition, who taught in the painted porch or *stoa* in Athens which gave its name to the school he founded. The Stoics concerned themselves with the same problems as the Epicureans, but they taught the existence of a single world soul of which all human souls were a part. Real satisfaction was to be found in agreement with the world soul. This was achieved by undergoing unflinchingly the tribulations presented by the world and holding firmly to one's duty in whatever position one was found. The true Stoic sage with his mind fixed on his unalterable path would not even feel the evils of the world. The promise of the Stoic doctrine gave it an enormous vogue, not only in the Orient but later in the Roman world. At the same time, its teaching that all men, even slaves, were brothers since all shared in the world soul, gave it an equal appeal for all classes of society and had a profound influence on later ethical and humanitarian teachings.

THE WESTERN MEDITERRANEAN

The early development of Hellenistic civilization took place in the eastern Mediterranean basin, and its great centers were to be found there. Even the greatness of Athens paled before the splendor of the cities of Miletus, Ephesus, Halicarnassus, Antioch, and above all, Alexandria. The beam cast far out to sea by the great lighthouse erected in the harbor of Alexandria is a perfect symbol for the influence of its Museum on contemporary culture. Nevertheless, the western regions of the Mediterranean were by no means a desert in this period, but the home of a number of well-established states based on the Northern African coast and the Italian peninsula.

Carthage

In Africa the ancient colonies founded by the Phoenicians in the beginning of the first millennium B.C. had prospered. The great port city of Carthage

THE WEST in the Sixth Century, B. C.

Greeks
Phoenicians
Etruscans

Loire R.
Danube R.
Gauls
Alps
Gauls
Po R.
Ligurians
Apennines
Etruscans
Adriatic Sea
Pyrenees
Perusia
Clusium
Massilia
Elba
Veii
Rhodae
Tarquinii
Corsica
Caere
Italians
Iberians
Rome
Capua
Cumae
Naples
Tarentum
Poseidonia
Elea
Sardinia
Sybaris
Balearic Is.
Tyrrhenian Sea
Croton
Gades
Mediterranean Sea
Panormus
Messana
Ionian
Locri
Sea
Tingis
Utica
Sicels
Rhegium
Numidians
Carthage
Sicily
Syracuse
200 MILES

controlled an extensive domain along the African shore as well as numerous colonies in Sicily and Spain. No political ties bound Carthage to the Phoenician homeland, but many characteristics of Phoenician civilization were still clearly visible. Carthage worshipped the old Semitic gods of the Phoenician coast, and it was ruled by a small and wealthy merchant aristocracy such as dominated every Phoenician city. Although Carthage depended on paid mercenaries for an army, its fleet was unmatched in the West since it carried the extensive trade on which the city's wealth was founded. By Hellenistic times Carthage was one of the richest cities in the world and a constant threat to the Greek colonies of southern Italy. Plato, visiting at the court of the tyrant of Syracuse could write apprehensively, about 350 B.C., that if the Greek cities continued their eternal quarrels, Carthage would conquer all of them. Nevertheless, the powerful African city does not seem to have added any significant development to the civilization of its parent Phoenician cities.

The Italian Peninsula

The main centers of civilization in the West, however, were to be established on the Italian peninsula. Numerous Greek colonies were settled in the southern part of the country from the eighth century B.C. and a flourishing Hellenic civilization made these *poleis* part of the Greek and subsequently the Hellenistic world. But the rest of the peninsula was not in the same condition. Scholars noted long ago that the geographical position of Italy was isolated. The mountain ranges of the Alps closed access to it from the north, and its geographical configuration forced it to turn its back on the more civilized East. The great range of the Apennines cut the peninsula from north to south and left the more habitable plains to the west. Furthermore, Italy boasted few harbors in the East or the North of the country. Thus early Italy remained outside the mainstream of Mediterranean civilization and lagged behind it.

Nevertheless the most recent scholarship indicates that the cultural pattern of early Italy has been grossly oversimplified and was in fact extremely complex, with waves of invasions coming from east to west. From the second millennium on, various Indo-European languages were used by the inhabitants of the peninsula, and the appearances of Bronze and subsequent Iron Age cultures correspond generally to the chronological pattern found in Greece, with a considerable time lag. By the ninth century B.C. numerous Italic tribes inhabited the interior of the peninsula. These were mostly primitive semi-nomadic shepherds without important cities or elaborate government, although some loose tribal leagues seem to have existed as well as small settlements in the fertile western plains of Campania and Latium.

The Etruscans

The only cultural center to be found on the Italian peninsula, other than the ones provided by the Greek cities, was located in the north-central region now called Tuscany which was inhabited by the Etruscans. To this day the Etruscan language cannot be understood, and the origin of this people remains obscure. It was long believed that the Etruscans had come from the East in the eighth century B.C., and indeed their art shows many oriental affinities. The latest opinion, however, holds that the so-called Etruscan civilization was created by a mixed people. A population predominantly native may have been directed by a very small military or commercial aristocracy coming from the East. The main reasons for abandoning the earlier thesis of a great Etruscan migration are the absence of a sharp cultural change in Italy such as would have been provoked by a conquest and the fact that no Eastern sources around the eighth century speak of a large-scale movement to the West.

By the sixth century B.C. the Etruscans formed a sort of federation of cities stretching northward from the valley of the Tiber. Their wealth came from the control of important iron mines on the island of Elba. Their monuments and tombs show an elaborate and sophisticated civilization with traces of Oriental and Hellenic influence. Gradually the Etruscans extended their overlordship over the central peninsula, as well as southward, until their interests clashed with those of the northernmost Greek colonies of the western coast. Thus, at the end of the sixth century B.C., Italy was roughly divided into two spheres of influence—the Greeks in the South and the Etruscans in the North.

THE EARLY DEVELOPMENT OF ROME

Roman legendary tradition tells of the foundation on the Palatine hill of the city destined to be the mistress of the world by the semi-divine brothers Romulus and Remus, in 753 B.C. Legend recalls a period in which the city was ruled by Etruscan kings who were finally overthrown with the establishment of a republic in 509 B.C. Obviously this account is not to be taken at face value, and scholars have long since abandoned it as a source of historical information. Yet some of it is interestingly paralleled by archaeological evidence. The plain of Latium near the Tiber was one of the main Italic settlements. Some fifteen miles from the sea archaeologists have found traces of an eighth century settlement on a hill near a place where the Tiber can be forded. This settlement extended to the nearby hills and finally to a central swamp. The first traces of habitation are on the very hill which later bore the name of Palatine in Rome, corroborating the legendary tradition. The central swamp was the site of the later market place or *forum*. The region around this settlement constituted part of the Etruscan territory, but it was near its boundary. By the late sixth century the Etruscans and the Greek cities were in open conflict. Early in the next century Etruria was seriously defeated by the Greek cities of Cumae and Syracuse, and the text of a treaty between Rome as an independent state and Carthage, signed precisely in 509 b.c., still exists. Consequently, it is more than likely that at the end of the sixth century the city of Rome was already emerging from its first Etruscan overlordship.

Primitive Roman Civilization

The little settlement by the Tiber showed no signs of divine origin or future greatness. It was a small agricultural community with a market, perhaps a transfer point for goods carried across the Tiber. Indeed the absence of any coinage or ships until a very late date did not point to an important commercial center. Agricultural communities, with relatively few outside contacts and a fear of innovations which might wreck the all-important crop, tend to be conservative, and conservatism was the leading characteristic of Rome. Outwardly the city had, from the beginning of its independent existence, the usual framework of a *polis*. But its guiding spirit differed profoundly from that of the Greek city-states. Ancestral tradition rather than public service united the community, and its fundamental institution was the family. The head, the *pater familias,* was the guardian of all traditions which he expected to pass on to his children since Rome, unlike the Greek cities, provided no public education for its citizens. He taught them a trade and respect for their ancestors, he answered for their good behavior, and he supervised the family worship. As long as he lived, the *pater familias* had absolute authority over his entire household, which included the slaves and servants of the house as well as its adult children. This absolute authority included the right of life and death. Even a magistrate owed obedience to his father.

The religious institutions of early Rome were no more advanced than its social development. In time the Romans learned from the Etruscans and the Greeks of the southern cities the worship of the great gods of the Olympian pantheon, but their original devotion was directed toward far more primitive deities. Every person, object, or action was watched over by a spirit or *numen* who had to be propitiated. Sacrifices were offered to these spirits, who protected the house, the crops, and the state, so as to keep their goodwill and avert catastrophe. In these relations ritual was all important since any error of procedure might break the contract which bound humanity and these protecting genii. Gradually the Romans learned from their neighbors. New gods came to them and the alphabet apparently reached the city from the Greek city of Cumae. From the Etruscans the Romans received most of their political institutions, as well as much of their religious tradition and such practices as divination and gladiatorial games. Still the city remained faithful to its old agricultural tradition in which commercial, intellectual, and artistic developments had little or no place. Its commerce was left in the hands of the Carthaginians, and its children were sent to school in Etruria until the end of the fourth century B.C. The basic virtues of a citizen were considered to be courage, loyalty, discipline, seriousness, and respect for the past.

Internal Political Development

The political institutions of the city were as conservative as its society, and the government was controlled by the aristocracy. Even before the creation of the republic the body of citizens had been divided into two uneven halves, the patricians and the plebeians. The question of the origins of the two groups is still unresolved, although it is possible that the division of the two groups came relatively late as the wealthier patrician families succeeded in seizing the monopoly of power and excluding the others.

The actual institutions of the state were similar to those of the *polis* but they were also large-scale reflections of those found in the family. The two consuls were elected annually and, as the heads of the community, they held the *imperium*. That is, they were granted absolute civil authority within the city, and military authority with the power of life and death over citizens outside of it. They presided over the senate and the assembly and offered the official sacrifices for the welfare of the state. As advisers, the consuls had a senate of three hundred patricians whom they appointed, and from among whom they themselves were chosen. Similarly, tradition expected the *pater familias* to consult his friends, before coming to any important decision. Just as the assembled family approved the decisions of its head but could not change them, so the assemblies ratified the laws and elected magistrates. Several assemblies existed, but the most important was the *commitia centuriata* which was composed of the entire citizen body drawn up in military formation and subdivided into small units of unequal size known as centuries. As had been the case with the Athenian *ekklesia,* the *commitia centuriata* voted only "yes" or "no" to a previously prepared program or electoral slate, but its ratification was still necessary to make a decision legally binding.

With the elaboration of the administration other offices were added: *praetors* for the administration of law, *aediles* to supervise public works, *quaestors* for finances, and *censors* who supervised public morals and could expel any senator whose finances or behavior did not conform to the position and seriousness expected of an aristocrat. Only in times of public emergency could an appointed dictator suspend the proper functioning of the government and replace the consuls, but his emergency powers were granted for no more than six months.

All of the government offices were originally in the hands of the patricians; the plebeians were excluded and left unprotected. Gradually, however, they came to have their full share in the administration. The beginning of the evolution is confused by legendary traditions, and the entire development proceeded with a slowness suitable to Roman conservatism. The plebeians first acquired protectors, the *tribunes of the plebs,* eventually ten in all, elected by them to defend their interests. A tribune's person was sacrosanct, that is to say he could not be injured, and his murder was punished as a case of religious sacrilege rather than a mere secular crime. More important, although a tribune could not propose laws, he could interpose his veto to halt any piece of legislation or action of the magistrates. By 471 B.C. the plebeians had their own assembly, the *commitia tributa,* which, though it could still not pass laws, could make its will known in a decision or *plebiscite,* which acquired the force of law if approved in the *commitia centuriata.* Up to this time the law was known only to patricians, but the publication of the so-called *Twelve Tables* in 445 B.C. revealed it to all, as had the *Draconian Code* in Athens some two centuries earlier. Plebeians soon also obtained the right of inter-marriage with patricians. Nevertheless, their major victories were slow to come. Only in 367 B.C., the *Licino-Sextian Laws* stipulated the election of one plebeian consul every year. Nearly another century passed before the *Hortensian Law* of 287 B.C. gave the plebiscite the full power of law. More than two centuries had elapsed since the creation of the republic.

With the passage of the Hortensian law the plebeians shared in all the rights of the patricians, except a few religious occasions. But the government of Rome was still in the hands of the aristocracy. The powerful *commitia centuriata,* to which the plebeians had been admitted, was the only one empowered to approve or reject laws, declare war, ratify treaties, or elect magistrates. This assembly contained all of the citizens, as did the Athenian *ekklesia;* but its organization made it a tool of the ruling class rather than a democratic institution. The entire assembly was divided into 193 centuries on the basis of financial status. The centuries were uneven in size but each had only one vote. Votes were invariably taken beginning with the first and wealthiest century, and, as soon as an absolute majority was reached, the voting was brought to an end. Consequently the poorest, 193rd century, which contained the majority of the population of the city, had almost no occasion of making its opinion known during the course of the Roman history.

The Expansion of Rome

By the time Rome had completed the development of her political institutions, she was well on the way to dominating the Italian peninsula. A century later she was the dominating power of the Mediterranean. Neither the early history of the city nor the Roman dislike of innovation foretold such an expansion, but a number of elements made it possible. First among these was the geographical situation of the city. The plain of Latium was one of the largest and most fertile in Italy, especially in early Roman times when the vast northern valley of the Po was in the hands of hostile barbarians, the Gauls. Rome was assured of a sufficient local food supply. At the same time the central position of Latium was of great importance. At first it put Rome between Etruscan and Greek influence, and so free of both; later it allowed the city to prevent coalitions of its enemies and to dominate the whole peninsula.

Geography helped Rome to raise a large military population. But much of her success was due to the city's own tradition. The new Roman military formation, the legion, which replaced the Macedonian phalanx, owed as much to its discipline and endurance as to its new armament and flexibility. Far more important, Rome successfully achieved what the Greeks had been unable to do, the extension of its citizenship. From its earliest contacts with its immediate neighbors of the Latin League, Rome took the military leadership but did not try to overwhelm the League. The rights of Latin cities were recognized, and gradually full Roman citizenship was granted to them. This capacity for recognizing the rights of others and sharing its institutions with them is one of the greatest Roman achievements and constitutes its claim to superiority over far more brilliant Athens. It meant also that Rome would never face the coalition of the Peloponnesian war.

Later tradition always showed Carthage as the eternal enemy of the Romans. Historical evidence, on the contrary, shows an early alliance with Carthage, witnessed by the already mentioned treaty signed in 509 B.C. and its subsequent repetitions. The early history of Roman expansion was falsified to bring it into agreement with a later situation. In reality, the support of the Carthaginian fleet was of crucial importance in early Roman campaigns. The Romans first attacked their recent masters, the Etruscans to the north; then they concentrated on dominating the Italic tribes of whom the most threatening were the Samnites. The Roman advance, slow and occasionally checked by disaster, provides much of the material for Roman legendary history. A sudden invasion of Gauls broke through from the northern valley of the Po and captured Rome itself in 390 B.C., nearly putting an end to all Roman development. The psychological shock of the Gallic invasions was frightful. The Romans were long haunted by the horrifying and humiliating memory of their senators slaughtered by the barbarians, but the Roman recovery was amazingly rapid. Exactly one hundred years later Rome controlled all of the Italic confederation. Pushing steadily southward, the Romans inevitably came into conflict with the great cities of *Magna Graecia,* long since established in that region, and gradually overwhelmed them, receiving for the last time the cooperation of the Carthaginian fleet. By 274 B.C. all Italy south of the Po was in the hands of the Romans.

The Mistress of the Hellenistic World

The interests of Rome and Carthage had not clashed while the expansion of the former had taken place within the peninsula. But good relations could no longer be maintained when Rome was drawn into the quarrel of two local cities in Sicily where Carthage had numerous colonies. The beginning of the hostilities was slow. The Roman Senate was reluctant to embark on distant expeditions and hesitated before sending the requested help to Sicily. The struggle with Carthage over Sicily, known as the First Punic War, brought few advantages to the winner, Rome, under the terms of the peace treaty.

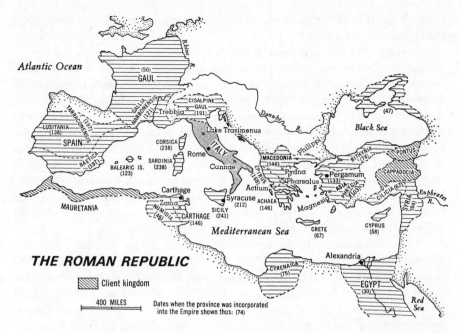

THE ROMAN REPUBLIC

Atlantic Ocean

GAUL (50)

Rhine R.

GALLIA NARBONENSIS (121)

CISALPINE GAUL (191)

Trebbia

Danube R.

Black Sea (47)

TARRACONENSIS (197)

LUSITANIA (138)

SPAIN

BAETICA (197)

CORSICA (238)

Lake Trasimenus

ITALY

Rome

Philippi

MACEDONIA (146)

BITHYNIA (74)

PONTUS

BALEARIC IS. (123)

SARDINIA (238)

Cannae

EPIRUS (168)

Pydna

Pharsalus (133)

Pergamum

ASIA

PHRYGIA (129)

CAPPADOCIA

CILICIA (67)

SYRIA (64)

Euphrates R.

Carthage

MAURETANIA

Zama

NUMIDIA (46)

CARTHAGE (146)

Actium

SICILY (241)

Syracuse (212)

ACHAEA (146)

Magnesia

SICILY (146)

Mediterranean Sea

CRETE (67)

CYPRUS (58)

Alexandria

CYRENAICA (75)

EGYPT (30)

Red Sea

Client kingdom

400 MILES

Dates when the province was incorporated into the Empire shown thus: (74)

The one exception was the fleet now built for the first time to oppose the famous Carthaginian navy. Rome was not ready to exploit its victory for several decades. The new fleet, however, made possible the creation of an empire in regions already held by the Carthaginians, and a war party grew at Rome. An uneasy and tenuous balance between the two spheres of influence in the western Mediterranean was maintained during this period, though revolts of Carthaginian mercenaries found backers at Rome. Finally in 219 B.C. the great struggle for the control of the western Mediterranean, the Second Punic War, broke out over an obscure Spanish town, Saguntum.

The beginning of the war was disastrous for Rome. The great Carthaginian general Hannibal Barca, by a stroke of genius, reached Italy in a lightning march from Spain, crossing the Pyrenees and the Alps with soldiers and elephants to find the Roman armies divided and unprepared. Three overwhelming victories at Trebbia, Lake Trasimenus, and particularly at Cannae in the southeast of the peninsula, where the Romans lost nearly 80,000 men, seemed to make Hannibal the master of Italy. Mistakenly he expected a rebellion which would force Rome to surrender without further struggle. Hannibal's miscalculation eventually cost him the war. Roman discipline did not fail in defeat, and most of the allied cities sharing many of Rome's privileges did not revolt. Gradually Rome recovered and Hannibal, cut off from his supplies and poorly supported by unpaid mercenaries, could not hold out. The relieving Carthaginian army commanded by Hannibal's brother was routed at the Metaurus river. A Roman landing in Africa and a final victory at Zama in 201 B.C. crowned the Roman victory. This time the peace terms were harsher than after the First Punic War. Carthage, stripped of her empire and fleet, had to pay a heavy war indemnity and the victorious Roman general, Scipio, received the title of Africanus to celebrate Rome's successful advance beyond the boundaries of Italy.

At the very moment when Rome came to dominate the western Mediterranean, the balance of power precariously maintained by the great Oriental monarchies was broken. Making the most of an internal revolt in Egypt, the Seleucids attacked the Ptolemies. In the political chaos that followed it was reasonable for the combatants to turn for help to the greatest military power of the time. Much has been written of Rome's reluctant imperialism in the early part of her struggle with Carthage. Roman conservatism was suspicious of foreign alliances, and early Eastern embassies were sent away. Nevertheless, in 200 B.C. Rome could put in the field an army unequalled by any other Hellenistic power. As the French historian Fustel de Coulange observed, she was "the hidden magnetic pole" which attracted all other powers and could no longer avoid entanglements.

In the beginning Rome repeated the pattern of the Carthaginian wars and resisted interference in the affairs of other lands. The first two so-called "Macedonian Wars" were victorious but ended merely in the proclamation in 196 B.C. of the independence of the Greek cities which had been dominated by the Kingdom of Macedonia. Once recognized as the protector of Greece, however, Rome could not avoid hostilities with Seleucids, who were attempting to dominate the East. The defeat of the Seleucid king Antiochus III at Magnesia in 189 B.C. and of the Macedonian king Perseus at Pydna in 168 B.C. put an end to the Macedonian kingdom and gave Rome a true protectorate over the East at the end of the Third Macedonian War. Even this step proved insufficient; half-measures merely provoked intrigues and rebellions. Simultaneous campaigns in 146 B.C., the Fourth Macedonian and Third Punic Wars, destroyed Corinth and Carthage whose very site was obliterated. The kingdom of Egypt was allowed to linger another century as a Roman protectorate, but in 146 B.C., willingly or not, Rome found herself the mistress of the Hellenistic world.

The Meeting of Rome with Hellenistic Culture

From the third century B.C. Rome no longer was able to preserve her isolation or to avoid contact with the intellectual and artistic Hellenistic culture spread through the Mediterranean. This contact brought about such great changes in Rome that its civilization has often been confused with that of the Greeks. The attitude of the Romans themselves was ambiguous and never overcame a certain antagonism toward the more developed civilization it had conquered. Roman gentlemen spoke Greek and went to study philosophy in Athens; Roman artists and writers copied Greek models. One Roman general, Flamininus, was such an admirer of the Greek *poleis* that he went to proclaim their independence at the Panhellenic games at Corinth in 196 B.C. one hundred and fifty years after such independence had any meaning. At the same time Greek philosophers were driven from Rome as undesirables. The Roman statesman, Cato the Elder, opposed all things Greek and wrote he preferred to see his son dead rather than treated by the newfangled Hellenistic medicine. The best indication of Rome's attitude is contained in the body of legendary history first written during the Punic wars and subsequently included in the national Latin Epic, the *Aeneid*. The Romans at the time of the creation of this historic tradition were no longer willing to be satisfied with the background of a minor barbaric tribe in Italy and wished to share in the great experience common to the entire Greek world, the Trojan war celebrated by Homer. The Roman Epic identified one of the heroes of the Trojan war, Aeneas, as its legendary ancestor and so achieved a place in the Hellenic tradition. But the merging of the two traditions was not intended. Aeneas, instead of being one of the Achaean chieftains, was always represented as a leader of their enemies. The hostility of Rome to Greece was carried all the way back to its legendary origin.

FURTHER READING

The Hellenistic world as a whole, that is to say including both the eastern and the western half of the Mediterranean, has not yet received a survey of manageable size. Consequently separate studies of the East and the West still have to be consulted.

The best short accounts of the achievements of Alexander are W. W. Tarn, *Alexander the Great* (1948); C. A. Robinson, *Alexander the Great* (1947); and A. R. Burn, *Alexander the Great and the Hellenistic World* (1948). For the expansion of the Greeks in Asia, see P. Jouguet, *Macedonian Imperialism and the Hellenization of the East* (1928).

The most satisfactory introduction to the culture of the period is W. W. Tarn, *Hellenistic Civilization* (3rd ed., 1952); see also J. B. Bury, *The Hellenistic Age* (1923), and particularly B. Farrington, *Greek Science II* (1944), for a study of the great Hellenistic intellectual advances. The *Hellenistic Philosophies* (1923) are discussed by P. F. More, and a survey of *Art and Literature in Fourth Century Athens* (1956) has been given by T. B. L. Webster. W. D. Ross, *The Works of Aristotle* (1908–31), is an introduction to the intellectual father of the Hellenistic age, and a good selection of philosophic and religious texts from the period has been published by F. C. Grant, *Hellenistic Religions* (1953).

For the Western Mediterranean, B. H. Warmington, *Carthage* (1960), and M. Pallotino, *The Etruscans* (1955), are excellent introductions to their respective subjects.

For general surveys of Roman history, see E. Bickerman's edition of M. Rostovtzeff, *Rome* (1960); C. Starr, *The Emergence of Rome* (2nd ed., 1953); and for all periods of Roman history consult A. E. R. Boak, *A History of Rome to 565 A.D.* (4th ed., 1954), which is both detailed and precise. For the earlier period of the Republic, L. Homo, *Primitive Italy and the Beginnings of Roman Imperialism* (1926), and T. Frank, *Roman Imperialism* (1914), can still be consulted with profit. W. E. Heitland, *The Roman Republic,* 3 vols. (1909) is still a basic work for the entire period.

General introductions to Roman civilization can be found in R. H. Barrow

The Romans (1949), and E. Hamilton, *The Roman Way* (1932). More detailed study of the whole range of Roman culture is made by A. Grenier, *The Roman Spirit in Religion, Thought and Art* (1926), and these various aspects are also considered in C. Bailey, ed., *The Legacy of Rome* (1923). A general treatment of religion can be found in F. Altheim, *A History of Roman Religion* (1938).

For political institutions consult, F. F. Abbott, *History and Description of Roman Political Institutions* (1911), and the first part of the general study of L. Homo, *Roman Political Institutions from City to State* (1929).

M. Hadas, *A History of Rome* (1956), is a very successful chronological sequence of excerpts from ancient sources covering the whole of Roman history, while A. De Selincourt, *Early History of Rome* (1960), is a translation of the first five books of Livy. Plutarch, *Lives,* tr. A. H. Clough (1859) includes the biographies of both Greek and Roman statesmen.

3 • The Roman Revolution and the Principate

With the conquest of the Mediterranean and the destruction of the Hellenistic political structure, Rome was faced with the overwhelming problem of finding a suitable government for the civilized world. The first response to the challenge was a crisis at home. The Roman institutions nearly gave way under the weight of the new problems thrust upon them, and a century of civil war followed the conquest of the East. At the height of the crisis the Roman genius for government intervened to save the situation. Avoiding the anarchy of the Greek city-states and the despotism of the Oriental monarchies, Augustus fashioned a system based on the Roman sense of compromise and respect for the rights of others, which provided a working solution for most of the problems raised by the conquest. The Augustan system, combining a maximum of centralization with a maximum of local autonomy, was not perfect—eventually the flaws of the system destroyed it—but the Augustan Principate in the two centuries of its duration gave to the world its longest period of uninterrupted peace and a pattern for a working administration of the world. For a thousand years after its destruction, the Roman Empire provided the ideal which one nation after another attempted to re-create.

A CENTURY OF REVOLUTION

The Greek historian Polybius, brought to Rome in 167 B.C. as a hostage after the battle of Pydna, saw the Roman government as a tripartite constitution, each part balancing and checking the others. Using the Greek terminology familiar to him, Polybius spoke in his *History* of monarchy, aristocracy, and democracy to describe the magistrates, senate, and assemblies of the Roman people. Outwardly Polybius' description was perfectly correct. To regularize the government still more, a law of 180 B.C. had fixed the order in which offices might be sought (*Cursus Honorum*) and the minimum age at which they might be held. But within the framework of well-balanced institutions the senate held the actual power in the state. We have already seen how the organization of the powerful *commitia centuriata* made it the mouthpiece of the aristocratic point of view. At the other end of the political framework, the consuls, drawn from the senate, were rarely at odds with a body containing most of their friends and relatives. The Licino-Sextian law of 367 B.C., opening the consulship to plebeians, often had the additional result of making the tribunitiate of the plebs, the only office closed to patricians, one of the early steps in the career of a young man of good family on his way to the consulship. The great plebeian families now shared all the privileges of the patrician aristocracy as well as their prejudices. As a result the traditional defenders of the interests of the plebs came more and more from senatorial families and shared their aristocratic convictions. Closed in their conservatism and respect for family tradition, the senatorial aristocracy did not allow outsiders to reach the consulship. A *novus homo* (new man) coming from a family without political experience had little hope of making his way in the government. No more than three or four might hope to reach the consulship in the course of a century.

The Impact of World Conquest

The Romans had been drawn step by step into the acquisition of an empire without any preconceived imperialistic scheme. When no serious enemy remained in the world, the Romans found themselves faced with a series of critical problems, none of which could find a solution within the framework of the city-state. Economic, military, and social problems at home accompanied the central question of how to extend the institutions of a small city to the government of the civilized world. The continuous foreign wars of the third and early second centuries B.C. had provided Rome with a multitude of slaves and, at the same time, an acquaintance with the scientific methods of Hellenistic agriculture. The result was the introduction of new crops into Italy where mostly cereals had been cultivated previously. The new olives and vines brought greater incomes, but they required an initial outlay of capital and were more efficiently grown on large slave-run estates than on small individual plots. Furthermore, the large-scale importation of wheat from the provinces made the cultivation of cereals in Italy unprofitable. Consequently, the second century saw the growth of large estates or *Latifundia* owned by the senatorial aristocracy, while the small farmers, unable to compete, lost their lands and swelled the discontented poor of the city.

The problem created was not only economic and social. In classical antiquity only a man owning property could serve in the army since he was responsible for his own equipment. Hence, every dispossessed farmer was a soldier lost to the army at a time when wars had sharply reduced the military potential of Rome and new men were constantly needed for the struggle still continuing in Spain and soon to flare again in other regions.

The question of the enormous new territories acquired was equally critical. When first faced with it, the Romans had adopted the makeshift arrangement of leaving all local institutions as they were; appointing a Roman governor drawn from among the ex-magistrates in each area, called a province, and levying taxes on the provincials who were not considered Roman citizens. Such a primitive arrangement was evidently not workable for very long. The small Roman administration did not provide enough ex-magistrates to supervise the government of the world, while other men were inexperienced.

Roman tradition, based on agriculture, had looked down on trade, which was closed by law to Roman senators. Consequently, the ruling class had no experience in business affairs, and the taxes raised in the new provinces had to be farmed out to private companies drawn from non-aristocratic classes. These companies bought from the state for a fixed sum the right to levy taxes in a given province, and made their profit by raising the maximum amount possible. The officials of the companies, brought up outside the aristocratic tradition of responsibility and public service, fleeced the provincials mercilessly in spite of the creation of some courts of appeal for extortions. The danger of provincial rebellion became constant. The shameless plundering of the provinces was pilloried and perhaps exaggerated by the great orator, Cicero, in his *Orations Against Verres.* At the same time, the new middle class growing rich on the increased financial transactions reached the social and financial level of the second class of Roman society, the Knights, who served in the army on horseback rather than in the infantry; but they found their way to political power barred by the senate jealously guarding its prerogatives. To all of these problems Rome in 146 B.C. had no solution.

The Beginning of the Crisis

In accordance with Athenian tradition, the first innovations in the Roman system of government came from the aristocracy. Two young noblemen thoroughly acquainted with Hellenic culture, Tiberius and his brother Gaius Gracchus, attempted to bring some improvement to the existing situation. The evidently noble intentions of the Gracchi and their tragic death has surrounded their memory with the aura of martyrs in the cause of liberty; but their activity, no matter how well-motivated, provided no effective solution and served only to aggravate the situation. Tiberius Gracchus, elected tribune of the plebs in 133 B.C., tried to pass an agrarian law sharply limiting the size of the *latifundia* and restoring the land to small proprietors. The law was vetoed by another tribune, Octavius, who represented the interests of the aristocracy. The veto of a tribune was final under the constitution, but Tiberius Gracchus appealed to the *commitia tributa* to override Octavius' veto, depose a tribune betraying the interests of the people, and vote in the new agrarian law. The assembly carried out his illegal proposition. The anger of the senate soon manifested itself. Tiberius was murdered within the year while seeking reelection. When, ten years later, Gaius Gracchus renewed his brother's legislation and went on to add revolutionary measures requiring the state to clothe and arm its soldiers and putting the new middle-class knights on the juries trying cases of provincial extortion, the senate responded for the first time by proclaiming martial law (*Senatus consultum ultimum*) thus interrupting all due process. Gaius was forced to commit suicide, and his followers were mercilessly hunted down.

The measures proposed by the Gracchi did not have the expected results. Small farmers would not stay on the land where they could not compete with the more profitable methods of the great estates, and the exodus to the cities continued. The law of Gaius Gracchus, putting on the investigating juries the very people whose financial extortions were being tried, only worsened the situation in the provinces. The actual consequences of the attempted reform were to create an evident opposition between the interests of the senate and those of the people and make the senate suspicious of any innovation whatsoever. Even more serious, Tiberius Gracchus' illegal if well-founded disregard of Octavius' veto and the Senate's equally unprecedented countermeasures broke down the Roman tradition of constitutional government and due process of law. Illegality and violence became the answers to political difficulties.

The Optimates and the Populares

The potentially explosive inheritance left by the Gracchi was made worse by a succession of wars which filled most of the early half of the first century B.C. The last Punic war had left conflicts in North Africa and Spain. In 106 a new invasion of the Gauls, whose first appearance from northern Italy had left a terrorizing memory, and of newly-come Germanic tribes threatened the peninsula once again. Only several years later were they driven back and annihilated by the Roman general, Marius. Once the threat of invasion lifted, the Latin allies of Rome, resenting their unequal status in Italy, revolted and formed a republic of their own. Hardly had the danger at home been allayed by the grant of full Roman citizenship to all Italy than the long expected trouble in the provinces exploded. In 88 B.C. one of the small independent rulers left in Asia, Mithridates of Pontus, attacked the Roman provinces. Simultaneously a frightful massacre disposed of some 80,000 Roman citizens living in the cities of the East. The exactions of the tax collectors were bearing their fruit. For the next twenty-five years successive Roman armies were to struggle to reconquer the Orient from Mithridates and his son-in-law, King Tigranes of Armenia.

In themselves the wars were serious enough for Rome, but the greatest danger was their acceleration of the constitutional crisis within the state. In the panic resulting from the Gallic invasion the successful Roman general Marius though a *novus homo,* was re-elected to successive consulships, in the face of a law which forbade consecutive terms of office for a consul. Even more dangerous, he obtained the passage of a law whereby army service was paid for the first time. The size of the army was increased, but the new soldiers who were drawn from the poorest classes and had never had a voice in the government, naturally gave their allegiance to the general who led them to victory and booty rather than to the state which had shown no concern for their welfare. In the new militarization of the state, a successful army career led to a political career. In opposition to Marius, a young officer named Sulla, who had won renown in the war against the Latin allies, demanded the command against Mithridates which legally belonged to him as consul elect. Unable to obtain this command, he marched on Rome with his army and seized it by force. The country found itself divided into two opposing camps, the *Optimates* and the *Populares.* Most of the senate was to be found among the *Optimates,* whose leader was Sulla, but the two groups were factions rather than political parties, equally irresponsible politically, using the same violent means and bent on the same goal, the acquisition of power and the destruction of the opposing faction. As Marius and Sulla alternated in power, a reign of terror was instituted as a series of proscriptions hunted down the enemies of the man in power. Thousands of individuals became the victims of public or private vengeance, and the rift between the parties was no longer reconcilable.

The Civil War

On his victorious return from the Mithridatic war in 82 B.C., Sulla received the special office of dictator, carrying with it full political power without the constitutional restriction which limited the office to six months. Sulla used his office to undo the work of previous decades. The tribunes of the plebs found their way barred to further office, the knights were driven from the juries, and the senate received for the first time by law the authority they derived from tradition in the delicately balanced constitution observed by Polybius. Such a violent turning back of the clock could hardly be successful, and the senate, decimated by prosecution, could no longer live up to the meaning of aristocracy and provide leadership for the state. After the death of Sulla the crisis accelerated. The new candidate of the Optimates against the successors of Marius was a young general, Pompey, who defeated the Marians and went on to bring the Mithridatic wars to a successful end. But the demoralized senate, fearing Pompey's growing popularity with his soldiers, would not support its own candidate. During Pompey's absence in the East in 63 B.C. the senate hurriedly pushed the election of a civilian consul, though their choice of candidate, the great orator Cicero, who was a *novus homo,* indicates that the aristocracy could not obtain the election of one of its own members. Armed bands of hoodlums roamed the streets of the capital; conspiracies brewed against the state; the consul maintained the government only through the proclamation of martial law. Nevertheless, when Pompey returned to Italy the following year, leaving his army outside the country as the law required, the senate would neither ratify his laws nor vote a bonus for his victorious soldiers.

Driven into the opposition, Pompey in 60 B.C. entered into an informal association with two other men, the millionaire Crassus, who had gained popularity by putting down a dangerous slave rebellion in the South, and a young man, Julius Caesar, whose only claim to importance was his extremely aristocratic background which made him eligible for the vacant office of *pontifex maximus,* an office controlling all the religious institutions of the state. The association of Pompey, Crassus, and Caesar, to which historians have given the name of *First Triumvirate,* was a private agreement that had no legal standing. The framework of the republican constitution was maintained, but the triumvirs saw to it that intimidated or bribed electors kept them in control of the government. At best the first Triumvirate was only a breathing spell; its unofficial standing provided no solution for the problems of the state. In 53 B.C. the death of Crassus in a disastrous eastern campaign left

Pompey and Caesar face to face. In its last phase the civil war was no longer a political contest or even the struggle of factions. It was the opposition of two individuals for absolute power.

After the death of Crassus the struggle was relatively brief. Caesar was in Gaul, where his brilliant conquest provided him with a following and military glory equal to that of his rival. Pompey stayed at Rome, reconciled with the senate in the face of Caesar's daily increasing might. Warned of danger by the friends he had left at Rome and summoned by the senate to return without his army, Caesar neither hesitated nor repeated Pompey's error of 62 B.C. Illegally crossing the Rubicon into Italy with his troops in 49 B.C., he marched on Rome. Pompey, hindered by the multiplicity of senatorial leaders, fled to Greece. Defeated at Pharsalus, he was subsequently murdered in Egypt. A series of campaigns in Africa and Spain disposed of the senatorial opposition and by 46 B.C. Caesar had obtained the dictatorship for life.

The Dictatorship of Caesar and the End of the Republic
Most of Caesar's brief period of sole rule was filled by his last campaigns against the Pompeians, so that his policies are unclear and have led to considerable speculation. Caesar was accused by his murderers of trying to overthrow the republic and make himself king and god. The truth of the accusation is possible. The only known system for world rule at the time was the semi-divine monarchy which had existed in Persia and the Hellenistic kingdoms where Caesar had the occasion to observe it during his pursuit of Pompey. The system offered a solution for Roman political problems, which he could not overlook. Nevertheless, Caesar up to his death had maintained the republican institutions and contented himself with the title of dictator last worn by Sulla. The chief characteristic of Caesar which may be at the base of the accusation is a brilliance and independence of mind which resulted in a total absence of Roman conservatism. He stopped at no innovation. Many of his laws, such as the reform of the calendar which had known no change from Egyptian times, and the foundation of new colonies for his veterans, were highly beneficial. He extended Roman citizenship to provincials and even appointed senators from Gaul, to the great scandal of the old aristocracy. No respect for the constitution halted him in his march on Rome. To such a man the solution of world monarchy might be acceptable as an efficient system, even if it ran counter to all Roman tradition. We cannot guess at his intentions, but his contemporaries were frightened by his lack of respect for tradition, and on March 15, 44 B.C., Caesar was murdered by a senatorial conspiracy spearheaded by Brutus and Cassius.

The solution of Caesar may have been too radical for Rome, but his enemies had no program to offer. The thirteen years following Caesar's death are an accelerated repetition of the decades that preceded it. A temporary triumvirate, now official, again ruled from 43 to 36 B.C., but after the defeat and death of Caesar's murderers at Philippi the contest gradually resolved itself into a duel for power between Caesar's heirs: Caesar's closest collaborator and chief of staff, Marc Antony, and his grand-nephew and adopted son, the young Octavian. The loyalty of the soldiers first went to the better-known Antony, but Octavian profited from Antony's lengthy sojourn in Egypt. A campaign of propaganda awakened the fear of the Orient, lingering at Rome since the Mithridatic wars, and rallied to Octavian the remains of the senate and the troops in Italy. A great defeat at Actium in western Greece spelled the doom of Antony and his consort Queen Cleopatra VII of Egypt. In 31 B.C. the last remains of the past were swept away. The last great Hellenistic monarchy passed to Rome with the death of Cleopatra, the last of the Ptolemies. The republican senate had been wiped out on the battlefields of Pharsalus and Philippi, or, like Cicero, in the great proscription of the Second Triumvirate. Octavian was the master of the world.

THE PRINCIPATE

The problems which faced the new ruler were still those left unsolved by the Gracchi and aggravated by several generations of civil war. The institutions of the city-state still had to be adapted to world government, and the only known system, the Oriental monarchy, was unacceptable to Romans. Slowly and cautiously, Octavian set out to find a different solution which would not be an innovation but rather show the respect for tradition suited to Roman conservatism. In his political testament to the Roman people, inscribed on public monuments throughout the Empire and commonly known as the *Res Gestae Divi Augusti,* Octavian, who bore by then the name of Augustus, boasted: "I restored the republic which had been oppressed by the tyranny of a faction." This sentence has often been criticized as rank hypocrisy, but before his death Augustus had achieved a compromise which assured the bases of his power, provided for the government of the provinces, and was acceptable to Roman tradition.

The Bases of the Power

The power of Augustus was based on three elements. The first of these was his holding of the *imperium proconsulare* conferred upon him by the senate. This was the *imperium,* similar to that of a consul, by which republican governors had ruled their provinces. As in republican times this *imperium* conferred on the holder all civilian and military powers, the right to command an army in the field and the right of life and death over citizens outside the capital. The second was the *Tribunicia potestas,* the power of a plebeian tribune which made the holder's person invulnerable, made him the spokesman of the people, and gave him the right to halt any legislation by veto. Finally, as *pontifex maximus* Augustus was chief priest of the state and supervisor of all religious affairs. Already a member of the senate as an ex-consul, he was granted by this body the title of *princeps* (first) always given to the senior member, with which went the privilege of speaking first to any matter before the house. Through these offices, of which the first two were renewed periodically, Augustus could control all of the workings of the state.

Provincial Administration

Augustus laid the foundation for a true provincial administration, although it was actually worked out under his successor, Tiberius. The entire territory of the Empire which by the end of Augustus' reign successive campaigns had extended to the Atlantic Ocean, the Rhine, the Danube, the Euphrates, and the Syrian and Sahara deserts, was divided into two sections. The provinces of long standing and peaceful character were under the supervision of the senate; border or rebellious provinces in need of closer attention were under the direct power of the emperor. In each province a governor with *imperium* oversaw the administration, and a financial officer, or *quaestor,* supervised financial affairs and taxes. The administration of all provinces but Egypt was identical, but in imperial provinces the administration was appointed by the emperor at will, while in senatorial provinces the old rule of ex-magistrates with fixed terms still existed. Appeals from the decision of a governor could be forwarded to the emperor himself, and the imperial legions were normally stationed only in imperial provinces, leaving the emperor in control of the army. Egypt, from which came most of the grain that fed the city, was administered as the private estate of the emperor, who therefore also controlled the food supply of the capital. The allegiance of the provincials was assured by the creation of a cult of Rome and Augustus unknown in Italy, and the festivals connected with this cult permitted the gathering of provincial assemblies where local grievances might be expressed.

The Republican Facade

Augustus' real authority rested on the allegiance of the army stationed in the imperial provinces, on the supernatural elements in his title which appealed to all provincials, and in the cumulation of powers within the state. Nevertheless, the republican institutions, far from being overthrown, were preserved in every detail. The cumulation of offices could find precedents in the days of Sulla and Pompey, as well as Caesar, and all the illegal additions of the Triumvirates were abolished when, in 27 B.C., Augustus formally returned the administration to the senate. This was not an empty gesture. Augustus drew all his administrators from the senatorial aristocracy. He watched jealously over its composition, excluding Caesar's provincial senators and seeing to it that the morals and finances of the senators were suited to the highest advisory council in the world. He consulted with them, as tradition required of the magistrates, and at Rome wore the senatorial title of *princeps* which indicated that he considered himself merely the first among his equals.

Although the constitutional work of Augustus contained a number of flaws which soon manifested themselves disastrously, and his intentions were often ambiguous, still his achievements were impressive. Adequate government was provided for the provinces and, after the violence of the opposition between Optimates and Populares, reasonable relations were reestablished with the senate. The devotion of the soldiers given to various generals since the days of Marius was redirected toward the state, whose head was the general of all the armies. Most important, after more than a century of increasing violence, an enduring civilian administration based on legal process had been re-created.

The Golden Age

The court of Augustus was the center of one of the most brilliant artistic and literary developments of all times. Outstanding artists and poets, such as Horace and Vergil, celebrated the new age. The subjects and methods of Augustan art were not new but mostly copied from Hellenic or Hellenistic models. Yet the themes of this official art were purely Roman and furnish a clear indication of the republican and traditionalistic form in which the new empire had been cast. On the walls of the Altar of Peace erected by Augustus, the princeps and his family mingle with the senatorial aristocracy, undifferentiated from it by either dress or position. Similarly, the great epic, the *Aeneid*, turns back to the old themes of the creation of the city. When Aeneas' father prophesies the future greatness of Rome, he adds:

> ... remember, Roman, that this is thy mission,
> to hold the nations under thy sway.
> (Let these be thy arts)
> To impose the ways of peace,
> To spare the vanquished and cast down the proud.

Here all of the themes and virtues of the ancient tradition reappear: the divine origin of Rome and its mission, the disciplined seriousness and responsibility which must accompany the high destiny of the city. The relief of the Romans at the end of the civil war and the reestablishment of ancient values is expressed by Vergil: "A God is he indeed who has granted us this leisure."

The Successors of Augustus

Augustus died in 14 A.D., leaving most of the work of reconstruction finished but no direct heir to continue his work. His first successors, who were members of his family, are known as the Julio-Claudian emperors since they belonged to those two ancient Roman clans. Four in all, the Julio-Claudians were Tiberius (14–37 A.D.), Gaius or Caligula (37–41 A.D.), Claudius 41–54 A.D.), and Nero (54–68 A.D.). After a brief civil war which followed the suicide of Nero, the last member of the clan, another family of much less distinguished origin, the Flavians (69–96 A.D.), took the power for two generations. The first of the family, the successful equestrian general Vespasian, was followed by his two sons, Titus and Domitian. Finally, through most of the second century (96–180) the five so-called "good emperors" reigned, the emperors known collectively as the Antonines, though they did not belong to one family: Nerva, Trajan, Hadrian, Antoninus Pius, and Marcus Aurelius.

The Julio-Claudians have often been presented as an incompetent group of criminal idiots and madmen. This picture is to a great degree the work of hostile writers belonging to the senatorial aristocracy who resented the existence of an emperor with authority surpassing its own; or, in the case of Nero, to a persecuted minority that grew later to unexpected greatness, the Christians.

The Julio-Claudians unquestionably plotted against each other and all died violent deaths, yet personal extravagances and court intrigues did not prevent them from being good administrators and continuing the work of Augustus. The violence in the imperial palace did not spread, and the civilized world remained in peace. Even the year of civil war which followed Nero's death was succeeded by the reestablishment of stable government for more than a century.

The main achievement of Augustus' successors was the completion of his work. It has already been said that the perfection of the provincial administration was the work of Tiberius, rather than Augustus. Even the victories which carried the Roman armies beyond the Rhine were won under the leadership of Tiberius, who was Augustus' greatest general. However as Augustus had decided not to extend Roman territory beyond the Rhine into the barbarian lands, Tiberius maintained the river frontiers. Only under Claudius was the far northern island of Britain added to the Empire. The consolidation of the eastern frontier on the Euphrates was the work of Nero, who achieved a compromise with the empire that had arisen as the heir of the Persians and the Seleucids beyond the river, the Parthian empire, which was the only existing serious threat to Roman domination. The last weak point of the border, the triangle formed by the upper Rhine and Danube, was consolidated by Domitian.

Even more important as an achievement was the gradual extension of Roman privilege to outsiders, which was part of the Roman tradition, even though Augustus himself had not encouraged it from deference to senatorial prejudices. Roman citizenship was gradually granted to the provincial aristocracies. From the time of Claudius on, provincials reappeared in the senate, and by Hadrian's reign they filled nearly half of this body. The Flavians brought with them to power their equestrian friends, and the old Roman aristocracy was transformed by the influx of a new social class bringing with it new ideas. With the second century, the provincials shared in all the privileges of Rome as Spanish emperors came to the throne with Trajan and Hadrian. Roman citizenship was no longer the preserve of Italians. Its meaning, transcending the boundaries of the city, had reached its fullest expression.

Serious difficulties still remained without solution and would become critical in the future, but in the early period of the principate the full extent of their danger was not always apparent. The relation between the senate and the emperor was ambiguous and easily strained as the senatorial aristocracy came to resent the imperial authority. But as long as the administration required the services of trained senatorial officials in the provinces, the precarious balance established by Augustus was maintained with reasonable success. Another source of danger was the army on which the emperor's real power rested. The civil war of 68–69 A.D. served as a warning of the crisis which would come when the choice of imperial candidates could be dictated by the army. In 69, however, the memory of the revolution was still fresh and civilian government was rapidly reestablished. The dictate of the army would not reappear for more than a century.

At the root of all the perils menacing the state was the question of succession. How was the enormous power of the emperor to be transmitted peacefully? Rome had a tradition of elective office, and any hereditary succession reminiscent of monarchy was abhorrent to its tradition. On the other hand, imperial elections, between the jealousy of the senate and the power of the army, would probably precipitate the state into war at the end of every reign. Augustus had left the problem unsolved and the imperial power had passed to his successors amidst disastrous family quarrels and senatorial plots punished with growing severity. The attempt of the Flavians to establish a hereditary system ended with the murder of Domitian. Only the Antonines found for a time a system which theoretically solved all difficulties.

The Antonines

The murder of Domitian in 96 A.D. brought to the throne an elderly civilian, Nerva, who died two years later after having adopted the Spanish-born Ulpius Trajanus, the best general of the Empire. The system of adoptions, once found, was continued three more times. In each reign, the emperor selected his successor, trained him for his future duties, and adopted him as a son. Consequently, the imperial power was given to the man most able to serve the public good, and at the same time adoption turned the government into a family affair in the spirit of the oldest Roman tradition. The result was a century of spectacular administrative ability and world government in the true sense of the word.

The imagination of contemporaries as well as of posterity was struck especially by the exploits of the great general Trajan, who crossed the Augustan frontiers to add Dacia beyond the Danube to the Empire and led victorious campaigns into Mesopotamia and Arabia. From an administrative point of view, however, the most important reign was that of his successor, Hadrian (117–138 A.D.). Abandoning Trajan's new conquests, which weighed heavily on the imperial treasury, Hadrian preserved only Dacia, whose gold mines made it profitable. The enormous circuit of the frontiers was surrounded by heavy fortifications known as *limes,* reinforced by towers, and continuously patrolled by sentries, as the legions were settled along the entire border instead of being concentrated in a few provinces. Hadrian's wall still stretches for miles in northern Britain to show the formidable defenses opposed by the empire to the barbarians beyond the frontiers.

Hadrian was a great patron of artists and intellectuals, but his most significant accomplishment was the establishing of a civil service for the administration of the Empire. Adequate administration of the provinces and particularly of the imperial finances was beyond the capacities of the senators who were not always competent or loyal. Already in the time of Claudius the emperors began to look for a new source of officials. The merit of Hadrian is to have regularized the system and given it its definitive form. Provinces continued to be governed by senators who commanded the armies, but most of the administration was in the hands of the new bureaucracy. All officials who had the rank of knights were appointed, promoted, or dismissed at the will of the emperor, according to their competence. They were paid for their services and could rise along a definite hierarchy to the command of the imperial fleets, the governorship of a few minor provinces, particularly of Egypt, or to the central government offices in the capital. The heads of the services were secretaries or ministers of state who supervised the main branches of the administration. Senior among them was the *Praetorian Prefect* who commanded the imperial guard and was responsible for the safety of the emperor. He soon came to be the chief legal authority in the state and to hold the supreme authority whenever the emperor himself was absent.

The excellence of this civil service reinforced the authority of the emperor, on whom the entire hierarchy depended; it assured the state of competent administration; and it provided an outlet through which any man might rise as far as his abilities could carry him. Such a system was revolutionary. Never before had a state relied for its administration on an organized, paid, and professional civil service whose fundamental criterion was loyalty and excellence.

ROMAN IMPERIAL CIVILIZATION

In the second century A.D. the Roman empire reached its greatest expansion and prosperity. Peace reigned everywhere within the imperial frontiers, and an efficient administration provided for the government of the inhabitants. The power within the state was highly centralized. Yet it has been pointed out that this power was not despotic and allowed for a remarkable amount of local autonomy.

Civic Life

The Roman empire has been called a network of city-states. Indeed, the Romans generally did not interfere with the local institutions of a conquered territory as long as peace was maintained. In the Oriental provinces the existing *poleis* were kept; in the new western provinces of Gaul, the Germanies and Britain, cities were founded by the conquerors. Most of these cities were self-governing and ruled their own territory. Civic institutions were maintained, magistrates elected locally, and no artificial uniformity enforced. Each *polis* kept its characteristics, and in barbarous regions not yet accustomed to urban life, local chieftains kept the peace according to their own traditions. Except in cases of gross mismanagement or open disturbance, such as the race riots at Alexandria in the time of Claudius, the government did not interfere. The only demand made from the cities, aside from orderly government, was the payment of taxes which were collected by local officials.

The result of this local freedom was the remarkable growth of the cities. Wealthy men, most of whom had already received Roman citizenship, vied with each other to adorn their native cities with magnificent buildings according to the ancient system of *leiturgies*. Such distant communities as Arles in Gaul, Gerasa in Transjordan, and Timgad in the African desert boasted the same wide colonnaded forums, paved streets, elaborate temples, theatres, arenae, and baths as the great cities of the Empire. Antioch and Alexandria rivalled

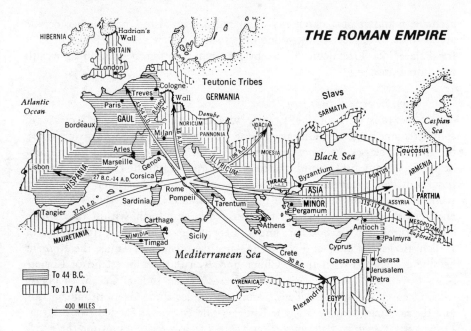

Map labels: HIBERNIA · Hadrian's Wall · BRITAIN · London · Teutonic Tribes · Cologne · GERMANIA · Slavs · Atlantic Ocean · Treves · Wall · Paris · SARMATIA · Caspian Sea · GAUL · Danube R. · NORICUM · DACIA · Bordeaux · Milan · PANNONIA · Caucasus · Arles · MOESIA · Black Sea · ARMENIA · Marseille · Genoa · ILLYRICUM · THRACE · Byzantium · PONTUS · Lisbon · 27 B.C.-14 A.D. · Corsica · Rome · ASIA · PARTHIA · HISPANIA · Pompeii · MINOR · ASSYRIA · 37-41 A.D. · Sardinia · Tarentum · Pergamum · 115-117 A.D. · Tangier · Carthage · Athens · Antioch · MESOPOTAMIA · MAURETANIA · NUMIDIA · Sicily · Crete · Euphrates R. · Timgad · 30 B.C. · Cyprus · Palmyra · Mediterranean Sea · Caesarea · Gerasa · Jerusalem · Petra · CYRENAICA · Alexandria · EGYPT

To 44 B.C.
To 117 A.D.
400 MILES

in splendor the capital itself. Electioneering inscriptions scribbled on the walls of the famous city of Pompeii, destroyed by the eruption of Mt. Vesuvius in 79 A.D., show that local elections were actively contested and that the population took great interest in these contests.

Most of our knowledge of life within the Empire comes from the cities. About life in the countryside, where a population largely composed of slaves worked on great agricultural estates, we know very little. Within the cities all was not pleasant or prosperous. The large population of slaves was often abominably treated, and the poorer classes lived in crowded tenements several stories high where fire was a perpetual threat. But even here mitigating circumstances were present. Humanitarian laws passed under the influence of the Stoic doctrine of the brotherhood of man gradually improved the situation of the slaves. Poor artisans belonged to craft guilds called *collegia* which provided some relief from the difficulties of life. These were in no sense protective unions, but rather associations with halls for members where banquets were given, and mutual assistance societies which provided help for the sick, burial of dead members, and some assistance to the widows and orphans.

In spite of its difficulties, life during the Empire showed considerable social flexibility. The senatorial aristocracy followed by the knights formed the upper classes, but wealth and prestige were not the monopoly of a closed aristocracy. Numerous inscriptions show that through the civil service a man who had started in life as a minor noncommissioned officer in the army could reach the rank of governor of Egypt or praetorian prefect. The baker Eurysaces became rich enough to erect for himself an enormous tomb, which is still standing in Rome. In a famous novel, the *Satyricon,* Petronius, a friend of the emperor Nero, pokes merciless fun at the ignorance, poor taste, and regrettable manners of a newly-rich man called Trimalchio, but the aristocratic author fails to appreciate the value of a society which made it possible for a freed slave like Trimalchio to rise by his own efforts to a position of wealth and importance.

Commerce and Industry

The prosperity of the Empire was due to an enormous increase in commerce and industry. Old aristocratic tradition had looked down on trade, but the new classes were not burdened with such prejudices. The magnificent network of roads, built mainly for strategic purposes and the rise of an imperial post, provided excellent means of communications throughout the empire, while Roman navies had cleared the sea of pirates. Customs duties were few and relatively light. Merchants travelled back and forth within the empire and ventured far beyond its limits. Benefitting from the explorations of Hellenistic geographers and continuing to investigate new lands, the Romans became acquainted with India, China, and even the distant island of Ceylon. Ships travelled down the Red Sea and crossed the Indian Ocean, to obtain silks, incense, and spices. Metals, wood, and hides came from Britain, Spain, and the northern provinces of the Rhine, while ivory was carried from Africa. Distant cities, such as Palmyra or Petra, grew rich as warehouses for the goods brought by caravan across the desert. Alexandria, the greatest port of the Mediterranean, was also the terminus of shipping that came up the Red Sea from the Orient.

Together with this trade, an active industry developed. Wool cloth, wine, and particularly pottery had long been manufactured in Italy, but the provinces soon caught up with and outstripped its production. The western provinces provided mostly articles of immediate necessity. Extensive mining was carried on in Spain, Britain, and Dacia. Gaul rapidly became a center for wine and pottery industries and particularly heavy woolen cloaks required by the army. The oriental provinces were the centers of luxury industries. Alexandria, in addition to its commercial activity, produced perfumes, cosmetics, papyrus, and highly prized glassware. The cities of the Syrian coast, continuing the ancient Phoenician tradition, manufactured purple-dyed textiles, often richly embroidered with gold. From Asia Minor came high quality woolens and rugs. Every article of necessity for daily life and every luxury to adorn the villas of the rich became available throughout the Mediterranean world; isolated regions ignored by civilization before or after this period reached a remarkable cultural level.

Roman Culture

Roman civilization has often been treated as an inferior repetition of the achievements of Greece, but this is a misleading oversimplification. We have seen that an original Roman tradition had existed before it was overlaid with Hellenistic cosmopolitanism at the time of the Roman conquest of the Mediterranean. Both elements are present in the Imperial civilization. It is true that the Roman genius was not directed toward the fine arts or abstractions. As artists and philosophers the Romans added little to Hellenistic achievements, but their sense of reality, order, and moral discipline produced important original contributions. The cultural role of Imperial Rome was twofold: it was the heir and transmitter of Hellenistic civilization, and it was a creator in its own right.

As the heir of the Hellenistic world, Rome continued many of its themes. The institutions of the city-state were brought to western regions previously inhabited by nomad barbarian tribes. Greek was the official language of the eastern provinces and was familiar to all cultured society. The ancient Epic tradition of Homer found its counterpart in the work of Vergil and the Hellenistic romance flourished throughout the Imperial period. The artistic tradition of Greece not only adorned all the cities of the Empire but was carried beyond its limits to influence the art of India. The scientific work begun at the Museum of Alexandria continued long after the end of the Egyptian monarchy, with the *Geography* of Claudius Ptolemy or the encyclopedic *Natural History* of Pliny the Elder. Rome produced no new speculative philosophies, but both Epicureanism and Stoicism flourished in the environment of Roman moral preoccupation. The most exalted glorification of Epicurus' release of mankind from the fear of death and the gods was written in the last century of the republic by the Roman poet Lucretius in his masterpiece *On the Nature of Things*. Late in the second century A.D. the last of the "good emperors," Marcus Aurelius, practiced all the Stoic virtues on the imperial throne. The great historic work begun by Herodotus and Thucydides appealed particularly to the Romans' sense of reality and their respect for tradition. An enormous historical literature beginning at the time of the Punic wars continued uninterrupted with Sallust, Livy, Tacitus, Suetonius, and Plutarch. Even as late as the middle of the fourth century A.D., in a period which as we shall see enjoyed little of the peace of the Antonine age, Rome could still bring forth a historian such as Ammianus Marcellinus, whose breadth of information, judgment, and integrity place him among the greatest writers of history.

As creators, the Romans made their mark in human affairs rather than in abstraction and imagination. Individual Roman buildings rarely matched the perfection of the Parthenon, but the Romans were master city planners, and the haphazard grouping of buildings on the Athenian Akropolis is not to be found in the carefully laid out imperial forums. The great systems of imperial roads maintained from year to year provided communications, and great aqueducts carried water to make life possible far in the desert. Similarly, in literature the Romans might not equal the greatness of Greek drama, and the great poetic achievements of the Augustan age were not matched in the second century, but Roman writers developed new literary genres, such as satire, to provide a commentary on the morals and weaknesses of mankind.

The most brilliant innovations of the Romans, however, are to be found in the area of government and its foundation, the law. We have already seen how the Empire succeeded both in reconciling a centralized government with the preservation of local freedom and in developing the first efficient civil service. Peaceful and efficient government based on law rather than despotism was something unknown both to the Hellenic *poleis* and the Oriental monarchies. Indeed it is in the law that Rome made its greatest contribution to the future. Originally, Roman law was not written but was administered by special officers, the *praetors*, according to tradition. Then new officers were added to cope with the presence of non-citizens with different traditions in the city and later the Empire. During the Empire an elaborate system of courts culminated in the emperor himself. The chief minister of the state, the *praetorian prefect*, was usually the most distinguished legal mind in the Empire. These great lawyers gradually came to formulate certain fundamental principles, which were finally written down late in the Empire, and lie at the base of most subsequent legal thought. From an early period the *ius civile* was established as distinct from *ius divinum*, recognizing that human law and religion were separate. The extension of Roman territory and the respect of the Romans for the institutions of other people brought about the development of the *ius gentium*, which included the traditions of all foreigners instead of imposing on them the particular customs of the Romans. Legal rights were not the exclusive privilege of the citizen body as they had been in the Greek *poleis*. Even in cases involving a Roman and a foreigner, Roman law was not necessarily used. With the continuous growth of the *ius gentium*, many general principles based on natural law common to all mankind also came to be recognized. With the extension of citizenship to all free men in 212 A.D., a single legal system could begin to be formulated. To many future societies the principles recognized by Roman jurists—that free men are equal before the law, that government is a contract between the ruler and the ruled, that all men have certain unalienable rights and that ultimate sovereignty in the state lies in the will of the people—seemed indispensable and self-evident.

FURTHER READING

Many of the general works suggested in the preceding chapter also deal with the period of the Roman Revolution and Empire.

An overall treatment of the later republican period is found in T. R. Holmes, *The Roman Republic and the Founder of the Empire*, 3 vols. (1923). R. E. Smith, *The Failure of the Roman Republic* (1955), is a very interesting analysis of the causes for the disintegration of republican institutions. R. Syme *The Roman Revolution* (1943), and L. R. Taylor, *Party Politics in the Age of Caesar* (1949), are fascinating studies of the inner workings of the revolutionary period. The numerous biographies of the leaders of this epoch: G. P. Baker, *Sulla the Fortunate* (1927); G. Boissier, *Cicero and his Friends* (1865), old but still valuable; M. Radin, *Marcus Brutus* (1939); C. Oman, *Seven Roman Statesmen* (1902); W. W. Fowler, *Julius Caesar* (1904); etc. . . . can also be consulted.

For the creation of the Empire the most useful works are: T. R. Holmes, *The Architect of the Roman Empire*, 2 vols. (1928–1931); M. Hammond, *The Augustan Principate* (1937); and J. Buchan's biography, *Augustus* (1937). Many studies of separate emperors of the first two centuries are also available: F. M. Marsh, *The Reign of Tiberius* (1931); A. Momigliano, *Claudius the Emperor and his Achievement* (1934); B. W. Henderson, *Five Roman Emperors A.D. 69–117* (1927) and many others.

Good studies of Roman imperial civilization are to be found in H. Mattingly, *Roman Imperial Civilization* (1957); C. Starr, *Civilization and the Caesars* (1954). M. Charlesworth, *The Roman Empire* (1950), is a very useful brief introduction, and M. L. Clark, *The Roman Mind* (1956), is an illuminating analysis. A general survey of *Roman Literature* (1954) is given by M. Grant, and S. Dill, *Roman Society from Nero to Marcus Aurelius* (1920), has not yet been replaced. E. Strong, *Art in Ancient Rome* (1929), is a useful introduction to the subject.

The best studies of imperial administration are H. Mattingly, *The Imperial Civil Service* (1910); F. F. Abbott and A. C. Johnson, *Municipal Administration in the Roman Empire* (1924); G. H. Stevenson, *Roman Provincial Administration to the Age of the Antonines* (1930); and for the provinces in general, still Th. Mommsen, *The Provinces of the Roman Empire from Caesar to Diocletian* (1881).

M. L. W. Laistner, *The Greater Roman Historians* (1947), is an indispensable guide to the subject. Good English translations of Tacitus, *Imperial Rome;* Suetonius, *The Twelve Caesars;* Vergil, *The Aeneid;* Petronius, *The Satyricon;* and *The Satires of Juvenal,* are now available.

III

THE FORCES OF DISRUPTION

1. The Forces of Disruption

2. Christianity and the Empire

Romans saw a single, stable world; but beyond its boundaries and within the state itself new forces were attacking the security and the very bases of the classical world. Although some of these forces were imperceptible at first, their influence grew steadily. Others changed the aspect of the Mediterranean world suddenly and radically. The problem of the end of the classical world and the beginning of the Middle Ages is one of the most highly disputed in our time. No watertight compartments separate the continuing experience of mankind, but from the second century after Christ many elements began to come together to produce what would become a civilization far different from that of the Mediterranean World.

1 · The Forces of Disruption

The great English historian Edward Gibbon called the second century A.D. the happiest period mankind had known, but the perfection achieved under the Antonines could not be maintained for long. Many elements of weakness, hidden within the efficient functioning of the state, created a friction which gradually brought the machinery to a standstill. From the end of the second century on, new movements of population threw new barbarian tribes against the imperial frontiers on the Rhine and the Danube, while in the East the powerful Sassanid Empire overthrew the Parthians and threatened Rome on the Euphrates. The combination of constitutional conflict, economic and social crises, and barbarian invasions brought about profound changes in the structure of the Empire. The *dominate* of the third and fourth centuries bore little resemblance to the republican institutions on which the Augustan principate had been based. The great reforms of Diocletian at the end of the third century checked a descent into anarchy, but they could not halt the process of destruction altogether. Part of the Empire was saved and even found a new vigor in the fourth century; but the renaissance of the eastern provinces was won at the price of the destruction of the West. A little more than a century after Diocletian's death a barbarian army sacked Rome, and barbarian kingdoms sprang up throughout the territory of the western empire.

INTERNAL DIFFICULTIES

Some of the serious difficulties underlying the smooth working of the administration have already been glimpsed. The relation of the senate to the emperor was ambiguous, especially when the creation of a civil service made the senate all but superfluous in the government. At the same time, the abandonment of a senatorial system and with it of the republican institutions would reveal the true power of the emperor and, more dangerously still, his dependence on the army, which would then be tempted to play the part of kingmaker. The key to all these problems was still the question of succession. The perfection of the administration culminating in the emperor depended on the equal perfection of the man at the top. The Antonine system of adoptions had provided for the training of the best man for the job. It was an admirable piece of constitutional machinery, but it made no concession to human weakness or human affection. Following exclusively his duty as first citizen of the state, the emperor was expected to disregard the claims of his family and pass the power to a distant relative or a stranger. Miraculously, the system worked three times; then, upon the death of Marcus Aurelius in 180 A.D. the imperial crown passed to his son Commodus, who had few of the virtues needed for his position.

The Growing Power of the Army

The break in the constitutional system of succession came at a time when the Empire embarked on an unceasing period of wars. The philosopher-emperor Marcus Aurelius spent his time in yearly campaigns on the Danube and died far from the capital. Thereafter the frontiers were never free from the attacks of foreigners whose raids penetrated deeper and deeper into the Empire. Under the circumstances the full military strength of the empire was needed, and the dictates of the army could hardly be disregarded. The first of the great generals raised to the imperial throne was Septimus Severus (193–211), but soon emperors came to be made and unmade at the will of the various army corps, each of which backed its general to power. From 235 until 284, military anarchy reigned in the Empire. Roman historians referred to the period as the time of the "Thirty Tyrants." Few emperors remained on the throne more than one or two years; at times several candidates disputed the throne while their armies ravaged the countryside; and provincial emperors were installed in Gaul and the Orient.

Economic and Social Crisis

Economic chaos accompanied military anarchy. Even in the period of great imperial prosperity some signs of danger had appeared. Italy could not compete with the developing economies of the provinces, and Trajan was forced to order all senators to invest a third of their income at home. The promise of a high career in the civil service drained the best men away from provincial cities leaving them at the mercy of second rate administrators. The cities vying with each other in splendor overstrained their finances, and imperial supervisors who interfered with local freedom had to be appointed. Industry had not succeeded in developing beyond the small workshop level. The road system functioned admirably as long as peaceful conditions permitted repairs, but the failure to make crucial technological improvements limited trade. The absence of the rudder made large ships ungovernable, and the failure of antiquity to invent a horse collar drastically reduced the loads that could be carried by wagon overland. The small quantities that could be transported were suited to the precious items of a luxury trade, but not to the efficient transportation of bulky supplies. The breakdown in communications and the ravaging of the land because of war interrupted commerce, and because they no longer had to meet serious competition local industries stagnated. To meet the financial demands of continuous warfare and an elaborate administration, increased taxes had to be raised from an impoverished territory. The coinage was systematically debased until the Empire found itself in a dizzying spiral of inflation. In 270 the banks of Egypt refused to accept the imperial currency.

Social changes accompanied the economic crisis. The large slave-operated estates, characteristic of Roman economy since the days of the Gracchi, became too expensive since, under the influence of Stoic humanitarianism, slaves had to be housed and fed even when they were too old or ill to work and their families given at least minimal maintenance. As a result the land was let to small tenant farmers. These tenants, called *coloni,* could not afford new technical methods, and they had little incentive to improve land which did not belong to them. Hence, as the productivity of the soil declined, large tracts of cultivated land were abandoned. To keep land under cultivation, and provide sufficient food, forcible means came to be used. With time, the *coloni* were forbidden to leave the estate on which they worked. They were not slaves in that personally they were free, but they no longer owned the land nor could they move at will; they were serfs attached to a particular property. In the cities the aristocracy suffered heavily. Personally responsible for the taxes of the city in the face of a falling revenue, they found themselves ruined and tried to flee from their obligations. Brought back by force, they were compelled to assume charges they could no longer bear.

Transformation of the Imperial Power

Side by side with the militarization of the state and its economic decline, the outer aspect of the imperial power underwent a profound, if gradual, transformation. The principate of Augustus had been based on republican institutions, although these masked an absolute power. Faced with danger on every side, from the senate jealous of his authority and the army dictating his choice or removal, the emperor tried to protect himself from attack by new means. Early emperors from the time of Augustus had been deified at their death though never in their lifetimes. The cult of the imperial genius, which first began in the provinces to provide a common link for the multiple peoples living in the Empire, spread throughout it. This cult was the expression of allegiance to the state while the gesture of burning incense, before an imperial image, was the traditional expression of loyalty to the Empire, expected of all. Gradually a new attitude toward the person of the emperor developed. Domitian (81–96 A.D.) demanded to be called "lord and god," though this arrogance resulted in his murder. By the time of Septimus Severus (193–211 A.D.) a supernatural aura began to surround the emperor, perhaps in imitation of the semi-divine Persian power across the Euphrates. The Severi claimed to belong to a "Divine House," imperial portraits were surrounded by halos, and during the third century the emperor was often identified with the all-victorious sun. By the end of the century the Empire bore little resemblance to the peaceful and republican principate of Augustus. Outwardly it was plunged in chaos, and its ruler, called *dominus* (lord), had a semi-divine power which has given to the late Roman political system the name of *dominate.*

The Reforms of Diocletian

In 284 A.D. a general from the Danube ascended the imperial throne. He was a man respectful of tradition, and his intention was to re-establish the Empire on a firm foundation. Many of the institutions he developed were not innovations but merely formalized changes which had gradually taken place during the preceding two centuries. Nevertheless, at the end of the twenty-odd years of Diocletian's reign, anarchy had been checked and the appearance of the Roman Empire had undergone a radical change. The despotic government and rigid society Diocletian left behind him would have been foreign and repellent to the contemporaries of Augustus, and even of Hadrian.

The first necessity was to strengthen the authority of the government and to provide for the defense of the frontiers. Diocletian still preserved the republican institutions of a distant past, but they were empty shells devoid of political meaning. In the fully developed form of the *dominate,* the emperor was a god hidden in his palace from the eyes of mankind and approached through an elaborate ceremonial. Although his power might still theoretically come from the will of the people, his will was absolute. Military and civilian offices were completely separated to remove any military control of the administration. The civil service was increased and strengthened. An identical threefold pattern was applied to the entire Empire without variation. The basic unit of administration was the province ruled by an appointed governor. Several provinces were grouped into a diocese supervised by a vicar, and the dioceses were included in the still larger prefectures which divided the Empire into four north and south segments and were the responsibility of the four prefects. Every subordinate was responsible to his superior, so that the government had the aspect of a pyramid culminating in the emperor. A large secret service kept track of the loyalty of all officials. The army was outside the administration; some still guarded the frontiers, but the main corps were under command of officers called *masters of the army,* appointed directly by the emperor. As we shall see, most of the army consisted of barbarian mercenaries, and the *masters of the army* had no relation to the vicars or prefects of their district.

To remedy the main problem of the Empire, that of the transmission of imperial power, Diocletian established a system known as the *tetrarchy.* During the third century the main difficulty connected with the imperial power had been to hold together the two halves of the Empire which were gradually pulling apart. The emperor could not be simultaneously on the Danube and the Euphrates. After his death the armies of the East and the West fought to put their candidate on the throne. Under the tetrarchy a solution was offered for both halves of the problem. The Empire was to be ruled by two emperors rather than one. The imperial power remained theoretically undivided, but Diocletian took a colleague to aid him in his huge task. To the two emperors, who were known as *Augusti,* were joined two assistants called *Caesars* who would succeed in their turn at the death of the senior emperors. Hence no part of the Empire would now remain without direct imperial supervision, nor the imperial throne stay empty as an invitation to civil war.

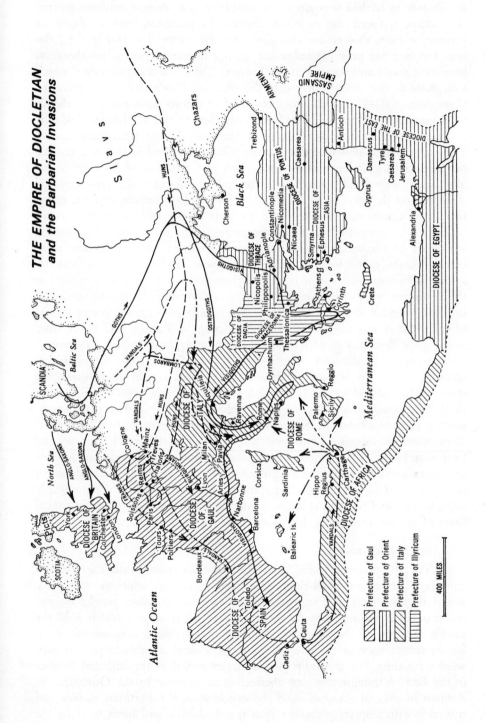

THE EMPIRE OF DIOCLETIAN
and the Barbarian Invasions

Slavs

Chazars

SASSANID EMPIRE

ARMENIA

Black Sea

Trebizond

Caesarea

Antioch

DIOCESE OF PONTUS

Nicomedia

Damascus

Tyre

Constantinople

Caesarea

Cyprus

Jerusalem

Nicaea

Chersón

DIOCESE OF ASIA

Smyrna

Ephesus

Alexandria

DIOCESE OF THE EAST

HUNS

DIOCESE OF THRACE

Nicopolis

Adrianople

Athens

VISIGOTHS

Philippopolis

DIOCESE OF EGYPT

DIOCESE OF DACIA

DIOCESE OF MACEDONIA

Corinth

Crete

Thessalonica

Dyrrhachium

Mediterranean Sea

Baltic Sea

SCANDIA

GOTHS

VANDALS

OSTROGOTHS

LOMBARDS

Reggio

Palermo

Sicily

North Sea

ANGLO-SAXONS

VANDALS

HUNS

Cologne

Mainz

Treves

BURGUNDIANS

DIOCESE OF ITALY

Aquileia

Ravenna

Rome

Naples

DIOCESE OF ROME

Corsica

Sardinia

Hippo Regius

Carthage

ANGLO-SAXONS

DIOCESE OF BRITAIN

York

Colchester

London

Lyon

Milan

Pavia

Arles

FRANKS

Reims

Soissons

Chalons

Paris

Narbonne

Barcelona

Balearic Is.

DIOCESE OF AFRICA

VANDALS

SCOTIA

Picts

Atlantic Ocean

Tours

Poitiers

DIOCESE OF GAUL

Bordeaux

VISIGOTHS

VANDALS

Ceuta

Cadiz

DIOCESE OF SPAIN

Toledo

Prefecture of Gaul

Prefecture of Orient

Prefecture of Italy

Prefecture of Illyricum

400 MILES

Diocletian tried to apply the same regularity in the economic life of the Empire as he had brought to its administration. A new uniform pattern of taxation replaced the oppressive system in existence, and a system of periodic revision allowed for changing financial status. To remedy the inflation, the emperor promulgated a law setting maximum prices for the most important goods and services in the Empire. The social transformation which took place at this time is primarily the work of Diocletian's great successor Constantine (311–337). Diocletian had tried to enforce uniformity in religion as in every other branch of life. Deeply attached to the old Roman gods, he had persecuted bitterly all religious innovations—though with little success. The new religious policy of Constantine will be discussed in the next chapter but his social legislation was the final touch to the reform of his predecessor. The *coloni* were legally attached to the soil to safeguard the production of supplies, and the sons of soldiers had to follow their fathers into the army. In 332 A.D. Constantine decreed even more drastically that every man would henceforth be compelled to follow the profession of his parents. The baker's son would be a baker and might marry only a baker's daughter to raise more bakers. Similarly, the wealthy citizens of provincial cities who had been responsible for the collection of taxes saw their obligation become hereditary at the very time when the economic crisis was destroying their revenues. The law was intended to assure the proper functioning of state services in a time of crisis, but it registered a fundamental change in Roman life. Every trace of the great flexibility of society found in the early Empire had disappeared.

Some of Diocletian's reforms were not successful. The religious persecutions failed, the law on maximum prices could not be maintained, the system of the *tetrarchy* never functioned, and within a few years of Diocletian's death six *Augusti* fought for the throne. However, peace and regular government were re-established in the empire, and the frontiers were held for a time. Even when his successors quarreled with each other, the result was not the total anarchy of earlier times. Finally the legislation of Diocletian and his successor Constantine marked a significant stage in the gradual abandonment of the outward forms and guiding spirit of the classical world. Consequently when in 330 A.D. Constantine left Rome for a new and more convenient capital founded on the Bosphorus, his action took on a symbolic aspect.

THE BARBARIANS

The Romans considered their Empire co-extensive with the civilized world and looked upon all those who lived outside its limits as barbarians. But at no time were they unaware of the existence of other peoples beyond the imperial frontiers. With the hellenized Parthian empire which held the eastern territory of the Seleucids, Rome had established a reasonably satisfactory compromise in the days of Nero. Occasional campaigns pushed eastward for a time, but generally the Euphrates served as the imperial frontier in the East. Although they saw themselves as superior to the Orientals, the Romans in general acknowledged the existence of the Parthian empire and treated it with respect; embassies even travelled back and forth between the two states. The attitude of the Empire toward its northwestern Celtic and Germanic neighbors was very different.

The Germans

The original home of the Germans is still a matter for controversy. In the absence of a written tradition, precise information is difficult to obtain. Furthermore, the home suggested for the Germanic tribes on the shores of the Baltic sea is ill-suited to archaeological excavations since the northern soil, alternately frozen solid and drenched during the spring thaw, does not preserve objects as does the dry sand of the Near East. By the time they had reached the notice of more civilized societies, the Germanic tribes spoke Indo-European dialects, but their relation to other people speaking similar dialects, such as the Greeks or the Celts, is not clear. Even before the second century B.C. the Germanic tribes had begun to move in various directions. The Romans first came to know the Germans in the west. Already at the time of Marius, Germanic tribes had appeared in Gaul, which was inhabited by an earlier population that also spoke an Indo-European tongue. These were the Celts, who had appeared in western Europe during the fifth century B.C. and settled in Britain, Gaul, Germany, and northern Italy. Marius had successfully defeated the first Germanic invaders, the Cimbri and the Teutons, in southern Gaul and northern Italy at the very end of the first century B.C. Fifty years later Julius Caesar, at the time of his conquest of Gaul, had found the country populated mainly by Celtic tribes, although he also fought Germanic tribes along the Rhine. In the time of Augustus and the Julio-Claudians, Germanic pressure increased along the Rhine, and repeated campaigns were needed to hold the frontier. Occasionally the barbarians trapped an imperial army and destroyed it, but generally they were no match for the highly disciplined legions and the defenses of the Empire along the Rhine and the Danube. Hence no serious trouble arose until the end of the second century A.D.

Germanic Society

Both Julius Caesar in his *Commentaries* to the Gallic Wars and the historian, Tacitus, in his essay, the *Germania,* have left accounts of Germanic life and customs. However, their information is now held to be inexact in many particulars, and our knowledge of early Germanic society is not extensive. In general the tribes seem to have been semi-nomadic groups moving about with their household equipment and cattle. Their chief occupation was fighting, and their leaders were primarily war chieftains. Around each chieftain were gathered his loyal followers who were rewarded with a share of the booty gained in combat. A simple tribal assembly existed to approve or reject a particular policy, but the Germans had no elaborate public institutions. The main ties of the tribe were those of kinship and the personal loyalty which bound the chieftain and his followers. There were no written laws, but tribal custom demanded the payment of a compensation to the injured party or his family in cases of theft, maiming, or murder. The intellectual life of the tribes was provided by an oral epic literature celebrating the deeds of the heroes and gods, and a primitive religion worshipped deities which were often incarnations of the forces of nature.

In spite of the imperial frontiers, Roman and German societies were by no means hermetically cut off from each other. Roman merchants travelled across the Rhine and the Danube to carry their wares to distant Germanic regions. Because of their military valor, Germanic tribesmen soon came to serve for pay under their chieftains as auxiliaries to the legions and were considered allies of the Roman state. By the late Empire the barbarians had so thoroughly penetrated into the imperial army that most of its troops had ceased to be Roman citizens, and the defense of the Empire was undertaken by foreign mercenaries.

The Sassanids

The first signs of danger from outside the Empire had come on the Danube frontier, but the most threatening enemy in the early part of the third century seemed to be in the East. In 222 a nobleman from the eastern province of Fars (Persia) revolted, against the ineffective rule of the Parthian king, and within two years the Sassanids, who took their name from an ancestor of the new dynasty, had established themselves on the Persian throne. From several points of view the Sassanids differed from their predecessors. Where the Parthian empire had been a loosely governed association of princes, sympathetic toward that Hellenistic culture which had so long influenced the East, the Sassanid realm was far more tightly knit under the royal authority, and the new dynasty spearheaded the hostility of the eastern provinces to the Hellenism of the Parthian court. A similar hardening appeared in the religious policy of the Persians. The Parthians had inherited the indifferent tolerance of the ancient Persian empire. The Sassanids, by contrast, were zealous Zoroastrians ready to support their faith through proselytism and persecution.

The consequences of the Persian revolution rapidly manifested themselves. A new hostility replaced the former half-hearted cooperation of Rome and Parthia. The danger was all the greater because new means of warfare were being introduced. For centuries the Roman infantry had been the best fighting force in the Mediterranean, but Roman cavalry riding without saddle or stirrups was incapable of serious fighting and good for little more than reconnaissance or occasional skirmishes. The new heavy armored cavalry of the Sassanids crushed the Roman legions, and the increased tempo of warfare, due to the use of mounted troops, carried enemy attacks far inside the imperial frontier. Hardly had the Sassanids strengthened themselves on the throne when their king, Shapuh I (241–271), attacked the Euphrates frontier. In 256 the great Syrian city of Antioch was taken and sacked, and a Persian army reached the Mediterranean for the first time in many centuries. Four years later Rome suffered the additional humiliation of seeing its emperor defeated by the Sassanids and carried off to die a prisoner in Persia, and Sassanid reliefs and inscriptions gloried in the victory of their ruler as had earlier Oriental civilizations. The initial success of the Sassanids could not be maintained. The Romans learned the use of heavy cavalry, and the Euphrates frontier was re-established, but for four centuries after the great raid of Shapuh I, war was endemic in the East. Part of the Roman forces always had to be reserved for the defense of her Empire from the Persians.

The New Migrations

Along the frontier of the lower Danube, the intensified fighting which had been carried on since the reign of Marcus Aurelius did not seem at first to be as serious as the Persian attack. Imperial armies were usually victorious, and the situation on the border outwardly seemed little changed from that of earlier times. Nevertheless, behind the immediate skirmishes along the frontier a violent shock had changed the configuration of the Germanic tribes in the East. Probably at the time when the early Germanic invaders moved westward into Gaul, other tribes had moved southward. By the second century A.D. an agglomeration of Germanic tribes, called the Goths, was settled in the area north of the Black Sea. The so-called kingdom of the Goths was in no sense a settled state but followed the usual nomad pattern. Gothic tribes wandered in the plains of southwestern Russia; a western confederation bore the name of Visigoths (Wise Goths); behind them, and again loosely associated, were the Ostrogothic (Brilliant Goths) tribes. The early pressure of the Goths on the frontier was not critical, though they infiltrated continually into the Empire, and various nomadic tribes from further east periodically disturbed the lower Danube, left open to attack by the destruction of the trans-Danubian kingdom of Dacia at the time of Trajan's annexation of this province.

In the fourth century the situation of the Goths was radically altered by the appearance of the Huns. The newcomers were a group of fierce mounted nomads coming from the east. The origin of the Huns is no clearer than that of the Goths, but their home was not in Europe, and the language they spoke was of the type called Mongolian. A break in the political equilibrium of Central Asia had sent waves of nomad populations, among them the Huns, toward the west. Reaching the south Russian steppes by the middle of the fourth century, the Huns swept out of their path the various tribes found in the region. The Visigoths, whose district lay furthest west, were hurled against the Danube by the shock and begged the permission of the imperial officials to cross the river to safety. Permission was granted, but the dishonesty of the officials aroused the anger of the Goths. In 378 a Roman army, commanded by the emperor in person, was annihilated by the Visigoths at Adrianople in Thrace. The immediate result of the battle was negligible, since the Goths retreated and did not try to exploit their victory. Nevertheless, they had shown that they could rout a Roman army in the field, the Danube frontier was breached, and the pressure from the east continued to increase as new tribes pushed westward from Asia. The Ostrogoths soon followed their kinsmen over the Danube.

The far western provinces of the Empire were not spared in turn. At the very time that the Goths finally crossed the Danube the frontier of the Rhine also gave way under the pressure of new Germanic tribes. The Alemanni, Burgundians, and Vandals poured into Gaul from Germany, and behind them still another confederation, the Franks, moved from its home on the lower course of the Rhine. Treading on each other's heels, the barbarians pushed and elbowed each other deeper and deeper into the Empire. Finally, the most distant province of the Empire, Britain, fell to the attacks of invading Angles, Saxons, and Jutes raiding from the German coast and the peninsula of Denmark. In 407 the last Roman governor left Britain, which was abandoned to the barbarians who settled in the country.

DISASTER AND SURVIVAL

The barbarian invasions had such a striking effect on the imagination of contemporaries that historians long attributed the destruction of the Roman empire to them. However, recent scholarship has rejected this single explanation for the disasters of the fourth and fifth centuries as an oversimplification of an extremely complex situation. The growing crisis of the late Empire has been assigned a multiplicity of interacting, internal and external causes. The failure to establish a firm law of succession; the imperial policy toward the barbarians; the shortage of manpower, as *coloni* and city officials fled from their imposed tasks; the destruction of the ablest classes of society; the vicious circle in which territories ravaged by war had to pay heavier taxes to support new armies for the continuation of the war; the demoralization of the rigid society, which, to be freed from its obligations, welcomed the invader—all have been cited as contributory elements in the crisis. At the same time, all of these evils were aggravated by the continuous pressure of the newcomers.

The Fall of the Roman Empire in the West

After the struggle following Diocletian's death, the Empire experienced a breathing spell in the first half of the fourth century. Constantine and his successors had succeeded in preserving a semblance of orderly government throughout the Empire, in spite of continuous warfare along the frontiers, and quarrels within the imperial family. As difficulties increased in the second half of the century and the beginning of the next one, however, order could no longer be maintained, and the separation of the two halves of the Empire, which had temporarily been checked, began anew. The great Spanish emperor, Theodosius I, succeeded in re-establishing Roman prestige after the disaster of Adrianople and holding together for the last time the entire Roman territory under a single rule; but his sons could no longer control the barbarians, and the two halves of the Empire split asunder.

The Visigoths, under their chieftain Alaric, became too demanding for safety in the early fifth century and the emperor sought to remove them from the vicinity of the new capital of Constantinople. Granting to Alaric the official title of *master of the army,* the emperor urged him toward the west whose doom was sealed by this action. To the horror of the civilized world, the Visigoths sacked Italy and the city of Rome itself in 410 A.D. before settling in southern Gaul, whence they infiltrated into Spain. At the same time the Vandals moving south across Gaul and Spain made their way to Africa, where they became the masters of the imperial provinces.

THE ROMAN EMPIRE about 500 A. D.

The disaster reached its height in the middle of the fifth century. In 451 the Huns under Attila broke from their home on the Danube and swept across Europe as far as Italy and Gaul before returning to the East. Four years later the Vandals, sailing from Carthage, sacked Rome which had been spared by the Huns. The weak successors of Theodosius I could do nothing to save the country. Hidden behind the marshes of their northern capital of Ravenna, they were the playthings of successive Germanic chieftains whom they honored with pompous titles. By 476 the invaders dispensed with these puppet rulers, the imperial insignia was sent back to Constantinople, and Italy was ruled by the Germans in the name of the distant eastern emperor. The last decades of the fifth century brought the last barbarians to the west. The Ostrogoth, Theodoric (490–526), was sent from Constantinople with an imperial mandate to reconquer Italy, and the Franks under Clovis (482–511) established their rule over Gaul from which they drove the Visigoths.

The Barbarian Kingdoms

By 500 A.D. the western provinces of the Empire were in the hands of various Germanic tribes. The Vandals held Western Africa; the Visigoths held Spain. The Ostrogoth Theodoric ruled in Italy and Clovis, king of the Franks, ruled over most of Gaul. In addition, smaller territories were held by the Burgundians on the Rhone river and there were various Anglo-Saxon principalities in Britain. The settlement of the barbarians in the lands of the western empire did not spell an immediate and total destruction of Roman culture. The Goths had long lived in the vicinity of the Empire and were acquainted with its civilization, for which they had considerable respect. The greatest of the barbarian rulers, Theodoric the Ostrogoth, despite occasional acts of violence and cruelty, tried to rule justly over a mixed Gothic and Roman society. He surrounded himself with educated Romans and protected arts and letters in his capital of Ravenna. The picture of life in the West during the fifth century, obtained from contemporary sources, shows a twofold aspect. On the one hand, the horror of invasion and destruction is described in the darkest colors. But on the other, for example, a Roman gentleman named Sidonius Apollinaris, living in central Gaul at the height of the chaos, wrote letters to his friends in which he described the idyllic peace of country life. Not all Romans were dispossessed, but in most regions kept a part of their lands. Some of the barbarian rulers, such as Theodoric and Clovis, even seemed to recognize the eventual authority of the emperor of Constantinople and received titles from him.

The relative mildness of the Goths should not blind us to the reality of change in the western empire. Even Theodoric ruled Italy as the chieftain of the Ostrogoths and not by virtue of any recognition from the eastern empire, whose interference in Italian affairs would never have been tolerated. In other parts of the West, the barbarians were far more hostile. The Vandals devastated Roman Africa with a violence that made their name a synonym for brutality. The principalities of Britain seem to have lost all contact with the Mediterranean world. The barbarians regarded themselves as the masters of the regions they had conquered, and Germanic customs were imported into the imperial territory. The uniformity of Roman law was replaced by the various customs of the Germans; the public institutions of the Empire gave way to the more primitive personal loyalty of the barbarians. The land had been ravaged again and again, industry and commerce almost wiped out, and the earlier economic pattern replaced by a subsistence agriculture. Throughout the West, the invasions generally resulted in the destruction or abandonment of the cities which had been the centers of cultural, economic, and political life. Consequently, the urban civilization which had characterized not only Roman but all of classical culture began to be eradicated from the western provinces of the Empire.

Survival in the East

Generations of scholars, concentrating their attention on the catastrophes which had all but wiped out Roman influence in the West, borrowed the title of Edward Gibbon's epoch-making book and spoke of the *Decline and Fall of the Roman Empire*. Contemporary historians, however, speak more cautiously of the fall of the Roman Empire in the West. The reason for such caution is provided by numerous studies which have demonstrated that no disaster in the eastern provinces of the Empire balanced that of the West, and that the evolution of Roman civilization at Constantinople showed little interruption from the foundation of the city in 330 by Constantine the Great.

Some of the experiences of the crisis of the fourth century were common to both parts of the empire. Barbarian attacks, imperial incapacity, and economic difficulties are found in the East as well as in the West. The older son of

Theodosius the Great ruling at Constantinople under the supervision of a Gothic chieftain seemed to be in precisely the same situation as his younger brother at Ravenna. But by the end of the fifth century, the two halves of the Empire were very different. Freed of the tutelage of the barbarians, the eastern emperors returned to the Roman tradition of orderly civilian government, and in 491 an elderly civil servant named Anastasius successfully ascended the imperial throne of Constantinople, at the very time that Clovis and Theodoric were establishing themselves in Gaul and Italy.

Part of the success of the eastern emperors was due to their policy of driving the barbarians toward the West. Both Alaric and Theodoric were bought off with gifts and urged westward to remove them from the neighborhood of the capital. The policy was probably motivated by no more than blind egoism and weakness in the face of the invaders, but it had momentous results. The eastern provinces did not experience the devastation undergone by the West in the fourth and fifth centuries. Concessions had to be made to the Persians on the Euphrates, but the loss of territory was insignificant. The manpower shortage and economic crises caused by the invasions in the West had no counterpart in the East. The provinces saved were the richest in the Empire; they included Egypt, the granary of the whole Roman world, and Syria. The greatest commercial and industrial center of the world, Alexandria, was untouched, and Antioch, together with the cities of the coast, rapidly recovered from the raids of the Sassanids. Having preserved its source of food supply and its great economic centers, the eastern empire could afford to maintain an army and a professional administration, both of which had become too expensive for the impoverished West. The survival of urban centers assured the continuity of intellectual life.

As the western provinces began their downward spiral, the eastern empire showed a gradual and partial rebirth. The emperor ruled no more than half of his former territory, but the administrative tradition and the civil service continued, and the ancient Roman institutions of the consulate and senate still lingered on. The nearness of the imperial court revived the luxury industries. Improvements in the rigging of ships facilitated trade; the imperial navy dominated the eastern Mediterranean; and the great road system was maintained for the imperial post. An economic revival permitted the improvement of the financial system. The new gold coins minted under Constantine I became the standard of currency for the whole of the western world, and remained unadulterated for eight centuries. In this new prosperity, oppressive social legislation no longer had to be maintained. Men were no longer compelled to follow their father's profession, and a certain amount of flexibility returned to society.

Political and economic revival was accompanied by a brilliant cultural life. When Constantinople became the capital of the Roman world, the aristocracy which had followed Constantine eastward built itself luxurious palaces in the new city. Imposing monuments bore witness to the glory and wealth of the imperial administration. The intellectual tradition received particular attention from the emperor Theodosius II, whose long reign covered the first half of the fifth century. Every type of literary activity was carried on in the great cities of the east and especially in the capital, but the emperor did not wish to leave matters to chance. An imperial commission was entrusted with the task of systematizing legal practices, and in 425 an imperial edict created the University of Constantinople. This institution, which contained chairs of philosophy and law, as well as Greek and Latin, rhetoric and grammar, maintained both the intellectual and cosmopolitan tradition which Rome had inherited from its Hellenistic teachers.

One of the standard questions of historians is the date of the fall of the Roman Empire. Many answers, more or less suitable, have been suggested. But the complexity of the question increases with study, so that no clean-cut division is to be found. Some aspects of the classical world had died before the reform of Diocletian; others were still flourishing. The western provinces, in the hands of the barbarian rulers, were profoundly transformed, but the Roman world was not dead. In Constantinople the imperial tradition, though sharply reduced, lived as a model and inspiration for the future.

FURTHER READING

In addition to the works mentioned in the preceding two chapters, the best general studies of the late Empire are S. Katz, *The Decline of Rome and the Rise of Medieval Europe* (1955), and F. Lot, *The End of the Ancient World and the Beginning of the Middle Ages* (1931). The classic account of late Roman society is S. Dill *Roman Society in the Last Centuries of the Empire* (2nd ed., 1906). T. R. Glover, *Life and Letters in the Fourth Century* (1901), is also very useful. An analysis of the possible causes for the fall of the western Empire is given by F. W. Walbank, *The Decline of the Roman Empire in the West* (1953).

On the Barbarian invasions, excellent surveys are to be found in the *Cambridge Medieval History I*, chapters ix–xv, or in J. B. Bury, *The Invasion of Europe by the Barbarians* (1928). The accounts of the period are discussed by C. J. H. Hayes, *Introduction to the Sources Relating to the Germanic Invasions* (1909). On the survival of the Empire in the East see J. B. Bury, *History of the Later Roman Empire*, 2 vols. (1923, 1958) and the general works listed in Part IV, Chapter 3. For the religious transformation of the Empire see the bibliography of the next chapter.

2 · Christianity and the Empire

The transformation of the Classical world which took place during the late Empire was not limited to political and economic changes. A profound alteration marked intellectual and religious life as well. The entire loyalty of the citizen had been claimed by the state of which he was a part, but little additional satisfaction was given to the emotional demands of humanity. As the disasters of the later Empire made earthly life progressively less secure, men turned from the civic gods, who were too deeply involved in the political catastrophes, to new religious concepts. In the spiritual revolution overtaking the classical world, the Christian doctrine grew gradually from humble and obscure beginnings until it reached a dominant position. The triumph of Christianity was impeded by exterior and particularly interior difficulties, but for all that it was singularly swift. Within three centuries of the death of its founder, Christianity had built an institution capable of contesting the ultimate allegiance of mankind with the state, and in so doing it had contributed to the destruction of one of the basic elements of classical civilization. The supremacy of the state had been challenged, and the Christian was no longer an interchangeable citizen but an individual soul.

RELIGIOUS TRANSFORMATION AND THE APPEARANCE OF CHRISTIANITY

The first dissatisfaction with classical gods appeared as early as the Hellenistic period. The traditional protectors of the *polis* were too closely identified with their particular locality to adapt themselves to the new cosmopolitan world. At the same time they were incapable of satisfying the emotional and ethical needs of a sophisticated but deeply perturbed society. The vacuum left by the state worship was filled by new moral philosophies, such as Epicureanism or Stoicism, while *syncretism* tried to adapt the old gods to a wider world. As the Romans emerged from the isolation of the Italian peninsula their primitive religion became clearly inadequate. Hellenistic beliefs and the growing cult of the imperial genius, common to all the inhabitants of the Empire, provided the answer for a time, but with the end of the period of imperial peace and prosperity, society began to feel once more the insufficiency of the existing order.

Ethical Philosophies

For some the answer was provided as before by philosophy. Epicureanism, and particularly Stoicism, reached their widest development in Roman circles. Philosophers concerned themselves with the central problem of good and evil, and a new school, the Neo-Platonists, applied the Platonic doctrine of images, in which physical manifestations were only the reflection of eternal abstract ideas, to moral problems. To the Neo-Platonists only the good had reality, while evil did not exist and was an illusion. The Neo-Platonists used the image of a light shining in the darkness to illustrate their doctrine, an image which struck profoundly the imagination of mankind. One of the best known uses of it is found in the Gospel of St. John.

The Mystery Cults

Moral philosophies were attractive to an educated minority, but they never reached the mass of population, which sought relief for its troubles in various mystery cults. Under the republic the worship of the Great Mother goddess and the orgiastic cult of Dionysus had been imported to Rome from the East to the dismay of the senatorial aristocracy who found the new rites unsuited to the Roman tradition of seriousness and dignity. These cults flourished primarily in the lowest classes of society; but with the accession of the Flavians, who were themselves of nonaristocratic background, the new beliefs spread among the nobility, and a temple of Isis was built in Rome itself.

At the beginning of the crisis of the third century, the population, oppressed by continuous wars, economic distress, and social rigidification, turned more and more from a world growing rapidly unbearable to revelations of a better future and promise of supernatural protection. The cult of Isis, the great mother who watched over her devotees wherever they were, spread throughout the Empire. The worship of Mithra, the intercessor for mankind in the struggle between good and evil, a worship derived from Zoroastrian doctrine, found particular favor with the army.

In spite of their extension and elaborate rituals, the mystery cults were not organized religions, for they had no unifying structure or doctrine, and they were not exclusive, but shared their devotees with other cults, as well as with the gods of the state. The common trait of the mystery cults was the revelation to the new initiate of a secret information or ritual which would give him the knowledge necessary to obtain the god's protection in this world and particularly after death. The acquisition of this knowledge and the reception of the newcomer into the circle of initiates after preliminary purifications was usually marked by a symbolic act or sacrament which set him apart from the rest of the world. In the cult of Mithra, those desiring to be received into the group of initiates had to be drenched with the blood of a specially slaughtered bull.

The Palestinian Communities

The religious transformation was not limited to pagan society. Palestine had been violently shaken by revolts against Roman authority. The military campaigns of the Flavians put an end to all Jewish independence and destroyed the Temple of Jerusalem in 70 A.D. Political unrest continued and broke out again in a major revolt under Hadrian, but Jewish discontent had also taken another form. The promise of a Savior sent by God to lead his people out of servitude was part of the ancient Hebrew tradition, and even before the war of 70 A.D. numerous prophecies announced the coming of this Savior. At the same time, the philosophic speculations of the Hellenistic world were influencing Hebrew thought. The recent discovery of the *Dead Sea Scrolls* shows that Palestine was in a state of profound ferment. The ultimate significance of the Scrolls must await the finding and deciphering of all the manuscripts, but even now there is evidence that in the desert near Jerusalem ascetic and mystical communities lived according to a strict rule of discipline, concerned with the teaching and martyrdom of a "Master of Righteousness" and with the struggle of the "Sons of Light and the Sons of Darkness." It is against the background of this profound transformation of ancient civilization by a growing mysticism that early Christianity developed.

Christianity

Historical information about the beginnings of Christianity is unfortunately very limited. No external source, Jewish or classical, records the career of Jesus, and our entire knowledge comes from the subsequent writings of his followers gathered together into the *Gospels.* Modern scholarship no longer doubts the authenticity of these writings, but the Gospels were not composed simultaneously, and the earliest, that of St. Mark, was written one generation after the death of Jesus.

The *Gospels* relate that Jesus was born in humble circumstances, but from the Hebrew royal house of David during the reign of Augustus, and that he was acknowledged the Son of God at the time of his baptism. He briefly preached his doctrine in Palestine before being denounced to the Roman authorities as an enemy of the state and betrayed by one of his disciples. He was put to death, came back to life after his burial, and laid on his followers the task of spreading his message before ascending into heaven. The essence of the doctrine preached by Jesus was the unity of God and his mercy in sending his son to save mankind, lost in sin, by becoming part of it. He recognized the brotherhood of all men, promised eternal life after death to all who received his doctrine and shared it through the sacrament of baptism, and stressed that the Heavenly Kingdom to come with his return was not of this world.

Jesus himself never left Palestine, and his followers at first were found in only a few Jewish communities; but within a generation the new faith was given a significant expansion through the activity of one of its early opponents. A Hellenized Jew from the city of Tarsus in Cilicia called Saul had begun by persecuting the followers of Christ. But his sudden conversion, about 35 A.D., made him one of their leaders under the name of Paul. Paul had never known Jesus personally, but he preached his doctrine, travelling ceaselessly from one small community to the other, so that they did not remain isolated. Even more important, Paul preached that Jesus' message was not restricted to the Jews as had been believed hitherto but was given to all mankind. Freed from the limitations of a particular group, Christianity now had become potentially a universal religion.

The Relationship of Christianity to Contemporary Religions

Outwardly, the doctrine preached by the Christians resembled closely that of many of its contemporaries. The relationship to the Hebrew tradition was acknowledged by Jesus himself according to the testimony of the *Gospels,* which quote him as saying:

Think not that I am come to destroy the law or the prophets: I am not come to destroy but to fulfill.

The similarity to pagan beliefs of the time was noted by contemporaries. The concept of the brotherhood of man had long since been spread by the Stoics. The concept of a faith revealed to mankind and shared through the participation in a sacrament was common to all the mystery cults. The Christians themselves, seeing this similarity, looked on the Mithraic initiation of blood as a sacrilegious parody of their own baptism. Consequently, to many contemporaries, Christianity appeared either as a Jewish sect or as one of the multiple cults flourishing in the Empire.

Intrinsically, however, Christianity differed from both traditions. The activity of Paul of Tarsus had removed the new faith from its purely Jewish beginnings, but even earlier it had contained elements foreign to the Hebrew tradition. Participation in a sacrament was never a Hebrew practice, and strict Hebrew monotheism could not accept the existence of a Savior who was both God and man. At the same time, the resemblance to the mystery cults was by no means complete. Initiation into the mysteries required preliminary ritual purity, but once the secret knowledge was revealed, nothing more was asked of the new member, who could pursue his former life secure in the possession of immortality. Christian baptism, which for nearly two centuries remained the only sacrament of the new religion, could remit past sins but gave no assurance for the future. It was seen as the beginning of a new life of rigid moral purity in which no transgression could be forgiven and for this reason was normally given only to the dying. In contrast to the early tolerance of the mystery cults which allowed members to be initiated to as many mysteries as they desired, Christianity adhered rigidly to the first commandment of the Hebrews: "Thou shalt have no other God before me"—which allowed no compromise whatsoever to its members.

Of great importance also was the internal structure of the new religion. We have seen that the mystery cults had no body of dogma, nor sacred literature, nor central organization. Some of the earliest Christian literature, such as the *Acts of the Apostles* and the *Epistles* of St. Paul, shows a very different picture. From the beginning the Christian tradition was one of consultation in common. The apostles met together to choose the successor of Judas, the betrayer of Christ. The letters of St. Paul kept the communities of

Asia Minor and Greece in contact with each other. From the beginning the signs of a common organization can be discerned. By the middle of the second century A.D., in the face of alternate compilations, the sacred books comprised in the New Testament had been identified, and all other tradition on Jesus' life and teaching rejected. Consequently, within little more than a century of its foundation, Christianity presented a homogeneity absent from the mystery religions. The Christian message of hope, love, and equality appealed to the same oppressed classes of society which had turned for relief to the worship of the mysteries, but its exclusiveness and organization soon attracted the attention of contemporary authorities, giving it a very different historical development. Subsequently, the long tradition of hostility between the Christians and the Roman state left Christianity untouched by the decline of Roman political institutions.

THE DEVELOPMENT OF CHRISTIANITY

The Roman tradition, though hostile to the emotional manifestations associated with eastern cults, saw religious beliefs as a matter of private or family concern, outside the competence of the state unless a public scandal took place. When in the early second century B.C. the orgiastic cult of Dionysus was introduced to Rome, the senate decreed that Roman citizens should not become priests of the new cult; that meetings should be small, private, and under police supervision, but it did not forbid its existence. Once the policy had been set, it was generally adhered to throughout the republic and the empire. The state demanded the loyalty of its citizens and the keeping of the public peace, but their private beliefs were not its concern.

The Persecutions

To the Christians even this tolerant compromise was completely un- acceptable. Allegiance to God and to the state were incompatible, and a true Christian could not perform the duties expected of every citizen. The gesture of burning a little incense before the imperial image was the minimum ex- pression of loyalty to the state, expected on innumerable occasions. It was demanded at all public ceremonies of all officials as well as of the soldiers. But to Christians such a gesture was an impossible denial of the one true God. Consequently, they would serve neither as civilians nor as soldiers. Even the mild words attributed to Jesus in the Gospel of St. Matthew: "Render unto Caesar the things which are Caesar's and unto God the things which are God's," introduced a division of authority which might well sound threaten- ing to a government in which Caesar was increasingly becoming god. The attitude of the Christians, claiming a higher authority for refusing the per- formance of the most elementary duties of a citizen, was revolutionary and in total opposition to the most fundamental principles of classical society. It was an expression of beliefs which the classical world could not understand and which could, under no circumstances, be tolerated by a state whose ultimate authority was brought into question.

The early relations of Christianity with Rome were not marked by excessive violence in spite of subsequent traditions to the contrary. The Empire did not at first distinguish the small, dissident minority from the Jews who normally enjoyed a special status. The attention of the authority was first attracted by the Christians' refusal to pay the special tax levied on the Jews. We do not know the reason for the violent persecution which flared briefly at Rome under Nero and took the lives of St. Paul, St. Peter, and numerous members of the small Christian community of the capital. The persecution was not continued, however. Even the historian Tacitus, who reflects a point of view hostile to the new sect, disapproved of the killing as unbecoming the Roman tradition. In the next century the emperor Trajan, in a famous letter to one of his provincial governors, formulated the official imperial policy. Christians were to be treated like the members of all secret societies dangerous to the state. They were not to be sought out nor were anonymous denunciations to be listened to by the authorities. If, however, they were found and convicted, they were to be punished as criminals.

The relative mildness of imperial attitude during the first two centuries of Christianity could not be maintained in the crisis of the third century. The Empire, menaced on all sides, no longer tolerated citizens who would neither manifest their loyalty to the state nor defend it. The persecution began intermittently in the early part of the century and reached its height under Diocletian, whose political opposition to Christianity was strengthened by his desire to enforce a uniform religious policy comparable to his other regulations, and by his personal attachments to the gods of classical Rome. The violence of the persecution of Diocletian created a real crisis for Christianity, but it was the last external difficulty it had to face. The Christian population of the Empire was too great to wipe out, and Diocletian's effort ended in failure.

Christianization of the Empire

Within a decade of Diocletian's death, the legislation against the Christians had been removed from the statutes, and Christianity had become a tolerated religion within the Empire. The precise form of the new imperial legislation is not certain; the famous "Edict of Milan" by which Christianity was supposed to have been recognized may never have existed, although there is no doubt that such provisions were made. However, Christianity was not yet a state religion; it was still recognized only on a basis of equality with all faiths permitted within the Empire. The Imperial legislation decreed that:

no one whatsoever should be denied the opportunity to give his heart to the observance of the Christian religion, or of that religion which he should think best for himself.

The intermediate position of the Christians was not of long duration. The emperor Constantine favored it and was baptized on his deathbed, as was the custom of the times. His children followed his faith. Brief pagan reactions still appeared in the fourth century. One of Constantine's own descendents, the emperor Julian, returned to pagan philosophy and the practice of mystery religions. The Christians were particularly alarmed at the law forbidding them to teach in the schools, thus cutting them off from the intellectual and official life of the state. But, although one more pagan emperor briefly ruled in the West, the reactions were not long-lived. At the end of the fourth century, Theodosius I formally proclaimed Christianity the state religion, and no pagan thereafter ascended the imperial throne.

The complete Christianization of the Roman world was still to come. Christianity was still a city religion concentrated in the urban centers; the gradually changing meaning of the latin word *paganus,* which had originally meant no more than a peasant but by the fourth century had its full modern sense of "pagan," shows the scant penetration of Christianity into the country-side. At the time of Constantine the Christian population was nowhere near a majority and was very unevenly scattered throughout the provinces. Far more pervasive in the East, where it had originated and where the great urban centers were located, Christianity is thought to have reached up to 40 percent of the population of the great Syrian city of Antioch; but the overall estimate for the entire realm of Constantine is usually given as no higher than 10 percent.

The Organization of the Church

The Christian Church recognized by Constantine in the fourth century was no longer composed of the small and scattered communities of the days of St. Paul. In the earliest period the communities had consisted of only a few members who met together in secret to hear Jesus' message and commemorate his last meeting with his disciples. The earliest Christians, expecting the imminent return of Christ on earth, were satisfied to wait for this event. The communities kept in touch through travelling teachers, such as St. Paul, but had little interior organization. Most Christians were simple and often illiterate people who felt no need of an elaborate doctrine beyond the message of salvation to all who had accepted baptism.

Toward the end of the first century the hope of the immediate appearance of the Heavenly Kingdom faded, and the Christian communities began to establish an earthly organization to provide for the lengthening interim until Christ's reappearance. In the second century the Christian Scriptures were unified, and by the end of the century the beliefs of the Church were gradually being clarified and extended. The first writings condemning perversions of the faith began to appear. At the same time provisions had to be made for the growing group of believers who had received baptism but had not succeeded in keeping free from subsequent sin. Gradually, the commemoration of the Last Supper with its sharing of bread and wine took on a sacramental aspect and became the central ceremony in the life of the Christian community. The full development of a doctrine of the sacraments, which eventually numbered seven, took centuries and was only foreshadowed in the pre-Constantinian Church. But very early the belief spread that the mercy of God preached by Jesus could not withdraw altogether from repenting sinners, who might still hope for salvation.

As the Christian communities grew in size, their administration became more elaborate. At first little had distinguished the teachers who were usually chosen from among the older members of the group and so were known as presbyters (elders). By the second century the Church was acquiring property which had to be cared for by deacons, and the entire welfare of the community, both its property and its doctrine, was under the supervision of an overseer or bishop who was superior to both presbyters and deacons. The bishops lived in cities because these were the centers of early Christianity, and gradually the bishop of the leading city in a province acquired authority over his colleagues and was called "metropolitan." Thus by the fourth century a definite hierarchy had been established within the Church. Among the metropolitans, those in the greatest cities of the empire came to have particular authority and prestige. These were the metropolitans of Rome, Constantinople (or New Rome), Alexandria, and Antioch, to all of whom was given the name of patriarch. Later the bishop of Jerusalem also received the title of patriarch, in spite of the insignificance of his city which had been destroyed under Hadrian, because he was the supervisor of the site of Christ's death and resurrection.

To preserve the homogeneity of the Church and the unity of the faith, all major decisions were taken in common, as had traditionally been done by the apostles. Three other bishops were needed to ordain a bishop after he had been chosen by the community. Problems of doctrine were discussed at meetings of the main religious authorities of the district. The need for secrecy limited the size of these meetings or councils before the time of Constantine, although a number of them took place. But with the recognition of Christianity the first Ecumenical, or World, Council attended by the bishops of the entire civilized world, was held in 325 at Nicaea, near Constantinople, under the presidency of the emperor himself. Thereafter, world councils met whenever major problems of doctrine had to be resolved.

The Church and the Empire

Constantine's presiding at the Council of Nicaea raised the question of who possessed the ultimate authority within the Christian Church. In the western provinces, of which he was the only patriarch, the prestige of the bishop of Rome, who shared with the patriarch of Alexandria the title of pope, became dominant. He was the overseer of the ancient capital of the Empire and the heir of the authority of St. Peter, the chief of the apostles, who had been martyred at Rome. All questions within the western provinces were subjected to his ultimate decision and many controversies in the East were brought to him for settlement. Nevertheless, to the four patriarchs of the Orient their Roman colleague was at best the first among his equals.

The emperor himself had little doubt as to his own position, though his opinion was not uncontested. After baptism he could no longer be the god he had been in pagan times, but his authority was still unquestionably of divine origin, and he saw himself as Christ's representative on earth and the head of the Church. He left doctrinal decisions to the great councils, but for some five centuries after Constantine's reign the emperor called and presided over the Ecumenical Councils, promulgated their decisions by imperial decree, and ratified elections to all the patriarchates.

Christian Literature

With the Christianization of the Empire came an enormous development in intellectual life. Christian literature had grown extensively during the period of persecution, but with the fourth and early fifth centuries the Christians, in spite of their still relatively small numbers, seem to have grouped together a majority of the great intellectual figures of the period. In the East, where the continuation of ancient cultural tradition brought Christian scholars into close contact with the philosophic teachings of Hellenism, great theologians such as St. Athanasius, St. Gregory Nazianzenus, St. Basil, and St. John Chrysostom struggled to clarify the subtleties of the Christian faith.

In the West, where Christianity was far less widespread than in the East, one of the main tasks was to make the new doctrine known and defend it against the attacks of the pagans. St. Jerome, though he spent most of his life in Jerusalem, provided the magnificent translation of the Bible into Latin known as the *Vulgate,* and continued the tradition of St. Paul in his voluminous correspondence. St. Ambrose, the bishop of Milan, made a major contribution to the ritual of the church through his development of church music. But the most outstanding figure for the future of the Church was St. Augustine, bishop of Hippo in Africa, who died in 430 as the Vandals attacked his city. St. Augustine was converted to Christianity as a grown man after a long acquaintance with Neoplatonic philosophy and various religious sects. The originality and emotional intensity of the new faith finds its greatest expression in his work. In the *Confessions,* the spiritual regeneration and hope of the new convert is described with an individualism and sensitivity of introspection never found in earlier literature. His monumental work, *The City of God,* was written to defend Christianity against the accusation of having brought disaster on the world through its abandonment of the old gods, but it contains the bases of the new Christian philosophy. The realms of this world, despite their achievements and evolution, are sinful and passing and doomed to eventual destruction; the true allegiance of all Christians belongs to the City of God, which is not found in this world and of which they have all become citizens through their baptism.

THE CRISIS OF THE CHURCH

Before its recognition by the state, Christianity had undergone considerable danger from persecution, but the Christians themselves recognized by the end of the second century that persecution, far from being a catastrophe, strengthened and unified the Church. Far more serious and ominous were internal differences whch threatened to split the faith into various factions. The efforts of the Church from the earliest times were directed toward the maintenance of a single faith.

The Causes of Heresy

Serious problems had arisen very early in the history of the Christian community. The earliest Christians had been simple men who had accepted the revelation given to them without question. As Christianity spread, however, it reached the educated classes of society who were trained in the theories and methods of ancient philosophy, and questions deeply affecting the very bases of the new faith were raised and debated. Innumerable questions were discussed, but the bitterest controversies raged around three fundamental problems: 1. The problem of good and evil—how could an all-merciful God permit the all-too-evident existence of evil in a world he had created? 2. The problem of the Trinity—how was the absolute unity of God to be reconciled with the existence of the Father in heaven, the son he had sent to save the earth, and the Holy Spirit which had descended upon Jesus at the time of his baptism; and furthermore, what was the relation of the three persons of the Trinity to each other? 3. The problem of the nature of Christ—how could he be both God and man?

Crucial as it was, the need to clarify the doctrine was not the only source of controversy and heresy. The changed status of Christianity after its recognition by the Empire was also a serious source of unrest. The Christian faith had been born outside the state, and its early development had been in direct opposition to a state it would not support and whose persecution it had endured. Christ had specifically said that his Kingdom was not of this world and that his message of salvation was addressed to the poor and oppressed as much as, if not more than, to the rich and powerful. With the creation of a Christian empire, the revolutionary character of early Christianity seemed to be fading. The emperor presided at ecumenical councils, and the Church seemed to some a tool in the hands of the mighty. The great Fathers of the West saw the danger very soon. St. Ambrose asserted that the emperor was no more than a sinful man and as such subject to the authority of the priests; on one occasion he refused entrance to the church to Theodosius I himself until he had repented. St. Augustine affirmed that the City of God was not to be found on earth and should not be identified with earthly institutions. Nevertheless, the Church, when in difficulty, often turned to the authority of the emperor to enforce its decision, and discontented minorities unconsciously came to identify religious conformity with imperial despotism. Under the continuous unrest that beset the Church in the fourth and particularly the fifth century lie both the necessary clarifications of difficult points of doctrine and concern over the growing association of the Church with the state. The center of controversy was in the eastern provinces, which contained the main intellectual centers and where imperial authority preserved all of its powers.

Gnosticism

The earliest crisis in the Church was brought about by the numerous heresies which are usually grouped together under the name of Gnosticism. The variations of the Gnostic sects are almost innumerable, but each represented an attempt to solve the problem of evil through a reconciliation of Neoplatonic philosophy with a fantastic mythology derived primarily from Persian sources. For most of the Gnostic sects, the world was divided into the realms of darkness and light, and the entire visible world belonged to the realm of darkness and evil. Consequently, these sects went on to deny the reality of the incarnation of Christ for his divinity could not come in contact with an evil world. The extravagance of most Gnostic doctrine had driven them outside the framework of Christianity even before the time of Constantine; but the greatest of the Gnostic heresies, called Manicheanism, flourished in the Orient, and Manichaean dualism reappeared to plague the peace of western Europe in the thirteenth century.

Arianism

The calling of the Council of Nicaea in 325 was intended to resolve the violent controversy raised in Alexandria by a priest named Arius, who maintained that since God was one, Christ had not always existed and he could not be of the same nature as his Father or his equal. The opposing doctrine of St. Athanasius affirming the con-substantiality and co-eternity of Christ with God triumphed at the Council of Nicaea and is expressly stated in the creed adopted by the council. Half a century later, another council held at Constantinople affirmed the same con-substantiality and co-eternity in the case of the Holy Spirit. But Arianism, though defeated, did not disappear at once. The successors of Constantine favored the condemned doctrine, and it was carried by missionaries to the Goths on the Danube. As both the Visigoths and the Ostrogoths entered the West, they carried Arianism with them, and the Vandals also adhered to the heresy, so that most of the barbarians in the West found themselves in religious disagreement with both the imperial authorities, who soon abandoned Arianism, and the pope at Rome.

Christological Heresies

The last major quarrels which agitated the Church in the fifth century were centered in the nature of Christ. The problem had been raised by the patriarch of Constantinople, Nestorius, who had gone so far as to separate the two natures of Christ, the divine and the human. Condemned at the council of Ephesus in 431, Nestorianism provoked a reaction which went too far in the opposite direction and led to the Monophysite doctrine which saw only one nature in Christ. The reconciling solution was found by Pope Leo I and the Council of Chalcedon in 451, which decided that in the person of Christ two natures were indivisibly united. Despite its rejection by both Nestorians and Monophysites, who lived mostly in the extreme eastern provinces, the compromise doctrine of Chalcedon was accepted in most of the Christian world.

The Changed Focus of the World

With the settling of the Christological controversy at Chalcedon, the first main period of crisis was passed for the Church. Other heresies arose and had to be combatted by new councils, and dissatisfied minorities survived on the fringes of Christian society. Nevertheless, the problems of the following centuries were not as acute as those which followed immediately upon the Christianization of the Empire. The compromise solution of Chalcedon given by the pope and enforced by the emperor was in a sense symbolic of the undefined cooperation between the Church and the state. It still left open the question of whose authority would eventually prove the greater. Even more important, a new division had been introduced into the world with the triumph of Christianity. For centuries to come, no Christian state could command the undivided loyalty which had been given to the city-state. The Christian revolution had divided the allegiance of mankind between the world and the City of God.

FURTHER READING

For the new elements in Roman religion in the imperial period, the best studies are, C. Bailey, *Phases in the Religion of Ancient Rome* (1932); T. R. Glover, *The Conflict of Religions in the Early Roman Empire* (1912); L. R. Taylor, *The Divinity of the Roman Emperor* (1931); F. Cumont, *Oriental Religions in Roman Paganism* (1911) and *The Mysteries of Mithra*. Apuleius' *The Golden Ass* is a second century religious tract in praise of the cult of Isis presented in the form of an adventure story. E. R. Goodenough, *An Introduction to Philo Judaeus* (1940), can serve as an introduction to the study of neo-platonic philosophy.

Since the discovery of the Dead Sea scrolls, innumerable interpretations of them have appeared, but as yet no definitive study. E. Wilson, *The Scrolls from the Dead Sea* (1959), is the first account of the discovery of the scrolls in 1947 and of their subsequent vicissitudes. A translation of such scrolls as have been deciphered so far is given by Th. Gaster, *The Dead Sea Scriptures* (1957).

Scholarly research on the life of Jesus developed with the publication of E. Renan's epochmaking book, *The Life of Jesus* (Eng. tr., 1863). More recent interpretations have been: A. Schweitzer, *The Quest of the Historical Jesus* (1910); J. Knox, *The Man Christ Jesus* (1941); A. T. Olmstead, *Jesus in the Light of History* (1942); and the warning of H. J. Cadbury, *The Peril of Modernizing Jesus* (1939). For the background of Christianity, see C. Guignebert, *The Jewish World in the Time of Jesus* (1939), though it must be remembered that it was written before the discovery of the Dead Sea scrolls. The various influences on early Christianity are studied by R. Bultmann, *Primitive Christianity in Its Contemporary Setting* (1956).

On the early development of Christian doctrine, the best introductions are J. Bethune-Baker, *Early History of Christian Doctrine* (8th ed., 1959), or A. Harnack, *Outlines of the History of Dogma* (1957), which is an abridgement of his monumental work on the same subject. A brief account of the early church can be found in E. R. Goodenough, *The Church in the Roman Empire* (1931), and the lectures delivered on this subject by H. Mattingly, *Christianity in the Roman Empire* (1955), are particularly interesting for their presentation of the changing attitude of both the church and the empire. The intellectual relations between the two institutions are analyzed by C. N. Cochrane, *Christianity and Classical Culture* (1944), and M. L. W. Laistner, *Christianity and Pagan Culture in the Later Roman Empire*

(1951). Useful collections of early Christian texts are to be found in A. Freemantle, *A Treasury of Early Christianity* (1953); H. Bettenson, *Documents of the Christian Church* (1947); and R. M. Grant, *Second Century Christianity* (1946). The best survey of Christian literature is P. de Labriolle, *History and Literature of Christianity* (1924).

For Constantine and the creation of the Christian empire, the best introductions are A. H. M. Jones, *Constantine and the Conversion of Europe* (1948), and N. H. Baynes, *Constantine and the Christian Church* (1929). Two opposing interpretations of Constantine's conversion spanning a century of controversy on the subject are J. Burkhardt, *The Age of Constantine the Great* (first published in 1852), and A. Alföldi, *The Conversion of Constantine and Pagan Rome* (1948).

Very useful chapters on the early heresies are to be found in the *Cambridge Medieval History I,* Chapters v, xvii, xviii. The problem of Gnosticism is treated in F. Burkitt, *Church and Gnosis* (1932), and more recently in H. Jonas, *The Gnostic Religion* (1958).

IV

NEW SYNTHESES

1. The Empire Re-created

2. New Forces

3. From Monarchy to Anarchy

The first effective world government had disappeared, destroyed by internal and external forces. In the centuries that followed, a number of political and social patterns evolved gradually to bring order out of the existing chaos. Some of these attempts were limited and included only part of the old Roman world; some were largely outside it. Some tried consciously or unconsciously to re-create the past, while others sought new solutions and new institutions. Many proved abortive and were separated by intervening periods of disorder and regression. But they were steps toward re-creating a form of stable and civilized government, which will be our concern from now on.

1 · The Empire Re-created

We have seen that the emperors in Constantinople succeeded in maintaining the eastern half of the Roman Empire approximately as it had been at its height. The cities of Asia Minor and Syria, untouched by the barbarian invasions, still flourished, and the grain of Egypt still supplied the demand of the eastern provinces. The manpower needed to defend the frontiers had not been destroyed by continuous wars, as it had been in the West. Merely to maintain the *status quo* was, however, far from the achievement expected of a Roman emperor whose predecessors had ruled most of the civilized world. It is not surprising, therefore, to see a gifted man take the first opportunity of aiming for a higher goal.

JUSTINIAN (527–565)

In 518 an Illyrian peasant named Justin who had served in the army and become commander of the imperial guard was elected emperor. He was a man of very humble origin, illiterate and modest, but he brought with him to the capital a nephew, Justinian, who in his long reign was to go far toward re-creating the world empire of the Caesars. For the first nine years Justinian remained behind the throne as an assistant ruling in his uncle's name, but upon Justin's death and his own accession, he inaugurated a program of consolidation and reconquest almost at once. Supported by his lowly-born but brilliant and ambitious wife Theodora, Justinian aimed at the twofold program of a single empire and a single faith. By 532 an "eternal peace" had been signed with the Persians who were the perpetual enemies of the Empire in the East. The emperor was then free to turn his attention to the West.

Military Reconquests

The most immediately threatening of the barbarian kingdoms in the western Mediterranean was that of the Vandals. Established in Africa and possessing a powerful fleet, they were in a position to cut all navigation routes between the East and the West and thus interfere with military operations as well as with trade. Making the most of internal quarrels within the Vandal royal house, Justinian sent a powerful fleet under the command of his greatest

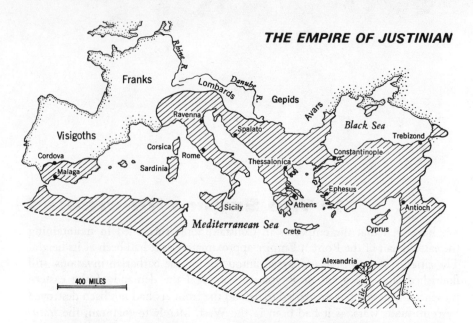

Franks

Rhine R.

Lombards

Danube

Gepids

Avars

Ravenna

Spalato

Black Sea

Trebizond

Visigoths

Corsica

Cordova

Rome

Constantinople

Sardinia

Thessalonica

Malaga

Ephesus

Sicily

Athens

Antioch

Mediterranean Sea

Crete

Cyprus

Alexandria

Nile R.

400 MILES

general, Belisarius, to attack the African shore. The Vandal kingdom collapsed rapidly under the onslaught, but a violent insurrection of Berber tribesmen delayed the final victory for many years. The complete pacification of Africa took fifteen years (533–548).

The main goal of the emperor was, however, the reconquest of Italy and of the city of Rome. Two years after the beginning of the Vandalic war, another expedition, again under Belisarius, sailed to attack the kingdom of the Ostrogoths. Here, too, Justinian diplomatically made the most of opportunity. The daughter and heiress of Theodoric the Great, Almalasontha, who ruled in Italy, had appealed for help to the emperor before she had been deposed and murdered by her husband. Hence Justinian could and did claim that the imperial armies were the defenders of Ostrogothic legitimacy against the usurper. The struggle for the Italian peninsula was even more bitter and protracted than against the Vandals. Following a number of initial successes, the imperial armies ran into formidable opposition from the last of the great Ostrogothic chieftains, Totila. The city of Rome, taken and retaken by rival armies, was reduced to ruins, and Belisarius was recalled in disgrace. Only in 552, after years of continuous fighting, did a new general, Nerses, defeat and kill King Totila at the battle of Busta Gallorum and put an end to Ostrogothic rule in Italy. Even before this final success, however, still another imperial army had landed in southeastern Spain in 550 and begun the attack upon the Visigothic kingdom. Justinian's dream of total reconquest seemed about to be realized. The lands of the western Mediterranean, except for much of Spain, westernmost Africa, and the whole of Gaul, were brought back under imperial control, and viceroys, known as *exarchs,* with full military and civilian power ruled in the name of the emperor at Ravenna and Carthage.

Internal Activities

The activities of Justinian were by no means limited to military operations. The Roman empire had been famous for its monuments, and the contemporary historian of Justinian, Procopius, from whom we get most of our knowledge of the period, devoted an entire book to the *Buildings* of the emperor. A chain of fortifications protected the imperial frontiers; cities were adorned with fine structures of all types, and the great churches of imperial Ravenna still testify to Justinian's reconquest of the West. But the greatest monument of all was erected in Constantinople itself. The huge church of Haghia Sophia, or the "Holy Wisdom" of which the emperor considered himself the earthly representative, was designed to be the visible symbol of the imperial power. Inaugurated on Christmas Day, 537, its walls were covered with multicolored marbles sent from all over the Empire, and its great central dome, set atop forty windows and decorated with gold mosaics, seemed to float more than one hundred and fifty feet above the ground, or as Procopius described it, "hang from heaven itself." Later barbarian beholders of this splendor did not know whether they were in heaven or still on earth.

The attention of the emperor was given also to trade and industry. To supply the realm with the luxuries of the East, the emperor sponsored expeditions to India and China designed to break the monopoly of the eastern trade enjoyed until then by the Persian empire. One of these travellers, Cosmas Indicopleustes (the Indian sailor), has left us descriptions of the Red Sea, the Indian Ocean, and the Abyssinian capital of Axum in Africa, as well as of the Island of Ceylon. To protect the new trade routes along the Red Sea, Justinian even tried to form an alliance with the Christian kingdom of Abyssinia, which also ruled Yemen. But this attempt was not overly successful, as the Abyssinians were never able to compete effectively with the Persians. Finally, luck intervened to help the Empire break the Persian monopoly of one of the most important articles of trade. According to Procopius, several monks succeeded in smuggling silk cocoons out of China, and they taught the inhabitants of the Empire how to work the thread. As a result, a flourishing silk industry developed along the Syrian coast in such cities as Tyre and Antioch, and in Egypt at Alexandria.

Justinian also took seriously his role as protector of his subjects. He tried to stop governmental oppression of the population and do away with the abuses which had gradually crept into the bureaucracy, particularly the sale of offices common at the time. Even more important for the future was Justinian's legal activity. An attempt had already been made in 438 under Theodosius II to eliminate the confusion existing in the Roman laws, but it remained for Justinian to accomplish the task. At the order of the emperor, a commission presided over by the great jurist Trebonianus labored for four years, reading through some two thousand volumes, to produce the great Civil Code known as the *Corpus Juris Civilis*. The work was divided into three parts: the *Codex Justinianus,* the Code itself, promulgated in its final form in 534 and containing the laws of the Empire; the *Digests* or legal opinions on these laws; and the *Institutes,* a manual for law students based on the other volumes. In addition to the *Corpus* which was written in Latin, new laws, or *Novellae,* written in Greek so that they might be understood by all, were promulgated whenever the need for legislation arose. This entire body of laws, which was rediscovered by the West after many centuries, provides the basis for much European legislation to this day.

The numerous military ventures of Justinian and his administrative occupations do not seem to have distracted him from the second half of his program. Master of the world, he wished to see his will obeyed in the spiritual realm as well. Authoritarianism seems to have been the besetting sin of the emperor, who fancied himself an outstanding theologian. Urged by a genuine piety and the unwillingness to tolerate any opposition, Justinian wanted to reunite all the branches of the Christian church and to abolish all heresies. Already in 529 the last great center of pagan learning, the Academy of Athens, had been closed by the emperor's orders and its teachers scattered. A number of dissenters such as the Manichaeans, Jews, and Samaritans were cruelly repressed by imperial legislation which reduced them to the level of second-class citizens. Justinian himself, who had been brought up in the Latin tradition prevailing in his native Illyricum, tended toward concessions to the western church, represented by Rome. However, the Empress Theodora, who was of eastern background, favored the Monophysite churches. It was only after her death in 548 that Justinian summoned a council of the entire Church to systematize the faith, as had already been done for civil law. The so-called Council of the "Three Chapters" met in 553 and, by condemning three theologians whom the eastern churches rejected as Nestorian, tried to work out a compromise which would be satisfactory to all. When Pope Virgilius, who had refused to attend the council, although he was present in Constantinople, also refused to approve the conciliar decision, he was brutally maltreated and exiled to an island for daring to oppose the imperial will.

Opposition to Justinian

Despite his many achievements, the absolutism of Justinian did not flourish unopposed. In 532 a formidable uprising nearly put an end to his reign at its very beginning. Political life in Constantinople was dominated by the so-called "circus factions" known from their colors as the Blues and the Greens. These were not sports clubs, as might be imagined, but opposing religious and political parties. Angered by heavy taxation and the oppression of dishonest imperial officials, these factions for once joined forces in support of the nephews of an earlier emperor. Shouting "Nika, Nika" (victory), the populace wrecked the capital for six days and invaded the Hippodrome from which they threatened the adjoining imperial palace. Justinian was terrified at first and wished to flee, but Theodora refused to leave, saying that she would never outlive the title of empress. Encouraged by his wife's stand, Justinian decided to remain and Belisarius' troops finally succeeded in surrounding the rioters in the Hippodrome and massacring them all.

After the "Nika" rebellion had been drowned in blood, serious efforts were made by the government to reform the administration and stop official abuses. However, the situation which had provoked the uprising was not altered, especially since the great military campaigns forced the exaction of heavier and heavier taxes. War dragged on year after year in Africa and Italy, requiring new troops and fresh supplies. In 540 the king of Persia, seeing Justinian occupied in the West, broke the "eternal peace." The imperial armies now had to wage war simultaneously on three fronts. The Persians, breaking through the frontier, again sacked the city of Antioch and reached the Mediterranean, ravaging some of the richest provinces of the Empire. It was not until 562 that a temporary peace with them could be achieved. New barbarians, who were to prove a major threat in the future, the Slavs, made their appearance in the Balkans.

Nor did the religious unity dreamed of by Justinian have any great success. The Monophysites rejected the compromise of the Three Chapters as insufficient, while the West refused to accept it, despite persecutions. When officials attempted to arrest a successor of Virgilius who had also refused to ratify the decision of the council, the population of Rome rose in protection of the pope and scattered the imperial troops. Local revolts had to be put down all over the Empire. Opposition to Justinian was so bitter that even Procopius, who had praised the emperor unqualifiedly in his book *On Buildings,* accused him in another book, *The Secret History,* of being the incarnation of the devil himself.

Historians are not agreed on the significance of the work of Justinian. Some have seen it as the anachronistic dream for a world long dead, doomed to failure from the beginning. For them the Empire of the sixth century no longer had the cultural unity or economic strength needed for the reconquest of the world. They cite the evidence of the restless population; the long drawn-out wars; the overstrained finances; the failure of the Three Chapters; and the rapid disintegration of Justinian's realm under his successors. On the other hand, at his death in 565 Justinian could well believe that he had fulfilled his program. Most of the barbarian Germanic kingdoms had been defeated or destroyed outright. Interior discontent had been kept in check and an attempt had been made to improve the administration. A single faith and a single law had been given to the civilized world. Finally some of the forces which were to help destroy Justinian's work appeared only after his death, and he could hardly have reckoned with them.

The most threatening of the new forces were the Slavs, who had barely made their appearance in Justinian's lifetime, and especially the new faith, Islam, in Arabia, which was to develop more than half a century after his death. We shall speak of these movements in the next chapter. Here let us only note that as a result of their appearance the eastern Empire, fighting for its very existence as it had not been forced to do against the Germanic invaders, had for a century at least no attention or help left to spare for the concerns of the West, with very serious consequences for the historical development of both areas.

The Lombards

The first break in the Empire came in the West. Only three years after the death of Justinian a new Germanic people, the Lombards, who had settled on the middle Danube in the sixth century, penetrated into the northern part of Italy which was no longer protected by the Ostrogothic kingdom. The imperial *exarch* lacked troops to repel the barbarians, who overran much of the peninsula, although they could not capture the cities of Ravenna and Rome. For the next two centuries a loose Lombard kingdom with its capital at Pavia was established in northern Italy, and additional Lombard duchies which did not recognize the authority of the king at Pavia were founded further south at Spoleto and Beneventum. The situation was particularly serious since the Lombards seem to have been among the most savage of the Germanic tribes. Far from attempting to adapt themselves to surviving Roman customs, as the Goths had done, they slaughtered the inhabitants and seized their lands. The violence of the barbarians was increased by the fact that the Lombards entered Italy as fanatical Arians and as such were particularly opposed to the Catholic population. A Lombard historian of the eighth century speaks of one of the kings who had a drinking cup made from a human skull. The *exarch* was helpless in surrounded Ravenna, but he managed to maintain himself there until 751. The roads between Ravenna and Rome were cut by the Lombard kingdom. The attention of the emperor of Constantinople was occupied in the East, though he still kept his holdings in Venice, Sicily, and southern Italy. The population of Rome did not know where to turn for help in the absence of its traditional protector.

THE CHURCH

The first force which appeared in the vacuum left by the failure of imperial authority in Italy was the Church. Even before the fifth century the Church had provided cultural centers in the West. In the absence of secular learning, such as had survived at Constantinople, the learning of the West was preserved exclusively by religious institutions.

Monasticism

Monasteries, which had originated in the East, found great favor in the West as cultivated men gathered together to seek refuge from the violence of the world. As early as the fifth century Saint Patrick founded a number of monasteries in Ireland, which were to become great centers of artistic and missionary activity. Cassiodorus, the great minister of Theodoric the Ostrogoth, founded in 534 on his property at Vivarium in Southern Italy a cultural center where a library was assembled and learning carefully preserved through the translation of Greek works. The most important foundation was made by an Italian nobleman, Benedict of Nursia. In 529 Saint Benedict, after a stay near Rome, founded at Monte Cassino, further south, a monastery which still stands today, although it was almost destroyed by bombardment in 1944. The Benedictine rule written for this monastery spread rapidly through western Europe. It enjoined among other things that every monk, in addition to prayer and meditation, should spend several hours a day at work. Much of this work was manual labor in the fields and in the monastery, but some of it was more intellectual, and most of the ancient texts which we still possess were saved only because they were at some time laboriously copied in a Benedictine monastery.

The Papacy

From the monastic tradition also came one of the great leaders of the Church, Pope Gregory the Great (590–604). While a number of outstanding figures had occupied the chair of Saint Peter, much of the ultimate authority in the Church still belonged to the emperor. As we have seen, it was Justinian who called the Council of the Three Chapters and enforced its decision. All papal elections had to be confirmed by the approval of the emperor. With the election of Saint Gregory, the Church in the West assumed not only much of the authority of the Empire, but also many of its secular responsibilities. When he came to the papal throne Gregory the Great had already had considerable administrative experience. He was a Roman nobleman and had been prefect of the city before entering a monastery. He had also served as papal ambassador at the court of Constantinople for six years and, though he failed to learn Greek, he had ample opportunity to observe the imperial administration at firsthand. Papal elections continued to require imperial ratification for a time after his election, and Saint Gregory himself wrote respectful letters to the imperial authorities. Yet upon his accession he assumed, both in spiritual and temporal affairs, the active leadership of Rome. Not only did he defend the city against Lombard attacks, but he took over internal administration as well and supervised the police, the law courts, markets, schools, the water supply, and all the necessary services of the state.

Moreover, Gregory the Great did not limit his activity to Rome. Denouncing the ambition of the Patriarch of Constantinople, who had taken the title of Ecumenical Patriarch (Patriarch of the Entire World), the pope, assuming the title of "Servant of the servants of the Lord," asserted the primacy of the see of Rome over all others. For the guidance of the clergy he wrote a *Rule* which laid down their duties and responsibilities, and his enormous correspondence covers almost every subject of interest to the Church. Finally, the pope concerned himself particularly with the spread of the Christian faith through missionary activity. In Spain he succeeded in obtaining the conversion of the still Arian king of the Visigoths. In 596, after his interest was aroused by the appearance of blond slaves in the Roman markets he sent one of his monks, Saint Augustine, to England where Augustine established Christianity among the Anglo-Saxons with the conversion of the king of Kent and the foundation of the see of Canterbury in 601; Britain was linked once again to the civilized world. From Britain, Saint Boniface was to spread Christianity still further among the Saxons of northern Germany. The final triumph of the pope, one year before his death, was the conversion from Arianism of the heir to the Lombard throne. These manifold activities spread the prestige of the Roman see far afield and supported the claim of the pope that he was the true head of Christendom.

In spite of the conversion of the Lombards and the increased spiritual authority of the papacy, the pressure of barbarians on Rome did not decrease. The popes did not have the temporal means to defend Italy. In the absence of the eastern emperor, who was by now pursuing his own policy, and with whom the Roman Church had also broken over religious matters early in the eighth century, a more vigorous protector had to be found at once. Since the other Germanic kingdoms had been destroyed or seriously weakened, the popes turned to the Franks, to whom the emperors of Constantinople had also appealed for assistance against the Lombards in the seventh century. As Christians, they could be looked to as faithful supporters of the papacy. The moment was propitious for such a move.

THE CAROLINGIANS

The Frankish Merovingian dynasty which was established by Clovis at the end of the fifth century and controlled most of Gaul after his victory over the Visigoths in 507 was dying out by the beginning of the seventh century. The family of Clovis, weakened by bloody internal feuds and a succession of child kings, was represented by rulers whose helplessness was acknowledged in the name given them—"the do-nothing kings." The real power within the country belonged to the nobles and particularly to the king's chief minister, the Mayor of the Palace.

By the beginning of the eighth century one of these Mayors named Charles Martel (Charles the Hammer) acquired particular prestige through his defeat of the Arabs who had swept through Spain destroying the Visigothic kingdom and who were raiding northward into France. The battle of Poitiers near the Loire in 732 halted the Arab advance in the West and consolidated power in the hands of the victor. Nevertheless, though Charles Martel was in effect ruler of the Franks, he did not dare to assume the actual title but continued to govern in the name of the shadowy Merovingian king. The reason for this was that according to Frankish custom, the crown belonged irrevocably to the house of the Merovingians, and no one outside that family might lawfully wear it. It was left for Charles Martel's son, Pepin the Short (741–768) to find a solution to this ambiguous situation and to the civil wars resulting from it.

After having consolidated still further the achievements of his father, Pepin decided to assume the title of king, but mindful of the danger of such a step he sought some additional support. To obtain this he turned to the chief spiritual authority of the West, the papacy. Pope Zacharias received the request favorably and decreed that henceforth, for the welfare of the realm of the Franks, the real holder of the royal power should also bear the title. The last of the Merovingian rulers was relegated to a monastery, and Pepin was anointed and crowned king by the Pope's delegate, Saint Boniface in 752.

A little later, in 754, Zacharias' successor, Pope Stephen II, alarmed by the fall of the exarchate of Ravenna to the Lombards three years earlier and the consolidation of Lombard power in northern Italy, decided to leave Rome for France. There he encountered Pepin and before the assembled nobility crowned

The Empire of
Charlemagne, 814 A.D.

Tributary to
Charlemagne

Byzantine Empire

Northmen

North Sea

Danes

Anglo-Saxons

Saxons

THURINGIA

Slavs

Atlantic
Ocean

Aix-la-Chapelle

Paris

Strasburg

Magyars

AQUITAINE

BAVARIA

Roncevaux

KING OF
ASTURIAS

SPANISH
MARCH

BURGUNDY

LOMBARDY

ITALY

Venice
(Byz.)

Avars

Danube

Bulgars
R.

Black Sea

Under
Moslem Rule

Corsica

Monte Cassino

Constantinople

Sardinia

Sicily

400 MILES

Crete

Mediterranean Sea

him again, together with his sons Carloman and Charles I, the future Charlemagne, and conferred on all three the title of Roman Patrician. The new Frankish dynasty, the Carolingians, had received its consecration at the price of accepting the crown from the hands of another person; its legitimacy was not automatic but required a special new ceremony, the anointing, although at the time probably no one was aware of the implications of this act. In return for the honor he had received, Pepin agreed to defend the pope against the Lombards. He succeeded in defeating them on two occasions, and presented the lands he had conquered to the pope. This gift, the so-called "Donation of Pepin," which included most of the lands of the former exarchate of Ravenna together with the city of Rome, formed the basis of the future Papal States. By this alliance the Carolingians had become the temporal protectors of the spiritual head of the western world. Under Pepin's son Charlemagne they were to revive in the West the long-vanished idea of empire.

Charlemagne (768–814)

In 768, at the death of Pepin, Charles I came to the throne together with his brother Carloman. Both had been crowned in 754, and according to the German custom in which all sons inherited equally, they were expected to divide their father's kingdom. A critical situation was avoided by Carloman's lack of ambition and his early death. Left sole ruler, Charles I began by carrying on his father's policy. Answering the appeal of the pope, once again threatened by the Lombards, the king of the Franks brought an army to Italy. He visited Rome at Easter 774 and confirmed the Donation of Pepin. In June of the same year he succeeded in capturing the Lombard capital of Pavia. Crowned king with the iron crown of the Lombards, he added their kingdom to his own. Thus the power of the Lombards in northern Italy was destroyed forever, though additional campaigns were needed to maintain the original victory. Only the Lombard duchy of Beneventum succeeded in preserving its independence despite repeated efforts of the Franks to conquer it.

The destruction of Lombard power was only the first move in Charlemagne's pattern of conquests. Mindful of the fact that he was both a Germanic king and the defender of Christendom, he turned his attention away from the Mediterranean world to the still pagan German tribes of the North. Repeated campaigns against the Bavarians, Thuringians, and Saxons extended the frontier of the Frankish kingdom eastward as far as the Elbe. However, this frontier was never secure. The heathen Saxons in particular took every opportunity to rebel against conquest and baptism and had to be put down again and again by force. Although Saxony had not yet been completely pacified at the time of his death, Charlemagne had added to his realm territories which had never belonged to the Romans.

Further south, Charlemagne was more successful. Several campaigns destroyed the Asiatic Avar kingdom which had established itself in the plain of Hungary. By 796 the Avar power was crushed, its armies scattered, and the last remnants of the nation were fleeing eastward. Christianity and the authority of the king of the Franks had reached almost as far as the middle Danube.

In the West Charlemagne also fulfilled his duty as a Christian king by protecting the last small Christian principality left in northern Spain against the Arab invaders. The beginning of the Spanish expedition was not auspicious. An army commanded, according to tradition, by Count Roland, Charlemagne's nephew, was totally destroyed in 778 at Roncevaux in the passes of the Pyrenees. The disaster of Roncevaux became the subject of one of the greatest medieval epics, *The Song of Roland,* but Charles did not abandon his undertaking in Spain. Though he never attempted to drive the Arabs out of the Iberian peninsula, he established a secure frontier zone, known as the Spanish March, south of the Pyrenees. By 796 Charlemagne ruled from his northern capital of Aix-la-Chapelle (Aachen) a kingdom which stretched from the Atlantic and the Pyrenees to the Elbe, the Danube, and the center of Italy.

The Imperial Coronation
In the year 800 Charlemagne set out once more toward Italy where the Pope, Leo III (795–816), was in serious trouble with the rebellious population of the city of Rome. After quelling the disturbance, Charles remained in Rome to put the city in order. On December 25, 800, while the king of the Franks was attending the Christmas mass in the Church of Saint Peter, Pope Leo III placed a crown on his head and saluted him as Emperor of the Romans.

We shall probably never know exactly what took place on this famous occasion, and historians still discuss almost every one of its aspects. The contemporary accounts agree only on the fact that Charles was crowned emperor by the pope. Consequently, numerous interpretations of the event have been possible. Was Charlemagne taken by surprise, as his official biographer Eginhardt assures us, or had he planned the coronation in advance? At least one of the king's ministers, Alcuin of York, had pointed out in a well-known letter written the year before the coronation that because of the failures of the pope and the emperor of Constantinople, Charles himself was the only guardian of Christendom; yet Eginhardt, who was also close to the court, writes that "he [Charles] would not have entered the Church that day if he had known in advance the plan of the Pope." Did the king accede to the wishes of the people of Rome and receive the homage of the pope after his coronation, as we are told by the official Frankish chronicle, or was he granted the crown by the pope for his protection of the city of Rome and his respect for the papacy, as is asserted by the biographer of Leo III? Even if we do not raise the question of the background of the ceremony, additional problems were created by the coronation itself. Charlemagne had been crowned by the pope, and he had apparently been proclaimed Emperor of the Romans. What were the relations of the new emperor to the Church and to the emperor at Constantinople?

Charlemagne could not fail to realize that his assumption of the new title could only be regarded as an act of defiance by the rulers of Constantinople. Both Alcuin and the contemporary chroniclers felt the need of justifying Charlemagne's pretensions by the fact that the throne in the East was occupied by a woman, the Empress Irene, who had deposed her own son, and whom they did did not consider a legitimate ruler. The problem was particularly serious because the eastern emperors still held both Venice and Sicily and were intriguing with the still independent Lombard duchy of Beneventum for the reconquest of Italy. For this reason, Eginhardt tells us, Charlemagne sent many envoys to Constantinople. The newly crowned emperor even seems to have proposed marriage to the Empress Irene, but the plan failed when the empress was overthrown in 802. It was only at the end of his life that Charlemagne obtained some recognition of his title from a hard-pressed Emperor of Constantinople, though even this concession was later withdrawn. To counterbalance the danger from the other Emperor of the Romans, Charlemagne even entered into relations with the enemy of the Eastern Empire, the distant Arab caliph of Baghdad, Harun ar-Rashid. The negotiations never led to an alliance, but the presents brought by the ambassadors of the caliph, magnificent silks embroidered with elephants and a water organ unknown in western Europe, testified to the luxury and refinement of contemporary oriental civilization.

The problems of the relations between Charlemagne and the Church were of another nature. Charles had been anointed and crowned emperor by the pope, as earlier his father, Pepin, had been anointed king of the Franks. In the West, therefore, there were now not one but two heads. Though the matter was not considered at the time the question might well be asked in the future: Could a man truly become emperor without the papal consecration, and which of the two, emperor or pope, was superior to the other and thus the head of Christendom? Charlemagne himself does not seem to have had any doubt of his own position. Though very pious and conscious of his duty as a Christian ruler, we have seen him negotiating with an enemy of the Christian world, the caliph of Baghdad. He relied heavily on churchmen as personal advisers and official administrators; he endowed numerous churches and monasteries and took care of church affairs; but he too never hesitated to act on occasion as a master. When the need arose, he summoned councils, promulgated edicts in his own name, and even addressed letters of advice or admonition to the pope himself.

Internal Administration

Regardless of the meaning and implications of the event of 800, Charlemagne concentrated on trying to bring order to the vast territory under his control. In 802 a great assembly was held at the palace of Aix-la-Chapelle at which the nobility was summoned to take an oath to Charles as emperor, replacing the one they had sworn to him earlier as king of the Franks. At the same time Charlemagne ordered that the laws of his various lands be written down, though he did not attempt to systematize them into a single code, as had been done by Justinian. On all important matters, secular or religious, however, the emperor promulgated throughout his reign general edicts, called *capitularies,* which were to be obeyed everywhere in his dominions.

In the matter of administration much needed to be done. Almost all pretense at central government had disappeared under the helpless rule of the late Merovingians and local nobles had become more and more independent and unruly. The local officials, or counts, who had originally been appointed by the king as his representatives settled in their districts. Because of poor communications, their distance from the court, and the incapacity of the king to enforce his orders, they became local chieftains pursuing their own ends and disregarding or openly opposing the interests of the crown.

Charlemagne sought to curb these nobles and re-establish a degree of central control over them. He was not completely able to break the power of the local landowners, as he could no longer maintain an effective system of public communications. Furthermore, since he had no regular army, he was dependent on the good will of the chieftains, who appeared to serve when summoned in the spring for a campaign and returned home in the fall. Nevertheless, he tried to make the counts once again government officials, appointed and dismissed by the ruler and his representatives. Some taxes were collected and the government re-established its monopoly over the currency. Charlemagne also tried to keep some control over the administration of justice by having the major cases tried before a count who, advised and assisted according to German tradition by the freemen of the place, judged in the emperor's name. Finally, Charlemagne tried to establish a system of itinerant supervisors. Whenever the need arose, two officials, usually one count and one bishop called *missi dominici,* were sent from the palace on an overseeing tour of a given district. These *missi,* who were men trusted by the emperor, supervised the administration of the local count, heard appeals on judicial decisions, corrected any abuses they found, and generally reported back to the court on the state of the district to which they had been sent.

The emperor also tried to revive some education and culture in his realm. He himself never succeeded in learning to write, although he spoke both German and Latin, and even understood some Greek, but he was profoundly interested in intellectual activities. Among his intimates were such scholars as Eginhardt (Einhard) and Alcuin of York, and he even founded in the palace at Aix a special school, of which Alcuin became the head, for the children of the nobility and some commoner children.

Personality and Legend

We know something of Charlemagne's personality from Eginhardt's biography. Despite his imperial title, he seems to have been more of a Germanic chieftain than a Roman gentleman. He always dressed according to the manner of the Franks and enjoyed hunting. Although he was abstemious in food and drink, his numerous marriages and illegitimate children were hardly suited to a civilised Christian ruler. In later centuries, however, the memory of the great emperor was surrounded by many legends in which his real personality was totally lost. Attended by a dedicated group of twelve companions, ever victorious over the unbelievers whom he pursued in a pilgrimage to the Holy Land, the Carolingian Emperor became a supernatural figure still revered in some parts of Europe as a saint. This legendary character was to have an historical significance of its own as an imperial symbol, but it was far removed from the able and harsh warrior and administrator of reality.

The empire of Charlemagne did not long survive its founder. Even the emperor had been unable to free himself from Germanic tradition and had planned, as early as 806, to divide his realm between his sons. Fortunately, by the time of his death in 814 Charles had only one surviving son, Louis I the Pious, who had already been crowned emperor so that the succession occurred smoothly. But Louis could neither control his father's realm nor transmit it peacefully. In 843 Louis' three sons divided the Empire at Strasbourg by the Treaty of Verdun. This was the first document in the vernacular French and German languages, for the brothers swore friendship in the native tongues of their troops. As the variety of languages indicate, the French and German parts of the Empire were pulling apart into separate realms. In the middle the eldest brother Lothair was given, along with the imperial title, an awkward strip of territory running from Rome to Aix-la-Chapelle which bore his name, Lorraine (*Lotharii regnum*). This strip was still to disturb the peace of Europe in the twentieth century. By 888 the Carolingian house had destroyed itself in quarrels reminiscent of those of the earlier Franks. The last direct descendant of Charlemagne was dead, and little of his administrative system remained.

In its own time the appearance of the new emperor in the West created two political and cultural focuses for the old Roman world, as well as two leaders for western Christendom. To some historians Charlemagne's achievement was a temporary military conquest with little significance and little inner cohesion, doomed to rapid disintegration. For others it was an attempt to re-create an empire and a reminder to the West after many centuries that the idea of world government and centralized administration still survived.

General syntheses for the period are H. B. Moss, *The Birth of the Middle Ages 395–814* (1935), and the less extensive R. Sullivan, *Heirs of the Roman Empire* (1960). Most other works treat either the East or the West.

For bibliography on the early Byzantine empire see also Part IV, Chapter 3; most of the general works listed there contain an adequate treatment of the reign of Justinian. In spite of its age, J. B. Bury's detailed *History of the Later Roman Empire,* 2 vols. (1923), remains extremely useful. A briefer introduction to the various aspects of the reign can be found in P. N. Ure, *Justinian and His Age* (1951). A good biography of Justinian's famous consort Theodora is included in Ch. Diehl, *Byzantine Portraits* (1927). Many of the contradictory interpretations of the reign can be traced back to the ambiguous main source for the period, Procopius, tr. H. B. Dewing, *Works,* 7 vols. (1914–1928), which contains the factual *History of the Wars,* the panegyric of Justinian, *On Buildings,* and the libellous *Secret History.*

The visual setting of the period can be found in D. T. Rice, *Byzantine Art* (1935), and the more general introduction of G. Downey, *Constantinople in the Age of Justinian* (1960). Magnificent reproduction of the art of the period may be found in W. F. Volbach, *Early Christian Art* (1961), and D. T. Rice, *The Art of Byzantium* (1959).

For the West, good introductions are provided by W. C. Bark, *Origins of the Medieval World* (1958), and J. M. Wallace-Hadrill *The Barbarian West* (1962). On the growing leadership of the church, in addition to general works, see L. Duchène, *The Beginning of the Temporal Sovereignty of the Popes,* 2 vols. (1908) and F. H. Dudden, *Gregory the Great,* 2 vols. (1905). A good if very brief introduction to monasticism is given in the *Cambridge Medieval History I,* chapter xviii, see also parts of E. Duckett, *The Gateway to the Middle Ages* (1961).

Several excellent works exist on the intellectual developments of the period: M. L. W. Laistner, *Thought and Letters in Western Europe A.D. 500–900* (1957); also E. K. Rand, *Founders of the Middle Ages* (1928, 1957); and H. O. Taylor *The Emergence of Christian Culture in the West* (1958) (formerly *The Classical Heritage of the Middle Ages*), both of which discuss the dependence of the Christian tradition on the classical past. For a treatment of purely literary aspects, see W. P. Ker, *The Dark Ages* (1958). S. Dill, *Roman Society in Gaul in the Merovingian Age* (1926), is a thorough and most useful study, and E. Kitzinger, *Early Medieval Art* (2nd ed., 1955) is a particularly good introduction.

Most of the sources of the period have been translated. The *Letters* of Gregory the Great are published in the *Library of Nicene and Post-Nicene Fathers,* Series II, vv. xii–xiii and there is a translation of *The Rule of St. Benedict* by F. H. Gasquet (1908). The translation of the *History of the Franks* by Gregory of Tours (1926) provides a good picture of the barbarization of the West, while Bede's *A History of the English Church and People* (1955) demonstrates that not all scholarship and learning was lost in this area.

The best treatment in English of the period of Charlemagne is H. Fichtenau, *The Carolingian Empire* (1937). As introduction to the subject, there is an excellent essay by S. C. Easton and H. Wieruszowski, *The Era of Charlemagne* (1961), which is accompanied by a translation of a number of relevant documents. Very valuable also is the pamphlet in the series *Problems in European Civilization* edited by R. Sullivan, *The Coronation of Charlemagne. What Did It Signify?* (1959), in which the main interpretations of this event have been collected. For an easy introduction to the Carolingian court see, E. Duckett, *Alcuin, Friend of Charlemagne* (1951); also the biography by Th. Hodgkin, *Charles the Great* (1891); and for the contemporary accounts, A. J. Grant, *Early Lives of Charlemagne* (1907).

2 · New Forces

The successor states created by Justinian and Charlemagne did not prove durable. In neither case had the world unity of Rome been achieved. In both cases failure may be traced in a large degree to internal defects of structure: the excessive ambition of Justinian straining the resources of his empire, and the inability of Charlemagne to create a centralized administration. Some of the causes of failure, however, must also be sought in external and unforseeable elements. The transformation of Europe and the Mediterranean world begun at the time of the Roman Empire was not yet completed. Between the seventh and the ninth centuries, even later in the East, the constant appearance of still new peoples altered the existing situation and destroyed all plans based on past experience. Arabs in the East and Normans in the West brought destruction and change. Parts of the old Roman world were lost to European civilization for more than a millennium, and the split between the two halves of the Roman Empire was accentuated by the wedge driven between them by the newcomers: the Arabs, the Slavs, and the successors of the Huns, the Avars and the Magyars. Ancient institutions were no longer suited to the new times and their memory grew dimmer with distance. By the tenth century Europe was divided in two, and it had taken on a new aspect. The West was struggling to emerge from total political chaos while the still surviving Empire in the East bore only remote resemblance to its original form.

THE ARABS

The most serious threat came in the seventh century from an unexpected source. For centuries the Romans had been acquainted with nomad tribes who roamed the desert of Arabia and Syria beyond the borders of the Empire. A few trading cities on the caravan routes had a stable population, but most of the tribes wandered over the desert, following the flocks which were their main source of subsistence, according to the traditional pattern of the Semitic society to which they belonged. The chief occupation of these Arabs was warfare, either among themselves or in sudden raids on the settled communities bordering the desert. Because of their skill as soldiers, the Arab tribesmen had been used as mercenaries by both sides in the wars between Rome and Persia. In the days of Justinian some of the loyal Arab chieftains were Christians, and had received imperial titles. At the time of Justinian's death nothing indicated that these minor border auxiliaries would be a danger to the very existence of the Empire.

Muhammad

The momentous change in the position of the Arabs came with the work of the great religious reformer Muhammad. Little is known of Muhammad's early life, and even the date of his birth is not certain: He was not a desert nomad but was born into a poor branch of the local aristocracy in the commercial city of Mecca in western Arabia. He was soon left an orphan and as a young man entered into the service of a wealthy widow whom he later married. At about the age of forty he received the first revelation of the religious doctrine he was to preach. At first Muhammad had little success outside his immediate family. Mecca was a center for pilgrims worshipping some of the numerous deities of primitive Arab paganism; and its citizens feared a loss of income from attacks on the ancient cults. In 622 Muhammad was compelled to seek refuge in the northern city of Medina. This flight, called the Hejira, was the turning point in his career and is still used as the first date of the Muslim calendar. In Medina, Muhammad had his first successes; he then returned triumphantly to Mecca, which accepted his doctrine. By the time of his death in 632 A.D. most of Arabia had rallied to the new faith.

Islam

Muhammad called the doctrine revealed to him *Islam* which means submission in Arabic. Medieval Europe, noting the great similarities between Muhammad's faith and Christianity, often saw Islam as a Christian heresy. There seems to be no doubt that Muhammad, who had travelled with caravans in his youth, was acquainted with and strongly influenced by the doctrines of Judaism and Christianity. Abandoning the several gods of early Arabic paganism, he preached that there was but one God, Allah. He was all-powerful and all-merciful, and the only duty of mankind was absolute submission to his will. The rigid Monotheism of Islam could accept neither the Christian doctrine of the Trinity nor the divinity of Jesus Christ, but all the prophets of the Old Testament, and most of all Jesus, were to be revered for having received the divine revelation of which Muhammad brought the final and perfect form. Like Judaism and Christianity, Islam was the religion of a book. All the revelations granted to Muhammad were gathered in the Muslim holy scriptures, the *Quran* (*Koran*), whose final form was set after the prophet's death. Beyond the obligation of submitting to the will of the only God, the duties of the faithful were simple. They must publicly confess the faith and defend it, pray to Allah five times daily, give alms to the poor, fast during one month in the year, and if possible accomplish the pilgrimage to Mecca once in their lives.

Muhammad had provided no institutions for the preservation of his doctrine beyond the revelation of the *Quran*. Islam had no ritual and no clergy. At his death he had no sons to be his heirs. Consequently, authority passed at first successively to his nearest companions, each taking the name of Caliph or "Successor." Since Allah's power had no limits, Islam recognized no division of authority into separate spheres. The Caliph's position as both political and religious leader is evident from his title of "Commander of the Faithful." In spite of the Caliph's enormous authority, however, divine revelation had closed forever with the *Quran*. Consequently, no Caliph might change the divine law or add to it; it could only be re-interpreted. As the Islamic state grew under the Ummayad (661–750) dynasty and subsequently the Abbasid (750–1258) dynasty, the Arabs were forced to borrow from their neighbors, in Persia and the Empire, all the administrative and cultural institutions which they lacked.

The Expansion of Islam

Immediately after Muhammad's death his entire work seemed threatened as the Arabs revolted against his successors. But the check was brief. After the pacification of the Arabian peninsula, Muslim armies moved almost simultaneously in various directions. By 636 the first imperial army sent from Constantinople had been defeated on the Yarmuk in Syria. In the next few years Arab armies destroyed the Sassanid empire, captured Egypt, and marched westward both in Africa and in Asia Minor. Nothing was to stop the advance of Islam for the rest of the century, and in 711 the Arabs, who had reached western Africa, crossed the Strait of Gibraltar into Spain, where they overthrew the last of the Gothic kingdoms. The first years of the eighth century marked the apogee of Arab expansion, as their lands stretched from the Atlantic across Africa to the Near East and well into Central Asia.

The victorious advance of Islam was checked only in 717, when the Emperor of Constantinople, Leo III, successfully hurled the Arabs back from the walls of his capital and began the laborious reconquest of Asia Minor. Almost simultaneously, the grandfather of Charlemagne, Charles Martel, saved Gaul by a decisive victory at Poitiers near the Loire, in 732. Soon after, the Umayyad Dynasty of Caliphs ruling from Damascus was overthrown. The new dynasty of the Abbasids came to the throne as the result of the discontent of the eastern provinces of Persia and Iraq, which felt themselves slighted by the Umayyad's favor to Arabs and Syrians. Consequently the Abbasid caliphs moved their capital to the new city of Baghdad on the Tigris, and though an Arab fleet dominated the Mediterranean in the ninth century and the Arab advance in the West added Sicily to the earlier conquests, the attention of the Abbasid caliphate turned gradually more to the East. The enormous Arab empire began to break into smaller and often hostile states, and its immediate threat to the West gradually receded.

The Causes of Muslim Expansion

The rapidity and size of Muslim expansion have long been a puzzle to scholars. The warriors from the desert had overwhelmed the two major powers of the times, the Eastern Empire and the Persians, and gone on to conquer most of the Mediterranean world. The overwhelming victory of Islam is particularly difficult to explain because the sizes of the conquering

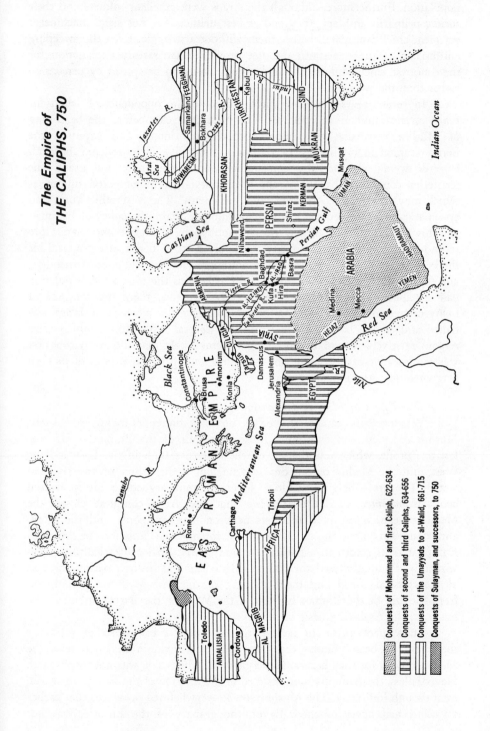

The Empire of
THE CALIPHS, 750

Indian Ocean

Jaxartes R.
FERGHANA
Samarkand
Bokhara
Oxus R.
Kabul
TURKHESTAN
snpul
SIND
Aral Sea
KHWARESM
KHORASAN
MUKRAN
Caspian Sea
PERSIA
KERMAN
Shiraz
Musqat
Nihawend
Baghdad
Persian Gulf
UMAN
ARMENIA
Tigris R.
AL-EZEREH
AL-IRAQ
Basra
HADRAMAUT
Euphrates R.
Kufa
Hira
ARABIA
YEMEN
SYRIA
Medina
Black Sea
Constantinople
Brusa
Amorium
CILICIA
Mecca
Red Sea
Konia
TARSUS
Damascus
HEJAZ
E   A   S   T   R   O   M   A   N   E   M   P   I   R   E
Jerusalem
NILE R.
Alexandria
EGYPT
Mediterranean Sea
Tripoli
Danube R.
Rome
Carthage
AFRICA
AL MAGRIB
Toledo
ANDALUSIA
Cordova

Conquests of Mohammad and first Caliph, 622-634
Conquests of second and third Caliphs, 634-656
Conquests of the Umayyads to al-Walid, 661-715
Conquests of Sulayman, and successors, to 750

armies were very small; the desert had never been able to support a large population. Furthermore, although the Arabs were excellent soldiers and their society primarily military, they had at first neither fleet nor siege machinery; yet great cities capitulated before them without a struggle. Even the sweeping enthusiasm of the new faith did not provide a satisfactory explanation for the conquest, since Muhammad had urged that Islam be spread by persuasion rather than the sword.

In recent years historians have turned to the opponents of Islam for many of the causes of its victories. Less than ten years before the beginning of Muslim expansion the emperor of Constantinople had captured the Persian capital in retaliation for the sack of the city of Jerusalem, and both empires were exhausted by continuous war. Even more important, the territories conquered by the Arabs contained large, discontented minorities which may well have cooperated with the enemy. The Visigothic kings had systematically persecuted the Jewish population of Spain, the policy of Justinian and his successors had turned the Monophysites of Egypt and Syria into second-class citizens. The simplicity of Islamic doctrine had a strong appeal for the lower classes of society who could not appreciate the subtleties of theology, and the Muslim's tolerance of other faiths as long as the conquered population paid a tribute—often lower than earlier taxes—earned them the welcome of many oppressed groups. In view of the fact that the advance of Islam was halted and turned back both in Gaul and Central Asia Minor, which were regions relatively free of heresy, it now seems likely that the Arab conquest was as indicative of discontent and weakness among its enemies as of its own overwhelming strength.

The Effect of Muslim Expansion

Whatever its causes, the effect on the contemporary world of the Muslim conquest was enormous. More than half of the Roman world was lost to Europe, which found itself on the defensive both in the East and the West, and the Mediterranean Sea was no longer the center of the civilized world. The great Belgian historian Henri Pirenne argued in his influential book *Mohammed and Charlemagne* that the Arab conquest closed the Mediterranean, interrupted relations between Constantinople and the West, and destroyed international trade, thus forcing the isolation of Western Europe and its return to a natural economy based on local agriculture. Consequently, Pirenne altered the traditional divisions of history, dating the end of the classical world and the beginning of the new Medieval period, not from the end of the Roman Empire in the West or the Barbarian invasions, but from the Arab conquests of the seventh century.

Subsequent historians have criticized almost every aspect of Pirenne's thesis. It has been pointed out that the Arab invasion did not close the Mediterranean for they had no fleet at first and that trade was not interrupted. Nevertheless, the Arab invasion resulted in the division of the European world, even though indirectly. The Muslim attack overwhelmed provinces that earlier invasions had never touched. Egypt, the granary of the Empire, was lost together with the great commercial cities of Syria. The enemy was at the gates of Constantinople. In their desperate struggle to survive, the emperors had neither the will nor the power to defend their western provinces from the Lombards or the Arabs, who raided southwestern Europe from bases in Southern Italy, Spain, and the Alps. When, in the ninth century, the difficulties of the Abbasid caliph at Baghdad gave Constantinople a breathing spell, it was too late for the emperor to re-establish in the West the prestige that he had so long neglected. Other forces filled the vacuum left by Constantinople. Leadership in the West had passed to the Church and the Franks, and Charlemagne had created a rival empire which did not recognize the authority of Constantinople. The successors of Roman culture were irretrievably divided, and in this sense Pirenne had been partially correct when he attributed the success of Charlemagne to the actions of Muhammad.

By the end of the ninth century the Abbasid caliphate was beginning to decline. The unity of Islam had long been split between two sects, the Sunites and the Shiites. The political unity of the Muslim had long since vanished as Spain, loyal to the Umayyad dynasty, refused to recognize the Abbasid usurpers. Numerous principalities arose in Northern Africa and throughout the East. The ruler of Egypt even had the insolence to claim the religious title of Caliph. The Abbasid heirs in Baghdad were pathetic puppets, made and unmade at the will of the barbaric Turkish palace guard, which controlled the capital after the middle of the tenth century. Nevertheless, the caliphate, once created, was a political power which could never be disregarded. The Muslim principalities might quarrel among themselves, but all were normally hostile to the Christian world. Leo III and his successors slowly fought back across Asia Minor in the eighth and ninth centuries, Charlemagne conquered the March of Spain, but the Arabs remained the masters of most of the Mediterranean, which was controlled by their fleet in the ninth century. All European political calculations had to take into consideration the ever-present Arab threat, and very soon embassies, such as the one sent by Charlemagne to the Abbasid caliph Harun-ar-Rashid, tried to placate or even win over the Muslim princes.

The effect of the development of Islam was not exclusively negative for Europe. The Abbasids in the ninth century succeeded in creating a brilliant civilization. Baghdad under Harun-ar-Rashid was truly the city of the Thousand and One Nights whose splendor could be matched only by imperial Constantinople. The Arabs had learned from the conquered populations both Greek philosophy, taught in the great Syrian school, and Oriental science, preserved in India. Consequently, they were the keepers and transmitters of much ancient knowledge lost in the destruction which had overtaken Europe. Greek classics and philosophic works passed from the Eastern Empire into Arabic translation, and many of the great works of Aristotle survived only through these means. Arabic science and medicine made enormous progress, and on the basis of the decimal system, first brought from India, the Arabs elaborated the new mathematical science of algebra. Arab geographers, astronomers, and travellers added much to the exploration of the world. Gradually this accumulated knowledge began to pass to western civilization, first through Sicily and Spain, and later in the East, during the eleventh and twelfth centuries in the western attacks on Muslim Palestine, which are called the Crusades. The lost works of Aristotle were re-translated from Arabic to Latin and the decimal system was accepted as the basis of mathematics. When the first medical school in Europe was created at Salerno in Southern Italy, it was in a region which had long been in direct contact with Muslim civilization. For all of its very real benefits, however, the value of Islam for western civilization came at a relatively late date. During the first centuries of its existence the Islamic state was primarily destructive for European culture and unity.

CENTRAL EUROPE

Long before the creation of a fleet gave the Arabs mastery of the Mediterranean and imperilled the communications between Constantinople and the West, another wedge had been driven between the two halves of Europe. Starting at the end of the sixth century, the Slavs and various Mongol and Turkic tribes, such as the Avars, Bulgars, and Magyars, began to infiltrate eastern and central Europe, rendering land communications practically impossible and bringing disorder and ruin to both halves of the old Roman world.

The Slavs

The home most recently assigned to the Slavs by modern scholarship is the area of the Pripet marshes of western Russia. As in the case of the Goths, the swampy nature of the land there makes archaeological investigation exceedingly difficult. Nevertheless, various groups of tribes speaking Indo-European dialects of the type known as Slavic seem to have been scattered through the district, though they formed no political unit and were still at a primitive level of culture. Their first appearance in the ancient civilized world came at the end of the sixth century; they began to pass into northern Greece soon after the death of Justinian and eventually filled the plains of occidental Russia. Westward and southward, they gradually reached across eastern Europe until their way was blocked by the Adriatic Sea, the Italian border, and the Germanic tribes stretched across central Europe.

In Greece the political power of the Slavs was brief. By the middle of the seventh century the emperor of Constantinople had regained much of their territories in the south, and the defeated Slavs in the north of the peninsula fell to more warlike new invaders, the Bulgars. All of Greece and the Balkans had been so thoroughly populated by the invaders, however, that a nineteenth century German scholar could argue that not a single Greek was left in all Hellas. Even though this claim now seems exaggerated, the slavinization of the Balkans in the seventh century is unquestioned. The main line of imperial land communications (the Via Egnatia) connecting Rome and Constantinople was cut as the Slavs settled along most of its central course. A series of more or less defined Slavic communities stretched between the world of the Eastern Empire and that of western Europe. In the ninth century a powerful

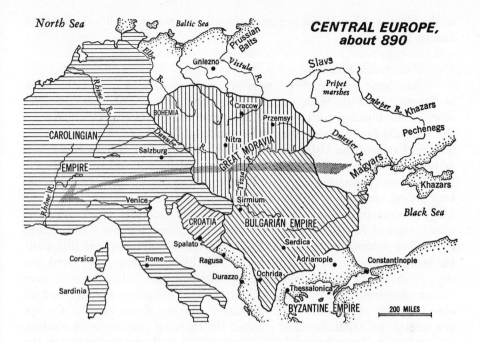

North Sea   Baltic Sea

Prussian Balts

Gniezno   Vistula R.

Slavs

Elbe

Rhine R.

BOHEMIA

Cracow

Przemsyl

Pripet marshes

Dnieper R. Khazars

Danube

CAROLINGIAN

Salzburg

Nitra

GREAT MORAVIA

Tisza R.

Dniester R.

Pechenegs

Magyars

EMPIRE

Rhône R.

Venice

Sirmium

Khazars

CROATIA

BULGARIAN EMPIRE

Black Sea

Spalato

Corsica   Rome

Ragusa

Serdica

Adrianople

Constantinople

Durazzo

Ochrida

Sardinia

Thessalonica

BYZANTINE EMPIRE   200 MILES

Slavic state, Great Moravia, dominated the area later known as Bohemia, and new principalities arose in the Balkan peninsula.

The first results of the Slavs' appearance had been destruction to the lands they entered and disruption of communications. But as they settled into more stable communities their presence created a serious additional problem, with lasting consequences. When they first came, the Slavs worshipped primitive gods; but in contact with more developed civilizations, they gradually came to accept Christianity as had the Germans and Goths before them. The Christianization of the Slavs came primarily from the Eastern Empire, as did most of their culture. The great missionaries St. Cyril and Methodius came from Constantinople to convert Great Moravia in 863, and they created the special alphabet modelled on Greek for the notation of the Slavic language, still called Cyrillic. But at the same time missionaries had also come from the West, particularly from German lands newly conquered by Charlemagne. The Slavic principalities became a bone of contention in the hostility existing between the new Carolingian empire and its older rival in the East. With the increasing coldness between the pope and the Ecumenical Patriarch, Rome and Constantinople vied with each other to establish their cultural and religious domination, and the Slavic rulers, who soon realized the advantages of the situation, turned now to the East and now to the West. For centuries the presence of the growing Slavic states increased not only the physical separation of what had been the northern provinces of the Roman Empire, but also their political and religious hostility. After the establishment of these states all hope of reunion between the two halves of Europe was at an end: a wall had been erected, and the lasting character of the struggle for the cultural domination of the Slavs is still reflected in the checkered religious and political pattern of eastern Europe.

The Asiatic Invasions

The Slavs and the Arabs were not the only ones to disturb the peace of Europe. From the fifth century on, successive waves of Asiatic peoples repeated the invasion pattern of the Germans and the Goths. Destruction in the West did not end with the reconstruction of an empire by Charlemagne. The brief raid of the Huns in the mid-fifth century had been only the first of many to come as the Avars, Bulgars, and Magyars emerged successively from Asia and penetrated deep into Europe. The destruction they brought was even greater and ranged further than that caused by the Slavs. For, unlike the Slavs, who moved as slowly and ponderously as the Germans, the Asiatic newcomers were of Mongol origin. They were magnificent horsemen and archers descending suddenly on an unprepared population at full gallop and disappearing before opposition could be organized. Tireless and savage, they lived and slept in the saddle and spared none of their enemies. Only horsemen were capable of meeting and pursuing such elusive and dangerous enemies, and all older methods of defense were no longer effective. Consequently, the appearance of the Asiatic invaders changed the character and tempo of warfare, and, as we shall see, helped bring about a profound transformation in the social and political pattern of western Europe.

The similarity of the successive Asiatic groups and the necessity for horsemen to follow well-defined routes produced a pattern of attack which varied relatively little. The nomads, starting from the steppes of southern Russia, usually first came in contact with the Eastern Empire which they attacked. Later they moved westward in a series of hit-and-run raids until they were eventually destroyed or forced to settle down.

The Avars

The appearance of the Avars came close upon the entrance of the Slavs into the Balkans, and their threat was increased by their cooperation with the Sassanids, who pressed the Empire in the East while the Avars attacked in the Balkans. Twice during the early part of the seventh century they besieged Constantinople with Persian help, but failed to take the capital. With the disappearance of the Sassanid Empire, they moved toward central Europe, where they were finally annihilated by Charlemagne in 796.

The Bulgars

The Avars had hardly moved toward the West when their place was taken by another Mongol people, the Bulgars. Some of the newcomers moved northward to settle on the Volga, but several tribes entered the Balkans in the seventh century and conquered the local Slavic tribes. At first the Bulgars had been typical Mongol horsemen, offering sacrifices to the forces of nature, ruled by chieftains called Khaghans, and speaking a Mongol dialect. In the Balkans, however, they became completely slavicized through their contact with the far larger population they had conquered. Gradually they settled in communities, adopted the Slavic language and many Slavic customs, and created a state which became Christian in the second half of the ninth century.

From the time of their earliest raids, the Bulgars were uncomfortable neighbors for the emperors at Constantinople. In 803 a Bulgar Khaghan had appeared under the walls of the City, and less than ten years later the emperor was killed fighting the barbarians. Christianity did not halt the warlike tradition; in 926 a new Bulgar ruler was again besieging Constantinople. A horrendous rout at the beginning of the next century, at the hands of the Emperor Basil II whose single-minded policy earned him the title "Killer of the Bulgars," put a temporary halt to the constant Bulgar threat in the Balkans but failed to destroy it. As early as the tenth century the Bulgar rulers had shown their ambition by claiming the title of Emperor. In the thirteenth century their power was sufficiently revived for their king Joannitza to upset the balance of power of his period and make another bid for the mastery of eastern Europe.

The Magyars

The brunt of the earlier raids had been borne by eastern Europe, though the Avars had also pushed their way toward the West. But the lands of the Carolingian Empire were to have their share of destruction. Starting like their predecessors from southern Russia in the ninth century, the Magyars swept directly westward. By 863 they had reached Germany and, by the end of the century, northern Italy. They inaugurated the tenth century by destroying the state of Great Moravia. For the next fifty years, western Europe was never free from the terror of almost yearly Magyar raids, which wrought havoc through Germany, Italy, and France. By 937 the Asiatic horsemen reached the south of the Italian Peninsula and just missed taking the city of Rome. It was not until 955 that the German Emperor Otto I succeeded in defeating them at the battle of Lechfeld and forced them back to the plains of Hungary, where they settled down. At the same time he defeated the Slavs and halted their expansion, so that by the tenth century the battered lands of western Europe were at last freed for a time from the constant threat from the East.

THE NORTHMEN

Arab raids from the south and Magyar attacks from the east were not the only trials faced by the successors of Charlemagne. The northern and westernmost fringes of Europe were not to be spared their share of sorrows in the ninth and tenth centuries when the raids of the Northmen from Scandinavia struck all around the coasts of Europe. These centuries in some respects were the lowest point of civilization reached by the West since the defeat of the Romans.

Except for the fact that they came by sea rather than overland, the raids of the Northmen or Vikings were very similar in their destructive effect to those of the Magyars. The pirate raiders appeared from Scandinavia in ships driven by oars and sails, which allowed them to come and vanish with the destructive speed of horsemen and find the settled population equally unprepared. Since the northern ships were small, they could sail far up the main rivers of western Europe, such as the Thames, the Seine, or the Loire, so that inland cities and territories were no safer from attack than the coasts. The actual number of the invaders was never very great, but their yearly incursions brought increasing damage as they penetrated further and further afield, until the Northmen ceased to return to their homes between raids and settled in the lands they had previously devastated. Like the Mongol invaders, the Northern pirates were heathens; consequently, they had no respect for religious buildings but rather singled out for attack churches and monasteries where precious vessels and ornaments were kept. Much of the ancient culture preserved in these monasteries perished in the flames which marked the passage of the pirates.

The Raids of the Ninth Century

The first raids of the Northmen in the West came in the reign of Charlemagne, while other bands of Scandinavian pirates, called the Rus, began almost simultaneously to move in the opposite direction to attack the northern districts of Russia. Through the ninth century the raids increased in frequency and violence. By the middle of the century the Northmen came regularly to Ireland, England, and France, as well as down the great rivers of Northern Russia. All the western chronicles record the endless destruction and the terror of the helpless population. By 845 the city of Paris, miles up the Seine, had been sacked by a band of Northmen who returned again and again. Further south, neither the coasts of Spain nor those of Italy, which were simultaneously undergoing Arab attack, were spared by the raiders. The enormous reach of the Northmen's raids is perhaps best illustrated by the events of the year 860–861. In 860 a band of Rus, starting from the city of Kiev on the Dnieper, sailed their canoe-like boats into the Black Sea and tried to storm the walls of Constantinople. The following year, another band of Northmen came around from the Atlantic, pillaged the coast of Spain and an Italian city they mistook for Rome, and sailed across the Mediterranean to attack Constantinople, from which the Rus had just been driven back. Both the attempts failed before the formidable defenses and superior military skill of the city. The immediate succession of assaults was pure coincidence and not strategic planning, since the Northmen had no organization which could have undertaken such an expedition, and the various raiding bands had neither knowledge nor interest in the undertakings of others. Nevertheless, the ability of these men to reach Constantinople from the two opposite ends of Europe showed that neither the Atlantic nor the Mediterranean nor yet the Black Sea was beyond the reach of their ships. Far out in the Atlantic, northern ships reached Iceland and Greenland, and it is even possible that some may have actually gone as far as the coast of North America, though no actual proof of this has been found.

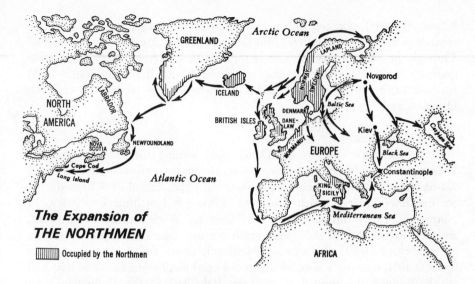

**The Expansion of
THE NORTHMEN**

▨▨▨ Occupied by the Northmen

The Settlements of the Northmen

The local population in most cases had been able to offer very little effective opposition to the raids of the Northmen. The scattered Slavic tribes of Russia, the ineffectual successors of Charlemagne, and the small Anglo-Saxon principalities all lacked the strength and the organization to resist. By the latter part of the ninth century the Northmen found it more profitable to winter far from home and to create new principalities.

Russia

In Russia the Northmen established a number of small settlements of which the most important was at Kiev. From their cities the Viking princes watched over the trade going up and down the rivers and continued to send raiding parties against the Eastern Empire. Gradually, a loose confederacy of principalities grew up under the senior prince of Kiev. Treaties established trade relations with the Empire and a Russian merchant quarter developed in the suburbs of Constantinople. At the end of the tenth century, the new Viking aristocracy had been absorbed by the Slavs, as had the Bulgars in the preceding centuries. Christianity had also come to Kiev from Constantinople, with an imperial princess, Anna, the sister of the Emperor Basil II, who married prince Vladimir of Kiev in 988. The Russian realm subsequently remained in the cultural orbit of Constantinople, even though a Kievan princess, Anna, became queen of France in the middle of the eleventh century by her marriage to Henry I.

The Danelaw

In Ireland and particularly in England, the northern raids coming from Denmark also resulted in permanent settlements. In Ireland, they brought to an end the brilliant culture which had flourished around the monasteries from the fifth to the ninth centuries. In England, the Anglo-Saxon king of Wessex,

Alfred (871–889), checked the encroachment of the Danes but was forced to concede to them a large section of northeastern England, called the "Danelaw." Through the next century a fusion of the Danish and Anglo-Saxon population gradually took place, and in the reign of Canute the Dane (1017–1035) England briefly became a part of his northern empire which also included Denmark and Norway.

The Normans

At the same time as the Danes were settling the Danelaw, another Viking chieftain, Rollo, settled on the continent in northwestern France. In 911 he wrested from the helpless Frankish ruler the control of a large district on the lower Seine which took the name of Northman's country, or Normandy. From this new base the Normans, as they came to be called, sent new expeditions in the mid-eleventh century. One such expedition under a minor chieftain called Tancred d'Hauteville drove the Arabs out of Sicily in about 1041, creating a state which spread northward from its island base and which disputed the control of southern Italy and of the Dalmatian coast with the emperor of Constantinople.

Some twenty-five years after the departure of Tancred, William, the bastard son of the duke of Normandy, led an expedition across the channel to reconquer England, which had briefly reverted to Anglo-Saxon rule after the death of Canute. The victory of Hastings in 1066 gave to William the Conqueror the control of the country which his descendants were to rule for many centuries. The Norman rulers of the island soon came to hold their homeland of Normandy on the continent so that their rule stretched on either side of the English Channel.

The Norman States

The vigor and enterprise of the Vikings brought new vitality into Europe. They were daring explorers and always willing to adapt themselves to local customs and usages, unhindered by traditional prejudices and customs. Wherever they came, the Viking conquerors gradually mingled with the conquered population to form new mixed cultures. Particularly in the Norman kingdom of Sicily, the Viking rulers successfully created a semi-oriental state in which northern elements were dominated by the Greek and Arab traditions of the area. The remarkable wealth and brilliance of the mixed Italo-Norman culture can still be seen in the magnificent monuments of the capital city of Palermo on the northern coast of Sicily.

However, all the audacity and ability of the Normans did little to retrieve the initial damage they had done to the West. Much of the culture they destroyed during their raids was irretrievably lost, and almost all large-scale political units disappeared with the final fragmentation of the Carolingian empire. The establishment of Norman principalities on the periphery of Europe did nothing to re-create the unity they had destroyed. In spite of their common origin, the Viking states never formed a unit. Except for the eighteen years of Canute's rule, it is impossible to speak of a northern empire. The Norman-Saxon kingdom of England, the Slavic-Russian Kievan state, or the Italo-Norman kingdom of Sicily had no relations to their Scandinavian homeland or to each other. They did not speak the same language, and they had no common culture or institutions. Hellenized in Russia, Oriental in Sicily, and Germanic in England, Norman civilization had no unifying traits. The very adaptability of the Normans led them to create differing cultures which made any thought of a Norman empire impossible. In addition to displaying these centrifugal tendencies, the Normans, as well as the Slavs and Bulgars, helped turn the two halves of Europe against each other. The ambition and aggressiveness of the Sicilian princes in the eleventh century did much to envenom the relations between the Western and the Eastern Empires and eventually contributed to the failure of the Crusades.

The Fragmentation of Europe

Five centuries after barbarian kingdoms had first been established within the limits of the Roman world, little could be found to recall the unity of the classical ages or even the relative reconstruction of Justinian or Charlemagne. During the ninth and tenth centuries the political pattern tended toward increasing complexity, fragmentation, and isolation. The Carolingian empire vanished among the quarrels of its rival claimants. The Eastern Empire closed upon itself. The Abbasid caliphate survived at Baghdad until 1258, but its authority was not recognized by most of the Muslim princes of North Africa and the Syrian coast. The Norman principalities pursued their independent and often selfish ends. In central Europe the Slavic and Mongol principalities, which had developed largely in the orbit of Constantinopolitan civilization, gradually came to feel increasing pressure from Germany and formed a no-man's land between the two halves of Europe, the separation of which eventually led to open hostility.

After the seventh century, half of the Roman world was lost to the West as the result of the Arab conquest. At the same time it is impossible to speak of a single Europe. From this period on, historical study is forced to differentiate increasingly dissimilar areas. In the East the imperial tradition survived for seven more centuries after the failure of the great Arab assault of Constantinople in 717: it was the guardian of the past. But the new Empire, painstakingly rebuilt on a drastically reduced territory, bore little resemblance to the realm of Justinian. In the West, the transformation and innovation were even more profound. At first western Europe, all but destroyed by the attacks which battered it from every side, lagged far behind the reconstruction of the East. But from the institutions which gradually developed to protect it in its time of troubles evolved a new world and new concepts of civilization.

FURTHER READING

The standard general history of the Arabs is P. Hitti, *History of the Arabs* (6th ed., 1956), but an excellent brief introduction to the subject can be found in B. Lewis,

The Arabs in History (1958). See also, E. Atiyah, *The Arabs* (1955). The best introduction to Islam is H. A. R. Gibb, *Mohammedanism: A Historical Survey* (2nd ed., 1953). The structure of Muslim society is analyzed in M. Gaudefroy-Demombynes, *Islamic Institutions* (1954), and an excellent study of Muhammad has been made by Tor Andrae, *Mohammed the Man and His Faith* (1935). For the medieval period see G. von Grunebaum, *Medieval Islam* (1937), and A. Mez, *The Renaissance of Islam* (1937), gives a particularly good reconstruction of the civilization of the Abbasid caliphate at its height. A very good selection of the main Muslim scriptures has been made by A. Jeffery, *Islam: Muhammad and His Religion* (1958), and the translation of *The Koran* by N. J. Dawood (1956) is readily available.

The classic statement of the thesis on the effects of the Arab closing of the Mediterranean is to be found in H. Pirenne, *Mohammed and Charlemagne* (1939). The subsequent fate of this thesis at the hands of scholars can be traced in the compilation by A. Havighurst, *The Pirenne Thesis, Analysis, Criticism and Revision* (1958).

For the Slavs, the best introduction is F. Dvornik, *The Slavs: Their Early History and Civilization* (1956) or *The Making of Central and Eastern Europe* (1949), which though more general indicates the place of the Slavs among the contemporary powers. S. Runciman has given a thorough treatment of *The First Bulgarian Empire* (1930) and for the Magyars see C. A. Macartney, *The Magyars in the Ninth Century* (1930). The best account of early Russian history is G. Vernadsky, *Ancient Russia* (1943) and *Kievan Russia* (1948).

The main general study of the Northmen is still C. M. Haskins, *The Normans in European History* (1915); see also T. D. Hendrick, *History of the Vikings* (1930). The civilization of the raiders is studied by A. Olrick, *Viking Civilization* (1931), and G. Turville-Petre, *The Heroic Age of Scandinavia* (1951). For the creation of the northern Viking empire including England see also L. M. Larson, *Canute the Great* (1912). The expansion of the Northmen into Russia is treated in the first volume of Vernadsky's history of Russia cited above.

3 • From Monarchy To Anarchy

In the chaos of the second period of barbarian invasions only one state survived in Europe to carry on the tradition of organized government lost everywhere else. As in the fifth century, the Eastern Empire had survived the attacks of the Goths and Huns to provide the base for Justinian's reconquest, so again in the seventh and eighth centuries the same Empire withstood the onslaught of Arabs and Bulgars. Nineteenth-century historians following the lead of Edward Gibbon looked on the thousand years separating the time of Constantine from the capture of his new capital of Constantinople as a period of "Decline and Fall." The term "Byzantine," taken from the former name for Constantinople, which historians gave to the Eastern Empire, was used in a derogatory sense. Twentieth-century historians, however, have tended to reverse this attitude and have been far more impressed by the vitality of Byzantium than its decline. Again and again for a thousand years, the imperial government weathered exterior attacks and internal crises to re-create a stable administration.

The cultural achievement of Byzantium was even more important for the development of humanity than its political resiliency. To the inhabitants of the Empire their capital was always "the city," the *polis;* and indeed until the twelfth century Constantinople was "the city" of the western world. It had an eastern rival, Baghdad, but none in all of Europe. The wealth and beauty of the city filled westerners with awe and envy. It was the one center of culture and higher education which had escaped the destruction of the barbarians. For centuries it remained as the model of what a civilized society had been and could be while its contemporaries struggled for bare survival. Consequently, the role of Byzantium as the preserver and transmitter of ancient wisdom can hardly be overemphasized.

The Byzantine Empire was conservative as had been its predecessor, the Roman Empire; and in fact its inhabitants called themselves Romans until the capture of Constantinople in 1453. Nevertheless, changing circumstances transformed the Empire profoundly. From a world-state with a culture common to that of the West, it developed increasingly into a relatively small and orientalized monarchy. The separation between Byzantium and the West began in the seventh century and grew wider. Not only were the two civilizations different; they were hostile. The new states growing in the western world came to look upon Byzantium as an enemy, and the powerful western church considered the Eastern Empire heretical after the eleventh century. This enmity exploded in the beginning of the thirteenth century, as a German and French army which should have been fighting the infidel in Palestine was persuaded by the Venetians to turn aside and sack Constantinople in 1204. The Byzantine Empire survived even this catastrophe, but the last two and a half centuries of its existence were a slow agony. Hopelessly weakened internally, receiving little or no help from the rest of Christendom, the Empire went down after eleven centuries under the last wave of barbarian invaders, the Ottoman Turks.

THE EASTERN ROMAN EMPIRE

One of the early, modern historians of the Byzantine Empire, J. B. Bury, marked an important break in the development of this state at the beginning of the eighth century. Up to that time he spoke of the "Later Roman Empire," but after that date he spoke of the "Eastern Roman Empire." The division made by Bury has usually been accepted by scholars. The Empire of Justinian was still a world state; his successors more or less successfully maintained their relations with their western provinces and their supervision over the church at Rome. At the beginning of the seventh century an emperor who came from the western exarchate of Carthage had marched as far as the Persian capital of Ctesiphon to sack it and destroy the power of Rome's traditional equal and enemy. The *Code* of Justinian continued to be the law of the land. The great Arab attacks of the seventh century brought this world to an end. For nearly one hundred years, besieged again and again, its lands ravaged and lost, Constantinople was caught in a crisis it had never known before, and it bent every effort on survival. The West was abandoned to its fate; culture came to a standstill. The seventh century has been called by historians the "Byzantine Dark Ages." The state which emerged with Leo III's successful end to the siege of Constantinople in 717 was very different from the one which had been attacked by the Arabs.

The Imperial Territory

Physically, the Empire of Leo III was far smaller than it had ever been. All of North Africa was gone, together with Egypt, Syria, and much of Asia Minor. Most of the western provinces no longer recognized the imperial authority. Slavs and Bulgars filled the Balkans. During the course of the ninth century, some of Asia Minor was reconquered, but Crete and Sicily were lost to the Muslims, and Arab pirates controlled the eastern Mediterranean. The imperial possessions consisted of part of Asia Minor and most of Greece, with some possessions in Italy and along the Dalmatian coast. Most serious of all were the losses of Egypt and the commercial cities of Syria, whose survival had permitted the imperial continuity of the fourth and fifth centuries. Now, for the first time, the whole economic structure of the Empire had to be altered and based on the single area of Asia Minor which was slowly won back from the enemy.

The Themes

The first consequence of the years of constant warfare was the militarization of the Empire. From the days of Diocletian military and civilian administration had been separate. In a time of acute crisis this division could no longer be maintained. Civilian administration continued to exist, but on the territory of the Empire were established military units known as *Themes,* or garrisons. Each Theme was commanded by a general responsible directly to the emperor and having full power. The origin of the Themes is still debated and may go back to the viceroys or *exarchs* of Justinian, but when Byzantium emerged from its dark ages the system was in process of establishment. Eventually the entire imperial territory was divided into Themes whose number increased as land was reconquered. One of the Themes was not based on land but formed the imperial navy.

To supply the armies with recruits, a system of military landholds was developed. Soldiers were granted full ownership of small estates in Asia Minor in exchange for service in the army. The inhabitants of the coastal districts served in the navy. The peasant-soldier had full enjoyment of his land, which he could not sell, but might leave to his children. He was obliged to bring up at least one son to follow him in the imperial service.

Social Transformation

The militarization of the Empire brought with it important social changes. In western Asia Minor, great cities continued to exist as before, but in the hinterland the new soldier settlements created free peasant communities. The soldiers and their families were in no way bound to the land as had been the late Roman coloni. They could come and go at will, and no one might take their farms as long as the military service was performed. The grouping of peasants into communities was only for tax purposes; a community was responsible as a whole for the taxes of its members. The wealthy often attempted to encroach on the lands of their less fortunate neighbors, but the imperial administration watched for centuries over the rights of the poor.

Imperial Administration

Leo III and his successors took very seriously their duty as rulers. The main services of the state were maintained; taxes were collected, justice was administered, the defense of the Empire was kept up, and the postal system was maintained. Not only did the administration continue to function in the capital, but imperial officials also went forth to oversee the proper distribution of the taxes; and a system was created whereby the appeals of the poor could be brought to the attention of the imperial justice. A series of *Codes* regulating the rights of the peasants as well as questions of navigation and trade, show the imperial concern for the proper working of society even in periods of acute crisis. Leo III promulgated a new law code called the *Ecloga,* which replaced in part the legislation of Justinian. Conceived in a new Christian spirit, the *Ecloga* marks a change from pure Roman law. Although modern opinion is usually revolted by its insistence on mutilations, such as blindings, as punishment for crimes; to contemporaries these punishments, which replaced the death penalty formerly provided, indicated a new mildness and mercy in the administration of justice.

Cultural Isolation

The enormous effort to hold together the state made by Leo III and his successors, the Isaurian emperors, entailed a certain cost. The world culture of the Roman Empire disappeared with the world-state. Constantinople gradually came to turn its back on western Europe, not only physically, but also intellectually. The Empire of Justinian had been multi-national and bi-lingual, like that of the Romans. The realm of Leo III was still supra-national, as Greeks, Syrians, Armenians, Slavs, and Bulgars elbowed each other inside the Empire and were even found in the upper reaches of the administration; the emperors themselves came from as far as the Syrian frontier, but the cultural tradition of the Empire in the eighth century was much narrower than it had been in the fifth. Literary production was both small and of poor quality; the historical sources are deplorable. The impartiality of the great classical writers was replaced by bitter partisanship. The *Code* of Justinian, promulgated in Latin, could be read by the whole civilized world; but the *Ecloga,* written in Greek, could no longer be understood in the West. Soon Latin came to be considered as the language of barbarians. Byzantium tended to close upon itself in a dangerous intellectual isolation. Civilization was equated with the Eastern Empire, and outsiders were usually disdained and disregarded.

The Basileus

The changed atmosphere at Byzantium is perhaps best reflected in the increasingly oriental and religious concept of imperial power. Justinian had been an autocrat, but he still wore the classical titles of *imperator* and *augustus.* After their defeat of the Persians in 629, the Byzantine emperors assumed the title of *Basileus.* In itself the word, which meant "king" in Greek, suggested nothing that was startling; but the title came to confer on the ruler a super-natural aura. Especially as the emperors, in the seventh and eighth centuries, grew to know the Muslim caliphs, who were both religious and secular rulers, they emphasized the spiritual aspect of their power. The Byzantine emperor was no longer an ordinary man. Leo III may even have gone so far as to write to the pope "I am both king and priest." The preface of the *Ecloga* asserts his competence and obligation to legislate in religious matters. The division between Christianity and the state, fundamental to the religious tradition and reasserted by St. Augustine in *The City of God,* was disappearing.

Iconoclasm

The pretensions of the Byzantine *Basileus* could not pass unchallenged in a profoundly religious society. They were of course rejected by the Papacy at Rome; and the Eastern Church, usually submissive to the imperial authority, likewise rebelled. The quarrel which raged in the Byzantine Empire during the eighth and the first half of the ninth centuries is known as the Iconoclastic Controversy. At first the subject of the controversy was the excessive reverence paid to religious images in the Byzantine Empire. Early Christianity had observed rigorously the second commandment given to Moses against the making of "graven images," but gradually the practice of adorning buildings with holy images or "icons" had grown. An edict of Leo III ordered the removal of religious images from the reach of public adoration. In spite of violent popular opposition, the policy was maintained and Leo's son, Constantine V, went further by ordering the destruction of all icons and enforced his edict through a drastic persecution of all icon worshippers. Thereafter for about a century a violent contest opposed the destroyers of icons (iconoclasts) and their defenders (iconodules).

Many reasons have been suggested for Leo's action. To some it was the consequence of his disapproval of an un-Christian idolatry; to others, the imperial policy seemed directed against the multiple monasteries in Byzantium, which had grown rich on the donations of pilgrims coming to revere their icons, and so were disrupting the economy of the Empire through their control of extensive lands. An earlier theory that Leo had been influenced by Arab ideas, has now been rejected since recent studies show that Muslim aversion to images was of a different nature from Leo's iconoclastic activity. For the contemporary religious leaders the controversy had many theological implications, but on the political level it came down to a crucial point. Was the emperor the head of the Church: Did he have the right to legislate in religious matters? This the Church emphatically denied, and the Iconoclastic Controversy took on the aspect of a contest between the Church and the State.

For an entire century the struggle remained inconclusive. Images were re-established once at the end of the eighth century by the Empress Irene, who did not hesitate to have her own son blinded to keep the imperial authority. The policy of the empress provoked a violent reaction, which brought with it the end of the Isaurian dynasty, and Iconoclasm was once more established. Finally, in 843, an Ecumenical Council summoned at Nicaea condemned Iconoclasm once and for all in a decision which is still commemorated by the Eastern Church on the second Sunday in Lent as the "Feast of Orthodoxy." The partisans of images had won on this point, but their victory was deceptive, for they had lost on the most crucial aspect of the controversy for the Church. Images were restored in 843 by an imperial decision, as they had been removed a century earlier by an imperial decision: The emperor had kept his right to legislate in ecclesiastical matters. He was still the head of the Church with the title "Equal of the Apostles," even though he had to take public opinion into consideration. The patriarch remained to all intents an imperial appointee.

The repercussions of the Iconoclastic controversy were profound. In Byzantium, art, which had been primarily religious in subject, suffered a serious loss from the destruction of all icons during the eighth century. In the West, the popes, incensed by the imperial pretensions and supported by iconodule monks fleeing from imperial persecution at Constantinople, condemned Iconoclasm outright. Most of Italy turned away from its eastern allegiance and looked toward the Franks. The deterioration of relations with Rome helped bring about the coronation of Charlemagne by the Pope and the setting up of a rival empire. On the other hand, the Byzantine concept of the imperial power which had won out over its challengers was to have a significant influence in the future. This was the concept introduced to the Slavs and Bulgars as they came in contact with Byzantine civilization and religion. Consequently, the supreme rights of the emperor as head of the Church were accepted in Eastern Europe, both in Bulgaria and in Russia without question and preserved there after the destruction of Byzantium until the beginning of the present century.

THE MACEDONIAN DYNASTY

The iconoclastic controversy had shaken the solidity of the Isaurian's accomplishment. After the end of the dynasty, various emperors succeeded each other on the throne and often came to a violent death. Outside the limits of the Empire, the danger from the Carolingian was not great under Charlemagne's successors, but Arabs were holding the sea and Bulgar Khaghans were threatening Constantinople. Nevertheless, instead of collapsing under the new difficulties, Byzantium rallied to a period of particular brilliance in the tenth century—at the very moment when the West was reaching the depth of destruction.

The new dynasty was of oriental origin but is called Macedonian because the parents of its founder, Basil I, had migrated to that country. Basil was of peasant origin and came to the throne through the murder of his predecessor. But the dynasty he founded in 867 ruled for nearly two centuries. The prestige of the Macedonian house and its hold on the affection of the people of the Empire were so great that usurpers no longer dared to overthrow the legitimate emperors but associated themselves with the throne as imperial relatives by marriage or as tutor emperors ruling in the name of the Macedonian heir. Any attempt to remove the legitimate ruler provoked bloody insurrections. Even the ridiculous vagaries of the two old women who closed the Macedonian line could not destroy this allegiance, and both reigned to their natural death. Imperial power under the Macedonians was too great to be successfully challenged.

External Policy

The accession of Basil I marks an important turning in the military position of the Empire. Byzantium, which had been on the defensive since the early days of the Arab advances, now passed to the offensive. In Asia Minor the Arabs were rolled back to the frontiers of Syria, and in the middle of the

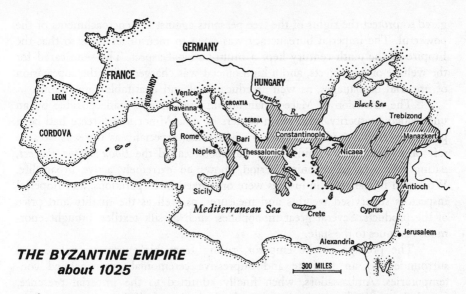

GERMANY
FRANCE
LEON
CORDOVA
BURGUNDY
Venice
Ravenna
CROATIA
SERBIA
HUNGARY
Danube
R.
Black Sea
Trebizond
Constantinople
Nicaea
Manazkert
Rome
Bari
Naples
Thessalonica
Sicily
Mediterranean Sea
Crete
Cyprus
Antioch
Jerusalem
Alexandria

THE BYZANTINE EMPIRE
about 1025

300 MILES

tenth century one of the tutor emperors, John I Tsimiskes, even reached as far as the suburbs of Jerusalem. In the Balkans the threatening Bulgar empire was first neutralized, then destroyed outright and Bulgaria became a Byzantine province in 1018. On the sea the re-created imperial fleet won back its superiority with the help of a secret weapon which had been invented as far back as the seventh century. This secret weapon, known as "Greek Fire," consisted of a liquid squirted through nozzles at enemy ships. Its composition is still uncertain, but its enormous advantage was not only practical but also psychological: The fact that the liquid burned on water and could not be extinguished like normal fire terrorized and demoralized the enemy. The pirates were cleared out of the eastern Mediterranean; Crete was reconquered and Constantinople found herself again the mistress of the sea. Finally, imperial troops returned once more to Italy. Although Sicily remained Muslim, large sections of southern Italy were reconquered and imperial Themes established in the lower part of the peninsula. The boundaries of the Empire had been sizeably enlarged.

Macedonian power was extended not only by force of arms. Skillful diplomacy furthered the imperial interests abroad. Enemies of the empire were turned against each other, and judicious bribes kept barbarian chieftains at peace. Imperial princesses married in Bulgaria, Germany, and Russia and helped to keep their husbands in the imperial orbit. Missionaries, such as St. Cyril and Methodius, saw to it that Bulgaria and Kiev received their religion from Constantinople. A sort of Byzantine cultural protectorate was established over eastern Europe and southern Italy.

Internal Policy

The internal policy of the Macedonian dynasty was a continuation of the work of the Isaurians. A new *Code* replaced the *Ecloga*, but the imperial authority remained unchanged. Repeatedly, imperial legislation was promulgated to protect the rights of the free peasants against the encroachments of the powerful. The imperial bureaucracy was open to men of all races so that the Empire of the tenth century kept a multi-national aspect. The state cared for the welfare of its subjects, and a high official was charged with the supervision of imperial orphanages, as well as educational and charitable foundations.

The extension of Macedonian administration was made possible by an unequalled prosperity. The urban centers of Asia Minor and Greece had been preserved so that trade and industry flourished, especially as the seas became safe once again. An administrative handbook called the *Book of the Prefect,* dating from the Macedonian period, shows an extremely active urban life. Workmen in the great industries were organized in corporations, and imperial inspectors supervised weights and measures, as well as the quality and price of the products. Several great monopolies, such as silk textiles, brought enormous revenues to the state.

The prestige of the emperor, ruling from his enormous palace and surrounded by an intricate and impressive ceremonial, overwhelmed contemporaries. Ambassadors, when finally admitted to the imperial presence, found the court dignitaries wearing the insignias of their rank, standing in silence while the emperor sat motionless on a golden throne, decorated with lions and birds, which moved upward and downward. When the curtain hiding the emperor was drawn aside the birds sang and the lions roared. The envoys were impressed, even when provoked by the contempt of imperial officials for them as barbarians, and went home to report that they had visited the greatest city in the world.

Macedonian Civilization

Byzantine culture under the Macedonians was not limited to childish mechanical tricks designed to overawe barbarians. Even before the accession of Basil I the University of Constantinople had been refounded to provide higher education in philosophy, mathematics, and classical literature. Instruction in this institution was free, and the professors were paid by the state. After the warlike reign of Basil II (976–1025) who had neglected education, the university was re-opened once again in 1045 with an added law school. At the same time, the capital boasted several hospitals and extensive medical training was given in connection with them. At a time when literacy in the West was the prerogative of a small minority of ecclesiastics, and when Charlemagne himself never learned to write his own name, all the upper classes of Byzantine society were literate. Imperial officials were expected to be able to identify Homeric quotations, and the ancient tradition of secular education was still maintained.

The leaders of Byzantine society set the example of culture. Photius, the great Patriarch of Constantinople at the time of Basil I, had been a professor at the university and continued his literary work the whole of his life. For the use of his friends, he composed a catalogue of his extensive private library which he called the *Myriobiblion* or "Thousand Books." This work contains not only titles, but also brief accounts and criticisms of the books, and many works of antiquity are known to us only through their inclusion in Photius' catalogue. In the middle of the tenth century, the grandson of Basil I, Constantine VII, better known as Constantine Porphyrogenitus, gathered a scholarly circle within the palace itself. The Emperor in person wrote numerous treatises on *The Themes, The Administration of the Empire,* and *The Ceremonies of the Byzantine Court,* while under his patronage various works of history and other research were compiled. The university of the eleventh century was another source of important scholarship, thus much of the classical tradition which eventually reached western Europe after the fall of Constantinople was gathered and clarified during the Macedonian period. At the same time as court literature exhibited its erudition and refinement, among the peasants of Asia Minor grew up a new popular epic which celebrated in vigorous verse the exploits of the national hero *Digenis Akrites* in the endless border warfare between the Empire and the Arabs.

Art flourished with particular brilliance under the Macedonians, following its partial eclipse due to the Iconoclastic quarrels. The dome of Haghia Sophia was rebuilt after its destruction during an earthquake, and new churches and palaces adorned Constantinople. The acquaintance of Byzantium with classical tradition was reflected in art as well as literature and philosophy. In the painting and the magnificently illustrated manuscripts of the Macedonians reappear a freedom, grace, and talent for form and proportion reminiscent of classical Greek models. As in the case of literature, the artistic rebirth was not limited to the capital. Such far-scattered monuments as the churches of St. Luke in central Greece, St. Maria Antica in the Forum at Rome, and St. Sophia in Kiev bear witness to the fact that the leadership of Constantinople reached through the provinces and even beyond the boundaries of the Empire.

THE END OF THE EMPIRE

The brilliance of the Macedonian period hid internal stresses which began to appear on the surface already in the last years of the dynasty and exploded violently after it had died out. The final decline of the Byzantine Empire, however, cannot be attributed exclusively to internal causes. After the settlement of the Magyars in the tenth century, western Europe was free of the eruption of barbarians except for a brief Mongol attack in the middle of the thirteenth century. Byzantium, however, had to bear the brunt of two Turkish onslaughts—first the Seljuks in the middle of the eleventh century, and later the Ottomans beginning in the thirteenth century under which it succumbed. In this desperate struggle the emperors found themselves largely alone, for partly through their own fault they had alienated the sympathies of western Europe, which failed to give help in moments of crisis, and in fact contributed to the destruction of the Eastern Empire by undermining it. Yet, even in its last period, the amazing vitality of Byzantium did not desert it. The crisis which followed the extinction of the Macedonian house was followed by another reconstruction under the Comneni (1081-1185). Finally in the early days of the last Paleologue dynasty in the thirteenth century, the Empire revived for a last Indian summer. But with the increase of Turkish pressure, this revival was not sufficient to save Constantinople.

The Alienation of the West

The initial break between Byzantium and the West, at the time of the papal condemnation of Iconoclasm and the coronation of Charlemagne, did not heal with time. Already in the ninth century friction between Constantinople and Rome over the respective prerogatives of the pope and the Ecumenical patriarch, aggravated by the desire of both to dominate the newly-created churches in the Balkans, led to an open break between the two. Though this first separation soon ended, relations did not improve. The ambassador of the German Emperor, in his account of his embassy to Constantinople, expressed the resentment felt by new western states because of the contemptuous treatment given them in the capital where they were considered equal or inferior to the Bulgars and other Barbarians. In the middle of the eleventh century, a break came again. At first the new separation of 1054, later called the Great Schism, seemed no more serious than earlier divisions. Much of the difficulty was due to the harshness of the papal envoy and the uncompromising haughtiness of the ambitious patriarch Michael Cerularius, who sought to profit from the weakness of the last Macedonian heiress to regain greater authority for the eastern Church. Unfortunately, this schism which started primarily as a clash of personalities was never healed. The Byzantines continued to view westerners as brutal boors unfit for civilized society, and the opinion was reinforced by a series of Norman attacks in the Balkans. At the same time, the religious division led the growing western states to believe that the heretical Eastern Empire was not only unworthy of protection but was also one of the enemies of the Christian world. This antagonistic attitude was to have serious repercussions on East-West relations at the time of the Crusades.

Internal Difficulties

The military strength of the Empire after the creation of the Themes was based on the free soldier-peasants of Asia Minor. Imperial legislation systematically tried to protect these small military holdings from the great proprietors. But this policy was finally defeated. Enormous estates began to grow in the tenth and eleventh centuries. These estates cut the revenues of the state from taxes, transformed the free peasant of the communes into serfs attached to the land, and gave a dangerous power to their owners. To gain allies against the threatening nobles, the emperor turned to the civilian bureaucracy, who found a dangerous system for cutting the power of the military aristocracy. Funds were refused for the defense of the Empire at the very moment when new enemies appeared in the East. In this period of crisis in the eleventh century, the control of trade began to shift from Constantinople to growing western cities, such as Venice and Genoa, which made the most of the difficulties and succeeded in wresting costly trade concessions from the Eastern Empire. The economic situation declined steadily. For the first time since Constantine the Great the currency had to be devalued. As the Turks advanced across Asia Minor, Byzantium lost its urban centers along with its last reservoirs of food and manpower.

The Turks

The emergence of the Turkic tribes from central Asia began relatively early, but their danger to Europe does not date further back than the eleventh century. In the ninth century they had begun to establish themselves in the eastern provinces of the Abbasid Caliphate, and by 955 one of the tribes called the Seljuks established a protectorate over Baghdad, where they made and unmade caliphs to suit their purposes. Moving eastward toward Asia Minor, they annihilated the Byzantine army at Manazkert in Armenia in 1071, and began to spread eastward across the peninsula. The new dynasty founded in 1081 by Alexis Comnenus succeeded in weathering the storm. Through a careful policy of fostering the army while pursuing cautious diplomatic relations with the Seljuks and the Western Crusaders, Alexis and his successors reestablished their authority over Asia Minor and part of Syria. However, one century after Manazkert the second military disaster of Myriokephalon, in 1176, destroyed all the painful reconquests of the Comneni in Asia Minor. Nevertheless the time for the final collapse of the empire had not yet come. In spite of their initial success, the Seljuks were not a formidable power. Their initial unity soon broke down into numerous small principalities, and their primary interests lay in the East. The real danger to the Empire and to the West was to come two centuries later when a small principality left in northwestern Asia Minor after the destruction of the Seljuk power began to develop with unexpected rapidity in the fourteenth century. This was the empire of the Ottoman Turks which was to terrorize Europe for centuries.

The Final Collapse

The initial blow to Constantinople came from the West, with which relations had steadily been deteriorating. In 1204 an army led by the Venetians and bound for Palestine turned northward to attack the heretical capital. For the first time since its foundation, the city was taken and systematically sacked. The loot from Constantinople embellished many of the cities of western Europe, and the city never regained its former splendor. After the capture of the capital of the Empire, the westerners set up a rival Latin empire and parcelled out the eastern lands among themselves, while the Byzantine rulers took refuge at Nicaea in Asia Minor. For sixty years westerners ruled at Constantinople, forcing their religious practices on the Eastern Empire and earning the undying hatred of the local clergy and population.

Even after this disaster, Byzantium found the strength to make a final comeback. The emperor of Nicaea, Michael I Paleologue, successfully retook Constantinople in 1261 and drove the Latins out of a large section of Greece. In the reconstituted empire of the Paleologues, the cultural tradition of Byzantium flourished again. A great literary revival reacquainted society with the Greek classics; philosophic and theological arguments were as active as they had ever been. The magnificent mosaics of the Church of the Savior in the Fields

(Karie Djami), which have recently been restored, show the magnificence and refinement of Byzantine civilization in its last centuries.

The energy of the Paleologues was not sufficient, however. Their territory was smaller than it had been at the worst moment of the Arab advances in the seventh century. The imperial finances were beyond repair, since almost no source of revenue remained. No soldiers were left to defend the Empire. The re-created Bulgarian empire and the still more dangerous new state of the Serbs threatened Constantinople from the west while the Ottoman Turks, starting from humble beginnings, engulfed Asia Minor and crossed into the Balkans by the middle of the fourteenth century. The capital of the Empire was cut off from Europe and surrounded. In this desperate situation the Paleologue emperors tried to win the help of the West by offering to make religious concessions which would bring about the reunion of the Eastern Church with the Papacy, but the antagonism of the Greeks, who remembered the oppression of the Latin Empire, brought all the attempted compromises to nought. In a last desperate attempt, the Emperor Manuel II Paleologue went in person to France and England in 1400, to plead in vain for aid. A Mongol attack on the Turks gave the Empire a last fifty years of life. But on May 29, 1453, the Turkish armies breached the walls of Constantinople, and the last Paleologue emperor died in the destruction of his capital.

The shock of the taking of Constantinople was felt by the entire civilized world, although the city's political significance had long been negligible. For centuries it had represented for the western world the model of culture; and even after its destruction it rendered one more service to the civilized world. The scholars fleeing from the capture of the city and the manuscripts saved from its ruins contributed enormously to the intellectual development of the West.

FURTHER READING

In addition to the works mentioned in Part IV, chapter 1, the best general studies of Byzantine history are A. A. Vasiliev, *History of the Byzantine Empire,* 2 vols. (1952); C. Diehl, *Byzantium Greatness and Decline* (1957); and G. Ostrogorsky, *History of the Byzantine State* (1957). An excellent brief survey is provided by J. Hussey, *The Byzantine World* (1957). A useful general introduction can be found in S. Runciman, *Byzantine Civilization* (1956), and N. Baynes and H. Moss eds., *Byzantium* (1948), is a series of introductory essays to various aspects of Byzantine society. Although both works concentrate primarily on the later, or Russian, aspect of their subject, E. Benz, *The Eastern Orthodox Church* (1963), and T. Ware, *The Orthodox Church* (1963), are useful introductions, particularly the first chapter of the Benz which deals with the Orthodox concept of icons. On the art of the eastern Empire, see D. Talbot Rice, *Byzantine Art* (1935), and the more recent, J. Beckwith, *The Art of Constantinople* (1961).

The great period of the Macedonian intellectual renaissance has received a detailed study in J. Hussey, *Church and Learning in Byzantium* (2nd ed., 1963).

The break between the two halves of Christendom is studied by S. Runciman, *The Eastern Schism* (1955), and the Latin conquests in the East following the fourth Crusade are surveyed by W. Miller, *Latins in the Levant* (1908).

E. Barker, *Social and Political Thought in Byzantium* (1957), is an excellent selection of contemporary sources, and a few of the main Byzantine historical works have been translated into English, e.g. Psellos, *Chronographia* tr. E. R. Sewter (1953), and Anna Comnena, *The Alexiad,* tr. A. S. Dawes (1928). *The Works of Liutprand of Cremona,* tr. F. A. Wright (1930), gives a very lively account of the worsening relations between Byzantium and the West in the tenth century. Historians of the Crusades listed in Part V, chapter 2 should also be consulted for these relations.

V

THE EMERGENCE OF EUROPE

1. Feudalism and the Rise of Feudal Monarchy

2. Medieval Economy and Society

3. The Struggle for Leadership in the West

4. Feudal Monarchy at Its Height

5. The Church and Medieval Culture

The two centuries or so following Charlemagne's death were the most chaotic of the Middle Ages. The tendencies which Charlemagne had held in check toward political and economic localism and the fragmentation of society accelerated. Central government broke down; economic and cultural contact with areas outside and even among areas within the crumbling Carolingian Empire, was cut off; and political and military power was divided among petty strong men, most of them dukes and counts of Carolingian origin. Men sustained themselves by drawing closer to the land, where they lived in fear and insecurity from one meagre harvest to the next.

Out of this chaos, European civilization arose. Heir of Greece and Rome, and of the barbarians, it drew also on Byzantium and Islam. Its ethos and spiritual foundation was Christianity, its political ideal the Roman Empire. But if it owed much to the past, there was also much about European civilization that was new in its culture, its institutions, its social relationships, and its sources and concepts of power. It began to grow in the tenth century, to cover the European peninsula, to reconquer the Mediterranean, to construct a network of trade routes, to organize its people into states, and to arm itself with an ideology. It would come in time to dominate the world. In these next chapters we shall examine the origins and the early life of European civilization.

1 · Feudalism
and the Rise of Feudal Monarchy

"Feudalism" is an historian's word, coined to describe the political order which was dominant in most of western Europe from about the tenth to the thirteenth centuries. In general terms, it was characterized by the dispersal or devolution of public authority into the hands of many private persons. It arose to fill the void created by the collapse of the Roman Empire and began to decline when strong monarchy appeared. Essentially, it was an interim phase between forms of centralized government. Feudalism was accompanied —some historians would say "caused"—by a corresponding movement in economic life. The centralized economy of the Roman Empire, with its emphasis on towns and trade and industry, gave way to local economic self-sufficiency based on agriculture. In short, Europe broke up into fragments more or less independent of each other. In these local units, most of the require-ments of daily life were satisfied by small groups of private persons. Feudalism was the system by which these groups organized themselves. At first simple, it eventually became quite complex, rationalized fully in law, and praised in song and story. Indeed, its tenacity was such that it was a powerful influence on the feudal monarchies, and vestiges of it remained until modern times.

ORIGINS AND GROWTH OF FEUDALISM

To trace the origins of feudalism and to define its character precisely is most difficult because source materials are scanty and practices varied widely from place to place. We can say, however, that some of its institutions were Roman, others Germanic, that its recognizable form dates from the Merovingian period, that it developed and spread under the Carolingians, and that it was virtually universal in much of France and western Germany by the twelfth century. By this time, too, it had appeared farther eastward in Germany and in parts of Spain and Italy, and had been carried by the Normans into England. It provided for an essential need, since none of the central governments possessed the economic resources, the manpower, or the administrative techniques to assert its authority over large geographical areas. Without unity, civil order was replaced by anarchy. Out of necessity, then, groups of individuals, usually led by a man of local prominence, perhaps an old provincial official of the crown such as a count or duke, or even an ecclesiastical official such as a bishop or abbot, assumed the basic functions of government. Of course, such men were ambitious for power and often encouraged lesser men to join them in taking the law into their own hands. Meanwhile, the transformation of the economy had made land ownership the basis of wealth. It gave to men with large holdings the dominant place in society, while depressing the man with only a few acres to the status of tenant or depriving him of his land altogether. Thus, a situation was created which fostered a hierarchical pattern of personal dependence.

The most important functions assumed by local groups were military and judicial, the right to enforce and interpret the law. In effect, government was by armed force. The peace was kept (and often broken) by bodies of knights who arrested lawbreakers and brought them to trial. This gave pre-eminence to soldiers and a military nobility grew up which controlled lay and, to a large extent, religious society. The profession of arms became the ideal to which every man aspired and in the beginning it was open to anyone with strength and courage. In time, however, its members drew their ranks together, substituting for skill and determination the requirement of heredity. The European nobility became a nobility of blood which was one of the first signals of the decay of the feudal system. On the other end of the scale, the layman who was not a noble was clearly a social inferior, even if he was not a serf. These social aspects of feudalism will be discussed at greater length in the next chapter.

Vassalage

At the heart of the feudal relationship was a contract between two men in which one placed himself at the service of the other in return for protection and maintenance. The one became *vassal* and the other *lord,* and the arrangement was called *vassalage.* The lord himself might be the vassal of a greater lord, a margrave, count, or duke, who in turn might be a vassal of the king. Thus developed a hierarchy of lords and vassals resembling a pyramid, with the king at the apex and knights without vassals at the base. A contract from the Merovingian period runs as follows:

He who commends himself to the power of another man. To the magnificent Lord (A), I (B). Inasmuch as it is known to all and sundry that I lack the wherewithal to feed and clothe myself, I have asked of your pity, and your goodwill has granted me, permission to deliver and commend myself into your [protection]. This I have therefore done, in such fashion that, you have undertaken to sustain me in food and clothing, while I have undertaken to serve you and deserve well of you in so far as lies in my power.[1]

In time, several formal acts became attached to the vassalage ceremony. One was *homage,* a rite in which the vassal knelt, bareheaded and unarmed, placed his hands between those of his lord and declared that he wished to be his "man." This was followed by an oath of *fealty,* taken by the vassal

[1] Quoted in F. L. Ganshof, *Feudalism,* 2nd English ed. (New York: Harper, 1961), p. 6.

with his hand on a sacred object such as the Bible. A ceremony of 1127 was described like this:

First they did homage in the following manner. The count demanded of the future vassal if he wished without reserve to become his man, and he replied "I wish it"; then, with his hands clasped and enclosed between those of the count, their alliance was sealed by a kiss. Secondly, he who had done homage engaged his faith . . . by the following words. "I promise by my faith that from this time foreward I will be faithful to Count William and will maintain towards him my homage entirely against every man, in good faith and without any deception." Thirdly, all this was sworn on the relics of saints.[2]

The obligation for lord and vassal to keep faith was taken very seriously; indeed, loyalty became, after bravery, the chief medieval virtue. It sometimes happened, however, especially by the later feudal period, that one man, usually through marriage or inheritance, would become the vassal of several lords. To overcome the problem of conflicting obligations, the system of *liegeancy* developed which provided that one lord was owed full service against all men. This lord was called the *liege lord*. In England, this lord was the king.

In time, too, it became the rule for the vassal to receive from his lord a *benefice* or *fief*, normally a landed estate or manor, as a means of maintaining himself. This might be of any size, from a few acres to thousands of acres, but included tenants, stock, and buildings as well as the land itself. The vassal did not hold this fief outright, as *allodial* property, but simply enjoyed the use of it as long as the feudal contract remained in force. At first, fiefs were neither divisible nor inheritable but fiefholding quickly assumed more of the character-istics of property-owning. Vassals took on vassals of their own and assigned pieces of their fiefs by a process called *subinfeudation*. In practice fiefs became hereditary, passing by primogeniture intact to the eldest son. Often the heir had to deliver to his lord a large sum in money and produce, perhaps his fief's entire income for one year as *relief* before his inheritance was confirmed. At the same time the heir, if he had not attained his majority (thirteen or fourteen years old in those days), would probably become the ward of his late father's lord who would train him to knighthood and then invest him with the fief. If the heir were a girl, the lord had the right to choose a proper husband for her.

The reason for this was that the lord wanted to assure his own military strength, for vassals were above all fighting men and their chief obligation was service in their lord's army. In the earlier feudal period, when disorder was most prevalent, there was no limit to this obligation. But in later times the normal length of service was forty days, about the time between spring planting and fall harvest when the weather was fine for battle. Each vassal was expected to report mounted and equipped with sword, lance, shield, and chain-mail armor. If he had vassals of his own, they were supposed to accompany him. Armies numbering several thousand knights could be assembled this way by the king or by a great magnate. Obviously, warfare consisted almost wholly

[2] *Ibid.*, p. 71.

of cavalry action, infantry being used sparingly and as a defensive arm. A battle usually consisted of disorganized milling about and hacking at one another. Man-to-man engagements were particularly favored as the ultimate in knightly combat.

Vassals were also expected to serve their lords in other ways. Next to war, justice and council were most important and required the attendance of a vassal at the lord's "court" to give advice, take part in ceremonies, or assist in legal deliberations. Questions that arose might concern a declaration of war or conclusion of a treaty, or a case in which another vassal had broken his oath of fealty. This service was known as "paying court" and the gathering of vassals around their lord was called the "council." It, together with the lord's own household, was the foundation on which rudimentary government was built. The vassals also owed their lord *aid* and *hospitality*. *Aid* consisted of a contribution for specific expenses. In France and Norman England these included the knighting of the lord's eldest son, marriage of the lord's eldest daughter, and ransom of the lord when captured. *Hospitality* was the vassal's obligation to provide food, a place to sleep, and entertainment for the lord and his attendants whenever they came to visit. Lords, in their turn, were expected to come to their vassals's defense in case of unjust attack, to give them advice and see that they received fair justice, and most important, to supply the wherewithal, usually a fief of land, with which they could maintain themselves.

Thus far we have assumed that vassalage was peculiar to the laity. But churchmen were also part of the feudal system and entered into feudal relationship with each other and with laymen. In the tenth and eleventh centuries the Church was in an extremely weakened state, morally and physically. In order to survive, many bishops made themselves vassals of great lords and became obligated to perform feudal services. The bishop, in turn, accepted the homage and fealty of vassals, some of them knights, some of them other prelates or monastic establishments. Monastic establishments sought the same means of protection. Since the Church held vast tracts of land, it could offer fiefs in abundance. A problem arose, however, when feudal obligations came due because churchmen could not kill or sentence to death. A few ignored the ban but most took a layman as *advocate* to lead their knights and dispense justice. A significant result of this involvement of the Church in the feudal system was to secularize the episcopal and monastic offices, for many bishoprics, abbacies, and lesser offices became plums for distribution to retainers and relatives by the lay nobility. Income was good because Church benefices were well-managed, and the duties light because a young noble bishop or abbot usually hired an assistant to do his work for him. Naturally enough, the spiritual nature of the offices was often lost sight of.

THE FOUNDATIONS OF FEUDAL MONARCHY

From this discussion, it is clear that political power during the feudal period resided in a hierarchy of lords and vassals. In theory, the king was at the top, the dukes and counts (his "vassals-in-chief") in the first rank, and the men of lesser importance in descending ranks. The *state* as it developed in later centuries did not exist. There was no central government extending its jurisdiction over a unified, clearly-defined territory, employing public officials, making laws, dispensing justice, and collecting taxes. Kings, in the two hundred years after the death of Charlemagne, retained real authority only in their own domains; that is, the lands they owned outright or over which they had direct personal control. Elsewhere they were bound by the same feudal relationship as any other lord. They could call on their vassals-in-chief to supply them with knights, to attend them at court, and to provide aids and other payments on special occasions, but that was all. Moreover, most vassals-in-chief were hardly less powerful than their royal lords and often willfully refused to abide by feudal law.

But government had not disappeared entirely. Remaining political power had simply devolved on the men who could apply brute force most effectively. An individual's prestige and authority depended on his physical strength, intelligence, leadership ability, and determination, and on such natural factors as favorable terrain and passable roads. A valley walled by mountains, for example, was easier to defend than a wide plain. In a sense, the feudal age was one of intense individualism within the apparently rigid hierarchic order. Once brought to heel, a group of territories could be welded into a rudimentary political unit. A well-known case is that of the counts of Anjou who gathered together a kind of feudal empire by the end of the twelfth century. Ignoring the weak king of France, they subdued their vassals, built and garrisoned fortresses, made advantageous marriages, and put a simple administrative system into operation. They made full use of feudal law to justify their actions, finding it an excellent means to control territories small in size but too primitive for the large agglomeration they eventually acquired. Loyalty to the feudal contract extended, in practice, only as far as the lord could enforce that loyalty.

The Supremacy of the King

A king, however, had advantages no count enjoyed. He was at the apex of the feudal pyramid, supreme over all lords and vassals in the hierarchy and, as such, he was the ultimate recipient of all legal obligations and the owner of all lands held in fief. This supremacy gave him, in law if not in fact, a kind of chain of command by which he could rule his kingdom. This was a bit of logic ambitious magnates could ignore but could hardly deny. Moreover, feudal supremacy was not far removed from sovereignty, from the idea that the king embodied all public authority, that kingship was a unique institution, and that kings were therefore intrinsically different from other men.

Other special qualities attached to kingship. The old Germanic tradition preserved the notion that the king was descended from the gods. This was modified, of course, but also reinforced in the process of Christianization. Christianity conceived of kings as earthly in origin but with an aura of divinity about them since they had been chosen by God to defend the faith and protect the faithful. Early writers saw kings as possessing something of the sacred power of priests, a quality derived from the holy oil with which they were anointed and the bishop's ring and staff with which they were invested at their coronation:

Both Kings and Priests are deified and sanctified by the grace of unction and by the consecration of their benediction. . . . If therefore the King and the Priest are both, by grace, Gods and Christs of the Lord, whatever they do by virtue of this grace is not done by a man but by a God and a Christ of the Lord.[3]

This is an extreme opinion and it was too theocratic to endure in the growing secularity of western Europe. But to the popular mind well into early modern times, certain kings possessed miraculous healing powers. The king of France, for example, had a "touch" that could cure scrofula. It was clear to most men that to obey their king was God's will.

Conceptions of Law and Justice

Kings also gained strength from new conceptions of law and justice. Indeed the judicial nature of royalty was perhaps its most important special quality, and one which has had profound effects on western political institutions. Its sources were several. Germanic kings were judges of their people, though their function was rather to apply existing laws than to make new ones, and the earliest coronation oaths contained clauses by which the kings promised to judge rightly. Feudalism parcelled out the responsibility for justice among many lords but recognized the king as the highest judge simply because he was the highest lord. Furthermore, as feudal society grew more complex, many questions of contract arose, making adjudication necessary. Justice became more regularized and men began to realize more clearly that they lived under law. By the tenth or eleventh centuries men also began to demand a more efficient criterion for judgment than personal combat and the ordeal. Judgment by their peers based on known rules and precedents was not so mystical but far more practical and consistent. The regularization and rationalization of justice tended to augment the practical judicial role of the king. The Church, which always held kings responsible for seeing justice done in their realms, encouraged this tendency.

So, too, did the doctrines of Roman law, which were revived in the twelfth century and put to use by the new, educated professional administrators who entered royal service. Writers such as John of Salisbury (1119–1180) and Bracton (1214–1268) developed theories that placed monarchy within the context of Roman law and kings made use of these theories in actual practice. The theories emphasized that kings were subject to the rule of law and could not act arbitrarily, but they also taught that kings were the recipients of the old and sources of the new law as well as the chief administrators of justice in their realm. It was a popular idea for it was in tune with the times. "God made the king to judge the people," went a medieval phrase and the picture of the

[3] From the "Anonymous of York," quoted by R. W. Southern, *The Making of the Middle Ages* (New Haven: Yale University Press, 1961), p. 93.

sainted King Louis IX sitting under an oak tree dispensing justice to his subjects lived as an ideal in France for centuries.

In the hands of strong, smart, and determined kings, these advantages and special qualities were formidable weapons. Moreover, the institution of monarchy had powerful friends in the Church and among the great mass of common people. Both the Church and the people desired peace and social stability above all else. Hence, clerics encouraged the growth of stronger government, particularly monarchy, so long as it did not threaten the independence of the Church in its own sphere of activity. We find St. Thomas Aquinas (1225–1274) declaring monarchy to be the best form of secular government because it is the most secure and enjoining Christians to remain at peace even when kings become tyrants.

The people suffered in silence. With the rise of the towns and urban business, however, a more articulate and influential group of non-nobles, the middle class, appeared. Its business was chiefly trade, and trade was possible only in areas where highways and waterways were free from brigandage. This strong rulers could provide. The middle class was willing to support monarchy with money and personal services in return for protection.

The rise of monarchy brought to western Europe the first territorial aggregates which we recognize as having some of the features of the modern "state." They arose on the ruins of the Carolingian Empire, to some of whose institutions they were heir, and they were at least in part erected on feudal foundations. The most important of these monarchies were three: the Anglo-Norman, established in the mid-eleventh century on the island of Britain; the French, born painfully in the tenth century, uncertain in its growth, but destined in the long run to be the strongest and most perfectly elaborated of all; and the German, the first to appear and the shortest lived.

ANGLO-NORMAN ENGLAND

William the Conquerer, duke of Normandy and first of the Norman English kings, was a man who could make feudalism work for monarchy, and he found the English situation particularly favorable. The Anglo-Saxon kingdom which William won in 1066 was better organized than any kingdom on the continent. It was located on a small, relatively homogeneous island, where feudalism had not yet destroyed the unity of the government or the loyalty of the people to the crown. There was a species of feudalism in England. Lesser men depended on greater men for protection and support in matters of justice, and there were warriors called *thanes* attached to the king and high nobility. But the crown still retained authority everywhere.

Technically elective, the Anglo-Saxon kings were chosen by tradition from the house of Wessex, founded by Alfred the Great. The elective body was called the *Witan,* an assembly of the highest lay and clerical lords of the realm who also served as the king's advisors. The Witan was the only important brake on the king's actions. The king's resources were sizeable. He had a fairly reliable armed force since he had the right to call every Englishman to military service. To support himself and his retainers, he also had a good

MEDIEVAL ENGLAND

SCOTLAND

NORTHUMBER-LAND

CUMBERLAND   DURHAM   • Durham

WESTMORLAND

North Sea

Isle of Man

Irish Sea

YORK   • York

LANCASTER

CHESTER   DERBY   NOTTINGHAM   Lincoln •
LINCOLN
Boston •

W A L E S

STAFFORD   LEICESTER   RUTLAND   NORFOLK

SHROPSHIRE

WORCESTER   WARWICK   NORTHAMPTON   HUNTING-DON   CAMBRIDGE   SUFFOLK

HEREFORD   BEDFORD   Cambridge •

OXFORD   BUCKINGHAM   HERTFORD   ESSEX

GLOUCESTER   Oxford •   MIDDLESEX

BERKSHIRE   • London

Bristol •   WILTSHIRE   SURREY   KENT   • Canterbury

Bristol Channel   Winchester •

SOMERSET   HAMPSHIRE   SUSSEX.

Hastings •

DORSET.

DEVON   Isle of Wight

CORNWALL   *English Channel*

Plymouth •   50 MILES

income from large domains scattered throughout the country, from fines collected at local courts, and from feudal dues. In addition, he had the right in wartime to collect the *danegeld,* a tax based on land. He also controlled the English Church, appointing the bishops and heads of the great monastic establishments. He treated the episcopacy as royal agents and advisors and for the most part they served him loyally. In addition, the king had a simple administrative force of laymen and clerics, and a number of agents in the *shires* or counties. These agents, called *shire-reeves,* or sheriffs, managed the royal domain, collected monies owed the king, and represented him in local affairs.

Local government in Anglo-Saxon England was largely in local hands, but even here the king exercised some influence. The basic unit of local government was the shire, and the chief local officials were the sheriff and, above him, the *earldorman* or *earl*. The earls were appointed by the king and Witan from prominent local families. They supervised justice and kept the peace, sitting with the sheriffs and bishops on the shire courts where both lay and ecclesiastical cases were heard, and commanding the local militia. The kings found the sheriffs more reliable than the earls, however, for the latter tended to identify themselves with local interests in opposition to the crown and to regard their appointive office as hereditary.

William of Normandy

This was the England that William of Normandy found when he crossed the channel and won the battle of Hastings against King Harold in 1066. William's claim to the throne was distant but legitimate. He was a cousin of the late Edward the Confessor (1042–1066), a pious but ineffectual monarch whose dubious service to his country was to surround himself with Norman friends. Edward died without heirs, and the Witan had elected Earl Harold of Wessex, who was not of royal blood, to succeed him largely because Harold was the most powerful man in the realm. William, however, refused to recognize the election. Gaining support from the papacy and from most of his Norman vassals by promising rewards to the latter in the form of booty and fiefs, he crossed the channel in early October. He and his army met Harold at Hastings near the south coast of England on the 14th. Harold's troops were put to rout and Harold and his brothers killed. The victory strengthened William's hand: now he was not only England's heir apparent but also its conqueror, a status which gave him the right to take all the land in personal possession and to distribute it as he saw fit. He was crowned William I (1066–1087) at Christmas time.

His immediate problems were to satisfy his followers and prepare for the defense of his government which, he believed, was threatened by native Anglo-Saxons and Scandinavian invaders. He solved both by imposing Norman feudalism on England. Since it was fully developed, this feudalism was particularly rigid and all-encompassing. All land was held in fief to the king; the Normans, who received most of it, and the remaining Anglo-Saxons were the king's vassals—the greatest are usually called *barons*—and owed him heavy dues and services. All of them were subject to royal justice and could be punished by confiscation of their fiefs. Each vassal was required to provide a quota of knights for the king's army and was encouraged to construct forts, castles or earthen mounds for defense. William himself put up a castle at the edge of each royal borough and England became a country of castles. Some 1200 of them were constructed before building stopped. That the English monarchy took on a more feudal caste is indicated by William's gradual transformation of the Witan into a *curia regis,* a king's court, of the continental type.

Justice and Finances

William I did not uproot Anglo-Saxon institutions though he added some of Norman origin. In the century and a half after the conquest, except for the twenty-year interlude of civil war under the weak Stephen (1135–1154), he and his successors created a monarchy stronger than any their predecessors had known; indeed, it was the strongest in all of Europe. William II (1087–1100) was a deplorable king but Henry I (1100–1134) was skilled in the arts of government and Henry II of Anjou (1154–1189), the first Plantagenet, was one of the greatest royal administrators in English history. The strength of the monarchy was founded on the efficient administration of justice and finances. William permitted local courts to continue enforcing local custom, but wherever possible he asserted the rights of the crown. This he left mostly to the sheriffs; the office of earl he made purely honorary. He introduced the continental practice of sending royal justices from shire to shire to hold local courts and apply the king's law. Henry I developed the practice further, and Henry II systematized it.

These two legal-minded monarchs extended the crown's jurisdiction to include all serious criminal cases and many civil cases arising out of property disputes. The latter were no longer subject to trial by battle, but were settled by "assizes," groups of sworn men or "juries" who testified as to which party had a just claim. Henry II also introduced the jury system, which traced its origins to William the Conqueror's time, into criminal trials. Trial by ordeal gave way to trial by a man's peers. Thus, the ancestors of our modern "grand" juries (those which decide if a crime has been committed) and "petty" or trial juries (those which declare a defendant guilty or innocent) were born. These legal innovations of Henry II were the beginnings of "common law," the law of the entire realm as contrasted to local custom. They served to increase greatly the prestige and authority of the crown.

William I and his successors also made innovations in the methods of collecting and managing money which strengthened the crown's position. William I and his son, the greedy and repulsive William II, exacted every penny owed them in dues from their vassals and from fines taken in by royal courts. Both collected the *danegeld,* the old property tax, and William II used his father's survey of all the lands and chattels in England to assure the most thorough collection of revenue. This survey is called the Domesday Book, a remarkable achievement for the time and one of our best sources for medieval English history. Henry I also instituted a system of accounting called the *exchequer* to replace the haphazard practices of his predecessors who kept their reserve funds in the castle of Winchester and cash for current expenses in a strong box in their bedchamber. Twice a year the sheriffs and those who owed the crown money appeared before a group of royal officials, the "barons of the exchequer," to render their accounts and pay their debts. Figures were recorded on Pipe Rolls, so called because they were stored in wooden tubes.

Henry II, though he continued the system, was more interested in collecting than managing money, and he contrived several new ways of wringing funds from the feudal relationship—payments in cash in lieu of military service, for example. His persistence in thus burdening his vassals, whose property was in land rather than money and whose only saleable commodity was knightly skill, infuriated them and set the stage for the great baronial rebellions of the following reigns.

Henry II also got into trouble with the Church. Traditionally, the English Church was a creature of the crown. William I had consented to clerical demands that lay and ecclesiastical justice be separated but had retained his control over the clergy and church affairs. Henry II, for whom royal authority depended on efficiency, tried to regularize the church-state relationship by the Constitutions of Clarendon (1164). These withdrew the jurisdiction of criminal cases involving clerics from the ecclesiastical courts, specified the king's right to appoint bishops and demand feudal allegiance from them, and severely limited papal authority in England. The Archbishop of Canterbury, Thomas à Becket, who was primate of the realm, protested vigorously, only to be slain in his own cathedral by three knights who misconstrued Henry's anger. Henry did public penance for the act but got most of the Constitutions put into practice. His quarrel with the Church, however, was only the first of many involving English kings.

CAPETIAN FRANCE

The French kings, like the English kings, conquered their kingdom, but with much more difficulty and over a much longer period of time. Indeed, at the very time when William of Normandy was establishing his mastery of all England, Philip I of France was losing battles to the rebellious vassals of his own domains. The disintegration of the Carolingian Empire had left its western part to seek political refuge in feudalism. By the tenth century, the kingdom of the West Franks had broken down into several large and numerous small feudal enclaves in which dukes and counts held nominal lordship over a mass of ill-organized, unruly vassals. The greatest of the enclaves were those of the dukes of Normandy and Brittany and the count of Flanders in the north, the duke of France in the center, and the dukes of Acquitaine and Burgundy and the count of Toulouse in the south. The lesser counties of Anjou, Champagne, Blois, and others were in being or in the process of building. Nearly all recognized the king as their feudal lord, but none took the relationship seriously, and the monarchy had ceased to have any but symbolic meaning. It was elective, hence at the mercy of the great lords who did what they could to preserve it without power.

The Capetian Kings

In 987, Hugh Capet was elected king. Though neither he nor his successors were able to break out of their feudal prison, they were able to found a dynasty. The monarchy remained elective in law for many more years but in fact it was transmitted thereafter in the male line of the house of Capet.

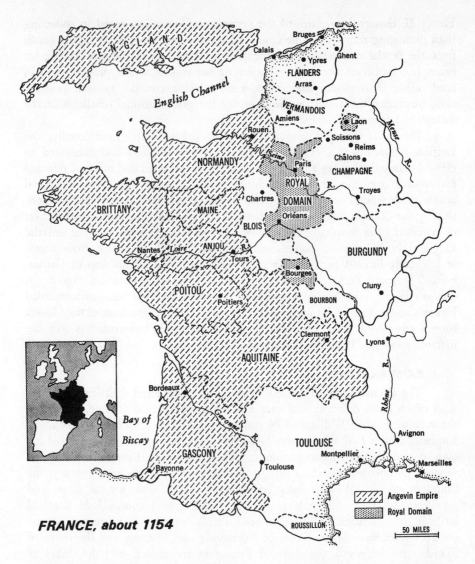

FRANCE, about 1154

Angevin Empire
Royal Domain

50 MILES

Hugh himself was the duke of France as well as king and, though weaker than the others, was one of the great lords of France in his own right. His actual authority was confined to only a portion of his duchy—the small area between the Seine and the Loire rivers called the Ile de France—and even there it was openly flouted by many of his vassals. But it was a base on which to build and from it the kings of France went forth to win the rest of their kingdom. On their side was little except the fact that they were kings, a position which commanded unique honor and prestige in the worst times. Further, they had active support from the Church and eventually from the middle class. These groups were particularly useful as a source of educated administrators, men who had ideas and could make the institution of kingship fulfill its promise.

The first task of the Capetian kings was to pacify their own domain. Only in this way could they guarantee themselves a regular supply of food, clothing, and men for their army while at the same time securing a nucleus from which to expand. Nothing effective in this direction was done before the reign of Hugh's great-great grandson, Louis VI, called "the Fat" (1108–1137). Indeed, the helpless kings, the worst being Philip I (1060–1108), let most of their remaining small authority slip away. They became politically isolated, abandoned by the great lords who in the past had at least given them token honor by occasionally paying court, and left dependent on the service of their immediate household staff. This staff was the royal government: the *chancellor* who drafted the king's letters; the *chamberlain* who looked after his bedchamber and guarded such valuables as clothing, jewels, money, and legal documents; the *seneshal* who provisioned the household; and the *constable* and *marshal* who took charge of the horses and served as the king's deputies in war. They moved about from castle to castle, the king and his tiny group of retainers, unsure of their own personal safety and of the loyalty of the *prévots,* the superintendents of the royal estates.

Louis VI, however, was not a man to be cowed by his vassals turned brigands; he was determined to bring peace and order to the royal domain. Tremendous in size, full of energy, courageous, he spent his life riding from one end of the domain to the other enforcing the crown's rights. He ruthlessly suppressed his rebellious vassals in the Ile de France, in several cases waging wars against them lasting many years. He destroyed their castles, freed bishops and abbeys from their control, and brought the peasants some measure of security. He also founded a number of new towns in his domain, whose middle-class citizens gave him support and money through taxes. Feudal-minded, he used the machinery of feudal law to excellent effect. He was backed by the authority and prestige of the French Church. His chief advisor was Suger, abbot of St. Denis, the great monastery near Paris. Suger was a noted canon lawyer and a firm believer in strong monarchy as the best defense of the Church. He was the first of many great clerical administrators of the French kings who very soon began to seek advisers from the rising middle class as well. But Louis VI and Suger made only a start. The royal domain belonged once more to the king, but the feudal magnates whose lands surrounded it were as independent as ever.

The impotence of the crown in most of France is clearly seen in the period of Louis VII (1137–1180), during whose reign the house of Anjou rose to prominence. Louis VII was promising enough as a young man but too soon lapsed into weakness and indecision, substituting humility and extreme spirituality for leadership and vigor. His marriage to Eleanor of Acquitaine was rather a handicap than a help. Eleanor proved too gay and too sensual for the pious Louis and Acquitaine was far too big a feudal bite for the feeble Capetian monarchy to chew. Hence, their divorce in 1152—whether on grounds of Eleanor's adultery or her failure to bear a male heir remains in question—seemed no great loss. Almost immediately, however, she married

Henry, duke of Normandy and count of Anjou and Maine, and the French king was confronted with a vassal more powerful than himself.

The Angevin Empire

Henry, nicknamed "Plantagenet," was the son of Count Geoffrey of Anjou and Matilda of England, whose rivalry with King Stephen had brought years of civil strife to the island realm. Henry's marriage to Eleanor added Acquitaine to his large holdings, and in 1154 he completed what some historians have called the "Angevin Empire" by succeeding Stephen as king of England. We have discussed some of Henry's accomplishments as king. He restored domestic peace and reestablished strong monarchy. But the English crown he regarded mostly as a source of prestige and money; his real interests lay in France. Indeed, he spoke no English and lived much of his life away from England. He expended his energies on generally fruitless ventures in Europe and in attempting to weld his disparate continental possessions into a rudimentary state. But he was unsuccessful. His possessions remained wholly feudal, bound together only by the tie to his person. After his death in 1189, they fell away one by one, and in the next century and a half most of them became part of France. The friction they created between France and England was continuous, leading to several short wars and culminating in the long and terrible Hundred Years' War of the fourteenth and fifteenth centuries (see pp. 275–281).

GERMANY AND THE EMPIRE

The German experience was different from that of England and France. "Germany," or more accurately the kingdom of the East Franks, was the first of the strong post-Carolingian monarchies, dating from the second decade of the tenth century. Carolingian tradition was still alive at that time, while feudalism was not yet fully developed. Hence, while the East Frankish kings were not confronted by a realm wholly decentralized and divided in its loyalties, neither were they recognized as feudal lord over all their people. This situation made their job both simpler and more difficult.

The last of the Carolingians, Louis the Child, died in 911, and Conrad I, duke of Franconia, was elected king. German historians have traditionally set this date as the beginning of German history. Conrad was an ineffectual king, hardly able to do more than his weak predecessors to overcome the two principal roadblocks to effective royal government. These were the barbarian Magyars and the great dukes. The Magyars, who had taken over the area formerly occupied by the Avars, modern Hungary, were the last important invaders from the east. After about 900, they carried out almost yearly raids into Germany, leaving destruction and anarchy in their path. To defend the kingdom successfully was the first business of a king who would be strong.

The dukes were the powerful military leaders of the principal districts ("stem," or tribal, duchies) of the kingdom: Lorraine, (Lotharingia), Saxony, Franconia, Swabia, and Bavaria. They were appointed to their high office by the king and possessed no legal authority other than that delegated to them.

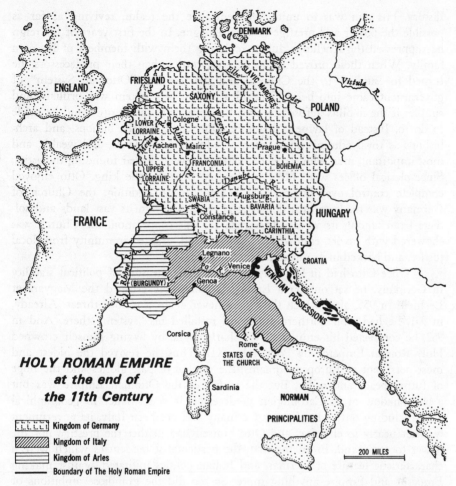

**HOLY ROMAN EMPIRE
at the end of
the 11th Century**

<table>
<tr><td>`⌐⌐⌐⌐⌐`</td><td>Kingdom of Germany</td></tr>
<tr><td>`////`</td><td>Kingdom of Italy</td></tr>
<tr><td>`≡≡≡`</td><td>Kingdom of Arles</td></tr>
<tr><td>`———`</td><td>Boundary of The Holy Roman Empire</td></tr>
</table>

200 MILES

Most of them, however, tried to gain an authority more permanent and personal. They used their wealth (they were numbered among the largest landowners in their districts), their military forces, and their prestige and influence with their people to build some sort of feudal structure headed by themselves. In the long run, they were successful, and Germany broke apart into separate petty "states." But for a time, the kings of the Saxon and Salian Houses who followed Conrad kept ducal ambitions in check, not by eliminating them or by greatly curtailing independent ducal power, but by creating a unique monarchical administration from which the dukes were excluded.

Otto "the Great"

The originator of this administration was Otto I, called "the Great" (936–973). Otto was the son of the first Saxon king, Henry I (918–936), a man of considerable military prowess, who had failed to tame the dukes but had prepared the way for the final defeat of the Magyars. Otto possessed far greater abilities; indeed, he was one of the outstanding rulers of German history. His aim was to unite and centralize the realm, reviving as far as possible the power and prestige of Charlemagne. In the first years of his reign he suppressed the rebellious dukes, replacing them with members of his own family. When these proved no more trustworthy than their predecessors, he turned for support to the Church, and the so-called "Ottonian System" of government came into being. The idea behind this system was brilliant and simple: if the nobility refused to obey the royal will, the clergy could be made to do so. Instead of laymen, therefore, Otto chose abbots, bishops, and archbishops as royal administrators, men of education, influence, and wealth, and most important, men whose rule of celibacy prevented their founding dynasties. Since clerical offices were filled in the first place by the king, Otto enjoyed complete control over his political lieutenants. In addition, the Church of Germany was made to provide material resources from its vast lands and soldiers from among its vassals. In return for this cooperation, the Church was showered with favors, endowed with more land, granted immunity from local justice, and backed in its missionary activities.

Once Otto had in this way achieved some measure of political stability in Germany, he set out on a European policy. He crushed the Magyars at Lechfeld in 955, after which they were never again a serious threat. Already, in 951, he had won northern Italy and installed his "system" there. And in 962, he completed his emulation of Charlemagne by having himself crowned Holy Roman Emperor by Pope John XII. Thus, he revived the oldest and most persistent of European dreams, the symbol of past glories and the hope of future peace and order. But the reality of the Ottonian Empire was but a pale shadow of its Carolingian predecessor. It was smaller in geographical area, including only what is now Germany and northern Italy, its government was not nearly so effective, and Otto himself had neither the prestige nor the power to command. From the first, the particularist tendencies which were a characteristic feature of German and Italian politics militated against making Emperor and Empire anything more. So too did the grandiose ambitions of Otto and most of his successors. Their aim was to conquer Italy, to restore the Empire's center at Rome, to regain the wealth of Italy and the Mediterranean, to rival the Byzantines. They were blind to the imperative need for consolidating and strengthening their position in Germany. For three hundred years, Holy Roman Emperors were drawn irresistibly south across the Alps, and with justice it may be said that whatever aspirations they might have had for a truly unified and centralized German kingdom were buried there.

Nor did their aim to conquer all of Italy succeed, and the chief reason was the implacable opposition of the papacy to imperial domination. From the time of Otto the Great, the interests of the two "heads" of Christendom were linked. Otto required Roman acquiescence in his "system," for only the pope could create new bishoprics and archbishoprics and grant special favors necessary to the German Church to carry out its governmental role. The pope, in his turn, depended on imperial arms for protection against his enemies and on imperial support for expansion into the frontier lands of central Europe. But Otto, like Charlemagne, believed his coronation entitled him to treat the pope as his puppet, while practicing a new form of caesaro-papism. When John XII refused to accept a subordinate role, Otto deposed him (963) and had a more amenable candidate elected. The new pope, Leo VIII, took an oath of loyalty to the Emperor, at the same time agreeing that no future pope could be consecrated without taking a similar oath. The strongest of Otto's successors would try to enforce this precedent, and all of Leo's successors would resist. The lines of conflict between popes and emperors were drawn, and the battle would be joined time and again in the next three centuries.

The Development of Monarchy in Germany

Otto the Great's son and grandson, Otto II (973–983) and Otto III (983–1002), were concerned chiefly with expanding imperial influence in Italy. Both spent the first years of their reign suppressing the rebellious dukes, for while the "Ottonian system" circumvented ducal power it did not eliminate ducal ambition, and Otto III was obliged to grant the rebels increased independence from the crown in order to be left free to pursue his Italian policy. Indeed, he turned his back on Germany, preferring to live in Rome, clothed in the traditional purple and looking for intellectual sustenance to Byzantium. He had medals struck reading *Renovatio Imperii Romanorum,* "Renewal of the Roman Empire."

The next two emperors paid the price of Otto III's fancies. Henry II (1002–1024), last of the Saxons, and Conrad II (1024–1039), founder of the Salian House, devoted their entire energies to recovering the ground lost by monarchy in Germany. Henry II developed the "Ottonian system" further, but he alienated many revenue-producing royal rights and much of the royal domain in his eagerness to reward his ecclesiastical supporters. Conrad II reversed this policy completely. He regained a part of what Henry had given away and replaced many clerical administrators with laymen, called *ministeriales,* drawn largely from the servile class and wholly loyal to and dependent on himself. Hence, when Henry III (1039–1056) came to the throne, he found his royal servants to be partly ecclesiastical and partly lay. He encouraged this mixed administration, and during his reign the imperial government was stronger than ever before. Nor was this strength confined solely to administrative efficiency. The hereditary principle of kingship seemed to be accepted now, Henry III being the first king not faced on his succession by rebellion. Furthermore, Henry's personal wealth made the crown virtually independent financially. And, using as an excuse the need to protect his extensive landholdings, he built and garrisoned many castles in Saxony and elsewhere. To further cow the nobility, he forced them to recognize long-forgotten dues and obligations to the crown. Finally, because of the tradition of the "Ottonian system" and because he had taken a special interest in its spiritual welfare Henry continued to enjoy the backing of the German Church in all of his activities.

But much of Henry's power proved transitory for the forces of antiroyalism were strong. The dukes and lesser nobility, whose progress toward feudal independence had never stopped, were restive under Henry's heavy hand.

They were prepared to rebel when opportunity offered. Nor were all church-men equally enthusiastic about monarchy. Some of them, imbued with new ideas of reform and freedom from royal control, were looking to the papacy for leadership. Meanwhile, the papacy had come a long way from the days of John XII. The popes were now men of character, purpose, and clear aim who were determined to cast off imperial shackles and assert the spiritual supremacy of their office over all Christendom. In the reign of Henry IV, successor to Henry III, the crown was challenged in Germany by a resentful nobility and a reform-minded clergy, and in Italy by the great Pope Gregory VII. Fighting on two fronts, unsure of where his real interests lay, the emperor was unable to prevent the royal authority from gradually slipping away (see pp. 222–225).

FURTHER READING

The classical analysis of the social and economic aspects of feudalism, based for the most part on French sources, is Marc Bloch, *Feudal Society* (1961). An excellent introduction, emphasizing the legal aspects, is F. Ganshof, *Feudalism* (2nd English ed., 1961). More elementary is C. Stephenson, *Medieval Feudalism* (1942). Some penetrating comments on the contractual relationship among medieval men (as well as on many other subjects) are contained in R. W. Southern, *The Making of the Middle Ages* (1953). R. Coulborn, ed., *Feudalism in History* (1956), is a suggestive if not entirely successful attempt to discover general characteristics of feudalism by comparing the western European variety with that found in other parts of the world. Feudal political thought is the subject of F. Kern, *Kingship and Law in the Middle Ages* (1939).

A brief introduction to the feudal monarchies is S. Painter, *The Rise of Feudal Monarchies* (1951). Excellent short histories of England are to be found in the Penguin series: D. M. Stenton, *English Society in the Early Middle Ages* (1952), and A. R. Myers, *England in the Late Middle Ages* (rev. ed., 1956). There is nothing comparable in English for France, but see R. Fawtier, *The Capetian Kings of France: Monarchy and Nation (987–1328)* (1960), and A. Luchaire, *Social France at the Time of Philip Augustus* (1912). C. Petit-Dutaillis, *Feudal Monarchy in France and England* (1937), is standard. A. R. Kelly, *Eleanor of Aquitaine and the Four Kings* (1950), is a fascinating account of that much married and crowned queen. The older, standard account of medieval Germany is J. Bryce, *The Holy Roman Empire* (rev. ed., 1904). A brilliant, interpretive essay is G. Barraclough, *The Origins of Modern Germany* (2nd ed., 1947).

2 · Medieval Economy and Society

The most important fact to remember about medieval Europe is that its economy was overwhelmingly agricultural. Cities and towns were relatively few and small in size; one with more than five or six thousand inhabitants was a rarity. Merchants and craftsmen were also few in number and engaged for the most part in local trade and industry. No less than nine out of ten Europeans gained their livelihood from the soil, and lived in small villages or hamlets, barely more than a group of farm huts, amid their produce and their animals. Only a village church tied them tenuously to the world outside. In such an agrarian environment, land was everything: the measure of wealth, the gauge of social status (hence a determinant of the structure of society), and the foundation of political power. Land was also an important factor in shaping medieval man's psychology and therefore his culture.

AGRARIAN EUROPE

Agrarian societies are slow to change. Traditional ways of living and doing things cling for centuries. This was an outstanding characteristic of medieval agrarian society which was little different in fundamental respects from the early to the late middle ages. But this does not mean that it was wholly static for there was quantitative if not qualitative change. Indeed, in the thousand years following Rome's decline, the frontiers of the old Empire were pushed back, forests were cleared, villages built, and people settled where none had been before. In short, Europe was occupied. This feat was accomplished by an agrarian society for trade and manufacturing were negligible throughout most of the period. Thus, we may consider the collapse of the Roman Empire an economic catastrophe but not one without certain beneficial consequences.

Since adequate records are not available, little is known about the exact nature of medieval agrarian society and its economic base, and even less about its origins. It dates from the later centuries of the Empire, a period of economic decline when commerce shrank and industry languished. An already chaotic situation was intensified first by the barbarian invasions and then by the expansion of Islam which drove the remaining trade from the Mediterranean. There was always a vestige of civilization left, of course, as the hints of early-day Venice and other Italian cities suggest, but for practical purposes it was gone and once-bustling cities slipped into somnolence. A predominantly money economy became an economy of barter, an "open" economy became a "closed" or "domestic" economy. There was a continuing struggle for land as it became more and more necessary to man's existence. Large estates tended to grow larger, smaller estates to disappear. The peasantry, that is the slaves and free tenants called *coloni,* were compelled to stay on the land where they were joined by former proprietors whose debts or inability to protect themselves had forced them to sell and who were now merely working the land they once owned. The large estate owners, meanwhile, assumed most of the day-to-day functions of the weakening central government. The arrival of the barbarians did not change much. They had an agriculture of their own onto which they grafted many Roman institutions and practices. Under the Merovingians and Carolingians, as anarchy grew and dangers threatened constantly, almost all the small, private owners who were left were forced to give up their land, becoming free tenants or one of the many grades of semi-free serfs (slavery had virtually disappeared). Variations on this pattern were countless, depending on exact time and place. But in general, the result was to produce the great medieval *seigneuries,* or *manors,* which we begin to see clearly by the tenth century.

The Medieval Manor

There was no typical manor and no typical manorial organization. Manors differed greatly from place to place depending on such factors as soil, climate, legal practices, or individual historical development. Some areas, such as Norway, never had manors and other areas, such as eastern Germany, got them very late. Nevertheless, for our purposes we can identify certain common characteristics. At the head of the manor was the lord, heir of a Roman estate owner or a Germanic chieftain. Doubtless, by the tenth or eleventh centuries, the manor was a fief which he held of a greater lord. He resided in a *chateau* or manor house, a crude but strong affair of wood or stone, with a courtyard attached. Sometimes the manor house was more along the lines of a castle, fortified against attack and surrounded by a moat or earthen mounds. If he had several manors—a not uncommon thing—his stewards or bailiffs managed those from which he was absent. The land he held directly was called the *demesne;* the rest he held through his tenants and serfs who worked both their own and the lord's land. Artisans who lived in the village provided such services as milling, weaving, and shoemaking. Of course, the lord was not always a layman. A great deal of land was held by clerical institutions, abbeys, cathedrals, or individual churches in fief or outright ownership. The land had been donated by pious souls over the years, and was inalienable and nonheritable by the law of *mort-main* (literally, "dead hand," meaning the church never died). Except for the lord's identity and the presence of a few monks in the field, clerical were much like lay manors.

If we could have flown over a manor, we would have seen first the

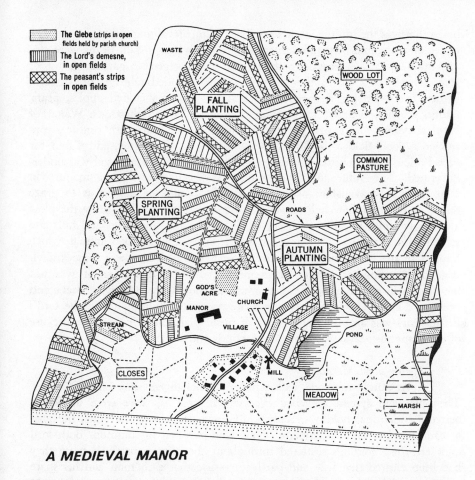

The Glebe (strips in open fields held by parish church)

The Lord's demesne, in open fields

The peasant's strips in open fields

A MEDIEVAL MANOR

village, a few houses, a church, a mill, grouped together or strung along a road. The manor house might stand near the village or at some distance from it, but in either case it would be obvious by its size and structure. Fields would stretch away on all sides, some planted, some fallow, some in grass for pasture. There would be no fences or hedges, but strips of uncultivated land (called "balks" in England) would separate the fields into large blocks. Scattered here and there would be scrubby waste and woodland, perhaps a third of the manor. A stream or two and a pond would complete the picture.

Manorial Economy

The manor was an economic unit, largely, though never entirely, self-sufficient. Except for salt, iron, such peculiar items as millstones, and the few luxury products consumed by the lord and his household, it provided for all the needs of its people. The population of a manor would seem quite small as would the yield of its arable land. The two were in balance in years of normal harvest so that bare subsistence without surplus was the rule. The chief crop was grain including wheat, barley, rye, and oats used to make the bread that was the indispensable ingredient of medieval man's diet. Frequently, barley or rye would be planted in spring, winter wheat in fall. Beans were also important, and each peasant had his own small vegetable garden. A list of seeds bought in 1360 for the king of France included cabbage, onion, leek, lettuce, beets, parsley, and mountain spinach. Fruits included apples, pears, plums, peaches, cherries, and such nuts as walnuts and chestnuts. Walter of Henley, who wrote a treatise on husbandry in the thirteenth century, considered a good yield to be 5 to 1 for wheat, 8 to 1 for barley, and 4 to 1 for oats. Ratios were no better because seed strains were weak and soil was undernourished. The values of fertilization were well known, but manure in quantity was unavailable; often the best that could be done was to graze the stock on the fallow field. Stock consisted of cattle, used to draw the plow and to give milk for cheese; sheep, which roamed the meadows and hills and served both as food and a source of wool; pigs, the chief food animal, which foraged in the woodlands, and in some areas horses. There was some knowledge of breeding, as Walter of Henley's treatise suggests, but it was not used to much effect. Hens (Walter says each should lay 115 eggs a year) and bees were kept. The woods were full of game, and hunting (with the lord's permission) was an important source of meat. Fish, eaten in quantity because of the many fast days, was available in ponds and streams.

Agricultural Methods

Agricultural methods had remained unchanged since ancient times. The open-field system prevailed everywhere; that is, there were no fences between individual holdings. Rather, divisions were by work units, the area a team could plow in a day, and fields were worked in common. Both lord and serfs had holdings scattered throughout the manor, partly because they had been cleared that way and partly to assure that each man had his share of good and bad land. The Roman "two-field" system was universal before the tenth or eleventh century. The land was divided into two parts, one part being planted and the other lying fallow each year. By rotating the planted and fallow fields, some fertility was preserved. The fallow field was plowed twice and animals were allowed to pasture on it. After the eleventh century a "three-field" system was introduced in a number of areas. With three fields instead of two in rotation grain production was increased by one-third, plowing was reduced, and such lesser jobs as harrowing and weeding were spread more evenly over the year.

The three-field system was only one of several improvements in agriculture made by medieval man. Another was wider use of the heavy wheeled plow to work the rocky soils of the north for which the Roman plow was too light. Still another was the introduction of horses to replace oxen in some places. Three technological developments made this practicable: the horse collar, the horse shoe, and tandem harnessing. The first of these permitted a horse to work at full strength without strangling himself, a real danger when he was harnessed with a strap around his neck in the Roman way. The second development increased traction and protected the horse's hooves against stones.

The third made it possible to team horses efficiently. Horses, however, did not wholly supplant oxen. The latter were slower at their work and needed more pasturage but did not require costly grain and were less susceptible to disease. Though most European manors retained the traditional agricultural methods, these improvements brought about an over-all increase in production.

Rural Life and Work

The work on the manor was done by tenants and serfs, under the eye of the lord or his steward. Tenants were generally freemen under the lord's jurisdiction while on the manor and owing him services but at liberty to leave. There were numerous grades between freeman and serf, and the lines separating them were often unclear. The serf's relationship was in some ways like the relationship of lord to vassal in that contractual protection was provided and justice was exchanged for labor services and payments. However, it was not a contract between free men for in making it the serf forfeited a part of his freedom. Moreover, it was perpetual and could not be broken by him or his descendants. It attached the serf for all time to the land on which he worked and made him subject in important ways to the lord. Superficially it might seem to have been harshly one-sided. But the serf benefited, too. He gained security for he could not be driven from the land so long as the contract was in force. He also gained membership in a community with some assurance of safety in a time when society was in chaos and individuals were prey to constant fear and danger.

Servile contracts and arrangements between lords and free tenants were of many kinds. Generally, all peasants owed the lord labor and payments in kind or money. Labor consisted of several days' work, either on the lord's land (week work) or at tasks (*corvées*) that he assigned, such as road-building, ditch-digging, and wood-cutting. Corvées were much resented by peasants everywhere because they were arduous and often arbitrary. To "week work" was added "boon work," seasonal tasks such as plowing, sowing, and reaping. Payments to the lord were usually in kind, occasionally in money. Money payments became more common in the later Middle Ages. There was an annual poll tax and a usually onerous exaction called a tithe. Altogether these payments amounted to perhaps a half of the peasant's income. In addition the lord demanded special fines, such as the *heriot,* a kind of inheritance tax, and he required the peasants to pay *banalités* for the use of his oven, mill, and wine-press. Thus, each peasant could devote only part, perhaps half, of his time to earning a living for himself and could expect to keep only a part of the fruit of his labor. Furthermore, he was subject to the jurisdiction of the lord's court, could not marry off the manor without the lord's permission, and could not hope to resist the tyrannical actions of a lord who was cruel or rapacious. In effect, the lord was the prince of a petty state and the serf his subject.

But these were things the peasant endured; indeed, he became accustomed to them. They were leavened by the many religious holidays when no one worked and by the great feasts held at planting time, harvest time, pig-killing time, and so on. They were leavened too by his family life and his few simple daily pleasures. The peasant's living accommodations were rough but adequate. His house, really a hut, was of mud, wood, or stone with a thatched roof, dirt floor and uncovered windows. Its one room served every purpose and was dark and probably smoky, for chimneys were not invented until the twelfth century and smoke had to find its way out through the windows or a hole in the roof. Furnishings were few and homemade. Clothing, too, was homemade: stockings to the waist, a short habit or jerkin, sometimes of leather, and perhaps a smock. The peasant's chief food was bread, made of wheat, rye, or barley, or a combination of several of these and nearly always black and hard. He enjoyed a fairly wide range of vegetables and fruit and ate meat once in a while. He drank wine or beer if available, water or perhaps whey if not. His greatest enemies were famine, disease, and war. In a year of bad harvest, starvation was common and epidemic a constant threat. A year of good harvest could become a year of bad at the hands of a robbing and burning soldiery. The result was that few babies survived long after birth, and those who did lived a short, hard life. One may doubt, however, whether it was much different from the life many millions of the world's peasants live today.

The lord's situation contrasted sharply with that of the peasant but we must not think of it as luxurious or even very comfortable. He and his household were better fed, better dressed, better housed, and far less work-worn, but the differences were only a matter of degree. More important was the fact that he was a nobleman, a member of an elite in feudal society. He was only a farmer by circumstance; his chief function was to fight. Fighting was his occupation and his pleasure, and everything in his life was directed toward it. In his early youth, he began to train rigorously, serving first as a page at court, where he picked up a little culture and a few manners, then as a squire to a knight, learning the simple military arts of the time. On reaching manhood, he was outfitted and mounted, becoming himself a knight by test of battle or simply through the ceremony of dubbing. He was probably not as yet a vassal to a lord or the possessor of a fief for knighthood and the feudal relationship were independent of each other. The remainder of his life, a life probably no longer than a peasant's, was devoted to armed combat or spent in service to a lord, in search of booty, or merely in fun. Sport consisted of sham battles, jousts, and tournaments to keep in fighting trim. A knight was particularly unlucky if he failed to survive his battles for death in combat was uncommon.

The lord's home life was determined by his profession, dominated always by the spirit of "eat, drink, and be merry for tomorrow you may die." His manor house was rude, damp, dirty, dark, and draughty. It usually consisted of two large rooms, the great hall and the chamber, and sometimes a third, the wardrobe. The hall was living room, dining room, guest room, and servants' quarters. The chamber was the sitting room and bedroom of the lord and his immediate family. The wardrobe was the lord's dressing room. The greater manor houses also had chapels. Straw covered the floors, a concession to tidiness, for it tended to absorb the refuse thrown from the eating table. There were numerous household servants, usually serfs, bound to the lord himself rather than to a parcel of land. These serfs were obviously better off than their peasant counterparts. If the lord were important, they might find themselves in positions of administrative responsibility and possessors of considerable political power for they cared for the lord's business as well as his person. The lord's clothing was similar to but of better quality than the peasant's. In addition, he enjoyed the privilege of displaying his noble rank by wearing fur, forbidden to commoners.

The lord ate much the same food as his peasants, but in more abundance. His meals were heavy and consisted of many courses cooked in an outside kitchen. He accompanied them with huge quantities of wine or beer. He demanded continual amusement, and the great hall was filled with entertainers ranging from jugglers and troubadours to prostitutes. His fighting companions frequently gathered around him to talk of war. Away from the table, his days not spent in actual fighting were filled with knightly sport. Hunting was a favorite pastime as well as a source of meat. Spears, bows and arrows, and hawks were employed, although falconry was considered more suitable to women. The lord's wife and the other women of his court were as boisterous and fond of crude amusement as he, but the lord and his fellow knights considered them useful only for love-making and motherhood.

For the lord and his peasants, religion was very much a part of daily life, governing many of their thoughts and actions. The village church, with its priest, was the visible expression of their membership in Christian society and the vehicle through which they could attain salvation. The Church also performed many important social functions, from registering baptisms (hence births) to settling disputes over wills. The priest was usually an appointee of the lord and therefore the lord's man, a circumstance which tended to separate and sometimes alienate him from the peasants. The peasants also resented the tithes they were forced to pay the priest to supplement his regular income from the church land of the manor, the *glebe*. But the priest's spiritual and social functions, as well as the fact that he was probably the only person on the manor who could read, made him necessary. The actual religion of the peasants, and often the lord as well, was larded with superstition. Good and bad spirits were everywhere, governing weather, health, and the success of the crops. Little of Christianity's civilizing influence rubbed off on the peasants. They were ignorant, immoral (by Church standards) and given to disrespect. Church attendance was fairly regular, however, and celebration of saints' days a periodic relief from the routine of toil. Saints were important as recipients of prayer, indeed they formed a kind of pantheon for most people. Their days served as a kind of calendar: weeding after St. John's day, winter sowing on St. Martin's day, and so on.

Expansion of Medieval Economy

The medieval agrarian economy was not static but expanding; the wildernesses of Europe were being opened to the plow. Expansion was slow in the centuries immediately following the fall of Rome, quite rapid after the tenth century. It came to a halt, temporarily as it turned out, in the early four-teenth century, only to resume a hundred to a hundred and fifty years later, continuing until the present time. In the process of expansion, the frontiers were pushed back, and new areas were settled and cultivated. Spain, central and eastern Germany, and the outlying regions of the island of Britain were made liveable, and older areas, such as northern France, were brought back under cultivation. The inundated coastal regions of the Netherlands were diked and made into farmland. Everywhere forests were cut and wastes cleared. At the same time, cities began to grow again and commerce and in-dustry to flourish. The causes of this expansion are obscure. Clearly there was a steady and sizable population increase beginning about the year 1000, but the reasons for it are unclear. Some historians have suggested that the develop-ment of the feudal system brought relative peace to a Europe long ravaged by anarchy and war and that under this stimulus society took on new life. More babies were born, additional sources of food were needed, and expansion was a natural consequence.

The Church, the only universal institution in Europe, took the lead in this expansion by means of its great monastic orders. The first phase was directed by Cluniac monks, who concentrated in already inhabited areas where they founded new monasteries and rehabilitated old ones. The great advances into the wilderness were made by the Cistercians at the end of the eleventh and the beginning of the twelfth century. The Cistercians' aim was wholly spiritual: to escape the world and practice the perfect life of continual religious devotion according to the Benedictine rule. Their austerity led them to adopt an additional rule by which they would not live off the fruit of inhabited land. Restoring Benedict's injunction that monks perform manual labor, they took to the "desert" which they put under cultivation themselves. They spread over all of Europe—France, Germany, England, first, then elsewhere. From their foundation in 1098, they grew to 328 houses by 1152. Each place was a wilder-ness to begin with, but they cleared forests, drained marshes and invited peasants in to settle as *conversi,* or lay members of the order. Quite unwillingly, they became rich along the way.

Naturally, their success was an incentive to other religious orders and to secular lords and princes. A general movement to open new lands and found new towns began. In France during the twelfth century, the monarchy gave charters to many *villes neuves,* or new villages, and established colonies of *hospites,* or settlers, in the royal domain. In Germany and England, great landholders did much the same, though to a lesser extent. In Spain, the settlement of lands reconquered from the Moors had begun in the eleventh century. Since all these villages and colonies were made up of volunteers who had entered into a contract with the landholder, the customary arrangement of lord and serf did not apply. The *hospites,* for example, were simply tenants who paid a part of their produce as rent. They were not usually subject to other services. This expansion movement continued at a somewhat reduced pace throughout the thirteenth century and ground to a halt sometime in the early 1300's. The reasons for this slowdown and its results will be discussed in a later chapter.

THE REVIVAL OF URBAN LIFE

The tenth and eleventh centuries also witnessed the revival of urban life and the appearance of a new group in medieval society, the middle class. Urban life is town life, and towns are primarily agglomerations of merchants and artisans buying, selling, and making things. Towns cannot thrive except on trade. We have seen that trade was not completely dead even in the darkest of the Dark Ages. No manor was fully self-sufficient but needed various commodities of a specialized kind to sustain itself. Furthermore, evidence suggests that manors trafficked to some extent with one another in food products such as grain, wine, and fish. Finally, a few spices, silks, and other items of luxury were carried to western Europe in the packs of Syrian and Jewish merchants and furs were brought from the Scandinavian lands and Russia. At the same time, handicrafts continued to be practiced on a much reduced scale, providing such essentials as weapons and clothing. But all together these activities did not make a significant impression on the overwhelmingly agricultural economy, and they had small effect on the growth of towns. The towns that had survived the centuries of strife had shrunk in size and served not as business centers but as seats of bishops and civil administrators. Paris consisted largely of the *Ile de la Cité* in the Seine, future site of Notre Dame Cathedral, where the bishop of Paris was headquartered, and of an area on the Right Bank where the Frankish king resided.

The Revival of Industry

Commerce and industry reached their lowest ebb after the collapse of the Carolingian Empire when government disappeared and European society fell into lawlessness. In the course of the eleventh century, they began to recover and to expand, and imperceptibly the shift toward an open, money economy began. The reasons for this recovery and its early course are obscure but some of them are the same as those which stimulated agricultural expansion: a marked rise in population and relative internal peace induced by the feudal system. As we have seen, new lands were settled and new farming methods introduced, and these produced agricultural surpluses. Greater social and political stability permitted these surpluses to be marketed. For the first time in centuries landholders made a clear profit, and with it they were able to purchase goods, both the luxuries of the Near and Far East and the manufactured products of Europe itself. At the same time, the increase in population fed the towns with workers on which industry could draw. Finally, there seems to have been an influx of precious metals from new mines discovered in the eleventh and twelfth centuries which provided wealth and a medium of exchange. Towns grew and townsmen themselves as they gained wealth became buyers. Expansion fed on itself.

The first area to benefit was along the shores of the Mediterranean. Slowly the ancient sea was recovered by the West from the Muslims, gone soft after their first great surge of conquest and unable to resist the vigorous Europeans. In the eleventh century, the Iberian peoples launched the *Reconquista,* a war to free their peninsula from the Moors; the Normans recaptured Sicily and southern Italy from the Muslims, establishing a flourishing kingdom there; and the Italian cities of Pisa and Genoa, with their combined fleets, drove virtually all Muslim shipping from the sea. Venice, which had heretofore traded under Byzantine protection, built a navy of her own which was superior to any and it was not long before Italians, having defeated the Muslims, were fighting over trade rights with each other. The Crusades finished off Muslim resistance, delivering into Christian hands the ports of the Near East and North Africa. The Crusades also created an important, though temporary, market for western goods in the crusader's newly-won kingdoms in the Near East. They also gave a significant boost to shipping, and in a general way enhanced the western taste for eastern products. The result by 1150 was to turn the Mediterranean into a Christian sea, a condition which prevailed for more than two hundred years. Italy, in a perfect position geographically, reaped the harvest. Venice, Genoa, Pisa, then Naples, Amalfi, and finally inland cities such as Milan, Florence, and Siena burgeoned on commerce in exotic Near- and Far-Eastern luxuries and on the industry and banking this commerce stimulated. Soon the Lombard plain and Tuscany were more urbanized than in Roman days. Under the circumstances, it is not surprising that Italy produced the earliest mature urban civilization in medieval Europe.

Northern Europe was not far behind, though the results were not as impressive. The North Sea and Baltic Coast were areas of flourishing commerce and industry by the end of the eleventh century. The chief commodity was cloth from the towns of Flanders: Ghent, Douai, Yprès, Arras. Cloth was a native product in contrast to the foreign products traded by the Italians. Flanders had the advantage of a farsighted, if mercenary, reigning house and the counts of Flanders gave their encouragement and protection to the cloth industry in return for taxes. Also important in the northern trade were goods such as English wool (which supplied the Flemish looms), French wines, and fish from the maritime provinces of the Netherlands. Transport was mainly by river and sea which was easiest and cheapest. Roads were poor and dangerous, and every lord, large or small, exacted a toll from merchants travelling over his land.

Trade between the trading centers of northern and southern Europe was difficult and irregular until the establishment of the great fairs in the French county of Champagne early in the twelfth century. These fairs were huge, year-round market places, run under the benevolent eye of the count who drew a handsome tax from them. Champagne lay on the main route between Flanders and Italy, a convenient place for merchants to meet and do business. Much merchandise was bought and sold, future sales were arranged, letters of credit exchanged, and simple banking operations carried on. The fairs of Champagne and their lesser counterparts elsewhere in Europe were the direct ancestors of later commodity and money exchanges at Antwerp,

**PRINCIPAL TOWNS OF
WESTERN EUROPE
in the Thirteenth Century**

North Sea

Baltic Sea

Edinburgh

Dublin

York
Lincoln

Nottingham
Oxford
London
Bristol

Lübeck
Danzig
Königsberg

Hamburg
Bremen

Dresden

Utrecht

Bruges
Ypres Ghent Antwerp Cologne
English Channel Arras Lille Cambrai Aix-la-Chapelle
Hastings Dover
Bayeux Amiens St. Quentin Frankfurt
Rouen Paris Reims Mainz Nuremberg Prague
Trier Worms
Metz
Meaux Toul Strasbourg
Rennes Blois Orléans Munich
Atlantic Ocean Basel Vienna Buda
Nantes Besançon Berne Salzburg
Tours Bourges Constance Innsbruck
La Rochelle Poitiers Geneva Zurich
Limoges Milan Pavia Mantua Verona Padua
Bordeaux Lyons Turin Venice
Cahors Parma Ferrara
Avignon Genoa Modena Zara
Bayonne Montpellier Arles Pisa Florence
Oporto Pamplona Carcassonne Marseilles Siena
Salamanca Rome
Lisbon Toledo Barcelona Naples
Salerno
Valencia
Córdova Palermo Messina
Seville Granada *Mediterranean Sea* Syracuse

Amsterdam, London, and finally New York. Early business practices were evolved along with a primitive kind of business or "merchant" law. The Champagne fairs were the most important link between north and south until well into the fourteenth century.

Commerce was the greatest stimulus to the development of urban life. Old towns grew and new towns sprang up along the routes frequented by merchants. Sometimes merchants simply settled down to trade in or near existing episcopal or administrative towns, most of them the ancient Roman urban centers called *civitates*. Paris and Rouen in Normandy are two examples. On the other hand, merchants might cluster outside the walls of a fortified place, a *burg*, giving rise to a new settlement called a *faubourg* meaning "outside the burg." Evidence for this is found in the term contemporaries used for merchants: *bourgeois*, or "burghers." New walls would be built to encompass the mercantile addition. In Italy the *civitas* formed the nucleus of most towns, in the north the *burg*. Whatever the town's origin, the merchant element in time swallowed up or drove away the knights, on the one hand, and bishops or counts, on the other.

These towns were remarkably small compared to modern cities. Accurate population figures are difficult to arrive at and at best are only rough estimates. But we believe that Milan, the largest town in Europe by the early fourteenth century, had 200,000 persons at most. Venice approached that and Florence had something over 100,000 as did Genoa and Naples. The northern European towns were smaller: Toulouse—25,000, Ghent and Bruges—40,000 at most, London the same, and Paris, the largest of all,—80 to 100,000. Europe was still in the earliest stage of urbanization, but the towns, with their governments and their businessmen-citizens, exercised an influence on European history out of all proportion to their numbers.

TOWN GOVERNMENT AND THE MIDDLE CLASS

Towns by their very nature were alien to the feudal system, although they were necessarily a part of it because they were situated on the land of a lay or ecclesiastical lord. And, since they were within the feudal system, they were treated legally and politically like vassals, that is, their overlords granted them a charter, or contract, specifying rights and privileges in return for dues in money and sometimes for soldiers. The lords were stingy, however. They wanted towns on their land but they wanted to control them, and townsmen chafed under the restrictions the charters imposed. Most charters provided that townsmen be free and that they be able to move about at will. Usually residence for a year and a day in a town lifted a man from servile status, hence the famous phrase: "Town air makes free." A third important provision was the right to own, therefore to buy and sell, property. But townsmen wanted more, chiefly the right to govern themselves, to administer their own justice, and to collect their own taxes. In most cases, the lords were unwilling to allow such fundamental authority to pass from their hands and conflict, sometimes bloody, ensued. In the twelfth and thirteenth centuries town revolts occurred all over Europe. The advantage lay with the towns for they had money behind them and their desire for freedom was strong. Furthermore, many were able to enlist the aid of kings when royal power began to rise again. Only in rare instances, however, was full independence achieved though in Italy, Flanders, southern France, Castile, and Germany many towns became, for practical purposes, free.

As a town gained its freedom, its citizens formed a government. This was most frequently a council elected by the citizens. At first the strongest political group was the urban nobility. They were the town's original inhabitants and its natural administrators and defenders. Their economic power was founded on the lands they held in the nearby countryside. But they were soon compelled to share power with the richest merchants and these men of the upper middle class dominated town government thereafter. The merchants were organized in a guild, the "guild merchant," an association dedicated primarily to furthering its membership's commercial interests but also possessing other responsibilities. It regulated trade, arbitrated legal disputes, provided security against financial loss through disaster or robbery, and even supported deceased merchants' widows and orphans. Where the merchants were very powerful in the government, the town council and the guild council might be the same men performing different functions. The urban nobility and the rich merchants were soon joined together in a ruling patriciate. Moreover, they became indistinguishable economically and socially as the former entered trade and the latter bought land. Both lived well and served mounted as knights in the town militia. It was this patriciate which fought the domination of the town's feudal lord, which united all the townsmen in the struggle for liberty, and which introduced the earliest municipal institutions.

However, as so often happens in history, these aristocracies tended to degenerate into oligarchies. By the thirteenth century in Italy, and somewhat later in Flanders and other northern areas, the aristocratic governments had become exclusive, abandoning their initial policy of allowing anyone to join them who could climb to their economic position. Many rich but "new" men were denied political rights together with men of average or below average wealth. These last were for the most part artisans rather than merchants for industry had advanced hand in hand with commerce. Industry, however, was almost wholly of the local handicraft variety, each artisan making a commodity himself whether bread, shoes, or armor, and selling it directly to the consumer. Not until the end of the thirteenth century did cloth manufacturing in Italy and Flanders assume characteristics of large-scale capitalistic production.

The artisans in each craft were banded together in craft guilds. These guilds were formed later than the guild merchants and are evidence of an increasing specialization in the urban economy. The craft guild, like the guild merchant, aimed at protecting the artisans' economic interests by securing a monopoly in a particular line of work, by fixing prices and setting standards of quality, and by regulating admission to membership. They were controlled by the full members, or "masters," who employed both "apprentices" as trainees and sometimes wageworkers, or "journeymen." Politically they also provided an organizational base for the artisans' attack on the patrician oligarchy. The later Middle Ages, when craft guilds developed most rapidly, was a period of almost continual social strife between merchants and artisans, punctuated by rebellions of wageworkers, the lowest group on the economic and social scale. (The social and economic aspects of guilds will be discussed in Part VI, Chapter 2.)

FURTHER READING

Two standard economic histories which contain short sections on the Middle Ages are S. E. Clough and C. W. Cole, *Economic History of Europe* (rev. ed., 1952), and H. Heaton, *Economic History of Europe* (rev. ed., 1948). The work of the great Belgian historian, H. Pirenne, remains standard though not wholly unchallenged: *Economic and Social History of Medieval Europe* (1937). On challenges to the Pirenne Thesis, see A. F. Havighurst, ed., *The Pirenne Thesis: Analysis, Criticism, and Revision* (1958). P. Boissonade, *Life and Work in Medieval Europe* (1937), is extremely valuable, and N. Neilson, *Medieval Agrarian Economy* (1936), is useful and suggestive. The classic explanation of the origins of towns is H. Pirenne, *Medieval Cities* (1925). A provocative short synthesis, with illustrative documents, is J. H. Mundy and P. Riesenberg, *The Medieval Town* (1958). Medieval society is briefly treated in S. Painter, *Medieval Society* (1951). L. White, *Medieval Technology and Social Change* (1962), is useful.

3 · The Struggle
for Leadership in the West

By the middle of the eleventh century a semblance of order was reappearing in the West. Under the power of the Saxon house the imperial concept had once more been revived and its Salian successors were actively carrying on its work. In England, the Norman conquest brought a measure of unity and order to the confusion of the last Anglo-Saxon period. The gradual reappearance of recognizable secular institutions in western Europe was accompanied by reform and strengthening of the Church which had shared in the general eclipse of western society in the late ninth and tenth centuries. The revival of the Church was relatively rapid but its success carried with it a momentous problem. From the time of the Christianization of the Empire by Constantine the Great the issue of the relation of the Church to the Empire had implicitly been raised. The problem had sharpened with the coronation of Charlemagne by Pope Leo III. Who was to be the head of Christendom, the emperor or the pope? The question was openly raised before the end of the eleventh century and the conflict it provoked, generally known as the Investiture Controversy, was to last in one form or another for more than a century. But in the beginning of the thirteenth century an answer seemed to have been reached. With the calling of the Fourth Lateran Council by Pope Innocent III in 1215 the Church proclaimed its assertion that Christendom was united under the ultimate leadership of the papacy.

THE REFORM OF THE CHURCH

The Feudalization of the Church. In its early stages feudalism had been secular in character and had had little to do with the Church. In time, however, the two institutions grew closer together until they merged at a number of points. This situation led in many cases to the deterioration of ecclesiastical ideals. On the one hand, the vast lands which the Church had received at various times as gifts from the faithful had to be administered. The only manner in which this could be done in the tenth century was through a feudal organization which involved the Church in a series of secular undertakings which could not but lower its moral tone. Episcopal and abbey lands were granted to feudal vassals who had to be supervised. The bishop or abbot in turn owed service to the lord of his lands. Custom frowned on the clergy's participation in battles, but the warlike archbishop of such a popular tale as *The Song of Roland* suggests that the custom was not always honored. Even when abbeys handed over all of their secular affairs, both military and economic, to a lay supervisor or advocate the presence of such a layman and his retinue necessarily interfered with the proper keeping of the monastic rule.

On the other hand the rulers of the Church, abbots and bishops, came more and more from the same families as the secular aristocracy. In order not to weaken the family holdings by too many divisions, the feudal nobles left their lands to the eldest son and looked to the Church as a career for the children unprovided for. Younger brothers of counts and dukes received bishoprics, and the abbots of monasteries were usually relatives of the nearby lords who in most cases appointed them. Many of these younger sons thrust into the Church, often as boys, had no religious vocation whatever. They shared the tastes of their class, fought, hunted, drank, and the rule of the monasteries under their supervision understandably deteriorated. There were unquestionably numerous pious and dedicated ecclesiastics but, hemmed in as they were by the feudal structure, their efforts to maintain Christian ideals were often doomed to failure and in many cases it was hard to tell whether a bishop was a spiritual leader or a secular ruler.

The Decline of the Papacy

The crisis seen in the provincial Church was also felt in Rome itself. It is true that in the period of disintegration of the Carolingian Empire the papacy had briefly raised itself from the relatively subordinate position it had occupied under Charlemagne. Pope Nicholas I (858–867) asserted his authority over the patriarch of Constantinople, over his own powerful bishops, such as Hincmar of Rheims, and even over the Carolingian rulers, when he compelled Lothair II, King of Lorraine, to take back his divorced wife. After his death, however, the position of the papacy rapidly declined. The popes had neither the authority nor the power to free themselves from the quarrels of the Roman nobility and their office was captured by successive aristocratic factions. These figurehead popes were the scandal of their own and successive generations and the early tenth century is considered by scholars as the lowest point in the moral prestige of the papacy.

The situation at Rome was so scandalous that the Saxon emperors felt it necessary to interfere. Otto I at the time of his coronation in 962 summoned a synod which deposed the reigning pope as unworthy and he insisted that future popes must first be approved by him. His successors saw to it that the popes swore allegiance to the emperor. With the appointment of Otto III's cousin and later of his tutor as popes under the names of Gregory V and Sylvester II the imperial supervision of the papacy was assured.

The Cluniac Reform

The sorry state of the feudal Church, which had provoked the concern of the Saxon emperors, did not pass unnoticed by contemporaries. The first attempt to reform the existing abuses was directed at the monasteries. In 910 Duke William of Aquitaine founded the monastery of Cluny on his Burgundian lands. The foundation of a monastery by a powerful and wealthy layman was entirely customary but the terms of the foundation were not. Instead of being left under the supervision of the neighboring nobles and bishop, the monastery of Cluny was freed from all feudal interference by being made subject to the pope alone. Under its first great abbots, Odo and Odilo, Cluny became a model monastery. No innovations were introduced, but the rule of Saint Benedict was again applied particularly in its concern for intellectual and religious activities, and the traditional routine of prayer and liturgical observances was once again demanded of the monks.

The reform of Cluny received support from a number of secular rulers and particularly from the Holy Roman Emperors who felt concern for the Church and at the same time needed the help of the intellectuals who came from Cluny in their governments. As the result of this, the influence of the new foundation spread, and numerous reformed monasteries were established to imitate its example. These new houses were not left to their own devices as had formerly been the case. They were considered the "daughters" of Cluny, and their heads or *priors* were answerable to the abbot of the mother house. Thus a tightly-knit, centralized network of reformed benedictine monasteries, culminating in Cluny, free from secular interference, and responsible only to the papacy, covered the greater part of western Europe.

The Reform of the Papacy

The abbots of Cluny were concerned with the reform of the regular monastic clergy, but a similar reform of the secular Church was equally necessary. Gradually the papacy in turn began to emerge from the degradation of the tenth century. We have seen that the Saxon emperors had tried to keep an eye on the affairs of the Roman Church, and the Emperor Henry II was sincerely concerned both with the welfare of the Church and with the monastic reform movement. The chief imperial figure in the reform of the papacy, however, was to be the pious Emperor Henry III. In 1046 he called a council at Pavia to condemn the sale of ecclesiastical offices, known as *simony,* and another at Sutri, to decide between the three claimants of the papacy. In 1049 he obtained the election of the reformer bishop of Toul as Pope Leo IX (1049–1054). With him the reforming party reached the very summit of the Church. Within a year Leo IX, at a Council held at Rheims, condemned simony and attempted to free the clergy from all secular and feudal ties by forbidding all churchmen to marry. The bishops of France, incidentally, had a foretaste of conflicts to come by being forced to chose between their feudal duty to their king, who tried to divert them from a council called without his permission, and their obedience to the pope who required their presence. The decisions of the Council of Rheims were not final. The problems of simony and of clerical celibacy were to reappear at innumerable councils thereafter, but the reform program had now been applied by Leo IX to the whole of the secular church.

The Creation of the College of Cardinals

Of equal importance was a development within the structure of the Roman Church which occurred soon after Leo's death. The greatest difficulty of the papacy in the tenth century had been its dependence on the turbulent Roman nobles who had turned it into a mere pawn in their quarrels. In 1059 a decree of Pope Nicholas II proclaimed that papal elections were henceforth to be free of secular intervention. Neither the Romans nor the German emperor were to have a hand in the matter. The pope was to be elected by the bishops of the neighboring dioceses and the priests of the main parishes of Rome. The creation of this new electoral body, later known as the College of Cardinals, marked a major step in the emancipation of the papacy. Up to this period the popes had cooperated with the Holy Roman Emperors and recognized their authority. For all his piety Henry III had unquestionably kept the initiative in ecclesiastical affairs and Leo IX himself had been an imperial appointee. The decree of 1059, promulgated at a time when Henry's son and successor was only nine years old, was a challenge to the imperial rights, even though some of the prerogatives of the emperor had been preserved. The Empire could scarcely condone such an independent attitude in the papacy whose reform it had partially brought about and the stage was set for a clash between the Empire and the Church.

THE INVESTITURE CONTROVERSY

From the time of the pontificate of Leo IX and the decree of 1059 the Church was in a moral position to throw off the tutelage of the Empire, but its practical power to do this was by no means as great. Imperial armies coming again and again from Germany to Italy had protected the papacy from the riots in Rome. The need of the emperor to be crowned at Rome by an acknowledged pope increased the imperial concern for the welfare of the papacy. But if the popes undertook to carry out a policy divergent from that of the empire they would lose their protector against the Roman aristocracy, and who was to say whether a new army might not appear in Italy to reaffirm the traditional rights of the emperor and oust an unwelcome pope, as had often been done before? This precarious situation of the papacy was markedly altered in the middle of the eleventh century, at the very time of its capture by the reformers. In 1059 Pope Nicholas II recognized the Norman conquest of Southern Italy by investing Robert Guiscard with the lands he had captured and receiving in exchange from the Norman leader the oath of vassalage. As the Norman state spread in the south the Church in Italy acquired through Nicholas' action a powerful ally in case of imperial displeasure. From this time on the papacy was not only morally but also politically capable of carrying out the reform program by denying the authority of laymen in ecclesiastical affairs.

Gregory VII and Henry IV

The accession in 1073 of a powerful and controversial figure precipitated the crisis. As the monk Hildebrand he had been a follower of Leo IX and an ardent supporter of the reform; now as Pope Gregory VII he set out to turn the reforming theory into reality. Maintaining the fundamental belief that the Church should everywhere be freed from secular supervision, Gregory VII decreed at a council held in 1075 that no churchman should henceforth receive lay investiture. That is to say, that he should not, as feudal custom demanded, receive from any layman a staff or ring as symbol of his authority nor in return swear allegiance to any lord. This decree was in full accordance with the reform program but it could hardly be accepted by the secular powers and least of all by the Empire. The right of emperors to appoint bishops had never been challenged. From the days of Otto I they had bestowed innumerable lands on the Church, and in return they expected loyalty and service. Constantly threatened by the rebellions of the warlike German nobility, the Holy Roman Emperors had based much of their administration on bishops and abbots of their own making. One of the practical reasons for the imperial support of the Cluniac reform was the imperial need for well trained administrators whose celibacy and consequent inability to transmit lands to their descendants would keep them loyal to the interests of the emperor rather than to those of their own family. Without the cooperation of his ecclesiastical nobles the position of the emperor was seriously jeopardized within his own realm.

Disregarding the papal decree, the Emperor Henry IV appointed a bishop for the imperial city of Milan, as had been the custom. Going further he answered the letter of remonstrance addressed to him by the pope by a violent attack on Gregory himself which was in effect a declaration of war. Henry had forced the German bishops to renounce their allegiance to the pope and now he challenged the legality of Gregory's election and bade him step down from the throne he had usurped in favor of a more worthy encumbent. Gregory was not a man to leave such a challenge unanswered. Reiterating his position, he excommunicated the emperor and in an unprecedented step freed his vassals from the oath of allegiance they had taken to him. Some of Henry IV's barons and even some of his bishops such as Herman of Metz remained loyal, but the majority of the German nobility welcomed the opportunity of decreasing the power of the crown and revolted. In this critical position Henry IV was forced to submit. Hastening in the winter of 1077 to the castle of Canossa in northern Italy, where the pope had come for safety, Henry in Gregory's own words:

laying aside all the trappings of royalty, . . . stood in wretchedness, barefooted and clad in woolen, for three days before the gate of the castle, and implored with profuse weeping the aid and consolation of the apostolic mercy . . .

Gregory as a priest was forced to grant absolution to the repentant sinner and Henry, once he had regained the allegiance of most of his vassals, resumed the quarrel, so that Gregory was forced to flee to the lands of his Norman supporters and to die in exile at Salerno in 1083. Consequently, a number of scholars have maintained that Henry's submission was really a diplomatic victory which put him again in a position to continue the struggle. We must not forget, however, that the unprecedented humiliation of the emperor had been unmistakable and had struck the imagination of contemporaries, and that the king had been forced to swear that he would give satisfaction to the pope.

The Gregorian Program

The program of Gregory VII was not only a challenge of the imperial authority but a total break with the current tradition of Church-State relations. When he wrote in the *Dictatus Papae* (1075):

> [the Pope] alone may depose bishops and reinstate them.
> He may depose emperors.
> No council may be regarded as a general one without his
>   consent.
> A decree of his may be annulled by no one; he alone may
>   annul the decrees of all.
> He may be judged by no one.
> The Pope may absolve the subjects of the unjust from
>   their allegiance.

it is little wonder that his contemporaries, even within the Church, considered such statements as revolutionary innovations. As the German bishops wrote to Gregory, he had "usurped and arrogated to [himself] a certain new and unlawful power." Since Constantine the Great, emperors had supervised the affairs of the Church, called and presided over councils, approved and revoked popes. Gregory's action in freeing the German princes from their oath of allegiance to Henry IV could only appear to the imperial party as an intolerable interference. Yet Gregory himself was not wrong when he asserted that he "reverted to the decrees and teachings of the holy fathers—decreeing nothing new, nothing of our own invention . . ." This challenge of the state was a revival of the original revolutionary tradition of Christianity such as it had been in its defiance of the Roman Empire before the reconciliation of the fourth century. And his assertion of the superiority of spiritual power over temporal had already been voiced by Pope Gelasius I as far back as the late fifth century.

The Search for a Compromise

The death of Gregory VII left the problem of lay investiture unresolved. His immediate successors were less intransigent than he but the issue once raised could not be disregarded. In 1111 Pope Paschal II even went so far as to propose that the Church be freed from lay control by the abandonment of all its temporal possessions. Such a drastic step was acceptable to no one, but soon after a compromise solution was finally reached by the Emperor Henry V and Pope Calixtus II in the Concordat of Worms signed in 1122. Under the terms of this agreement, the investiture of churchmen was split in two. The emperor kept the right of investing them with their temporal possessions but their spiritual consecration was reserved exclusively for the Church. On the face of it the Concordat of Worms was a compromise, but in reality it contained a victory for the Church. The emperor had been forced to abandon some of his traditional prerogatives in favor of the Church and the power and dignity of the papacy was thereby enhanced. Another alteration brought by the Concordat into the former state of affairs was in its conception of ecclesiastical dignity. Formerly the authority of a churchman had been simultaneously spiritual and temporal; by its institution of a double investiture, once by the secular powers and once by the Church, the Concordat split that which had never been divided before.

THE CRUSADES

The compromise of Worms had provided a solution for the immediate question of lay investiture, but the more serious question raised by Gregory VII, that of the superiority of spiritual authority over temporal power, still remained unresolved. This problem was to agitate Europe for the whole of the next century. Into this new controversy the pope brought a position of far greater prestige than had been his before. Some of this new authority was due to the partial victory won at Worms, but much of it was also due to the papal leadership of the great religious movement of the late eleventh and twelfth centuries known as the Crusades.

Church Sponsored Movements in the Ninth and Tenth Centuries

The reawakening of spiritual values in the western world which brought about the Cluniac reform had been attended by a number of other religious manifestations through which the growing influence of the Church could be observed. As far back as the ninth and tenth centuries, associations to promote the Peace of God had been organized with episcopal blessing. The members of these associations banded together to provide protection against robber barons and to prevent the wanton attack of peaceful populations and the destruction of undefended settlements. At the same time, the Church promoted the idea of the Truce of God by which all fighting was forbidden on holy days and during the holy seasons of the year, such as Christmas and Easter. Neither of these movements were completely successful but they introduced some order and humanity into the generally lawless society of the earlier feudal period.

Far more important than either of these undertakings was to be the enormous surge of spiritual enthusiasm at the end of the eleventh century which was to produce the Crusades. The idea of a Christian war against the infidel and of the freeing of the Holy Land from Muslim domination was not altogether a new idea in this period. It had been suggested by both Sylvester II and Gregory VII. The campaign of the Emperor Heraclius against the Persians in 626 and particularly the reconquest of Syria by the Macedonian emperors in the tenth century had been conceived of as holy wars. None of these, however, came near the scope and fervor of the eleventh century.

The First Crusade

In November 1095 Pope Urban II at the Council of Clermont in France called upon Christendom to free the Holy Sepulchre of Christ from the Turks who had overrun Syria some ten years earlier, capturing the cities of Antioch and Jerusalem. The response to the call of the pope was unprecedented. Nobles

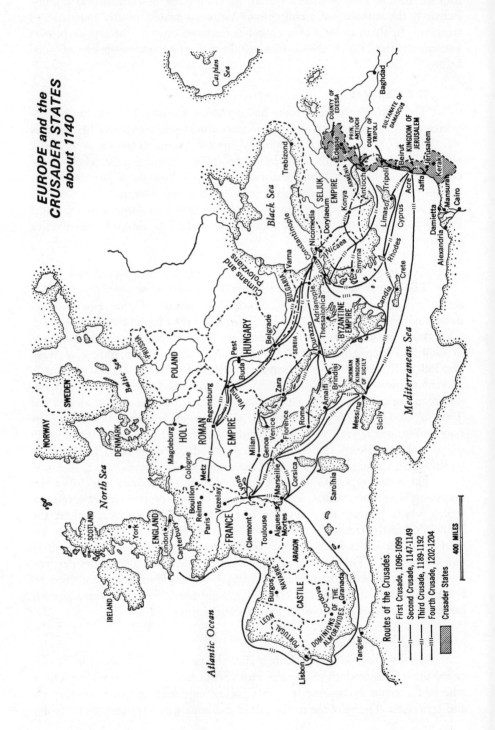

EUROPE and the
CRUSADER STATES
about 1140

Routes of the Crusades

——— First Crusade, 1096-1099
—+++— Second Crusade, 1147-1149
—•••— Third Crusade, 1189-1192
—|||— Fourth Crusade, 1202-1204
▧ Crusader States

400 MILES

and peasants, laymen and clerics, men, women and children, even the old and the crippled sought to take the cross and set out on the distant journey to Jerusalem. The attempts of the simple folk ended in disaster. Unprepared, badly guided, wandering through lands unknown to them which they looted for supplies, they never came within sight of their goal but were exterminated long before. Such were the fates of the Peoples' Crusade led by Peter the Hermit, as later, of the still more tragic Children's Crusade.

It was only a year after Clermont that the real First Crusade, composed of knights and barons, set out. The main contingents of the Crusaders were in no sense a disorganized rabble such as the groups that had preceded them. They were highly trained military contingents serving under their feudal overlords and led by some of the greatest nobles in Western Europe: Duke Godfrey de Bouillon of Lower Lorraine, Hugh de Vermandois, brother of the King of France, Duke Robert of Normandy, Counts Robert of Flanders, Stephen of Blois, and Raymond of Toulouse as well as the two Norman princes of Sicily, Bohemond and Tancred. Accompanying them as the pope's representative or legate was Bishop Adhemar of Le Puy. The absence of any royal figure, however, was to have considerable importance in the future.

The Crusaders in Constantinople and the East

The route of the Crusaders led them across Germany, down the Danube, across Hungary and Bulgaria to Constantinople. Here the Emperor, Alexis I Comnenus, received the leaders who, with the sole exception of Raymond of Toulouse, swore allegiance to him and swore to return to the Empire the lands lost to the Turks. In exchange the emperor promised them assistance and supplies. At first, the relations between the Latins and the Greeks were reasonably satisfactory, although their churches had separated from each other nearly half a century earlier as a result of the Great Schism. With Byzantine assistance the Crusaders safely crossed Asia Minor, defeating the Turks at Nicaea and Dorylaeum, and entered Syria through the pass of the Cilician gates. Here, however, the relations between the two powers took a sharp turn for the worse. At the siege of Antioch the Crusaders accused Alexis I of having abandoned his allies. Consequently they refused to return to him the captured city which had only recently belonged to the Empire. In Alexis' eyes this was a breach of the oath sworn to him by the Crusaders and a confirmation of his distrust of the Normans, his traditional enemies, who were among the leaders of the expedition. The imperial contingents returned to Constantinople. Alone, the Crusaders moved south and on July 13, 1099, they finally stormed into the city of Jerusalem in an attack which shocked later sensibilities by its savagery.

The Kingdom of Jerusalem

After their reconquest of the Holy Land the Crusaders set out to rule it according to the traditions to which they were accustomed. Godfrey de Bouillon refused to wear the royal crown offered to him in the city in which Christ had worn the crown of thorns, and was satisfied with the title of Advocate of the Sepulchre, but his brother and successor Baldwin had no such scruples. A feudal kingdom with its capital at Jerusalem was established to last with many vicis situdes a little less than two centuries. Together with the Kingdom of Jerusalem the Principality of Antioch, the Counties of Edessa and Tripoli and a number of smaller principalities were established to satisfy the ambitions of the Crusading leaders. In addition, special orders of military monks, such as the Templars and the Hospitallers, were created later for the defense of the Holy Land. Throughout its existence, the Kingdom of Jerusalem exhibited the major flaw of a feudal monarchy. Its king, crippled by the innumerable rights of his vassals, had but a shadowy authority over them and never succeeded in welding his kingdom into a single unit capable of resisting the growing Muslim opposition which culminated in the recapture of Jerusalem in 1187 and the expulsion of the Crusaders from their last stronghold in Palestine in 1292.

The Significance of the Crusades

Any final conclusion as to the importance of the crusading movement is still a matter for active discussion among scholars, but the enormous shift of population from the West to the East which accompanied the Crusades could not fail to have some effect on contemporary society. The Crusaders met in Constantinople and in the Muslim East civilizations far more advanced and refined than their own and naturally learned much from them. The demand for the new luxury goods of the East stimulated commerce, and the maritime Italian cities of Venice and Genoa grew rich on this traffic and through ferrying western knights to Palestine. Unruly knights, unprovided with lands in western Europe, found an outlet for their activities in the new principalities, and both order and royal control increased proportionately in the West. Intellectual activity was stimulated through new contacts. The most immediate effect, however, was on the position of the Papacy. The Council of Clermont had been called by Urban II. It was he who had preached the Crusade. Since the secular rulers of Europe, kings and emperor, had failed to join the movement, the pope, through his legate Adhemar, was its leader. At the time of the foundation of the Kingdom of Jerusalem, the princes of the Holy Land including their king had taken the oath of allegiance to the pope as their overlord and so held their lands directly from him and not a king or emperor. The claim of Gregory VII seemed to be vindicated. The Crusade had been a joint undertaking of all Christians, consequently its leader the pope must also be the leader of all of Christendom.

The Later Crusades

The spiritual upsurge which had produced the First Crusade was not spent with the capture of Jerusalem. The crusading states needed assistance against the Muslim counterattack and enthusiasm remained high for a time in the West. In the middle of the twelfth century the dominant figure in the Church was not so much the pope as the abbot Bernard of Clairvaux. St. Bernard was one of the greatest mystics of the medieval period and the great leader of the Cistercian order which brought to the Benedictine rule a reform still tighter than that of Cluny which it considered insufficient. Among his many activities St. Bernard urged the Christian rulers to assist the Kingdom of Jerusalem threatened by the Muslim recapture of the County of Edessa. In obedience to his call the kings Louis VII of France and Conrad III of Germany set out in 1147 on the rescue expedition of the Second Crusade.

The zeal of St. Bernard was enormous and the achievements of his Cistercians of major importance for European civilization. The western rulers were now supporting the crusading movement which they had neglected earlier. But the Second Crusade ended in failure. One of the main causes for this failure was the growing estrangement between the Latins and Constantinople. The princes of the Holy Land maintained reasonably good relations with Byzantium. The Emperor Manuel Comnenus succeeded in obtaining the return of Antioch, and he may even have received the oath of allegiance of the King of Jerusalem. To the Latins coming from Europe, however, the Greeks were heretics and traitors not to be trusted by true Christians. The immediate result of this lack of co-operation was the failure of the Crusaders to cross Asia Minor as had been done by their predecessors. Disobeying the guides provided by the Emperor Manuel whom he did not trust, Conrad III fell into an ambush and saw his army annihilated. By the time the kings reached Jerusalem, they could accomplish but little before their return home.

The Third Crusade, in spite of a glittering array of leaders which included King Philip Augustus of France, Richard the Lionheart of England, and the Emperor Frederick Barbarossa, was equally unsuccessful. Not only was the hostility of the Greeks now so great that the Latins, with the exception of the emperor, no longer dared to cross their territory but were forced to sail to Palestine, thereby putting themselves in the hands of the Italian republics, but the leaders quarreled among themselves. The emperor drowned accidentally in eastern Asia Minor and the conflict between the two surviving kings was so acute that it prevented their cooperation in the retaking of Jerusalem whose fall to Saladin had provoked their Crusade. Philip Augustus returned to France in 1191 and in the autumn of the following year Richard sailed away from Palestine abandoning what was left of the Kingdom of Jerusalem to its fate.

Even more disgraceful was the Fourth Crusade of 1204. The Crusaders indebted to Venice for their transportation, sought to pay off their obligation by destroying one of her commercial rivals, the city of Zara on the Dalmatian coast. Excommunicated by the pope for this action, the Crusaders then sailed to the scandal of Christendom not to Palestine but to take and sack Constantinople. The booty of 1204 enriched many a western city but the capture of a Christian city was a far cry from the ideals of Urban II and St. Bernard and the violent act of the Crusaders destroyed all future hope for the reunion of the two halves of the Christian world.

The Fourth Crusade was a disgrace to its contemporaries and the succeeding Crusades also failed to reach or save the Holy Land, but the entire movement should not be judged by its ultimate failure. We have already seen that the Crusades did much to alter the aspect of Europe and particularly to increase the prestige of the Church. The reasons for which men took the cross were numerous and some may not bear close scrutiny, but the religious aspect of the Crusades cannot be disregarded as it has occasionally been done. The greed of the looters of Constantinople should not be confused with the fervor of the Council of Clermont.

THE FINAL STRUGGLE FOR SUPREMACY IN THE WEST

The thirty-odd years between the signing of the Concordat of Worms and the imperial coronation of Frederick I Barbarossa in 1154 were not marked by any other major advance in the conflict between the Church and the State. The papacy was handicapped by disputed elections and a series of anti-popes so that the leadership of the Church was found at Clairvaux with St. Bernard rather than at Rome. The Empire likewise suffered from the conflict which arose after the death of Henry V without heirs and which opposed his nephews, the Hohenstaufen or Ghibellines, to the descendents of his elected successor, the Guelfs. In the second half of the century, however, the quarrel broke out anew with greater intensity. In a favorite image of medieval political theory, taken from the Gospel of Luke, Christ had given two swords for the rule of mankind, the sword spiritual and the sword temporal. For the first time St. Bernard interpreted this to mean that both swords had been given to the pope, who then delegated the temporal sword to the emperor.

The Empire at the Accession of Frederick Barbarossa

The second phase of the great controversy was played on a political checkerboard complicated by a number of circumstances which had not been present in the days of Gregory VII and Henry IV. In Germany, the quarrels of the Guelfs and the Ghibellines divided the allegiance of the princes and sharply reduced the power of the emperor. It is true that the young and ambitious Frederick I of Hohenstaufen had been unanimously elected King of the Germans and enthusiastically received, but his power was badly shaken and his Guelf enemies merely were biding their time waiting for a suitable opportunity to revolt. Hence, Frederick looked to Italy both for the authority which he would receive with the imperial coronation and for the power needed to curb the German princes.

Italy, however, was in no better condition than Germany. The growth of the commercial cities of Lombardy in northern Italy resulting from the increasing trade with the East brought forth a restless, ambitious class of merchants and artisans who demanded some say in the government of their community. They revolted against the local lords and founded independent communes. Since in most cases the lords of the cities were bishops, the agitation often took the form of an attack on the Church and of heresy. In northern Italy the *Patarini,* or Poor Men, denounced the growing wealth and power of the Church and demanded a return to apostolic poverty. In Rome itself, a commune was founded in 1145 headed by Arnold of Brescia who was in sympathy with the ideas of the *Patarini* and demanded self-government from the pope who was virtually his prisoner. The opposition of Arnold and of the *Patarini* to the Church does not imply, however, that the communes created in the Italian cities were necessarily all in favor of the emperor. The situation was still more difficult. On the one hand many of the bishops in north Italy continued to be the emperor's men so that any antagonism against them was automatically directed against the emperor as well. On the other hand, the cities were jealous of each other, so that neighbors would usually be found on opposite sides of the political fence. Thus, the great Lombard city of Milan could always count on the enmity of the nearby cities of Pavia, Cremona, and Como. It was against this shifting and complicated background that Frederick I entered Italy in 1154 to receive the imperial crown from Pope Adrian IV.

The Temporary Alliance of the Papacy and the Empire

At the time of the first appearance of Frederick I in Italy his interests were allied to those of the papacy. Frederick could only be crowned by the pope, while Adrian IV needed a protector against the commune of Arnold of Brescia. Consequently the year 1154 saw a brief alliance between the two traditional enemies, though at their first meeting the emperor had ominously begun by refusing to hold the pope's stirrup, as was demanded by custom. The subsequent relations were more cordial. Adrian IV crowned Frederick and the following year the new emperor hunted down Arnold of Brescia and had him executed. Once their respective goals had been achieved, however, the cooperation between the two opponents soon broke down.

The Diets of Besançon (1157) and Roncaglia (1158)

The first open break came with a small incident over a letter during the meeting of the imperial diet held by Frederick I at Besançon in 1157. The pope wrote that he had granted *beneficia* to Frederick and this was translated to the infuriated emperor as meaning fiefs, with the attendant legal implications, and the papal legate added fuel to the fire by asserting that the emperor was indeed the vassal of the pope. The incident was hastily glossed over and Adrian IV, who was still having trouble with the Roman commune, assured Frederick that all he had meant by *beneficium* was kindness, but the issue was clear. The emperor refused to recognize the superiority of the papacy and the former allies would be opponents at the first opportunity.

The Lombard cities were similarly antagonized by Frederick in the following year at the Diet held at Roncaglia. The emperor, reasserting the rights which had been allowed to lapse, refused to recognize the growing independence of the communes. He decreed that henceforth the emperor would control municipal elections and revenues and appoint a representative as governor or *podesta* in each city. The total destruction of the city of Milan, which had dared resist, temporarily cowed the opposition but in Lombardy as at Rome antagonism to the emperor continued to smoulder and the northern cities began to band together in a Lombard League.

The Failure of the Empire

The actions of Frederick at the Diets of Besançon and Roncaglia are readily understandable. The emperor could not admit his inferiority to the pope if he was to keep the respect of the German princes, nor could he forego the support and wealth of the Lombard cities if he intended to carry out his policy of consolidating and unifying his realm, but in the long run these actions were disastrous. A common enmity to the Ghibelline emperor drove the pope and the Lombard League into each other's arms and the name of Frederick's German opponents, the Guelfs, was also extended to his new Italian enemies. In 1159 the situation was aggravated by the election of Pope Alexander III of the legate who had defied Frederick at Besançon.

The growing opposition of the Lombard League which lay across the path to Rome turned the conflict between the emperor and the pope into a struggle for the control of Italy. Victory was not easily won by either side. Repeatedly Frederick brought victorious armies down from Germany only to be forced to retreat once again. Finally in 1176 the Lombard League, supported by the papacy, annihilated the imperial army at the battle of Legnano, Frederick was forced into a humiliating reconciliation with Alexander III at Venice the following year and at the Peace of Constance in 1183 he had to relinquish most of the prerogatives claimed by him at Roncaglia. Thereafter, until his death in 1190 on the Third Crusade, Frederick, though he did not concede defeat, concerned himself primarily with the affairs of Germany.

The Victory of the Papacy

The victory of Alexander III over Barbarossa was not as complete as he might have hoped, and indeed during the last decade of the twelfth century the papacy found itself in a most critical position. This reversal was due to a master stroke of the old emperor who in 1186 succeeded in having his son and heir, Henry VI, already recognized as King of Germany, married to Constance, the sole heiress of the Norman ruler of southern Italy. The marriage of Henry and Constance not only took from the papacy the Norman allies on whom it had counted since the eleventh century, but it trapped the pope between the two halves of Henry VI's new realm. Had Henry lived he might have succeeded in carrying out his father's ambitious program in Italy, but within eight years he was dead at the age of thirty-two leaving a child of four, the future Frederick II.

The turmoil in which the Empire found itself at the premature death of Henry VI was fully exploited by the new pope Innocent III (1198–1216), one of the dominant figures of the medieval Church. Innocent III was not a revolutionary as had been Gregory VII but he believed in all the aspects of the Gregorian program which he was to carry out. Commenting on the text of Matthew XXII, 21, he asserted:

Render unto Caesar the things which are Caesar's, and unto God the things which are God's, but it remains nevertheless that God is above Caesar and the Pope above the emperor, being the vicar of Christ.

Even more ominously the pope chose as the text for the sermon which he preached on his accession the verse from Jeremiah I 10:

See I have this day set thee over the nations and over the kingdoms to root out, and to pull down, and to destroy and to pull down, to build and to plant.

Innocent III soon demonstrated that he meant exactly what he had said. As the tutor of the little Frederick II, he administered southern Italy as a fief. In Germany, the imperial crown was disputed between Henry VI's brother Philip of Swabia and the Guelf claimant Otto of Brunswick. So great was the authority of the pope by this time that the German princes appealed to him as an arbiter, and even when Innocent changed his mind and shifted from Otto to Philip his decision was generally respected.

Innocent III never made the claim that the pope had the right to interfere in temporal affairs. He still saw the sphere of his activity as spiritual but as he pointed out "it is my province to judge when a sin is committed and it is my duty to prevent a public scandal." Basing himself upon this belief, the pope intervened in the internal affairs of most realms. Before his death, the kingdoms of England, Aragon, and Portugal had acknowledged themselves Innocent's direct feudal vassals and the papacy seemed well on its way to the claim that its authority extended over every sphere of human activity.

FURTHER READING

The best study available at present on the struggle between the Church and the Empire is G. Tellenbach, *Church, State and Christian Society at the Time of the Investiture Contest* (1940). For different interpretations of the controversy see the series of essays in S. Williams, ed., *The Gregorian Epoch—Reformation, Revolution, Reaction?* (1964). A survey of the Salian and Hohenstaufen empires can be found in G. Barraclough, *The Origins of Modern Germany* (1947), and for the situation in northern Italy, see W. Butler, *The Lombard Communes* (1906).

For the reform of the Church see the general survey in M. W. Baldwin, *The Medieval Church* (1953), and particularly the excellent section on "The Ordering of the Christian Life," in R. Southern, *The Making of the Middle Ages* (1953), a work valuable for the whole of the revival of the West after the tenth century. On the early center of the reform movement see, J. Evans, *Monastic Life at Cluny* (1931), and on the leadership of the papacy, W. Ullman, *The Growth of Papal Government* (1955). The standard biography in English of Pope Gregory VII is A. J. MacDonald's *Hildebrand, a Life of Gregory VII* (1932). *The Correspondence of Pope Gregory VII* has been translated by E. Emerton (1932), and the main documents of the controversy can also be found in J. H. Robinson, *Readings in European History I* (1904), which gives a larger selection than most collections.

A good survey of the Crusades is given by S. Runciman, *A History of the Crusades*, 3 vols. (1951–4) and a concise introduction to the subject can be found in R. Newhall, *The Crusades* (1927). On the Crusader states, see D. C. Munro, *The Kingdom of the Crusaders* (1935), and also J. La Monte, *Feudal Monarchy in the Latin Kingdom of Jerusalem* (1932). Among the sources on the Crusades available in English a sampling will illustrate the transformation of the movement with the passage of time: Fulcher of Chartres, *Chronicle of the First Crusade,* tr. M. E. McGinty (1941); William of Tyre, *History of Deeds Done Beyond the Sea,* tr. E. H. Babcock and A. C. Krey, 2 vols. (1943); and Villehardouin, *Memoires of the Crusades,* tr. F. Margiol (1933) on the capture of Constantinople.

4 · Feudal Monarchy at Its Height

By the last decades of the twelfth century, the pattern of royal authority in Germany, England, and France was becoming clear. In Germany, the monarchy would give way, and Europe from the Rhine to the Oder would fragment into its constituent parts, bound together by a monarchy in name only with a king stripped of most of his power. The cause was the centrifugal force of feudalism. Unlike the kings of France and England, the German emperors found few ways to make feudalism work for monarchy, and they found no way to limit its growth. In the end they watched royal authority slip from their hands into the hands of literally hundreds of great and petty princes, ecclesiastical lords, knights, and free-city magistrates. The first of the three great western states to establish central government was the first to lose it. Germany became "an anarchy in the form of a monarchy" and remained such until the nineteenth century.

In England and France, the institution of monarchy grew stronger each year. The English and French kings had set their thrones on feudal foundations, had placed themselves at the apex of the feudal hierarchy, and no one by this time dared challenge their right. Indeed, few Englishmen or Frenchmen would have wanted to do so, since the feudal monarchy benefited everyone. The kings were, after all, no more than "first among equals," legally bound by a contractual relationship to those below them in the hierarchy, to whom they owed justice and protection, and from whom they were expected to take counsel. Kings were subject to law and could not act arbitrarily. Moreover, they were supposed to "live of their own," as the English phrased it, that is, on the resources of their private domain. They could appeal for supplementary aid in cases of emergency, but such an appeal was by its very nature extraordinary. Finally, in time of war they were expected to rely on the traditional feudal levies and not hire mercenary troops whose ethics and social position were questionable. In short, medieval kings ruled in cooperation with their vassals in the accepted feudal manner.

THE CONFLICT BETWEEN FEUDALISM AND MONARCHY

For any king worth his salt, however, these were galling restrictions. A king was obviously in a special category, above the feudal herd, and smart young Roman lawyers, their heads filled with notions of "sovereignty," were ready to prove it. He wanted to treat his people as *subjects,* to be able to exercise his authority over them freely according to his pleasure. He also hungered after glory, which meant for him display and war. And to fight wars he needed a reliable and numerous army and plenty of available cash—neither of which the feudal system provided. It was inevitable that he seek ways of getting soldiers and money outside the normal feudal channels. He resorted to breaking feudal contracts or at least bending them badly, to encroaching on the financial preserves of the Church, and to devising entirely new sources of revenue usually involving the burgeoning towns and their rich merchants and manufacturers. These activities created the biggest problems for the English and French monarchs in the next centuries, for royalty could advance only at the expense of feudalism. The special rights and privileges which gave the feudal lords, the Church, and the chartered towns independent political power had to give way—though not quickly or without resistance. The conflict was long and hard, and each side won many battles, but economics and the evolution of society was on royalty's side. Out of the conflict came new political ideas and institutions; a clearer definition of monarchy and parliaments are two examples that will be discussed.

We must keep in mind several points while studying this conflict. For one thing, the participants—the kings and their opponents—were not aware that it was taking place or at least not in the way a historian would describe it. The policies of these kings were personal, expedient, and rarely the result of conscious planning. Moreover, they were simple policies on the whole and government was not very complex. If a king was strong and ambitious, he wanted power and glory and he asserted the royal rights. To contemporaries, most of whom preferred the status quo, such a king was often "bad." Boy kings, or kings who were weak in mind or spirit, usually ruled with mildness and earned the adjective "good." The reign of a feeble king frequently witnessed a feudal reaction, a political retrogression as far as the progress of monarchy was concerned. In other words—and this leads to another important point—a great deal of medieval, and indeed early modern, history may be correctly viewed in terms of the character of individual kings.

GERMANY: HENRY V TO FREDERICK II

The emperors of the Holy Roman Empire in the twelfth century were in no position to increase royal authority by trying out these newer conceptions and devices of monarchy. Rather, they were finding it increasingly difficult to hold on to the authority they already possessed. Henry IV had not rebuilt a strong central government because he could not. By incurring the enmity of Pope Gregory VII, he lost support of the reform party in the German Church and provided a cause around which the power-hungry German princes could rally against him.[1] Furthermore, his excommunication cost him dearly in

[1] On the Investiture Struggle between Henry IV and Gregory VII, see the previous chapter.

prestige; indeed, his defiance of accepted religious standards removed from the German monarchy its last vestiges of priestliness. We have noted the advantage their sacerdotal quality gave to the kings of France and England. That emperors after Henry IV had no such quality was one of the chief reasons for their failure to win out against German feudalism.

Guelfs and Ghibellines

Feudalism made long strides in the reigns of Henry IV's successors. His son, Henry V (1106–1125), continued his policy of enlarging the family properties in Saxony and Franconia and paid little attention to the rest of Germany. Henry V died without a direct heir, ending the long rule of the Salian House. The princes, whose independent power had been waxing steadily, took advantage of the situation to elect as emperor a man whose weakness seemed to offer no impediment to their ambitions. Lothair (1125–1137) found his principal support in the papal reform party, enemies of the Salians, who stood generally for a German Church free of imperial control and for feudal particularism. They were called "Welfs," after the Bavarian family into which Lothair married his daughter. This name has come down to us in the Italian form, "Guelf." A smaller party was made up of those who backed the Salian claimant, Frederick of Hohenstaufen, nephew of Henry V. This party retained the traditional policy of strong imperial government grounded on a subservient church. Its nickname, "Waibling," after a favorite Hohenstaufen residence, has survived as "Ghibelline," again the Italian form.

As emperor, Lothair proved something more than a figurehead, increasing his wealth and prestige tremendously through a marriage alliance. His Guelf supporters, in fright, elected on his death the Ghibelline younger brother of Frederick of Hohenstaufen, Conrad III (1137–1152). This time their choice was a good one, for under Conrad the imperial power virtually disappeared. Germany fell into political disorder, and the princes and nobles rapidly enlarged and consolidated their feudal gains. Their method was simple: usurpation of imperial and ecclesiastical rights by force, by subterfuge, and by default. Offices and fiefs, held of the emperor at his pleasure or for life, they turned into hereditary proprietary holdings. They seized crown lands, assumed the prerogatives of justice and taxation, and built castles to guard their loot against pirates like themselves. They took over monastery lands, treating them in much the same way. They made lesser lords and churchmen dependent on themselves, and they transformed their free tenants into serfs. They created a feudalism so strong that even the exceptionally able Frederick Barbarossa could not appreciably weaken it.

Frederick Barbarossa

The German monarchy was doomed, then, when that great Hohenstaufen came to the imperial throne in 1152. He did all he could to save it; indeed, even if he had not expended time and energy on a simultaneous Italian policy, he could have done little more. Frederick I Barbarossa had both Guelf and Ghibelline in his heritage and was the compromise candidate of those Germans who desired domestic peace even at the price of personal ambition. Frederick was a realist. From a family whose fortune had been made in the recent past of political chaos, he understood the avaricious habits of princes and nobles and the problems of a much diminished crown. He knew he needed the help of the great men of Germany to revive the monarchy; certainly he was not himself powerful enough to attack their now-entrenched feudal privileges. Hence, he cooperated with them, in effect sharing the rule of Germany with them. He may have intended ultimately to turn them into proper vassals and rule through them, in the manner of a true feudal monarch. But he succeeded only in agreeing to the limits they set for the crown, for by bowing to feudal custom, he gave legal sanction to the usurpation of royal rights.

Nor did Frederick succeed in creating a royal domain from which he might expand royal power as the kings of France had done. In his own lands of Swabia, the Rhineland, and Burgundy, he was able to revive and enforce his authority, establish a central government staffed by loyal *ministeriales,* and regain control and support of the bishops and abbots. But further accumulation of territory was virtually barred by the principle of *Leihezwang* which made it customary for lands escheated to the crown to be granted out to new vassals within a year and a day. Thus, the German princes and nobles held a fixed amount of land which they did not have to yield. The emperor was just another landlord, not the practical head of an operating feudal hierarchy.

On Frederick Barbarossa's death, his son Henry was elected emperor. Henry VI ruled only seven years (1190–1197), and his own death without heirs precipitated another constitutional crisis. The Ghibelline party elected Frederick's brother Philip of Swabia, who was challenged by the Guelf candidate, Otto of Brunswick. During the next eighteen years, the trend toward political particularism in Germany continued, as each claimant sought supporters by means of gifts of crown lands and royal rights. Pope Innocent III stepped in to settle the dispute in favor of Otto in return for Otto's renunciation of the traditional imperial church policy. Upon his election, however, Otto IV (1209–1215) once more took the reins of the German Church, and Innocent threw his support to Frederick of Hohenstaufen, young son of Henry VI. Frederick was confirmed as emperor with papal blessing in 1215.

Frederick II

Frederick II (1215–1250) was one of the fascinating personalities of the Middle Ages. Indeed, his modern conception of kingship, his ruthless application of power in political affairs, his religious skepticism, his broad cultural interests, the splendor of his cosmopolitan court in Sicily: all of these things have led historians to name him the first "Renaissance man." His long struggle with the papacy (as we have seen in the previous chapter) dominated his era. His goal was the old imperial dream, to restore the imperial power in Italy, and he sacrificed most of what little imperial power remained in Germany to that end. He made no attempt to check the ambitions of the princes and nobles; rather he confirmed the status quo and even gave them more

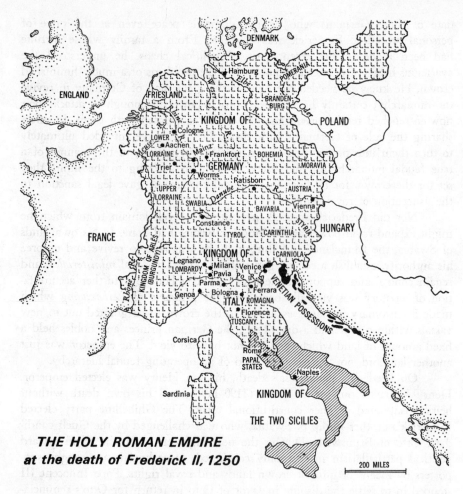

THE HOLY ROMAN EMPIRE
at the death of Frederick II, 1250

200 MILES

independent authority in return for their tacit support of himself, his son and heir, and his Italian adventures. In point of fact, Frederick was repelled by Germany and despised Germans as uncouth barbarians. His reign marked the definitive close of imperial greatness in Germany and the beginning of the age of the princes. A few later emperors tried to revive imperial fortunes, but without a hope of success. The crown of the Caesars became but a symbol of a glorious, vanished past.

ENGLAND: RICHARD I TO EDWARD II

Henry II, a tough, intelligent, hardworking king, had brought order to the realm following the civil wars of Stephen's reign and had done much to further the cause of strong monarchy. England was once again united as it had been under the Normans. Henry would have no peer among English kings for many generations. His heirs were his two sons, the legendary Richard I, "the Lionhearted," and the notorious John "Lackland," both of whom we know best, though inaccurately, from the stories of Robin Hood. Richard I

(1189–1199) was a handsome, irresponsible man, with the sensuality of his father and mother, Eleanor of Acquitaine, and a good deal of his mother's charm and artistic bent—he wrote excellent French and Provençal poetry. He was also brave and warlike, loving the chivalric life and a good battle whatever the cost. Indeed, he was the embodiment of all the best and worst in the feudal ideal. Most of his ten-year reign he spent away from England, in France and the Holy Land, fighting for his Angevin inheritance and his Church. He won his nickname on a Crusade and died of bloodpoisoning while besieging a French town. He left the English government to his secretaries and to clerks, notably Hubert Walter, archbishop of Canterbury, who continued the steady accretion of royal power begun by Henry II. Richard's chief concern was money for war and he went far toward draining England dry, angering particularly his vassals-in-chief who were forced to pay huge reliefs and other feudal dues. There were rumblings of protest, but the barons liked and respected Richard and did not rebel against him.

The Weakening of English Monarchy under King John

Feudal rebellion was left for the reign of John (1199–1216). John has been the target of hatred and abuse since his own time. Some have called him mean, cowardly, vulgar, even mad; others have been content simply to call him a failure. Certainly he was not the man his father was, nor was he the equal of his great antagonists, Philip Augustus of France and Pope Innocent III. But he was more conscientious and hard working than Richard though his unpleasant personality obscured his good qualities in any comparison with his popular brother. As one recent commentator has said, his "problems were immense and his near-successes brilliant."[2] The problems were his legacy: an empty treasury, a restless baronage, a Church chafing under royal control, and huge possessions in France almost impossible to defend. And his failures stand out more clearly in retrospect than they did to contemporaries who could neither perceive that most of the gains monarchy had made were slipping away under the rule of John and his feeble son, Henry III, nor foresee that in the long run a weakened monarchy would work to the benefit of the English people by giving a start toward parliamentary government.

John had hardly become king when his carelessness offered Philip Augustus of France an opportunity to take Normandy, Anjou, and Maine, the three large French fiefs John held of Philip. Using John's refusal to recognize his overlordship, Philip attacked John and defeated him wherever they met. The fighting lasted several years and was climaxed by Philip's decisive victory over a combined English and German army under Emperor Otto IV at Bouvines in 1214. To these large territories Philip's successor added Poitou in 1224, leaving the humiliated English only a strip of France along the coast of Gascony and Guienne to show for their once-great Angevin inheritance.

John's quarrel with Innocent III also ended in the king's defeat, though he emerged with some of the spoils. The question at issue was a fundamental

---

[2] F. Barlow, *The Feudal Kingdom of England, 1042–1216* (London and New York: Longmans, Green, 1955), p. 395.

one: whether the king or the pope had primary responsibility for appointing high ecclesiastical officials of the English Church. John believed, with justification, that prelates such as the archbishop of Canterbury enjoyed too much political power and controlled too much property to be wholly independent of the crown. Innocent, also with justification, was determined to secure the spiritual freedom of his bishops. After nearly a decade of acrimonious dispute, during which time England was placed under interdict and John himself excommunicated, the king accepted Stephen Langton, the pope's choice to fill the see of Canterbury. John also agreed to hold England in fief as the pope's vassal. But, in fact, John retained control over the appointment of English churchmen while recognizing the pope's right to confirm them in their offices. He also kept most of the Church revenues he had channeled into the royal treasury during the six-year period of interdict. Thus, the result was a compromise though it was a serious blow to the royal prestige.

The Magna Carta

The barons' revolt of 1215 and the crown's acceptance of Magna Carta climaxed John's reign. The great lords of the realm had never been happy with John, who was arrogant and arbitrary. The lords charged that he turned his back on tradition and the law by denying them a voice in his government. He also squeezed every penny in aids and relief from his feudal contracts with them and continued his predecessor's practice of taking "scutage," money payments in lieu of knights' service. John's recent defeats at the hands of Philip Augustus had emptied his treasury, and his loss of English lands in France had made the barons contemptuous of his person and his rule. The barons could look forward once more to paying through the nose to a king for whom they had lost all respect. Furthermore, most barons were opposed to his running battle with the Church and were jealous of his predilection for placing "foreigners," especially Normans, in government offices. English churchmen held many of the views of the barons, but were particularly incensed at John's highhanded treatment of the Church.

Pure selfishness, then, together with a sincere desire to regulate the crown's relationship to its subjects combined to drive many barons and churchmen into open revolt. The signal for the uprising was the defeat of Bouvines in 1214. After negotiations between the two sides failed to bring agreement, the barons formally renounced their oaths of homage to John, and he was forced to submit. On the field of Runnymede near Windsor in June 1215, the king affixed his seal to a long statement of baronial rights which had been prepared under the guidance of Archbishop Langton. This was Magna Carta, the Great Charter, the most famous single document in English history. Most of its sixty-three articles are purely feudal in character and applicable only to the immediate issues between John and his vassals-in-chief. For example, John guaranteed the "freedom" of the English Church, agreed to limit feudal dues and scutage to specified sums, and promised to ban "foreign" knights from the kingdom. Furthermore, all but a few articles concerned the baronage alone; the non-noble "knights of the shire" and businessmen of the towns reaped benefits from the Charter only later and indirectly.

The articles from which wider benefits derived were three, numbers 12, 14, and 39. Article 12 stated that no unusual scutage or aid "shall be imposed on our kingdom, unless by common counsel of the kingdom." Article 14 stated: "and for obtaining the common counsel of the kingdom anent the assessing of an aid . . . or of a scutage, we will cause to be summoned the arch-bishops, bishops, abbots, earls, and greater barons, severally by our letters; and we will moreover cause to be summoned . . . all others who hold of us in chief. . . ." These articles, which were not included in later reissues of the Charter even though they were observed by kings in practice, became the basis for parliamentary control of taxation. Article 39 stated that "no free man shall be taken or imprisoned, disseised [dispossessed] of his goods, or de-clared outlaw or exiled or harmed in any way and we will not advance against him or send anyone against him except by the loyal judgment of his peers according to the law of the land." This was not a new principle, but its in-clusion in Magna Carta gave it greater force and its explicit reference to all free men gave it broader scope. It is one of the foundation stones of our modern conception of the rights to "due process of law" and to protection against arbitrary actions by government.

Henry III and the Barons

The future held great things for Magna Carta, but for John it was simply an expedient to be ignored or repudiated as soon as possible. On his death in 1216, he was well on the way to suppressing the barons backed by the prestige of his new lord, Pope Innocent III, who had absolved John from his oath to them. But his son, Henry III (1216–1272), was a child on his ac-cession and remained throughout his life a weak and disinterested monarch, incapable of carrying out his father's plans. He confirmed the Charter and until he reached his majority left government to the barons. Then he turned from the barons to others he felt he could trust more fully, becoming prey to the whims of favorites and to the influence of the papal legates who virtually ruled England in the pope's name. The legates' principal concern was to raise funds and gain allies to support the papacy's struggle against the Hohenstaufen. The pious Henry was amenable, and money flowed from England to Rome. At the same time, he let his papal friends drag him into disastrous and ex-pensive foreign adventures, including one which aimed at seating his son Edmund on the throne of Sicily.

The result was to arouse once more the barons and the churchmen, again excluded from positions of influence and authority and burdened by heavy taxes which went to pay for unpopular policies. By nature, the great men of the realm were conservatives who favored cheap government and rule strictly according to law. Their opportunity came in 1258 when Henry was obliged to call on them to rescue him from his debts. Their answer was to demand re-forms, chiefly that they be given greater participation in government administra-tion and policymaking. The Provisions of Oxford (1258) placed England under the joint rule of the king and a "great council" of barons. It was retrogression of the worst sort from the point of view of strong monarchy, for the barons' political ideas were feudal anachronisms and most of their actions were motivated by a hatred of authority and a desire for self-aggrandizement. They tried, in effect, to establish the kind of feudalism never existent in England in which each would become a little king in his own barony. Their leader, Simon de Montfort, Earl of Leicester, was more statesmanlike, however. Supported by some of the barons and by many of the townsmen and knights, he made himself "protector," really dictator, of England after defeating and capturing the king at Lewes in May 1264. For fifteen months he ruled, only to be himself defeated and killed by the royal army under Henry's son, Prince Edward. The crown's revival began with the accession of Edward I in 1272.

Edward I and the Climax of Feudal Monarchy

The reign of Edward I (1272–1307) was the climax of feudal monarchy in England and one of the most significant reigns in the history of English monarchy. Edward was thirty-three when he gained the throne, active, resolute, everything a feudal king had to be to succeed in that day when personal qualities counted for so much. He was properly warlike, chivalrous, and courageous on the one hand; pious, just, and wise on the other. He was essentially a politician who knew how to restore and reinforce royal authority without appearing to trample on the privileges of his subjects. Indeed, he was careful to give lip service to the barons' traditional place in government. He was also deeply concerned about the general welfare and the greatness of the English state, and his policies were designed to promote both. Under his firm guidance the realm was consolidated and reorganized, judicial and administrative practices begun under his predecessors were regularized, and many feudal abuses were eliminated. Most important for the future, Edward made Parliament a regular part of the English government.

Like other strong kings of the Middle Ages, war was Edward's chief occupation and pleasure. But in his case war had constructive results for the realm. At home he first attacked Wales whose wild mountain people had for years been raiding the English border and retreating to the hills before the helpless English knights. He conceived the idea of using infantrymen, commoners armed with long-bows, from neighboring shires to garrison strategically placed castles. The conquest took most of his reign, but ended successfully with Wales divided into shires on the English style and the king's son bearing the title Prince of Wales. Welsh patriotism remained alive but Wales was never again independent. Edward's attempt to gain Scotland in the same way failed. Twice, in 1296 and 1305, he used a disputed claim to the Scottish throne to occupy the northern kingdom, only to be driven out both times. The hero of the Scots victory was Robert Bruce, who made his own royal claim good in 1314 by defeating an English army under Edward's son, Edward II, at Bannockburn.

Edward's domestic policy was aimed at strengthening the crown at the expense of the great men of the realm. His methods were to limit the barons' influence in government as much as possible and to assert his authority over all his subjects in the fields of justice, law-making, and finances. He was hard on the barons, forcing them to abide by the letter of their feudal contracts and making it plain that his wishes as overlord would be obeyed. He succeeded in recovering most of the royal rights the barons had usurped under Henry III. At the same time, he improved the administrative organs of the crown, staffing them for the most part with professional lawyers who were intelligent and loyal. As we have noted earlier, royal administration during the medieval period was rudimentary and ill-defined, deriving from the old feudal *curia regis,* or king's court and officials of the king's own household, called the "Wardrobe." By Edward's day a division into separate organs may be distinguished. The Exchequer, which dated from Henry I, was well-developed. Together with the Wardrobe treasurer (who was often treasurer of the Exchequer as well), the Exchequer regularly sat at Westminster, receiving the king's revenues, paying his debts, and keeping his accounts. Its administrative head was the Chancellor of the Exchequer. Other offices had also taken shape. The Chancery, from which issued writs initiating regular judicial proceedings, had also settled down at Westminster. Its chief, the Chancellor, was the highest judicial officer in the land, concerned particularly with grievances against the crown. He still kept the "great seal," but since he no longer travelled about with the court, the king now had a smaller "privy seal" of his own with which royal orders were authenticated. Edward's reign also saw the development of the "privy council," a group of intimate advisors to the crown which all but replaced the "great council" of barons and prelates. The great council was being transformed into "Parliament." This institution we shall examine a little later. Local administration, as in the past, was the responsibility of the sheriffs who collected the crown's revenues and maintained the public peace.

Edward I has been called, with some exaggeration, the "English Justinian." Certainly he was most interested in systematizing and standardizing England's judicial structure and the common law. There were three central royal courts by this time. The Court of Exchequer handled fiscal cases. The Court of Common Pleas tried civil cases between private persons. Traditionally, suits to which the king was a party had been tried in his presence but Edward abandoned the practice, establishing a third permanent court, the Court of King's Bench. This court also tried serious criminal cases. Important cases at the local level were still heard by itinerant justices representing the crown. All of the royal courts used common law. Edward contributed in another way to making common law the law of the realm. He checked the traditional practice of each justice more or less to invent his own law as needed by insisting that laws be made by statute only. During his reign he issued many legal statutes. Soon it became accepted that not even the king could issue such statutes except in full parliament. Many years passed before all local customs were eliminated but England, in contrast to France, was well on the way to becoming a country where a single law system prevailed. Nothing else was as important to the unity of the realm.

The Growth of Parliament

Edward's greatest contribution to the future of England was the Parliament. During his reign, the king's council of barons and prelates was transformed into a more representative body by the inclusion of knights of the shire and burgesses. A new institution was born. Historians trace the origins of Parliament to earlier reigns. The word "parliament" means simply "discussion," and barons and prelates had been called on to discuss problems confronting the king or to assent to aids and other feudal dues for revenue. Indeed, the "council" was a fixture of the feudal system, reiterated in Magna Carta. Knights, that is, non-noble landowners (usually but not necessarily soldiers) had also been summoned to court for similar purposes as early as the twelfth century, and the practice had become common by the reign of Henry III. Simon de Montfort's sturdiest allies were knights. The summoning of burgesses, that is, non-noble townsmen, began at a later date and only in 1265 did the king, again under pressure from Simon de Montfort, order that two men from each borough attend the council meeting of that year. The reason seems to have been simplification and improvement of taxation procedures. In the past, the crown's agents had levied taxes on chartered towns by striking bargains with each of them. Bringing their representatives all together, with representatives of the barons, prelates, and knights, was obviously easier and got results more quickly. In the early years of Edward's reign the knights and burgesses usually sat with the old council, now called the "Parliament."

It was the Parliament of 1295, the "Model Parliament," that regularized their position. Edward summoned it to ask for funds to prosecute the war with France. Philip the Fair had won back what remained of the Angevin Empire and was threatening to invade England. Quoting from Roman law, Edward declared that "what affects all should be approved by all," and that "common dangers should be met by means provided in common." Each sheriff was instructed to send two knights from his shire court and two burgesses from each city or borough in his shire. These would be joined at Westminster by barons and prelates. The only group of English left unrepresented were the serfs. As yet there was no clear separation between the "Lords Temporal and Spiritual" and the non-noble "Commons"; this division developed in the next generations. The Parliament became a body of two houses, a House of Lords and a House of Commons, in the fourteenth century. Though at first relatively insignificant, the Commons was to have the great role in the future, for it combined the vital elements of town and country. The knights and burgesses, allied politically, and in time socially and economically as well, would give to the Commons the strength and resiliency to survive every crisis and eventually to rule England.

This, of course, is not what Edward I had in mind when he began to strengthen Parliament. His purpose was certainly not to weaken royal authority. The Parliament possessed no sovereignty, could make no laws by itself, could do nothing more than discuss the requests put to it by the crown. Rather, Edward sought merely the convenience of such an assembly, the prestige it gave him, and the illusion it provided of popular support for his policies. However, he failed to foresee the inevitable. Within a few years it was generally recognized that only the king *in Parliament* could issue statutes of common law or levy taxes. The crown had created a monster that would be increasingly difficult to keep chained.

Edward II (1307–1327) was a pale shadow of his father, likeable, cultured, fond of poetry, but wholly ineffective as a ruler. Government fell once more into the hands of the barons as it would do whenever weak kings occupied the throne. But the Lords Ordainers, as the barons pompously styled themselves, were as incapable of ruling in the public interest as their predecessors had been in Henry III's day and their successors would later be. Their sole aim was to feather their own nests while avoiding responsibility. The climax came in 1327, when the king was forced to abdicate (he was murdered shortly afterwards) in favor of his young son, Edward III (1327–77).

FRANCE: PHILIP AUGUSTUS TO PHILIP THE FAIR

The French monarchy contrasted sharply in a number of respects with the English monarchy in the medieval period. The latter was characterized by a high degree of internal unity, by clear relationships between the king and his vassals, and by a well-developed royal administration. On the other hand, even after the size of the royal domain was quadrupled, France was characterized by disunity, by conflicting and unclear loyalties, and by a still primitive administration. However, the English kings were to a much greater extent dependent on their vassals-in-chief in governing their realm. Parliament was a vital part of government by the end of Edward I's reign and much local administration remained in local hands. The English barons had accepted monarchy; the more ambitious and greedy of them simply wanted to control it. The French monarchy was always more independent of its vassals and subjects throughout the administrative hierarchy, although it would be wrong to think of the French monarchy of this period as less *feudal* than its English counterpart. No king conceived of France as a "nation" or of himself as an absolute ruler. Each regarded himself primarily as the chief lord of a hierarchy bound together by ties of homage and fealty, governing within the law and with the advice of his vassals. Neither the king's unique judicial role, nor his quasi-divinity, nor his greater reliance on professional administrators seriously conflicted with this tradition.

The French monarchy rose to greatness in the thirteenth century. The royal domain was pacified, consolidated and much enlarged, institutions of government were developed, and strong kings made the crown a symbol of unrivaled power and prestige. These kings were Philip II, Philip Augustus (1180–1223); Louis IX, St. Louis (1226–1270); and Philip IV, "the Fair" (1285–1314). Philip Augustus contributed more that was new than either of the others. Shrewd, devious, untroubled by moral or religious scruple, he resorted to any method to advance his purposes. Louis IX was as different as a man could be. Just, wise, conscientious, he longed for the life of a monk, and was only persuaded by a sense of duty not to abdicate. Philip the Fair is something of an enigma, a king whose personality and aims are hidden behind a façade of conventional piety and a screen of bureaucrats. During his reign, however, the climax of feudal monarchy was reached, a climax that was prelude to collapse.

The Growth of the Royal Domain

During Philip Augustus' reign, the largest expansion of the royal domain took place. He acquired Artois, on the border of Flanders, by marriage and Normandy, Maine, Anjou, Touraine, and Auvergne by conquest from England. He refused, however, to take advantage of the crusade against the Albigensians of Languedoc to extend the domain farther south; he simply did not recognize that an area so far from the royal seat at Paris was worth the trouble (see p. 258). His short-lived son, Louis VIII (1223–1226), was more realistic. He joined the crusade and won a part of the county of Toulouse. The remainder of Toulouse fell by inheritance to the crown under Louis IX. Philip III (1270–1285), obtained the county of Champagne through the marriage of his eldest son to the heiress and completed the acquisition of Languedoc. Thus, in the course of the century the domain was enlarged more than five times. Of the great fiefs of an earlier day, only Burgundy and Brittany remained out of royal hands.

But, unfortunately for the future of the French monarchy, the feudal idea of provincial independence triumphed over the idea of centralization and unity directly under the crown. A good part of the domain was alienated to princes of the blood by the *appanage* system. The practice was not new at the time of Louis VIII though he went further with it than any of his predecessors. His oldest son became King Louis IX. His second son was given the county of Artois as an *appanage,* his third the counties of Anjou and Maine, and his fourth Poitou and Auvergne. If they or their heirs died without issue, the lands would *escheat* to the crown. By extending the appanage system, Louis believed that he could provide for each of his sons and, at the same time, "prevent the growth of discord among them." Later kings alienated other, lesser, areas for essentially the same reasons. Some historians have argued that the practice was justified because the crown was incapable of governing the full domain effectively. This was true at the time for difficulties did not arise until the fourteenth and fifteenth centuries. But it was shortsighted. Brothers could be friends and could rule their fiefs in peace and harmony but second and third cousins, several generations later, would bear no loyalty to each other and little to the king. Indeed, a new group of great feudal magnates arose who tried to create petty princedoms independent of the crown as other magnates had done three centuries before.

Royal Administration

The enlarged domain required a better system of royal administration than that provided by the unreliable and sometimes rebellious prévots. Local dignitaries could not be trusted, for their loyalty was to the local area rather than to the crown. Philip Augustus was an important innovator here. In newly-won areas he preserved local custom, some of which, like the custom of Normandy, was more advanced than his own. Thus France, in contrast to England, developed as a country of numerous local law codes with no *common* law. But Philip Augustus divided both old and new areas into administrative districts and put them under the charge of royal agents, called bailiffs (*baillis*) and seneschals. He may have patterned these on the Norman-English officers he found in Normandy for they combined the functions of sheriff and itinerant justice. They collected the crown's revenues, kept the public peace, and dispensed justice in cases involving the crown. The bailiffs were not members of the local nobility, but salaried, professional civil servants employed at the king's pleasure. The seneschals, who were sent to frontier areas and trouble spots and who commanded troops in addition to their administrative duties, were similar to the bailiffs but were knights, hence noble. The devotion of these officials to the crown's interest tended to dissipate with time. Before the reign of Louis IX was ended, many of them were administering their districts arbitrarily and for their own gain. Louis IX, honest, conscientious, and always concerned for the welfare of his subjects, established roving commissions of inquiry to supervise the bailiffs and seneschals more closely. But in the long run, no method of the French kings to govern local areas was truly successful. The crown was simply unable to exercise its authority over broad distances with the primitive communications available.

The expansion of the royal domain had increased the French king's revenues several times over. He was doubtless in this period, and generally in medieval and early modern times, potentially the richest monarch in Europe. Most of the sources of revenue remained feudal in character, though there was a slow evolution toward a system of public taxation. The crown's vassals were called upon to pay such dues as aid and relief and to supply contributions for such enterprises as crusades which became a huge expense under Louis IX. Philip Augustus devised a tax similar to the English *scutage,* money payments in place of military service, but unlike scutage it was borne for the most part by non-nobles. Another excellent source of income was the towns. Many towns, or *communes* as they were called, were franchised in new areas of the royal domain by Philip Augustus and Louis VIII. They were treated in a general way like vassals, owing the king militia and dues. Louis IX franchised many fewer communes but he was not averse to squeezing them for money. Louis IX also freed many serfs on the royal domain in return for a percentage of their goods. In this way he gained both additional revenue and popularity.

The crown's central administration was slower than the local administration to develop, but it gathered speed under Louis IX and his successors. As in England, it grew out of the king's court, the *curia regis,* and his household. In the time of Philip Augustus, the Knights Templars were assigned the task of auditing the royal finances based on reports of bailiffs and *prévots* in the field. Before long this was assigned to members of the household staff at the court, perhaps as a consequence of observing the Exchequer of Normandy. Under Philip the Fair it was given to a regular body of financial experts called the *Chambre des Comptes.* Meanwhile, a group of professional lawyers had begun to sit as the *Parlement* of Paris, the highest royal judicial body

and court of appeals. By the fourteenth century the *Parlement* had separated
into three divisions: the *chambre des plaids* which tried cases, the *chambre des
requêtes* which determined if a plea warranted trial, and the *chambre des
enquêtes* which carried out judicial investigations.

St. Louis

Despite the development of *Parlement,* the king remained chief justiciar
in his kingdom. Louis IX took the job seriously, not only because of his view
of the relationship of man to man but because it strengthened the monarchy,
made it popular, and added to its prestige. He was scrupulously fair and, at
the same time, firm, insisting on the rights of others as well as those of the
crown and his conception of justice went beyond the laws of feudalism. Indeed, he considered himself the court of highest appeal for all his subjects.
Thus, he was able to impose the royal will on all segments of the population.
Since he was a man of peace (except where heretics or infidels were concerned), he devoted much effort to curbing the warlike predilections of his
nobility. He restricted the opportunities to engage in petty feudal battle, so
much so as virtually to eliminate it. He also saw that lesser vassals were
permitted to appeal their cases from their lord's court to the court of the
king. Nor did he spare the Church in his zeal to have justice prevail. For
example, he refused to believe his bishops when they asked him to confiscate
the property of excommunicates until he had examined each individual case.

The half-century reign of Louis IX established the institution of
monarchy in France and made France the leading country of Europe. The
reason was chiefly St. Louis himself, partly the example of his holy life and
partly the character of his rule. As judge-king he earned the respect and
obedience of his subjects and raised his office to a height it had never known
before. At the same time, he fortified its spiritual character. He believed he
was God's minister on earth, a priest-king, duty-bound to protect the Church
and assure the salvation of his subjects' souls. His public policies and his
personal behavior reflected this belief. He was a saint on earth to Frenchmen
and to all Europeans; indeed, the Church canonized him in 1297. His crusades
(the first of which embraced the years 1248 to 1254 and the second of which
was cut short by his death) though military disasters, won him universal fame
as a chivalrous knight and courageous defender of the faith. Indeed, he
became the paragon of Christian monarchs, the embodiment of the medieval
ideal, and the moral arbiter of princes. Even the popes, at the height of their
power and prestige, listened humbly when St. Louis spoke.

Philip "The Fair"

Philip III (1270–1285) inherited few of his father's qualities, though
he, or rather his ministers, continued St. Louis' policies. Philip IV, called "The
Fair" (1285–1314), did the same. Historians have been unkind to Philip IV,
most of them writing him off as a mere figurehead for his ministers. Hence,
his reign is often viewed as one in which the traditions of feudal monarchy
were broken by a herd of wily and power-hungry bureaucrats, trained by

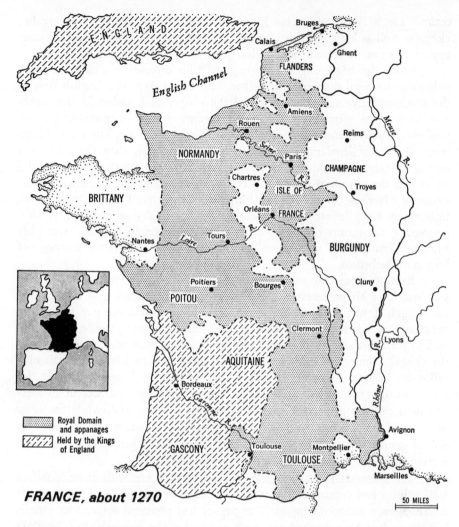

FRANCE, about 1270

Royal Domain
and appanages
Held by the Kings
of England

50 MILES

Roman law to despise feudalism and worship absolutism. This is greatly exaggerated. Philip seems to have tried his best to uphold the traditions established by Louis IX. Indeed, Louis' influence on him controlled his every action, for he slavishly emulated the sainted king in his devotion to law, his readiness to take council, and his preoccupation with spiritual matters. If he failed it was because he was Louis' intellectual inferior, though there is no evidence to support a contemporary who compared him to the owl: "the handsomest of birds which is worth absolutely nothing . . . such is our king of France who is the handsomest man in the world and who can do nothing but stare at men." Rather, he was hasty, lacked foresight and was easily persuaded by his advisors, many of whom were doubtless firm believers in stronger monarchy. As one of them wrote in 1307: the king has "supreme jurisdiction and dominion over everything within the boundaries of the realm," which he could employ "for the common welfare and defense of the realm." He is "emperor in his kingdom, and all the people of the realm, clergy as well as laity, are ruled by his imperial power." Thus, Philip's actions appear more modern than he ever intended them to be.

From the beginning of his reign, Philip directed his efforts toward enlarging the royal domain still further. His targets were the English fiefs in the southwest, especially Guienne, and the county of Flanders in the northeast. Both areas were lively centers of commerce and manufacturing, particularly Flanders, and both were held of him by the English king. Philip tried all sorts of legal maneuvers, finally attacking one, then the other and ending by achieving nothing. He was forced to sign a treaty with Edward I which left the territorial situation much as it had been. He overwhelmed the Count of Flanders, but the resolute burghers of the great Flemish cloth towns, fighting on foot, defeated the flower of French chivalry at Courtrai in 1302, permitting the return of the count. Philip's expansionist policies won only Franche Comté, the "Free County" of Burgundy, acquired by the marriage of his son to the heiress.

Even failures cost money and insufficient revenue was Philip's chief problem. Like his predecessors, his regular source of income was his domain, but though it was adequate for times of peace, it could not pay for almost constant war. His serious financial need led him to take unprecedented actions and, to lend them an air of popular sanction, he summoned representatives of the clergy, nobility, and middle class to a species of parliamentary assembly called an "Estates General." As in England, there was some tradition for doing so: the great ecclesiastical and lay lords (the First and Second Estates) had been called together for council from time immemorial, while the communes had been consulted now and then on such matters as taxation for several generations. But 1302 was the first time this "Third Estate" had met with the other two estates as advisors to the king.

The immediate occasion was Philip's controversy with Pope Boniface VIII. Philip had continued the normal practice of asking the French clergy for emergency financial support. The papacy had protested before, but usually something had been worked out, such as sharing the proceeds. But Boniface refused to cooperate; instead he quite unexpectedly issued the bull *Clericis Laicos* (1296) which forbade all kings and princes from levying taxes on the clergy without papal consent. Philip refused to obey, counterattacking by halting the flow of papal revenue from France. Boniface first retreated then attacked again, this time claiming the papal right to interfere in the affairs of secular kingdoms. The bull *Ausculta Fili* (listen, my son!) was, on paper at least, a clear threat to Philip's independence. He protested, appealing to the Estates General to back him up. It did so readily and there can be no doubt that it represented public opinion. The struggle between king and pope ended with the former having his way, the latter dying a humiliated old man. A series of events was underway which would culminate in removal of the papacy from Rome to Avignon. (These will be examined in a later chapter.) It is enough to note here that Boniface, not Philip, was the aggressor in the first place and he lost because popes could not treat kings this way by the opening years of the fourteenth century.

The Estates General was called a second time in 1308 to support Philip's attack on the Knights Templars. This was an old crusading order, out of work now and gone fat and rich on the profits of money-lending. Though somewhat unsavory, it was not the refuge of heretics, perverts and thieves Philip made it out to be. Rather, the Templars simply had money and Philip wanted it. He won the assent of the three estates to have the order disbanded and the pope, now at Avignon, reluctantly agreed. The order's property was confiscated by the crown. The Estates General was called again in 1314, to grant a tax for the first time. Thereafter, they met irregularly whenever the king wanted money or moral support. Each estate was allowed to present grievances, but not to initiate legislation. They merely confirmed or denied the program presented by the crown. Thus, more than the English Parliament, the Estates General was a creature of monarchy, and in the beginning it amplified and broadened rather than limited royal authority. However, very soon the three estates, clergy, nobility, and middle class, singly or together, discovered they could oppose as well as support the king. They did so and almost duplicated the career of their counterparts in England. Their near-success and ultimate failure will be discussed in subsequent chapters.

FURTHER READING

In addition to books cited for Part V, chapter 4, students may refer to S. Painter, *The Reign of King John* (1949), for a good discussion of the controversial ruler. An excellent short summary of the beginnings of the English Parliament is to be found in G. L. Haskins, *The Growth of English Representative Government* (1948). There is nothing comparable for France, though J. R. Strayer and C. H. Taylor, *Studies in Early French Taxation* (1939), contains material on the origins of the Estates General.

5 · The Church and Medieval Culture

By the opening of the thirteenth century the church had grown into an institution of unrivaled prestige and moral influence. Pope Innocent III (1198–1216) was justified in considering himself the ruler of Christendom. He was head of Europe's first well-organized monarchy, complete with a central administration, with judicial and financial systems manned by a hierarchy of officials extending to every corner of Europe, and with a subject people which included every Christian European. The Church touched all men. In doing so it gave to medieval civilization a basic unity. It provided its members with a common set of beliefs and a code of behavior. It recorded their births, performed their marriages, settled their estates, and attended to myriad other small but indispensable tasks. But the Church's primary function, its source of strength, was its great mission to save men's souls, for outside the Church there was no salvation. In carrying out this mission, the Church strove to establish as best it could a world ordered and at peace, a world conducive to preparation for life hereafter.

PAPAL MONARCHY

We must not think, however, of the Church as being monolithic and totalitarian. Never was its machinery perfected nor its authority wholly effective. Opposition from secular rulers was continual and popes were thrust into politics as often to protect what authority they had as to gain more. Nor was the secular clergy—the archbishops, bishops, and parish priests—ever free from the corrupting influences of secular society. Theological disagreement was the rule rather than the exception; indeed, great diversity in doctrinal matters was tolerated and try as it might, the Church could never eradicate all heresies and vestiges of paganism. Further, the pervasive military cast of medieval society worked against the Church's efforts as peacemaker; in point of fact, popes could do little more than direct this bellicosity outward, into such enterprises as the Crusades (see pp. 225–230). Finally, the era of Church supremacy was relatively short. If the high point was reached with Innocent III and his immediate successors, decline began to set in within a century of Innocent's death.

Innocent III and the Fourth Lateran Council

Innocent's authority was founded on the work of his predecessors, beginning with Leo IX (1049-1054) and Gregory VII (1073-1085). Innocent himself extended his authority over the papal territories in Italy and freed Italy from imperial influence for a time. He also completed subordination of the German Church to papal jurisdiction and enjoyed remarkable success in arbitrating disputes among Christian princes and asserting papal prerogatives in England and France. For Innocent there was no question that the spiritual authority conferred on him was superior to the temporal authority of rulers (see pp. 232-233).

This view and its general acceptance by the European community is no better illustrated than by the actions of the Fourth Lateran Council, which was called to meet in November 1215. Most of the great prelates of the Church attended and their work was wholly dedicated to augmenting and applying Church, particularly papal, powers. Important theological questions were settled and measures for clerical reform were promulgated. Raymond VI of Toulouse was declared a heretic and replaced by the leader of the crusade which Innocent had called in 1209 to stamp out the Albigensian heresy in southern France. A new Crusade (the Fourth) was proclaimed and Emperor Frederick II agreed to lead it. (Innocent had named him emperor after deposing Otto IV.) The orders of the council were obeyed because they were backed by the moral force of the papacy. This moral force was Innocent's only weapon. In that age, when it was applied justly and when as yet no counterforces had arisen to challenge it, it sufficed. But it could not withstand the assault of secularism and the growth of secular authority, nor could it survive the institutionalization, and thus the ever-increasing worldliness of the Church itself.

Papal Administration

The Church naturally evolved into the first, and in some ways the most perfect, absolute monarchy in European history. At the center of this monarchy was the pope himself and his *Curia* (court) consisting of the College of Cardinals and the administrators who assisted them. The Curia developed specialized branches: the chancery whose officials drafted correspondence (the most important letters came to be called "bulls," after the lead seal, or *bulla* which was attached to them); the *camera* or financial chamber, whose members collected papal taxes; and various judicial tribunals. Dispensing justice was the pope's chief administrative function, the one which consumed the efforts of most papal officials, and the one which contributed most directly to the growth of the papal bureaucracy. From all over Christendom appeals came to Rome for final decision. Most of them were of a minor nature, but some involved kings—for example Philip Augustus' divorce, a case which was decided against the king, who was made to keep his unwanted wife. Because papal justice was fair, if slow-moving, and because so many aspects of human affairs raised questions of canon law, the number of appeals to Rome steadily increased.

Papal Income

More business meant more personnel and higher costs for the papacy, and popes from Innocent's day forward were forever searching for ways to augment their income. Part of their revenues came from the Patrimony of St. Peter, the states of the Church which the pope ruled as a temporal lord, collecting rents, fines, tolls, and feudal dues. In addition there were taxes and levies of various kinds paid by the entire Christian community. Some countries paid Peter's Pence, in theory a tax of a penny on every hearth, but in practice badly collected and producing little income (England paid only 200 pounds a year). Also, by the thirteenth century, a number of kingdoms, including England, Portugal, Castile, and Aragon, were subject to tribute as papal fiefs; however, payment was irregular. More important were the special grants paid by the clergy of various regions when requested and the income taxes which at this time began to be collected regularly from the clergy.

A particularly lucrative source of papal income, and the one which would grow most rapidly and would stimulate much adverse criticism, was connected with appointments to Church offices. The popes tried resolutely to win the right of appointment from secular princes and enjoyed some success. By 1300 most prelates were papal appointees, even if nominated by the princes. With each appointment the pope received a gift called a *service*. This in time was expanded into all sorts of additional fees: *annates,* for example, a portion of the first year's revenues of newly-filled benefices. Finally, the sale of indulgences was fast becoming a leading moneymaker.

Bishops and Priests

Below the papacy in the ecclesiastical hierarchy were the archbishops and bishops, the Church's chief administrators. Church administration was centered in the *diocese.* Christian Europe comprised several hundred of these, large and small, each headed by a bishop. The archbishops headed larger circumscriptions made up of several dioceses. The bishop normally made his headquarters in the most important city of the diocese, where his cathedral church (so called because it housed his *cathedra* or throne), his administrative assistants, and his "chapter" were located. These administrative assistants saw to the day-to-day business of the parishes which comprised the diocese, collecting and disbursing revenues, managing the diocesan properties, and dispensing ecclesiastical justice through the bishop's court. The chapter, consisting of priests called "canons," carried out the various spiritual duties that were the bishop's responsibility, said the masses in the cathedral church, and supervised the cathedral school if there was one. Heading the chapter was the "dean."

The bishop's office was supported by his *benefice,* land and other property from which he derived his principal revenue. He also possessed wealth in church buildings and in gold and silver, and his income from dues and fines was considerable. A bishop, therefore, was a rich man, and a bishopric was a tempting plum for the avaricious. Most of the bishoprics found their way into the hands of the son of a powerful local nobleman. Disinterested, luxury-loving, even warrior bishops were common. Poorly administered dioceses were numerous from the beginning of Christianity, and not even the most thorough-going reform could eliminate them. Furthermore, by the thirteenth century, many thoughtful Christians were beginning to take note of the contrast between the visible Church with its riches and the ideal of poverty Christ had preached.

Inadequate supervision of the parish priests was perhaps the most serious episcopal failing. The dioceses were divided into parishes in each of which was an ordained priest. The priest's duty was to care for the souls of individual Christians, to administer the sacraments to them, and to direct their lives along properly spiritual lines. By the thirteenth century, it had come to be generally agreed that salvation was unattainable outside the Church of Rome because only the Church by means of the sacraments had the power to confer God's necessary grace. The priest alone was the agency through which this power was exercised; he was the essential intermediary between God and man. Ideally, all priests were pious and devoted, educated well enough to understand their spiritual role, and of sufficiently strong character to place the needs of their flock before any personal consideration. In practice, however, many were virtually illiterate, and some were dissolute and dishonest.

Clerical morality and clerical status were matters of immense importance to Innocent III. He was fully aware of the need for men of intelligence, virtue, and dedication in the hierarchy and priesthood, for he sought to separate the clergy from lay society to give it a special, mystical character in keeping with its sacramental function. The Fourth Lateran Council (1215) issued decrees which embodied this ideal. The council declared the theory of transubstantiation to be a dogma of the Church. This theory stated that when consecrated in the sacrament of the Eucharist, the bread and wine of the Mass change into the body and blood of Christ. The "accident" of their outward form causes them to appear to remain bread and wine. This miracle of the Mass could be performed only by an ordained priest. It was required that every Christian partake of the Eucharist at Easter and Christians were also required to say confession and perform the sacrament of penance once a year. Penance, too, could be imposed only by a priest. Other decrees were aimed at clerical reform, particularly at making the priesthood a special group. Priests and bishops were forbidden to wear lay dress or to engage in occupations and amusements not fitting their position. Bishops were required to preach or provide substitutes who would preach for them, and priests were prohibited from accepting fees for administering the sacraments. Enforcement was placed in the hands of the archbishops and bishops, who themselves were supervised by the pope. To Innocent, only a Church highly organized and disciplined could glorify God and prepare mankind for eternal life.

CHRISTIAN BELIEF

The worship of God and the salvation of man were the twin goals of the Church; only within the Church could they be achieved. To gain God's grace and be saved a man had to possess *faith,* sincere belief in the tenets of Christianity as taught by the Church, and he had to perform *good works.* Good works consisted of charitable acts, fasting, pilgrimages, and the like and, most important, those ceremonies and rites which came to be called "sacraments." By the thirteenth century there were seven sacraments, five for all Christians, one for priests only and one for laymen only. Each of them conferred a special grace but not all were necessary to salvation.

The Sacraments

The first, and only indispensable, sacrament was *Baptism.* It cleansed the soul of all sin, including original sin, and was administered only once, normally to infants as soon as possible after birth. *Confirmation,* usually administered by a bishop, was the sacrament by which young people received the Holy Spirit and were admitted to adulthood in the eyes of the Church. *Marriage* became a sacrament rather late. The Church consistently held that celibacy was a superior state and for many centuries looked upon marriage as an act requiring no more than consent of the parties involved. By the end of the twelfth century, however, the Church held that a proper marriage required special sanction and sanctification by a priest. *Extreme Unction,* the last rites of the Church, was believed to hasten the soul's passage to heaven. *Holy Orders* admitted a man to the priesthood by conferring on him the spiritual power to perform the miracle of the Mass and administer the sacraments. This power, once conferred, was irrevocable and did not depend on the moral condition of the priest himself.

Except for Marriage and Extreme Unction, these sacraments were administered only once. But men were constantly prey to temptation and sin, hence constantly in need of forgiveness. The sacrament of *Penance* was the means by which repentant sinners were permitted to avoid the penalty for sin. The sinner confessed his sins to a priest, and if truly contrite (sorry to have offended God and sincere in his resolution to sin no more) was assigned special prayers or other devotional acts as "penance." Although the stain of sin remained on his soul, he was saved from eternal damnation. Connected with penance was the doctrine of *purgatory.* Purgatory was considered a kind of half-way house on the road to heaven where all but the purest of saints suffered a period of punishment for guilt not expiated by penance.

By the later Middle Ages, time in purgatory might be shortened by means of an *indulgence,* a reward for such good work as participation in a crusade. The theory of indulgences derived from the belief that Christ and the saints, by their sanctity, had stored up an unlimited "treasury of merits" which the pope and his designated lieutenants could draw upon for the benefit of mankind. An indulgence did not forgive sin but only remitted punishment, though in the popular mind this important distinction was often overlooked.

In the thirteenth century, following the Fourth Lateran Council, the Church sought to enforce the new ruling that all Christians should confess and do penance yearly, and that all sins should be confessed and atoned for. Traditionally, penance was reserved for mortal sins and forgiveness could be granted only once in a lifetime. With the increased importance of penance, indulgences began to be awarded in return for money contributions. The Church, its wealth almost wholly in land, needed cash for its many projects, for its charities, for the building of new churches, and above all for financing the crusades.

Of all the sacraments, the *Eucharist* was the most significant. It was central to the celebration of the Mass and it alone both glorified God and conferred redemptive grace on man. The Eucharist was considered a miracle, a recreation of Christ's death and resurrection. In the priest's hands the plain bread and wine were changed (*transubstantiated*) into the Saviour's body and blood. The sacrament was completed when the priest and laity consumed the elements in communion, at which time a saving grace was conferred on the worthy. In time it became the practice for the priest alone to take the wine, further emphasizing his unique sacerdotal character.

Popular Religion

For most Christians, the sacraments and their theological underpinnings constituted only a small part of religion. Popular piety was more simple, more primitive, still mixed with a heavy measure of superstition. To the medieval man, the supernatural was the most important ingredient of every-day life, the explanation for all inexplicable phenomena. Demons were busy everywhere looking to trap the unwary, while the saints, who numbered in the hundreds, and especially the Virgin Mary, were always at hand, ready to protect their human charges. Most prayer and popular religious ceremonies were aimed at gaining the intercession of these allies in men's affairs and veneration of the saints became the most characteristic feature of late medieval religion. Churches and chapels were dedicated to a particular saint, festivals and processions in a saint's honor were frequent, and a saint's relics (bodily remains or personal belongings) were treated with particular reverence and were often reputed to cause miracles. The Virgin was held in even deeper reverence, ranking next to Christ in the heavenly hierarchy. She was believed to be especially sympathetic to the weak, to the fallen empty of hope, on whose behalf she might intercede directly with her divine Son.

Heresy

Though containing much superstition and vestiges of paganism, popular religion was not heretical. Heresy, however, was not uncommon; indeed, it was a recurring feature of Christian civilization and was particularly widespread in the thirteenth century. Many persons of that day were sincerely troubled by the contrast between the ascetic ideal taught by the Church and the worldliness and panoply of churchmen and Church practice. The Church seemed somehow to have lost touch with the common man. Other persons, equally sincere though fewer in number, were disturbed by the Church's theology, which was growing more complex and elaborate day by day and drawing further away from its Biblical origins. Such attitudes bred anti-clericalism and a desire among many Christians to reject ceremony and seek to follow a simple apostolic life. From there it was only a short step to heresy.

Among the more numerous heretics were the Waldensians, the Poor Men of Lyon, led by an ex-merchant named Peter Waldo. At first they were orthodox, simply renouncing their goods and travelling about as lay preachers. Soon some of them took up radical doctrines: that laymen could administer the sacraments, that the Bible was the sole authority in spiritual matters, that the Church was unnecessary to salvation. Here they struck at the institutional character of the Church. The Waldensians reflected a deep-seated need for a more personal relationship between God and man and prefigured the typical doctrines of the Protestant reformers, but they were essentially Christian.

More dangerous because it was less Christian and more anti-social was the heresy of the Albigenses, or *Cathari* as they called themselves. The Albigenses (after the town of Albi in southern France) took the basic Christian beliefs and threw them together with Manichaeism, a dualistic doctrine dating from the third century (see p. 135). They taught that all existence was a struggle between the forces of good and evil, between a god of light (truth, spirituality) and a god of darkness (error, materialism). Hell for man was imprisonment in a material body, heaven total release of the spirit. They shunned war, physical violence, sex, and meat and refused to take oaths or own property. There were large numbers of them in the southern French province of Languedoc where the nobles protected them, and particularly around the city of Toulouse where the count was well-disposed to their peculiar creed.

Innocent III was thoroughly alarmed at the rapid growth of the Albigensian heresy, for it combined an unacceptable doctrine with violent anti-clericalism. Expropriation of Church property was included in the Albigensian program. After trying persuasion unsuccessfully, Innocent III turned to force and preached a crusade, the first against heretics in Europe instead of infidels abroad. An army composed mostly of land-hungry French knights marched south in 1209 and proceeded to conquer Languedoc with relative ease. The count was replaced, the noble protectors wiped out, and the heresy virtually eradicated. The crusaders were wholly ruthless and massacres were common but the ends of the Church were served. So too were the ends of the French king, who stood aloof until the time was ripe for him to incorporate Languedoc into the royal domain, and of the knights who received their reward in land.

The Inquisition

An important immediate result of the Albigensian Crusade was the establishment of the Inquisition by Pope Gregory IX (1227–1241) in 1233. Prior to this date, heresy was a matter left to the bishops. Now the pope assumed the task. He set up a special tribunal, staffed by Franciscan or Dominican friars whose purpose was to ferret out heretics, to convert them, or failing that to bring them to trial. Its aims were purely spiritual: to save the heretic's soul and prevent him from corrupting others. Its procedures were regular, and a serious attempt was made to avoid the unpleasantness of a trial. The inquisitors first called upon all persons who held unorthodox religious views to confess and be welcomed back into the arms of the Church. Those who did so within a prescribed period of grace were treated leniently. Others were found out through the sworn testimony of witnesses and were interrogated and asked to recant. Most cases ended at this point. Confessed heretics were granted absolution and assigned an appropriate penance: a pilgrimage, flogging, wearing of a special badge such as a cross, or imprisonment. Their property was confiscated and they became social outcasts. Obdurate heretics were turned over to the secular authorities for sentence and punishment: burning at the stake.

Innocence was difficult to prove. The accused could not confront his accusers, nor was he even told who they were. He was not allowed defense council or witnesses in his own behalf. Torture was commonly used to elicit confessions. Contemporary civil judicial practice was hardly more fair but this fact does not justify inquisitorial methods. They were harsh in their own time and indefensible in modern eyes. But we must remember that heresy was the most heinous of crimes to the medieval mind, worse than murder. Furthermore, the Inquisition was designed to win back heretics, not to execute them, and it usually was successful. Very few died in the flames and these only the most recalcitrant.

Monks and Friars

To the medieval Christian, the ideal life was that of the monk who lived by a "rule" (*regulum*), his aim personal salvation. By the beginning of the thirteenth century monasticism had passed through several stages of decline and revival. Each time that the Rule of St. Benedict, the source from which most western monasticism sprang, seemed to lose its message and its urgency, a great reform movement took place. The first and most powerful of these began at the Abbey of Cluny in eastern France in 910. The Cluniac plan was somewhat different from traditional Benedictine monasticism. Individual houses were not independent but were joined together for purposes of discipline and uniformity. The Abbey of Cluny, as the mother house, became the center of a network of close to fifteen hundred dependent priories throughout Europe, over which its abbot exercised administrative control. The entire order was granted immunity from episcopal jurisdiction by the pope. The Cluniac reform breathed new life into the entire Church, reawakening its spirituality and setting a high moral standard for clerics and laymen alike to follow. It also strengthened the hand of the Papacy; without it the Hildebrandine program of ecclesiastical reform and revival would have been far more difficult to achieve. Gregory VII and his successors were inspired by the Cluniac plan of centralization. They used many Cluniac monks as papal administrators (see pp. 222–223). Gregory himself, it will be remembered, was such a monk.

But success bred complaisancy and laxity. The Cluniac houses acquired vast properties from pious laymen, eager to buy the monks' prayers in their behalf. Wealth sapped the Cluniac ardor, and the old abuses crept back into monasticism. At the end of the eleventh century a second great reform movement got underway at the Abbey of Citeaux in Burgundy. In the beginning, the founders of this abbey had no such thought in mind. They wanted simply to return to strict observance of St. Benedict's rule. They felt they could do so by founding their abbey in the wilderness which they would make flower with their own hands. But their idea, like that of their Cluniac forebears, had immense and immediate appeal. Others followed them and hundreds of *Cistercian* abbeys were founded in the uncultivated lands of Europe. Their organization was not centralized in the strict sense, although each new "daughter" house was the offspring of an older "mother" house and discipline and uniformity of rule was enforced by a system of annual visitations of senior abbots and a yearly conference of all abbots. The contribution of the Cistercians to medieval agriculture and to colonization of the European frontier, from Ireland to Poland, has been described in an earlier chapter (see p. 212).

The greatest of the Cistercians, and the man most responsible for the success of the Cistercian reform movement, was St. Bernard of Clairveaux (1090–1153). Bernard, through his writing, his preaching, and his indomitable will became the dominant figure in his order, his Church, and in all of Latin Christendom. For two generations he was the Christian conscience, ranting, cajoling, pointing the finger of righteousness at the erring, whether pope, king, or common man.[1] A true militant, obstinate and often wrong, he was uncompromising in his orthodoxy and wholly intolerant of weakness in others. Under his direction Clairveaux became the fountainhead of a widespread spiritual reformation. But the day of monasticism was on the wane by 1200. That Bernard could have been a European figure, advisor to princes, popes, and Church councils indicated that times were changing. Princely governments were gathering strength. Cities were expanding and commerce was breaking down localism and rural isolation. The ascetic ideal which Bernard so well personified did not harmonize with growing secularism and materialism. University men, armed with Aristotle and Roman law, and the preachers who followed St. Dominic and St. Francis would better serve the future than the great monk's simplistic anti-intellectualism.

The Dominicans and Franciscans were much more in tune with the thirteenth century than their older monastic brethren, for the *friars,* as the newer groups were called, forsook the ascetic life of contemplation in monasteries and went into the world to bring religion to men everywhere. The friars answered an important social need. The population of Europe had grown so rapidly that by the thirteenth century the establishment of parishes lagged far behind. The people of town and city, cut off from their traditional ties to the land, doubtful of the place of commerce and industry in medieval society, often living in squalor, were prey to temptation and to the heretical ideas which abounded in urban centers. They resented the wealth of the Church

---

[1] On St. Bernard's influence on the crusades see Chapter 3 of Part V.

and the worldliness of the clergy. They felt little attachment to the great institution which seemed to pay so little attention to their spiritual needs. The friars served where there were no priests, living with the townspeople, teaching them, and administering the sacraments to them. At the same time, the friars set an example of simple faith and poverty, fixed firmly to rigid orthodoxy. They seemed to the troubled souls of thirteenth-century Europe a reincarnation of the Apostles.

The Franciscans

The Order of Friars Minor, or Franciscans, was founded in 1210 when Innocent III gave his approval to the primitive "rule" drawn up by St. Francis of Assisi and his followers. Innocent proved his greatness in binding these strange, bedraggled men to the Church for they were different from monks in both their aims and their methods. They refused to live in isolation and practiced poverty so complete that they insisted they did not even own the ragged garments on their backs. Furthermore, they preached an inspirational brand of Christianity that might easily slip over into heresy. But Innocent saw their worth: the Church needed men such as these to help revive once more the ideals of the Founder.

The leader of the Franciscans was a remarkable man, a man whose personal vision was embodied in his order. St. Francis (1182–1226) was born in the Umbrian hill town of Assisi, son of one of the many merchants who were making Italy the center of thriving business activity. The young man was repelled by the materialism he saw around him and gave up the life of business his father had intended for him. His renunciation before the local bishop was described by one of his companions:

Going into the bishop's chamber, he cast off all his garments, and . . . stepped naked before the door and said "Listen all of you and understand. Up to now I have called Pietro Bernardone my father, but as I have now resolved to serve God, I give him the money . . . , as well as the clothes I wore which belong to him, and from now on I will say 'Our Father which art in Heaven,' instead of 'my father Pietro Bernardone.'"

Francis went forth with nothing but the cloak the bishop threw around him, barefoot, to beg. He soon began to preach humbly to whoever would listen, even to the birds and the beasts. He gathered followers wherever he went, and despite his unwillingness to do so was impelled by circumstances to establish an order. In 1223, again against his wishes, he prescribed a more elaborate rule; the "Franciscans" were organized and disciplined and made a part of the institution of the Church in spite of themselves.

Throughout the thirteenth and fourteenth centuries the Franciscans grew in numbers and influence, for their simple lesson of humility and love touched the hearts of all men. A "Third," or lay, order was attached to them, and found thousands of adherents, particularly in the busy, mercantile cities of Italy. That the anti-materialist doctrine conflicted with profit-making was, if anything, a reason for its success. Bankers and merchants renounced their wealth while humble people, already poor, gained hope and some measure of resignation with their lot. The ideal of St. Francis and his followers became, indeed, the most powerful psychological force among Europeans of the late Middle Ages.

Within the order itself, however, the ideal began to be questioned soon after Francis' death. Popularity brought many gifts of property and with wealth came a bitter controversy between the "spiritual Franciscans," who wished to live as St. Francis had lived, and the majority called "Conventuals," who wished to modify his absolute stand against property. Furthermore, many Franciscans entered universities and became leading teachers and scholars of theology, another development of which St. Francis, himself thoroughly anti-intellectual, would not have approved.

The Dominicans

The Dominicans, the second order of friars to be founded in the early thirteenth century, were not so popular as the Franciscans, but their influence within the organized Church was greater. The Dominicans were founded by St. Dominic (1170–1221), a Spanish priest, to extirpate heresy through preaching. Like the Franciscans, the Dominicans travelled about, living in the world, bringing the Word to the faithful. Like the Franciscans, too, they were mendicants, but relaxed the rules against owning property early in their career. There the similarity stopped. The Dominicans were the Church's guardians of orthodoxy—"hounds of the Lord" (*domini canes,* a pun on *dominicani,* "Dominicans") to keep the sheep from straying from the flock. As scholars they were unrivaled; as inquisitors they were tireless in their search for heretics.

Together the Franciscans and Dominicans revived the Church by bringing it once again into harmony with the changing times. As we shall see, they turned the new learning of the twelfth century to the Church's advantage, creating systems of theology which took Aristotle into account. They protected the interests of the Church in urban Europe, where it was in the greatest immediate danger. They took the place everywhere of parish priests, too few in number and lacking in inspiration. Above all they gave the Church and late medieval man an ideal, one that was rarely achieved but one which would prevail until the Renaissance.

MEDIEVAL LEARNING AND THE UNIVERSITIES

There were no "universities" as we know them until the twelfth century, and hence there was no organized system of higher education, no great centers of learning, and for that matter relatively little profound intellectual activity. Education, until that time, was more practical than speculative, designed by the Church which sponsored it to produce literate clerics capable of performing various ecclesiastical tasks. Many monasteries and cathedrals had secondary schools attached to them where young men looking toward a clerical career were trained in the elements of grammar, rhetoric, and logic, sometimes with geometry, arithmetic, astronomy, and music. These two groups of subjects, the *trivium* and the *quadrivium,* were the standard curricula of the time and had been for hundreds of years. Their purpose, essentially, was to assure that the students could read and write fluent Latin, the indispensable tool of their future trade. Students who wished to pursue their education beyond the secondary level—and there was a growing number of these by the twelfth cen tury—did so on their own, perhaps at the feet of a sympathetic older scholar. Intellectual life was unfettered, and secular studies contended for favor with theological. Theology had not yet come to dominate the stage.

Revival of Learning

In the course of the twelfth century a great revival of learning took place. At such cathedral schools as Chartres and Orléans a new interest in the classics produced what some historians have labeled a "renaissance" because it prefigured in superficial ways the later Italian Renaissance. Pagan texts were read avidly for their own sake and the classic style of prose and poetry was emulated. The leaders of this movement were primarily grammarians and rhetoricians, and they did much to develop the Latin language into a flexible and precise instrument by which medieval man could express his ideas. One of the most prominent was John of Salisbury, a writer of wide interests and almost wholly secular in his scholarly outlook. Meanwhile, other scholars were becoming deeply interested in logic as an intellectual tool. "Logic was an instrument of order in a chaotic world," a recent writer has noted. "[It] opened a window on to an orderly and systematic view of the world and of man's mind."[1] The most highly regarded logician was Aristotle, and the impulse to know all he had written on the subject was so great that scholars searched out his works and translated them, mostly from the Arabic, though some from the original Greek. In so doing they discovered other Greek and Moslem thinkers and a whole new body of knowledge was opened up to them, not only Aristotle's logic, but his *Physics, Metaphysics,* and other works, some of Plato's dialogues, Ptolemy's *Almagest,* Avicenna's *Canon of Medicine,* and Euclid's *Elements,* to name only a few. For the immediate future, however, it was Aristotle's rediscovery that had the most profound impact. It stimulated the study of theology on the one hand and of law on the other. Aristotle's method of proof and his ideas seemed to offer a means to explain the great truths of Christianity in rational terms. At the same time, they could be employed to systematize the *Digest of Justinian,* which had come to be the principal text for legal study.

The University

The expansion of scholarly resources increased the number of scholars. Cathedral schools burgeoned and vied for famous teachers, but could not keep up with the demand. Students gathered around individual teachers, paying fees to hear lectures. One gathering place was Bologna in Italy which was a

[1] R. W. Southern, *The Making of the Middle Ages* (New Haven: Yale University Press, 1961), pp. 179, 180.

center of legal studies; another was Paris where theology was the chief subject taught. The students at Bologna, preyed upon by townspeople and teachers, formed guilds for mutual protection, one for Italians and one for "ultramontanes." Each was called a *universitas,* and together they formed a corporate entity which became the University of Bologna. They hired the teachers, the "masters" or "professors," and to a large extent prescribed the content of the courses taught, although the masters set requirements for degrees. Four faculties existed: civil law, canon law, rhetoric, and medicine, and out of them began to flow the administrators for Church and secular government, men with a modern view (though learned for the most part from the ancients) of political authority and man's relationship to man. The greatest of the legal scholars was an Italian monk named Gratian who published his *Decretum* in 1148. This was a voluminous compilation of arguments pro and con in canon law.

At Paris, a large group of students and masters congregated under the influence of such brilliant theologians as Peter Abelard (1079–1142), whose *Sic et Non* (Yes and No) stimulated much controversy, and Peter Lombard (d. 1160) whose *Sentences,* employing logical analysis and synthesis, became a leading text in theology. Around 1200, the masters formed a *universitas* and before long they had subdivided into faculties of arts, theology, canon law, and medicine, each with an elected head. The rector of the faculty of arts became the chief officer of the University, though his place was bitterly disputed by the dean of theology. In contrast to Bologna, the students at Paris had no influence over university affairs. Most northern universities followed the organization of Paris; Italian and other southern universities followed the organization of Bologna. Oxford and Cambridge were founded shortly after Paris, as were many in the next century in Germany, Portugal, and Spain, as well as in Italy and France. The university was quickly recognized as an institution which would well serve God and men. In time, the universities became virtually independent entities, protected by charters from kings and popes.

But we must not visualize the university of 1200 as like the college of today. In formal terms, it consisted only of masters and students; there was no "campus" with classrooms, laboratories, and so on. Lectures might be held in the master's home or in rooms rented for the occasion. There were no dormitories or special dwelling places for either masters or students. In time, residential "colleges" sprouted in most places, often gifts of rich men like Robert de Sorbon, founder of Sorbonne College at Paris, and William of Wykeham, founder of New College in Oxford. But in the beginning, students and masters mingled with townspeople. They were, however, set apart from the townspeople by the fact that they were in minor orders and treated as clerics in law. And, since they were a rough and ready lot in that day, fond of drinking and carousing, they created much resentment. Unpleasant incidents between students and townspeople were common but on the whole, the students were little different from their counterparts in any age. A student at Oxford wrote his father in a familiar vein: "The city is expensive and makes many demands; I have to rent lodgings, buy necessities and provide for many other things which I cannot now specify . . . for you must know that without Ceres and Bacchus, Apollo grows cold!" And a father to his student son: "I have recently discovered that you live dissolutely, preferring play to work, and strumming a guitar while others are at their studies."[2]

But university life was not all easy. The average student was poor and full of hope that an education would improve his station. Hence he was willing to undergo a hard regimen of learning. He had needed a good command of Latin for admittance, and eventually the cathedral schools became in reality grammar schools whose principal purpose was to prepare young men for the universities. Once admitted, the student continued his study of grammar, rhetoric, and logic. He attended lectures in which masters would read and comment on texts. He probably had no book of his own, for books were all hand copies, rare and expensive. But since the masters spoke slowly and expounded each line at length, his notes comprised a textbook at the end of each course. After five or six years, the student became a master and was licensed to teach. A year or two previously he had received his bachelor's degree, and if he continued for several years more he might earn a doctor's degree in canon or civil law, in medicine, or in theology. To become a doctor of theology was a formidable task, requiring a dozen years of listening to discourses on Peter Lombard's *Sentences,* the Bible, and other texts, of disputing with other aspirants, and of lecturing on selected subjects before highly critical audiences.

Reason and Revelation

The supremacy of theology was not remarkable in an age when religion was the center of men's lives, both as a personal spiritual force and in the omnipresent institution of the Church. Of course, there was a Christian theological tradition extending back to the earliest days of the Church. More recently, in the eleventh and twelfth centuries, the controversy over the nature of "universals" had stirred much thought. Essentially this was a philosophical question: did individual objects have reality independent of themselves, in ideas which had existed eternally in the mind of God? Was there an ideal chair from which all chairs derive? Or were "universals" mere categories of objects with similar appearance, simply names used for convenience, not possessing independent reality? Adherents of the first position were called "realists," of the second "nominalists" (from the Latin *nomina,* "names"). The argument was not academic but had important theological consequences. Extreme realists were forced (like William of Champeaux) to hold that all men possess the same nature, a belief that could ultimately lead to pantheism, as Abelard pointed out. Extreme nominalists were hard put to explain the universal, invisible church except as a collection of individual, fallible men. In actual fact, most theologians took positions somewhere between these extremes.

Ancient thought, above all Aristotle, burst upon this theological scene and was taken up avidly by the masters and doctors of the universities, chiefly

[2] Quoted by C. H. Haskins, *The Rise of Universities* (New York: 1923), pp. 10, 15.

Paris. The entrance of many Dominican and Franciscan friars into these ranks seemed merely to intensify an already strong interest in the problems that ancient thought raised. Chief among these problems was that concerning the relative roles of *reason* and *revelation*. St. Augustine long before had taught that there was no conflict between the two, that what could not be proved of Christian truth should simply be accepted on faith. Augustine did not deprecate reason, but he was more concerned with "the mind's discovery of God through reflection on its own nature and activity than in working out any proof of God's existence of the type found in the *Metaphysics* of Aristotle."[3] The Franciscan Bonaventure (1221) adhered closely to the Augustinian view, with its strong mystical bent and its obligation to Platonism and his theology was influential at Paris and in his order, of which he was one of the first generals. Other Parisians, in the faculty of arts rather than theology, took quite a different tack along a course established by the Spanish Muslim Averroës in his commentaries on Aristotle. These philosophers held Aristotle in great reverence, even when his ideas did not coincide with Christianity, and they were forced to invent the notion of "two truths," one philosophical, derived by reason, the other theological, dependent on faith which might be directly contrary to each other. The finite nature of the world, for example, had to be taken on faith since Aristotle taught the universe had neither beginning nor end.

A third group of philosophers, theologians at Paris, attacked the problem head on, asserting not only that reason and revelation were in accord, but that one fortified the other. They used Aristotle as a tool, without accepting his thought uncritically, confident that only the most sublime mysteries (the Trinity, Christ's Incarnation) would remain beyond their ken. The greatest of these was Thomas Aquinas (1224–1274), an Italian Dominican whose *Summa Contra Gentiles* and *Summa Theologica* have been since their composition the most influential theological works produced at Paris. Aquinas was above all a practical theologian, whose aim was to prove the truth of Christianity beyond a doubt. His method was the one generally used in his day: he stated the problem in the form of a proposition, then listed all the known objections to it, finally contraverting each objection by his own arguments. His subject matter ranges from the nature of matter to proofs of the existence of God. Like most scholastics he depended heavily on authorities, Aristotle (whom he called "the Philosopher"), the Old and New Testaments, the Church Fathers; all previous western thought was grist for his mill. His works are not mere encyclopedias of other men's thought, however. To his authorities he brought immense powers of logical analysis and a creative imagination. Hence, he was in a real sense an innovator who struck down many contemporary sacred cows and stimulated much controversy. The most violent was against his moderate realism. In the fourteenth century, Nominalism was revived by Duns Scotus (1265–1308) and William of Occam (1280–1349), two English Franciscans. Occam was particularly influential in the next generations, his followers

---

[3] F. C. Copleston, *Medieval Philosophy* (Harper: New York, 1961), p. 62.

holding that religious truths could not be proven by reason but must be accepted on faith alone.

In fields other than law and theology, medieval thought was generally undistinguished. In science, the schoolmen were hampered by their often slavish reliance on authorities and by their deductive method of reasoning which discouraged observation and experimentation. Equally important, they lacked the advanced mathematics and measuring instruments necessary to true scientific investigation. Furthermore, though some Greek and Arabic learning was of great value in scientific studies, Aristotle as he was understood was a downright hindrance to the development of an inductive method. Hence, though some modern historians have made much of such "precursors" of modern science as Abelard of Bath, Robert Grosseteste, Roger Bacon, and William of Occam, the questions they asked were more useful for the future than the answers they supplied. Nevertheless, it is possible to trace the great scientific discoveries of the sixteenth and seventeenth centuries to the primitive theories and experiments of the thirteenth and fourteenth. By the fifteenth century, the center of scientific studies had moved from the University of Paris to the University of Padua in Italy. At Padua, theology took second place to medicine and the liberal arts.

LAY CULTURE

Inevitably, as feudalism matured it produced a culture peculiar to itself. A cult of knighthood and a whole set of knightly ethics called chivalry evolved along with a manner of daily life and a body of literature. Chivalry reached its fullest development after social and political feudalism had begun to decline; indeed, it was in a sense a substitute for the more practical aspects of feudalism and a means by which the idea of feudalism was preserved. Chivalric society was noble society. As we have seen, nobles in the middle ages were above all warriors; the qualities and virtues they admired and the spirit they sought to perpetuate were fundamentally martial in character: strength, bravery, loyalty, honor, and generosity in victory. Because the warriors were also Christians, they added piety and eventually the crusading spirit. The Church, pledged to peace, made use of this to mitigate the harsher aspects of feudal life. Finally, under the influence of their ladies, the warriors added courtesy to women which in time became an elaborate ritual of courtly love. Thus, the nobility took on an aspect peculiar, almost exclusive, to itself since by the end of the twelfth century the class had become hereditary.

Medieval Literature

Already, a literature had grown up around this chivalric society. Northern French writers took the lead, composing brief epics extolling feudal warfare called *chansons de geste* in the vernacular. The greatest of these was the *Chanson de Roland,* a description of Charlemagne's battle at Roncevalles in the Pyrenees. Written in the eleventh century, it predated most chivalric literature and served as a model for much of it. The *chansons de geste* were followed by longer stories and poems recounting the legends of King Arthur and the Round Table, Parzival and the Holy Grail, and others. Love, idealized and often unrequited, was the usual theme of the lyric poems of the troubadours. Originating in southern France, the love lyric moved north where it became somewhat more realistic. Courtly love was summed up and satirized in the *Roman de la rose,* a long and immensely popular allegorical poem written in the thirteenth century. Lyric poetry, though sterile in its old age, lived on in France well into the fifteenth century.

Medieval literature was not limited to works appealing to the ideals of chivalry. Among nobles and commoners alike, religious stories were popular. *The Miracles of the Virgin,* for example, were collections of stories begun in the twelfth century extolling the works of Mary on the behalf of men. The lives of saints were also favorite subjects and were written with the intent of uplifting and inspiring devotion in their readers. Poetry was a favorite form of secular literature. The *fabliaux* were humorous short stories in verse poking fun at the average man. The setting was usually urban and the butt of the joke often a pompous merchant. Satire in verse may also be found in the mock romances of Reynard the fox and the famous *Aucassin and Nicolette,* the latter a sentimental and ironic love story enjoyable to this day. More serious secular literature included history. Medieval historical writing was most often in the form of "annals" or "chronicles," a series of related and unrelated events noted in chronological order without interpretation or analysis. Most such histories were compiled by clerics and show a strong religious orientation. By the thirteenth century, however, laymen were writing a more secular and sophisticated history. One of the best is John of Joinville's *History of St. Louis,* completed in 1309.

Despite its numerous forms, literature was not the entertainment of the common man. Unable to read, he waited eagerly for the traveling shows and the religious dramas staged at certain seasons of the year. The latter were usually highly allegorical and stylized and always they taught a moral. Perhaps the common man's favorite form of entertainment, however, was a good sermon from the lips of a skilled preacher. By the thirteenth century, preachers were everywhere in the urban centers of Europe, particularly in northern and southern France and in northern and central Italy. People of the towns, rootless, insecure, felt a deep need for spiritual succor which the secular clergy was unable to provide. Preachers helped to fill this need. They also told funny stories and brought news of the outside world. Many of the earliest preachers were laymen like the *Humiliati,* a brotherhood of working men formed in Italy about 1200. But the greatest and most influential, as we have seen, were the Franciscans.

Medieval Art

The eye of the artist as well as the mind of the scholar was focused on God in the Middle Ages. Indeed, medieval art was the handmaid of religion. This is not surprising in an age so pervasively spiritual, when taste was oriented so completely toward spiritual things, and when the Church was art's chief patron. Only the Church could bring together the resources of money, of ideas, and of energy to support and sustain creative activity. Naturally enough the product of this activity was religious in content.

The supreme expression of medieval art was the building of churches. In unity of design, construction, and decoration, the church fulfilled the highest spiritual ideals of medieval man. Within the church God dwelt, the miracle of the Mass took place, and the faithful came to worship. What greater monument to God's glory could man provide? From the eleventh century onwards, magnificent Romanesque and Gothic structures rose throughout Europe. They were a clear break with the artistic past, both in esthetic conception and engineering principles. Western Christian civilization had made its first original contribution to art.

It is important to understand that, if the churches are a monument to the power and influence of the Church, they are also symbolic of an evolving society. The Romanesque style, which prevailed until the end of the twelfth century, is connected most closely with monastic establishments for in this period wealth was still concentrated in the land. Monasteries had immense holdings, a good labor supply and the patronage of the great feudal nobility. The greatest of all Romanesque churches, unfortunately no longer standing, was attached to the Abbey of Cluny. With the development of a money economy the towns and cities gained the resources for building; hence the next style, Gothic, which followed Romanesque, is found mostly in urban centers. There the bishops directed the work and most Gothic churches are cathedrals. More magnificent than the earlier style, Gothic reflects the rising status of the secular clergy on the one hand and of the middle classes on the other.

From an engineering standpoint, Romanesque and Gothic architecture was brilliantly inventive. Both, however, followed traditional ground plans. A *nave* with aisles on each side running east and west was connected at right angles to a *transept* to form a cross. The high altar was located at the point of the cross, and along the nave were often chapels. Behind the altar was an area, usually rounded, called an *apse* which in large churches might be separated from the altar by a section called the *choir*. The innovations consisted of construction methods, the *barrel vault* in Romanesque and the *ribbed vault* in Gothic. In Romanesque churches the nave and transept were roofed by barrel vaults, half cylinders of stone blocks supported by walls, which crossed to form a *cross vault* over the altar. In larger churches the vaulting was so heavy that windows could not be cut in the thick walls. A partial solution was to roof the nave and transept with a succession of cross vaults, supported by a succession of massive columns. But the basic problem remained: windows were small and the overall effect was of gloomy solidity and great strength. For some relief, interior and exterior was usually copiously decorated with sculptured scenes from Scripture. Indeed, in the Romanesque period, life-size figures were carved for the first time since antiquity, but naturalism was subordinated to didactic symbolism and the sculpture was subordinated to the architectural unity of the structure as a whole.

Where the Romanesque structure was heavy and dark, the Gothic structure was soaring and filled with light. The reason for the difference is the ribbed vault. The ribbed vault consists of six round arches over a square or rectangular area, four of them joining the corners along the sides and two of them joining the corners diagonally. Each arch is equal in height to its span, making the two diagonals higher than the others. Weight is concentrated at the four corners where columns instead of walls act as supports. A further development saw the side arches pointed, permitting higher and even less massive walls but making necessary the flying buttress, a bridge carrying the outward thrust of the walls to a stone pillar some distance away. Thus the entire structure was opened up to the light. From the first, the Gothic church was loftier and contained more windows than its Romanesque predecessor. Craftsmen in glass created marvelous window scenes to tell the stories sculptors in stone had told before. Hence, sculpture had a much less important place in the Gothic than in the Romanesque style.

The early Gothic period, which ended about the middle of the thirteenth century, saw the best examples of the style; the great cathedrals at Chartres, Amièns, Reims, and Paris express the transcendental beauty and grandeur of their spiritual message in a way that touches an observer deeply even today. After 1250, however, Gothic artists began to lose their inspiration and to compensate for the loss by overblown decoration and useless complexity. Later Gothic churches are not simple and functional but gaudy and even tasteless. By the age of the Renaissance there was good reason for critics to call the style "barbarous."

Art forms other than architecture, as we have suggested, played roles in creating the esthetic unity embodied in the Romanesque and Gothic churches. Carved figures and scenes, intricately designed and executed stained-glass windows, life-size wall murals—all formed a part of the whole. For each form the purpose and subject matter were essentially the same. Visual sermons were intended to tell religious stories and convey lessons to the unlettered. Nor did purpose or subject matter change in the transition from one style to the other. Gothic art, however, tended to become more naturalistic as time advanced, moving far from the heavy formalism of its predecessor. Indeed, it seems clear that Gothic artists of the thirteenth and fourteenth centuries, particularly sculptors, observed nature carefully, and if they did not copy her exactly the reason was more preference than lack of skill.

The deep emotional response produced by the Romanesque and Gothic churches was not entirely visual, but was also auditory. The liturgy of the Mass and the offices of the canonical hours were sung, and from morning to night the sound of voices filled the great buildings with music. In the course of the middle ages, music made great technical and esthetic advances. Church music began in the sixth century with the Gregorian chant or plainsong. Although not without form, this music had no fixed rhythm or any measured variation in the length of the notes. The relation of the text to the music varied greatly. Sometimes there was a syllable to each note, at other times several notes to a syllable. Some three thousand such Gregorian melodies survive today.

Sometime in the eleventh century, our present method of musical notation was invented. The staff and notes indicating pitch and time were described by the monk Guido d' Arezzo at this time. Church music developed both melody and harmony in the next two hundred years, or in the technical phrase became *polyphonic*. Gregorian was abandoned as too simple, and composers such as Perotinus were writing complex harmonies for several voices by the middle of the thirteenth century. Indeed, as happened in the plastic arts, music tended to become unnecessarily complex and over-elaborate in the later Middle Ages.

FURTHER READING

Probably the best work on Innocent III is S. Packard, *Europe and the Church under Innocent III* (1927). A shorter introduction is L. E. Binns, *Innocent III* (1931). On the subject of the Church as an institution, see W. Ullman, *The Growth of Papal Government* (1955). A more general work is M. Deansly, *A History of the Medieval Church* (1925). G. G. Coulton, *Five Centuries of Religion,* 4 vols. (1923–50), is a mine of information and provocative ideas. S. Packard, *The Organization of Medieval Christianity* (1929), is a brief survey. On medieval religious practices, consult C. Dawson, *Medieval Religion* (1934). The monumental work on heresy and the medieval inquisition is H. C. Lea, *A History of the Inquisition of the Middle Ages,* 3 vols. (1888). Shorter and from a Catholic viewpoint is E. Vacandard, *The Inquisition* (1938). G. G. Coulton, *The Inquisition and Liberty* (1959) is a generally unsympathetic view. Two interesting works of a more specialized nature are S. Runciman, *The Medieval Manichee* (1947), and N. Cohn, *The Pursuit of the Millennium* (1961), the latter a study of "revolutionary messianism."

On monastic reform and the friars, there is no single good work. See W. Williams, *St. Bernard of Clairvaux* (2nd ed., 1953), on the Cistercians, and P. Mandonnet, *St. Dominic and His Work* (1944), on the Dominicans. There have been many books, most of them of little value, written about St. Francis and the Franciscan movement. For background, one may profitably consult E. Gebhart, *Mystics and Heretics in Italy* (1923). The best biography of Francis, though uncritical in many respects, is still P. Sabatier, *The Life of St. Francis of Assisi* (1894). The story of the Franciscan movement is well told by Lea in the work cited above, but see also G. G. Coulton, *From St. Francis to Dante* (2nd ed., 1907).

A good introduction to medieval universities is C. H. Haskins, *The Rise of Universities* (1903). Haskins has also written a brilliant study of the first significant classic revival in *The Renaissance of the Twelfth Century* (1927). On the Goliards see H. Waddell, *The Wandering Scholars* (7th ed., 1934). Philosophy and theology are briefly and lucidly treated in F. C. Copleston, *Medieval Philosophy* (1952). More detail is contained in the works of the modern Thomist, E. Gilson: *Reason and Revelation in the Middle Ages* (1938); *The Philosophy of St. Thomas Aquinas* (2nd ed., rev., 1937); and *The Philosophy of St. Bonaventura* (1938). For science, see A. C. Crombie, *Medieval and Early Modern Science,* 2 vols. (rev. ed., 1959). On medieval culture, the standard work remains H. O. Taylor, *The Medieval Mind*

2 vols. (rev. ed., 1949), which may be supplemented by F. B. Artz, *The Mind of the Middle Ages* (2nd ed., 1954). A good brief account of court culture and its literature is S. Painter, **French Chivalry* (1940). A standard short work on architecture is K. J. Conant, *Early Medieval Architecture* (1942), to which may be added the stimulating E. Panofsky, **Gothic Architecture and Scholasticism* (1951). C. R. Morey, *Medieval Art* (1942), is a good introduction.

VI

THE CLOSE OF THE MIDDLE AGES

1. Politics and the Church

2. Economic and Social Developments

The light of the thirteenth century dimmed in the fourteenth and early fifteenth. In every way, the medieval civilization of northern Europe was in decay. Economic progress slowed, political life was disrupted by war and domestic strife, and the authority and influence of the Church began to decline. This century and a half was a period of economic depression with important social consequences. It was also a period in which the feudal monarchies reached the inherent limits of their growth. A new kind of "feudalism" arose which only a new kind of monarchy could suppress. The Empire of the Hohenstaufen distintegrated into separate, virtually autonomous political entities while the imperial crown devolved into a mere symbol of vanished power. The ascendancy of the Church over the lives of Christians gave way before the advance of secular forms of social and political organization. Overblown and complacent, the Church closed its eyes to the need for self-examination and internal reform, even though faced with revolt from within and heresy from without. Church and Empire, the two great universal institutions of medieval civilization, would never recover what they lost. Europe would arrange itself along new social and political lines. These lines begin to be visible at the close of the Middle Ages. Thus, in the midst of decay we can discern growth, as one phase of European civilization was transformed into another. By the middle of the fifteenth century modern history had begun.

1 · Politics and the Church

From the second quarter of the fourteenth to the third quarter of the fifteenth centuries, England and France were at war. Though actual fighting was sporadic, both great feudal monarchies remained on a war footing all of the time and war was the chief influence in political life. Its influence was immense, as we shall see. The excuse for it was an English claim to the French throne made possible because Edward III (1327–1377) was the grandson of Philip the Fair, while the reigning king of France, Philip VI (1328–1350), was only the elder Philip's nephew. In reality, the war's causes were more complex and less noble.

THE OPENING OF THE HUNDRED YEARS' WAR

Ever since the Angevins had mounted the English throne, bringing with them vast fiefs in France, there had been rivalry between the crowns of France and England (see p. 200). It was the goal of every French king to drive the "foreigner" out and over the years they had been quite successful. At Edward III's accession, only a fragment of the inheritance, a small stretch of territory along the Gascon coast, remained in English hands. Now the French were attempting to gather this in too. In 1294 and again in 1324, French kings seized Gascony on technical grounds under feudal law. This was intolerable to an English king for if successful it would end his chances of continental greatness. There were other sources of conflict, the most important being Flanders. France had taken over this prosperous industrial country, and the English feared disruption of the prime market for their raw wool. Finally, Edward III, like other monarchs of his day, sought glory in war. War was a king's truest occupation and success at it the only reliable way to earn the respect of his subjects, most particularly the great barons of the realm who tended to be quarrelsome and irreverent of royalty. The barons of England would certainly not look with favor on a pacific king, and even less so on a king who relinquished the last of the Angevin inheritance. We have noted the political disaster that followed John's losses in France (see p. 239).

All of these considerations influenced Edward to declare war on Philip VI in 1337, after he made careful, though in the end useless, diplomatic preparation to secure alliances with Emperor Ludwig and the Flemish towns. He crossed the channel and spent two years in desultory fighting before the English fleet won the decisive victory of Sluys, assuring the safety of the Flanders trade route. The same year, largely to please the scrupulous Flemish who were still vassals of the French crown, Edward had himself crowned "king of France" at Ghent. More indecisive fighting, punctuated by brief truces, followed in northern France, Gascony, and Brittany. Then, in August 1346, Edward and the English inflicted a crushing defeat on the French army at Crécy, close to the border of Flanders.

The Battle of Crécy

Crécy was the first great English victory that resulted from a clear superiority of English over French armies. This superiority was not in numbers since the French could always field more men but in weapons, organization, tactics, and skill. The French army at this time was much as it had been a century or more earlier. Its main strength was the mounted, armored man-at-arms, equipped with lance and raw courage, and imbued with the chivalrous spirit that brooked no discipline. A battle plan was scoffed at. The knights simply charged toward the enemy helter-skelter, and in battle it was every man for himself. Infantry consisted of a few mercenary crossbowmen, most of them Genoese. The basic element of the English army, on the other hand, was the infantryman, recruited largely from the rural yeomanry. He was armed with pike and longbow and had learned to fight in the hard campaigns in Wales and Scotland. The longbow was particularly deadly, the first really effective missile weapon in European history. Indeed, in good hands, there was none better before invention of the bolt-action rifle. A skilled bowman could fire an arrow every three or four seconds which was capable of penetrating chainmail at medium range and dropping horses at much longer distance. With the English infantrymen were the feudal levies of the baronage whose mode of fighting was like that of their French counterparts. Edward employed his forces brilliantly at Crécy, but he was given considerable help by the French themselves. Philip VI was a fool, blind to the needs of battle, tragically confident that his noble host was unbeatable. He went into the fight wholly unprepared and suffered for it.

The Battle of Poitiers

Following Crécy, Edward besieged and took the channel port of Calais, which became the distribution center for English continental exports. A truce was made in 1347 which lasted until 1355 when the English launched another assault against France, now ruled by a king even less effective than his father. John II (1350–1364) was called "the Good" on the strength of his chivalrous virtues rather than his intelligence or qualities of leadership. An English army under Edward, Prince of Wales, the "Black Prince" of legendary fame, marched northwest through Languedoc toward Paris, spreading devastation in its wake. In September 1356, it met the French under King John at Poitiers, a village some distance south of the Loire in east-central France. Despite some rudimentary planning by John, the battle that ensued was a repetition of Crécy. Its results were even more spectacular for the English, as the French king himself, his son, and a number of high-ranking nobles were captured and held for ransom. Exhausted, France agreed in 1360 to the Treaty of Brétigny which gave England outright possession of Calais and Ponthieu in the northeast and most of Gascony and Aquitaine in the southeast, and which also stipulated a huge sum for the king's release.

FRANCE AND ENGLAND DURING THE HUNDRED YEARS' WAR

Poitiers ended the first phase of the war, and the next years were given over to recovery by the two combatants. Already the war's effects were profound, contributing substantially to the economic ills from which both countries suffered and hastening the decline of royal power. In England, there was evidence that the monarchy had overextended itself before the war began; in France the fact became clear with the accession of John II. As we have seen in earlier chapters, feudal monarchy was limited monarchy. Kings governed, indeed were expected to govern, with strength and wisdom but within the accepted circumscription of law and custom. They were supposed to dispense justice clearly and fairly, pay their own expenses, and take the council of their "natural" advisors, the vassals-in-chief of the realm. Most of the time, things went fairly well, as during the reign of Louis IX, though even Louis, his piety notwithstanding, was inclined to assert his prerogatives more firmly than conservatives liked. Kings with the loftier view of royal authority being purveyed by Roman lawyers—kings such as Edward I and Philip the Fair— provoked widespread anger and discontent. The day when a king could act "at his pleasure" and contrary to traditional practice had not yet arrived. He simply did not command sufficient money or men. In an emergency, he was forced to appeal to his subjects and each appeal, however readily and humbly granted, sapped his power and prestige. Furthermore, his subjects soon found that they could use his appeals as bargaining points to gain concessions of their own. The situation for royalty was particularly dangerous if the king were stupid or weak and his subjects self-seeking and powerful.

France and England suffered from feeble kings during most of the fourteenth and fifteenth centuries. In France, the first three successors to Philip the Fair were his sons who were short-lived and, except for Philip V (1316–1322), were inconsequential.[1] Their reigns were uneventful as they coasted along on their father's reputation. But none produced an heir, thus ending the direct Capetian line and bringing Philip VI, a nephew of Philip the Fair and the first Valois, to the throne in 1328. Philip VI escaped the consequences of his own foolishness and the ignominy of the English victories. Instead, the work of repair and recovery fell to his equally incapable son, John II. Fortunately for the kingdom, John spent a good part of his reign a prisoner in England, while rule was in the hands of the clever and tough-minded Dauphin. The Dauphin's problems were serious ones. The peasants rose in revolt (see p. 299) and the Third Estate, headed by Etienne Marcel, provost of the merchants and artisans of Paris, led the Estates General to

[1] Besides Philip V, they were Louis X (1314–1316) and Charles IV (1322–1328).

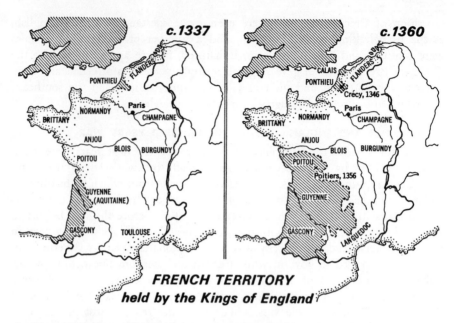

FRENCH TERRITORY
held by the Kings of England

c.1337

c.1360

challenge the crown's financial powers. In 1357, the audacious Estates, called following the defeat at Poitiers, refused the royal request for war taxes except on condition that its members collect them and supervise their expenditure. Marcel and his followers went even further, drawing up a "Great Ordinance" embodying liberal ideas which would have turned France into a constitutional monarchy if introduced. But the Dauphin proved adequate to the crisis. He won over the First and Second Estates whose clerical and noble members had little sympathy for middle-class radicalism, and in the process blocked the assembly's best opportunity to become a "parliament" in the English sense. Unlike the English Parliament, the Estates General remained divided, prey to class jealousy, a tool of the crown.

After the Dauphin had become king as Charles V (1364–1380), he continued to force the royal prerogative on a now compliant Estates General. Indeed, in every way he proved himself the strongest and most capable French monarch since Philip the Fair. Under his guidance France recovered from Poitiers and slowly but surely won back much of the territory that had been lost. To support the necessary military effort, Charles got the Estates General to agree to regular taxation: a *taille,* or hearth tax; a *gabelle,* or salt tax, and an *aide,* or sales tax on merchandise and wine. In theory, these were emergency taxes to prosecute the war, but in fact they remained permanent throughout Charles' reign. They permitted him to maintain a standing army, which he used sparingly but effectively. And he was blessed with good generals. The English were on the run and the foundations of a new, stronger French monarchy were laid by the close of the reign. But the king had a conscience, and on his death-bed he ordered discontinuance of the hearth tax, his principal source of revenue.

In England, Edward III's long reign also witnessed a reaction against

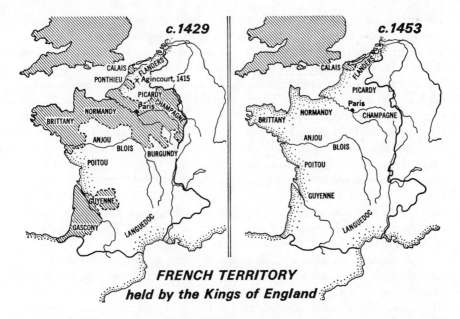

FRENCH TERRITORY
held by the Kings of England

royal authority, provoked largely by the high cost of the war. But Edward had neither the foresight nor the will to act in the manner of his French contemporary. In his efforts to raise money, Edward was obliged time and again to call the Parliament whose constitutional role was thereby greatly clarified and regularized over the years. The "Commons" in particular made gains. Quietly, peacefully, and in strict accordance with law, the middle-class country gentry and townsmen established precedents out of which would evolve the undisputed right to approve taxation and initiate legislation. Unlike the French Third Estate, which only represented the towns of France, the Commons represented both rural and urban interests and worked in harmony with the "Lords" of the nobility and high clergy.

However, Parliament was not yet the great representative body it would become, for it was not yet independent of the king on the one hand and the great barons on the other. During the tempestuous reign of Richard II (1377–1399), both the crown and its baronial opposition used the Parliament as a tool of their policies. Still, this in itself is significant for it meant that the Parliament enjoyed considerable prestige and was not something to be scoffed at, as was the Estates General.

"New" Feudalism

The most immediate threat to royal authority in the late fourteenth and fifteenth centuries was the high nobility, for the middle-class commoners, despite their aggregate wealth, were not truly influential in government. In both England and France, the high nobility had been immeasurably strengthened by the crown's practice of bestowing large chunks of the royal inheritance on younger sons. In France, this "appanage" system created a group of practically autonomous territories within the realm, each headed by a rich and powerful magnate of the royal blood whose natural inclination was to oppose monarchial centralization. The last and ultimately the most dangerous instance of the system occurred in 1361 when John II gave the duchy of Burgundy to his son Philip, who immediately set to work building a state that would soon rival France itself. In England, Edward III followed a similar practice, marrying off his younger sons to rich heiresses and awarding them large fiefs. Thus evolved what is usually termed "new" or "bastard" feudalism to distinguish it from the true feudalism of an earlier time. None of the great royal magnates on either side of the channel sought to do away with monarchy or even to make themselves independent of it. Rather, they used their wealth and the swarms of armed retainers which they gathered around themselves to dominate the crown to further their private ends. Of course, pride and self-interest drove them into quarreling, making French and English politics for nearly a century the story of brutal and unreasoning factionalism. The kings, helpless to defend themselves, saw monarchy sink to a low ebb.

Richard II was the first to suffer. Placated by favors in Edward III's day, the barons sought further privileges during the new king's minority. On coming of age, Richard tried to turn the tables on them. He was a thorough-going monarchist, with even a touch of the tyrant about him but his methods were clumsy and inadequate. In 1399 a faction of barons headed by Henry Bolingbroke, the duke of Lancaster, deposed him and Lancaster set himself up as Henry IV (1399–1413). His act was wholly illegitimate, a fact which dogged the Lancastrians thereafter. Henry never managed to satisfy his ambitious baronial allies and most of his short reign was given over to suppressing rebellion. Parliament, which had validated Henry's claim to the throne, made the best of his indebtedness, gaining more power than ever before. Henry was succeeded by his soldier son, Henry V (1413–1422), the "Prince Hal" to Shakespeare's Falstaff, who immediately renewed the war in France. At home, opposition to the Lancasters began to crystalize around the house of York whose heir called himself the rightful king.

In France factional strife among the high nobility broke out during the long and tragic reign of Charles VI (1380–1422). Charles, like Richard II of England, ascended the throne as a minor, and from the age of twenty-four was a madman, "the plaything of every kind of intrigue, a poor puppet whose name served to satisfy the most insatiable appetites." His first attack came in 1392, and thereafter his lapses into insanity were frequent. Government fell into the stronger and bolder hands of his uncles and cousins, first the duke of Burgundy and then the party led by the duke of Orléans, the Armagnacs. Neither side possessed a grain of public responsibility. An imaginative, though under the circumstances impractical, plan of governmental reform drawn up by the burgesses of Paris, heirs of Etienne Marcel, was adopted by the Burgundians but annulled by the Armagnacs. The French crown, for the next generation, would be solely a means to enhance the nobles' power and fill their pocketbooks.

The situation in France made Henry V's military task an easier one. He was a spirited and intelligent king who loved war and also saw it as a way to occupy his restless barons. In 1415 he landed in Normandy with a sizeable army which was soon decimated by dysentery and was forced to face the French in a much weakened condition. But the hard lessons of Crécy and Poitiers had still not wiped out the chivalrous prejudices of the French nobility. At Agincourt, English bowmen once more defeated French mounted knights with terrible losses, perhaps 4500 French to about 100 English. The Armagnac faction was wiped out and power fell once more to the Burgundians. A treaty was signed in 1420 at Troyes, giving Henry V everything he wanted. He married the king's daughter and was named heir to the French throne. Both Henry and the mad Charles VI died in 1422, and the crowns of both France and England passed to Henry's infant son (Henry VI of England, 1422–1461). The duke of Burgundy became England's ally, while the rightful Dauphin, Charles, to whom most of France south of the Loire remained loyal, fled to the town of Bourges in Touraine. Charles' enemies derisively called him "king of Bourges," and it was only with great perseverance that Joan of Arc persuaded him to accept the crown as king of France (see pp. 351–352).

GERMANY IN THE LATER MIDDLE AGES

By the death of the great Emperor Frederick II in 1250, it had been determined that Germany would pass to the princes. The following years simply confirmed this. The Hohenstaufen dynasty sank into insignificance. The papacy invited Charles of Anjou, brother of King Louis IX of France, to invade Sicily, which he did successfully in 1266. Northern Italy, which Frederick had failed to reconquer, became for practical purposes independent of imperial authority. Germany, which Frederick had permitted to continue full speed down the road to political anarchy, was virtually independent of imperial authority too. With the crown's resources and power gone, Frederick's successors had only their personal wealth and the authority they wielded in their own domains to set against the combined strength of the princes. The situation for Empire was hopeless. The princes, who zealously guarded their right of imperial election, time and again chose as emperors men whose resources were small and who would not pose a threat to them. Between 1254 and 1272 the princes could agree on no candidate, and this period of "Interregnum" gave them the opportunity to consolidate the privileges which made them virtually autonomous in their own territories.

In 1273, the electors chose Rudolf of Habsburg (1273–1291), a minor German count who they thought would make a "safe" emperor. Rudolf fooled them by working strenuously to recoup the declining imperial fortunes and managed to make his own house the most powerful in the Empire. By arranging the marriage of his son Albert to the heiress of Austria, Rudolf inaugurated the brilliantly successful marriage policy that made the Habsburgs the greatest of European dynasties and gave meaning to the phrase: *Bella gerant allii, tu, felix Austria, nube* ("Others make war, you, happy Austria, marry"). Albert I of Habsburg (1298–1305) also tried to revive imperial pretensions, as did Henry VII of Luxemburg (1308–1313). Henry went to Italy, hoping to re-

DENMARK
Baltic Sea
North Sea
Lübeck
Hamburg
Bremen
BRANDENBURG
POLAND
Meuse
Cologne
NASSAU
SAXONY
Rhine
Trier
Mainz
LUX.
PALATINATE
Prague
BOHEMIA
Danube
FRANCE
AUSTRIA
HUNGARY
STYRIA
SWISS
CONFEDERATION
TYROL
Drava
CARINTHIA
CARNIOLA
Danube
VENETIAN
REPUBLIC
Venice
Po
ITALY
Rhone
R.
Oder
R.

Hapsburg dominions
Lay electorates
Boundary of The Empire

Adriatic Sea

capture the authority and prestige enjoyed there by the Hohenstaufen three generations before, but he failed. Germany itself was prey to centrifugal forces too powerful to counteract. These forces were encouraged by the foreign policies of France and the papacy, the former in hopes of gaining territories along the Rhine, the latter in fear of a strong Germany. Later emperors, Ludwig the Bavarian (1314–1347), for example, accepted the inevitable and turned their whole attention to using the imperial crown to feather their own nests.

The Golden Bull

The failure of the German Emperors was recognized and written into legal form by Emperor Charles IV (1347–1378). Charles, once and for all, settled the question of whether the Holy Roman Empire was to be a monarchy or a loose confederation of princes in favor of the latter. Charles was a states-man, the most able emperor since Frederick II, but he was also a realist. He believed that if power lay with the princes, they should bear some constitutional responsibility for all of Germany; even a confederation could maintain internal order and present some sort of a united front to the outside world. The Golden Bull, which he promulgated in 1356, established electoral machinery and a kind of central authority. The Emperor was to be chosen by a majority vote of seven lay and ecclesiastical electors: the King of Bohemia, the Count Palatine of the Rhine, the Margrave of Brandenburg, the Duke of Saxony, and the

Archbishops of Mainz, Cologne, and Trier. The Bull also tried to establish a semi-permanent concert or committee of electors to supervise German affairs but nothing came of it. A *Reichstag,* or Diet, was called occasionally, in which the electors met as a first "estate," the lesser princes as a second, and urban representatives as a third, but its function was largely ceremonial. It could not raise money or maintain an army, or for that matter keep the public peace. The emperor was virtually powerless and the Diet was determined that he remain that way. This was in essential respects the constitution of the Empire until its dissolution in 1806.

The Golden Bull gave strong impetus to the evolution of princely power in Germany. Although far slower and never so complete, the political tendency in each of the large and small principalities was similar to that in the great monarchies. The rulers sought to augment their authority in their own territories, to suppress the remnants of feudalism, to introduce centralized financial and judicial institutions, and so on. Like the kings of England and France, they were continually in need of money and were obliged to appeal to their subjects. Thus, representative bodies of estates called *Landtage* appeared. Indeed, in most of the states they gained considerable influence. At the same time, free cities developed. Self-governing, and owing only nominal allegiance to the emperor, these cities grew fat on trade and industry. By the close of the fifteenth century there were more than two hundred separate political entities in Germany. It is not surprising, therefore, that disorder, crime and even petty war were continuous. The breakdown of imperial authority had brought chaos in its wake.

The Habsburgs

This was the political condition of Germany when the Habsburgs finally won *de facto* control of the imperial crown in the fifteenth century. From Albert V (1438–1439) in a line only momentarily broken in the mid-1700's up to the Napoleonic wars, scions of this house were elected emperor. Albert was insignificant and harmless. Frederick III (1440–1493) was perhaps the weakest of all the late medieval emperors, a man who made his monogram A. E. I. O. U. (*Austria est imperare orbi universo,* "Austria has imperial sway over the world") a joke. But he was lucky for the hereditary lands he frittered away were consolidated again under his son, Maximilian, whom he arranged to marry the daughter and sole heiress of Charles, duke of Burgundy. Thus, when Maximilian I became emperor in 1493, he joined the Austrian lands with the Netherlands.

Maximilian was also a dynast to whom the Empire was merely a stepping-stone to personal and family greatness and more specifically a source of money. He used the unsettled European situation as an excuse to bargain with the Diet, although with little profit. A charming man and a dreamer, he was known to contemporaries as *Massimiliano pochi denari* ("Maximilian always broke"). After assuring himself that the cause of monarchy was indeed hopeless in Germany, he acquiesced without heart to several constitutional innovations which might have strengthened the confederation and brought a measure of internal peace had not his and the princes' lack of interest and cooperation robbed them of their effectiveness. Maximilian's only real successes were dynastic. He joined his house with the recently united houses of Aragon and Castile by arranging the marriage of his son Philip to Joanna, daughter of Ferdinand and Isabella, and with the house of Hungary by arranging the marriage of his daughter Mary to the King of Hungary's son. The child of the marriage of Philip and Joanna was the great Emperor Charles V, heir to half the world.

THE DECLINE OF THE CHURCH AND THE PAPACY

The Roman Church, with the papacy at its head, also fell on hard times after the middle of the thirteenth century. Although it continued to wield immense financial and judicial power throughout Christendom, it slowly lost its political, and more crucial by far, its moral influence. It ceased to command the affection, the respect, and the unquestioned obedience it had done in the days of Innocent III. The Church had become secularized. In the two centuries since Pope Gregory VII had won its independence and bestowed on it the mission of unifying and pacifying feudal Europe, it had grown into a community of tens of thousands, its headquarters at Rome filled with a veritable army of bureaucrats, its papal court large, lavish, and immensely expensive. Spirituality had inevitably given way to worldliness. Participation in secular affairs had become the pope's chief task. The business of religion had become more important than religion itself and among most churchmen, defense and perpetuation of the institution more vital than the care of men's souls. The long struggle with the Hohenstaufen and the shorter but equally sharp battles with other secular rulers sapped the Church's prestige by emphasizing its worldliness. Furthermore, the rise of the secular states challenged the pope's claim to universal dominion. Every ruler, whether king, duke, despot, or free city council, sought to divest himself of foreign authorities, of which the Church was the strongest. Finally, and perhaps most important, by the late thirteenth century the mission provided by Gregory VII was becoming obsolete. A new force, the secular state, was unifying the people of Europe in a different way, at the same time demanding their undivided loyalty and allegiance. The Church could not halt this inexorable tide; it could only be hurt by it.

Pope Boniface

Although the papal decline had set in earlier, we first see it clearly in events which transpired at the turn of the thirteenth century, during the pontificate of Boniface VIII (1294-1303). Boniface was a terrifying figure, an old man of unremitting will and unconquerable self-confidence. Ambitious for personal power, dedicated to the interests of his family, he was also wholly convinced of the unlimited prerogative of the papacy to manage the affairs of Christendom. He doubtless talked his weak and saintly predecessor, the hermit Celestine V (1294), into abdicating and was accused by his enemies of using physical threats as a means of persuasion. Once settled on Peter's throne, he assumed all the traditional authority claimed by his great predecessors in defiance of the changes that had been wrought in society. He boldly entered into European diplomacy, asserting his right to arbitrate quarrels among Christian princes. At the same time, he made himself the champion of ecclesiastical privilege everywhere. To support his position he issued the strongest of all statements of papal supremacy. He was a man born out of his times and his defeat was tragic but inevitable.

Philip the Fair of France loomed largest in Boniface's defeat. The issue that divided them was a significant one: whether a secular ruler was master in his own house, in this case, whether the king had financial and judicial authority over all his subjects, both clerical and lay. Philip had no doubts in the matter, and in 1296 he ordered the French clergy to support him with money in his war against England. Complaints reached the Pope, who issued the bull *Clericis Laicos* forbidding such taxation without papal sanction under pain of excommunication. Philip's stubborn resistance caused Boniface to back down and peace was made by the canonization of Louis IX. But the fight resumed shortly, this time over Philip's claim to civil jurisdiction over a French bishop who had incurred his enmity. It seemed a trivial issue, but one on which Boniface chose to take his stand for papal privilege. He reiterated the points made in *Clericis Laicos,* and in a harangue opening the Jubilee Year 1300, he made even more extravagant claims for papal supremacy. A pamphlet war broke out, one side denying the pope's right to secular power absolutely, the other confirming it in strongest terms. King Philip took more direct action. With the support of the Estates General and armed with the ideas of a Roman lawyer named William of Nogaret, he had drawn up a list of charges against Boniface accusing the old man of heresy, sorcery, murder, and sexual perversion and declaring his election illegal. Nogaret then set off in the summer of 1303 to apprehend the culprit for trial. The lawyer with a few hundred soldiers found Boniface in his summer home at Anagni in early September. Seated fully robed on his throne, the pope was an impressive figure and Nogaret gave up his plan of capture. Indeed, the aroused citizenry of Anagni rioted until the invaders fled the city. But the shock and humiliation were too much for Boniface who died soon afterwards. His successor, Benedict XI (1303–1304), sensed the winds of change and let Philip have his way. The papacy was never again the same.

At the height of the battle of words in 1302, Boniface VIII issued the *Unam Sanctam,* setting out his claim of papal supremacy in uncompromising terms. In it, he propounded the doctrine of the "two swords":

We are told by the words of the Gospel that in [Christ's] fold there are two swords, a spiritual, namely, and a temporal. For when the apostles said, "Behold here there are two swords . . . the Lord did not reply that this was too much, but enough. . . . Both swords, the spiritual and the temporal . . . are in the power of the Church; the one, indeed, to be wielded for the Church, the other by the

Church; the one by the hand of the priest, the other by the hands of kings and knights, but at the will and the sufferance of the priest. One sword, moreover, ought to be under the other, and the temporal authority subjected to the spiritual. . . .[2]

The pamphleteers employed by Philip the Fair were clever, but not up to an adequate answer. Within two decades, however, several answers had been found, of which the most effective was the *Defensor pacis*, "Defender of the Peace," by the Italian, Marsilius of Padua, published in 1326 for Emperor Ludwig of Bavaria. Ludwig was at odds with Pope John XXII over the Pope's claim to decide a disputed imperial election. Marsilius was a theologian and Roman lawyer, a brilliant controversialist willing to attack the papal argument head on. He denied that the Church possessed any temporal authority whatsoever. Indeed, he relegated popes and priests to a position of simple spiritual advisors, possessed only of the powers of gentle persuasion. Furthermore, they were specifically "subject to the coercion, judgement or rulership of him who governs by the authority of the human legislator. . . ."[3] These propositions were extreme for their time but they indicate that the Church was no longer above reproach, that its waning power and prestige had exposed it to harsh criticism, at least from Europe's intellectuals.

THE AVIGNONESE PAPACY AND THE GREAT SCHISM

On the death of Benedict XI, the Bishop of Bordeaux probably with the connivance of Philip the Fair was elected Clement V (1305-1313), and took up his residence at Avignon, a city in Provence. For more than seventy years the popes remained at Avignon which became a papal possession, while Rome fell prey to banditry and economic decay. In the minds of the Avignonese popes the "Babylonian Captivity" (as the Florentine poet Petrarch bitterly called it) was temporary. Each intended to return to the city of St. Peter but each was a Frenchman with French loyalties and with obligations to the French king who found the situation to his advantage. Certainly, the papacy, as distinguished from the Church at large, suffered few privations. Indeed, this period was one of the most glorious in papal history, if glory be measured in administrative activity and monetary expenditure. The huge papal palace housed a court of unrivalled magnificence. Ostentatious display was the way of life of a curia which constantly expanded in numbers and duties. The Church had become a highly centralized government, the first in Europe. Its cost was immense, requiring new and larger sources of revenue. John XXII (1316-1334), the greatest of Avignonese popes and a financial genius, devised many new ways of securing money. Christendom was efficiently milked in every legal, and some illegal, ways. "Whenever I entered the chambers of the ecclesiastics of the papal court, I found brokers and clergy, engaged in reckoning the money which lay in heaps before them," wrote a Spanish official. "No poor man can

[2] This is the translation from E. F. Henderson, *Select Historical Documents of the Middle Ages* (London: George Ball, 1896).
[3] This is the translation of A. Genvirth, *Marsilius of Padua: the Defender of Peace,* vol. II (New York: Columbia University Press, 1956).

approach the pope. He will call and no one will answer because he has no money in his purse to pay."

The Great Schism

Such practices were not calculated to increase either the respect or the affection in which the papacy was held. Furthermore, however hard they tried, Avignonese popes could not escape the influence of the king of France, causing them to be distrusted by every other government. But the worst was yet to come. In 1377, Gregory XI (1370–1378) moved back to Rome which had become virtually a ghost city, gone to seed, plagued by constant feuding among the great families. On Gregory's death, the people of Rome and the surrounding countryside forced the College of Cardinals under threat to elect an Italian, Urban VI (1378–1389), who promised to remain in the city. But the French cardinals refused to recognize Urban's election and a few months later produced a new Avignonese pope who took the name Clement VII (1378–1394). Thus began the Great Schism; for close to forty years, scandalized Europeans watched as two popes, each convinced of his own legitimacy, each claiming the spiritual powers of St. Peter, each administering the Church, collecting taxes and naming prelates, vilified each other in the most terrible terms. Europe took sides, France and its friends supporting Avignon, and the rest, notably England, supporting Rome. These were loyalties that rested on purely political considerations, for no one could be sure who was the true pope. And the European, whatever else he may have been, was still a religious man. Hence, he felt a deep resentment and fear. Who could say whether a bishop had been rightfully consecrated, and more important, whether a priest the bishop had ordained was a true priest, capable of performing his sacramental duties? Some said that no soul entered heaven during the entire period of the Great Schism.

HERESY AND CONCILIARISM

Reactions to the Babylonian Captivity and the Great Schism were bitter and various. Governments opposed the growing centralization of Church administration during the Avignonese papacy. The money-conscious begrudged papal taxation. Ecclesiastical politicians resented papal interference in local Church affairs, in defiance of the traditions of local election. The pious everywhere were disturbed by papal worldliness and corruption and horrified by the spectacle of a two-headed Church. Of the secular governments, England acted most strongly. A number of laws, known collectively as the Statutes of Provisors and Praemunire, were issued in the second half of the fourteenth century seeking to limit papal administrative and judicial authority in England. Elsewhere, there were similar though less forceful efforts. The thinking that motivated them was to give impetus to the development of the so-called "national" churches, the "English Church," the "Spanish Church," the "Gallican (French) Church," and so on. These churches were considered by their leaders as members of the Universal Church, whose head was the bishop of Rome, but as possessing a large degree of administrative independence. Thus, the Gallican Church asserted a claim to elect a hierarchy, collect taxes, and in other ways manage ecclesiastical affairs in France with only nominal reference to papal supremacy. In general, secular government and princes favored this development for it simplified their job of unifying and centralizing the state.

Among the masses a widespread anti-papalism grew and a number of heresies flourished. The most typical of the latter were more than anti-papal; they were anti-institutional, stressing the idea of a more simple Church, stripped of material wealth and political power and reunified by a recrudescence of individual piety. The more radical envisaged a Church patterned on that of the days of the Apostles. The Spiritual Franciscans, strict observants of St. Francis' rule, were declared heretics by Pope John XXII for teaching that neither priest nor pope had the right to own property. The most famous and influential of the Spirituals was the theologian William of Occam (1280–1342), whose brilliant tracts against Thomistic theology on the one hand and papal authority on the other were used by such disparate figures as Emperor Ludwig of Bavaria in the fourteenth century and Martin Luther in the sixteenth. Marsilius of Padua also came under the influence of the Spirituals.

Lollards and Hussites

The Spirituals were mystics, adherents to Augustinian rather than Thomistic theology, but their doctrines were for the most part orthodox. John Wyclif (1320–1384), an Englishman, and Jan Hus (1369–1415), a Bohemian Czech, taught heretical doctrines and criticized the Church as an institution. Wyclif was a scholar, a master at Oxford, where the ideas of William of Occam survived. Argumentative and bold, he attacked the temporal claims of the papacy while asserting that the Bible was the sole source of spiritual authority. In many ways he prefigured the men of the Protestant Reformation in advocating salvation by faith alone and in denying the real presence of Christ in the bread and wine of the Mass. But he was a rebel born before his time. The Wyclifites, or "Lollards" as they were called, became fairly numerous, especially among the lower classes. The Church, however, supported by the crown, was able to suppress them.

The Hussites were more successful; indeed, under their banner the first successful revolt from Rome was accomplished. Jan Hus was a master at the University of Prague and a follower of Wyclif. Around him sprang up a religious movement which permeated the Czech population of Bohemia and took on a strong patriotic coloring when the German element at the university and among the population opposed it. Riots broke out in 1410 and both sides took up arms. Hus was summoned before the Council of Constance to answer charges of heresy, condemned, and burned despite a guarantee of safety. But the Czechs fought on, and the "Hussite Wars" continued for several decades. Both popes and emperors failed to quell the determined revolutionaries. In 1436, the Hussites, now split into "Utraquists" and "Taborites," conservatives and extremists, were granted religious concessions, chiefly the right to receive both bread and wine at communion. The Hussite Church, as it emerged from the conflict, was far more Roman in its beliefs and practices than Hus himself had been.

Conciliarism

Within the Church itself the Great Schism provoked another kind of rebellion, momentarily far more dangerous to the papacy than either secular legislation or heresy. This was "Conciliarism," the theory that the Universal Church, the body of the faithful as represented by their bishops assembled in "Council," held spiritual and temporal authority above the pope and cardinals. The theory's origins may be traced to the doctrines of the twelfth and thirteenth century canonists and were doubtless influenced to some extent by the evolution of the parliamentary idea in secular governments. But Conciliarism came to the fore only with the Schism, for which it seemed to provide an answer. By the very nature of their claim, neither of the rival popes could give way to the other voluntarily or submit to arbitration by authorities they considered their inferiors. The advocates of Conciliarism, however, held that the papal claim was false and that a Council was the pope's superior. Therefore, they said, the Council could depose one or both rivals and elect a true pope, healing the rupture in Christendom. At the same time, a Council could effectively extirpate heresy and reform ecclesiastical abuses. The more radical Conciliarists went even further, striking at the very heart of the papal claim to spiritual autocracy by claiming the right of Councils to help rule the Church. If carried out, the Church government would have been transformed into a constitutional monarchy.

The claim could not stand. Having gained the support of most churchmen and many princes, the Conciliarists called a meeting at Pisa in 1408. This achieved nothing except to elect a third pope, a soldier of fortune named Baldassare Cossa who took the name of John XXIII. In 1414, however, another meeting was called at Constance in what is now Switzerland. Its avowed purposes were three: to reunite the Church, to stamp out heresy, and "to reform the Church in head and members." The first purpose was accomplished by the death of the Roman pope, the deposition of the Avignonese pope, and the election of the Roman Cardinal Colonna as Pope Martin V. The second purpose was only in a small part accomplished by the burning of Hus. Accomplishment of the third purpose, so important to the future health of the Church and of all Christendom, was put off to a vague future date.

The Council of Constance adjourned in 1418, with plans having been made by the Conciliarists for periodic future meetings. Reunions of churchmen were held, the last ending in 1449, but the Conciliar Movement was doomed by the revival of the papacy under Martin V and his autocratic-minded successors. These "Renaissance popes" reestablished the old absolute papal monarchy, brought new life to Rome, and asserted their dominion once more in the Italian Papal States. But they were quite unable to recapture the spiritual and moral leadership of Europe they had enjoyed a century and a half before.

FURTHER READING

Two recent general works on the late Middle Ages are W. K. Ferguson, *Europe in Transition, 1300–1520* (1962), and S. Harrison Thomson, *Europe in Renaissance and Reformation* (1963). An older survey, still a useful interpretation though somewhat dated, is E. Cheyney, **Dawn of a New Era, 1205–1453* (1936), which contains an extensive, revised bibliography.

The best survey of France in the fourteenth and fifteenth centuries is contained in É. Perroy, **The Hundred Years War* (1951), which also includes much on England as well as an excellent detailed treatment of the war itself. A. R. Myers, **England in the Later Middle Ages* (rev. ed., 1956), is readable and good. G. M. Trevelyan, **England in the Age of Wycliff* (4th ed., 1909), is a classic work by a great modern historian. For Germany, the most easily available work, which is a bit sketchy on this period, is G. Barraclough, **The Origins of Modern Germany* (1949).

Of a number of general works on the Church in this period, M. Creighton, *A History of the Papacy,* Vols. I–IV (1887–94), is thorough and well-balanced. On special subjects, T. Boase, *Boniface VIII* (1933), and W. Ullman, *The Origins of the Great Schism* (1948) are worth noting. The best recent study of the Avignonese Papacy is G. Mollat, **The Popes of Avignon, 1305–1378* (1963). Two late medieval heresies are treated in D. L. Muzzy, *The Spiritual Franciscans* (1907), and K. B. McFarlane, *John Wycliffe and the Beginning of English Nonconformity* (1952).

2 · Economic
and Social Developments

The late Middle Ages was a time of economic and social, as well as political, crisis in northern Europe. The rapid and remarkable expansion which had proceeded without cease for three centuries slowed down. In some areas retrogression seems to have set in. Population stabilized sometime during the first half of the fourteenth century and perhaps began to shrink; commerce and industry contracted; land once tilled fell fallow. At the same time a series of disasters struck: famine, war, plague, social revolution. Europeans, who had greeted the new century full of optimism, were seized by a sense of confusion, even despair, as their art, literature, and religious practices attest.

The fourteenth and early fifteenth centuries were a bleak contrast to the prosperous ones which had gone before. Or so it would seem. The difficulty is that our knowledge is woefully limited. We are not sure when economic decline set in, what its exact causes or its character and its effects were, or when it ended. We do not know whether it was general throughout Europe or affected only those places most highly urbanized. We cannot satisfactorily explain why, in the midst of it, the cultural Renaissance began. At best, therefore, our conclusions must be tentative.

THE FALL IN POPULATION

One fact seems fairly clear: the fourteenth century was a time of decreasing population in most parts of Europe. Recent research suggests that the number of people began to outrun the available food supply around the year 1300. This is a phenomenon to be explained largely in terms of technological insufficiency. The land under cultivation simply could not support more people. Population leveled off and may have begun to decrease, and the decline was sharply accelerated by famine, war, and plague. Famine was common enough in that day of poor food storage and distribution, but it seems to have been more severe and more general in the first few decades of the fourteenth century than before, probably simply because there were more people, including now more townspeople, to starve. War, too, took on a more destructive character in these years. The Hundred Years' War in France and civil war in Castile, in southern Italy, and in Germany left crops ruined and stock dead. The reason is perhaps that armies were larger and fighting more organized than in an earlier time. Important, too, is the fact that many mercenaries were employed by these armies, and mercenaries were men who cared little for noncombatants or for the land in which they fought.

Nature capped man's work by loosing the bubonic plague, the fearsome Black Death, for which there was neither warning nor remedy, on an unsuspecting Europe. Infected rats, bearing fleas which transmitted the disease to humans, were perhaps carried from China in ships. They reached Italy in late 1347 and within months had spread throughout the Italian peninsula, into Switzerland, Germany, and Eastern Europe. The plague arrived in France early the following year, then moved on to Spain and England. For two years it raged, destroying between 35 and 65 per cent of the urban and somewhat less of the rural population. Nor did it stop after one attack, but became endemic in Europe, breaking out a number of times in the fourteenth and later centuries.

The fall in population seems to have been the major cause of economic decline. Commerce and industry contracted, for "the cities were the leaders of economic expansion," as the historian, R. S. Lopez, said. The home market was smaller than before and this at the time when many foreign markets were lost because of changing political conditions in the Near East. Workers were fewer and wages higher; goods cost more, but profits were less. The rural economy was also affected, but in ways that our meager research can only let us guess at. Fewer mouths in town and countryside meant less consumption of agricultural products and lower prices. Where famine conditions had prevailed before the Black Death, now there were surpluses in many parts of Europe. But surpluses were only temporary. Rural workers, already in short supply, moved to the towns where wages were high. Lords were obliged to let some of their lands go fallow and give in to the demands for lower rents and better forms of tenure put forward by the remaining peasants. Manufactured goods rose in value while land values declined and agricultural income shrank. Many lords were impoverished and entire manors were abandoned. This contributed to the breakdown of the manorial system already underway.

Social effects of depopulation and depression were many and complex. But it is not hard to conclude that the Black Death killed off many of the best Europeans, those who did not flee, but who stayed behind to care for the dead and dying. The generation after 1348 was overburdened with second- and third-rate men. The old nobility died, as did the clever and daring businessmen who had built the towns. The new men who replaced them were less steeped in tradition, less wise, less adventurous. Governments were in the hands of incompetents, and business in the hands of men who preferred the safe risk. The lower class savored its taste of freedom and wanted more. Insurrections, not of the oppressed but of those one step removed from oppression, swept over Europe. It was Europe's first age of revolution.

[1] R. S. Lopez, "Trade of Medieval Europe: the South," in *Cambridge Economic History of Europe,* II (Cambridge: Cambridge University Press, 1952), pp. 338–339.

BREAKDOWN OF THE MANORIAL SYSTEM

By the beginning of the fourteenth century, the traditional pattern of medieval agriculture was giving way and the pattern of the future was being established. The manor before 1300 had ceased to be isolated, as it came more and more under the influence of an urban, money economy. The rise of towns, the expansion of trade, the improvements in communications, the introduction of new commodities in quantity, and most of all, the greater amount of coin in circulation contributed to the uprooting of manorial self-sufficiency. The lord found the merchant's wares tempting. He sampled them, liked them, and came to depend on them. His taste developed and broadened, and what had before been rare luxuries became necessities, whether exotic spices from the Far East, elaborate armor from Milan, or fine wool cloth from Flanders. To acquire the cash he needed to buy, he began to sell the produce of his manor. The towns were a large and lucrative market. A few lords became capitalist farmers in areas where a single crop such as grain, fruit, or wine did particularly well. But most of them travelled an easier road. In effect, they abandoned active farming altogether, dividing up their demesne lands among free tenants who paid annual rents and commuting the dues of serfs who worked land held in tenure to money payments. For these lords, the manor became simply a source of money income.

This development had important economic and social consequences. The lord ceased to be the prince of a petty state, becoming instead a *rentier*, a modern "landlord." He no longer had personal ties to his peasants and often did not reside on his manor. As a *rentier*, he was prey to inflation, a condition that prevailed virtually throughout the late Middle Ages and early modern times. The arrangements he made with his tenants and former serfs stipulated fixed rents, and sums that may have been fully adequate at first shrunk as the years advanced. Lords with smaller holdings edged toward impoverishment, a movement hardly impeded by their extravagance and poor financial practices. These lords were often forced to sell out, usually to the rising men of the middle class, eager to better their social status by acquiring noble land. Other lords tried to supplement their income by entering the personal service of a greater lord or the king as mercenary soldiers or administrators. Thus, the social character of Europe's nobility was transformed.

The effects were no less important for Europe's peasants, who began to climb out of serfdom. This process had begun, as we have seen, on the lands opened up by colonizers such as the Cistercian monks. Prospective settlers on these lands were usually offered free leases as an inducement, and many of them grabbed at the opportunity to escape servile status. Indeed, a scholar writing recently has suggested that this, perhaps, was the chief method by which the western European peasant gained his freedom.[2] But many serfs also bought their freedom from lords in need of cash. The serfs paid a lump sum or regular installments in money or kind, signing a contract as free

[2] B. Lyon, "Medieval Real Estate Developments and Freedom," *American Historical Review*, LXIII (October, 1957), p. 61.

tenants or even leaving the manor to take up occupations in town. The effect over a period of time was to confuse what had formerly been a fairly clear relationship between the peasants and the land. For practical purposes, the tenants "owned" the land they held under contract and could even acquire more. Furthermore, they came to resent the rents they paid and sought to evade them for they had come to think of themselves as owners. On the whole, time worked to their advantage. Their quasi-ownership became traditional, however strenuously the lord opposed it. Then, too, the inflation that ruined lords with small properties helped the peasants for rents were established inalterably by contract. The depression did not arrest these general trends significantly. Instead, it stimulated them by further weakening the economic position of the lords. The progress of emancipation of the European peasantry was fastest in England, where all but a trace of serfdom disappeared by the end of the fifteenth century, and somewhat slower, though equally steady, in France and Germany.

The breakdown of the manorial economy and its replacement by an economy based on money undermined the feudal system. Feudalism did not provide for payments in coin, whether for military services or for agricultural produce and physical labor. Money depersonalized what was an essentially personal, one may say patriarchal, relationship. The process inevitably created profound social tensions. The traditional security of both lords and peasants, founded on their self-sufficiency and mutual dependence, was destroyed. Now each man fended for himself. Thus, occurred what appears superficially to be a paradox: the peasants with their financial positions improved, revolted. Royalty everywhere benefitted for it was the king that inherited the responsibilities and the loyalties given up by the feudal lords.

COMMERCE MATURES

Throughout the thirteenth and into the fourteenth centuries, commerce and industry continued to prosper and the towns to grow. The area of most striking development was still Italy. There, in Venice, Florence, Genoa, Siena, and other cities, as will be seen in later chapters, an ideal geographic position combined with favorable political and social conditions to produce a glittering urban middle-class civilization. In northern Europe, the development was slower and less spectacular and the imprint of urbanism on society less marked, but it was noteworthy nevertheless. The towns of Flanders retained their leadership in the manufacture and sale of woolen cloth. England, by the reign of Edward I, was the principal supplier of raw wool for the Flemish drapers, and the English crown was deriving considerable tax revenue from the wool trade. The wine trade of Bordeaux, the last important French port in English hands, was also lucrative. French trade did not compare with Flemish or English, although Philip V made some effort to improve it. Its center remained the northeast, the area close to and under the influence of Flanders. But the most significant commercial growth in the century or so before depression hit was in the towns of Germany, and even during the depression, Germany seems to have suffered less than the older commercial areas of Europe.

The German Leagues

The German towns had begun to trade in the eleventh and twelfth centuries, but their greatest period was the thirteenth and early fourteenth, for commerce, like agriculture, expanded to the east, beating against the frontiers and opening new areas to urban life. The earliest towns to flourish were in the valley of the Rhine, a natural trade route. Cologne led the way, causing the contemporary Otto of Freising to call it the richest city in Germany or Gaul. Mainz, Frankfurt, Strassburg, and Basel were rivals. Later, the towns closer to the heart of modern Germany rose to prominence, Hamburg and Bremen on the North Sea, Lubeck on the Baltic, and Frankfurt on the Oder River. Still later came Königsberg and Danzig in far-off Prussia. Some of these towns joined together in leagues for mutual protection and advantage in the thirteenth and fourteenth century. They were able to do so because, like the towns of Italy, they were virtually independent of higher authority.

The greatest of the leagues was the Hanseatic League, begun in the 1260's, formally organized in 1367, and not dissolved for some 250 years. At its height, this League comprised almost eighty towns scattered across northern Germany from the Rhine to beyond the Vistula. Besides Cologne, Hamburg, Bremen, Lubeck, and Danzig, these included such towns as Hanover, Dortmund, and Magdeburg. The League was, in effect, an alliance or loose confederation whose purpose was to secure trade monopolies, hunt out new areas of exploitation (it even founded new towns) and see that each member town benefited proportionately from the lucrative northern trade. It even had a species of government and carried on military campaigns. In the years of economic decline, the Hanseatic towns were not unaffected but their League did much to cushion the shock.

The Merchants of Bruges

The focal point of all European trade was first Bruges, later Antwerp in the Low Countries. There the northern and southern routes met and merchants gathered from everywhere to do business. Bruges replaced the Champagne fairs as the chief meeting place of merchants during the first half of the fourteenth century. The fairs declined for several reasons. Champagne was now in the hands of the French crown, which was not nearly so liberal in its tax policies as the counts had been. Furthermore, France and England were engaged in the ruinous Hundred Years' War, and the Champagne area was the scene of sporadic fighting. Most important, however, the fairs had been rendered obsolete by new trade routes and new methods of transportation. With the introduction of the sea-going galley by Venice around 1300, goods in large quantity could be carried by way of the Mediterranean, Atlantic, and English Channel to and from Italy and Flanders and England. The old overland passage through Champagne lost its former preeminence, though other transalpine routes continued to be used. At Bruges, the merchants founded *fondachi,* "countinghouses," and received many privileges from local authorities. Bruges was a "free" port with few restrictions to hamper business activities. Indeed, it was a foreigners' town, where Italians, Germans, French, Aragonese, Catalonians, and English bought, sold, and exchanged their wares on equal terms with the native Flemish.

The merchants who congregated at Bruges were a far cry from the dusty peddlers who travelled the roads of Europe with packs on their backs and settled the *faubourgs* in an earlier day. Nor were they like the traders who first visited the Champagne fairs. Rather, the new merchant was a capitalist entrepreneur who managed his affairs from his countinghouse. Most of his transactions were done on paper with bills of exchange (promissory notes) and letters of credit. Enterprises were usually undertaken by groups of such men, each man becoming a shareholder in an association resembling our modern stock company. This permitted large-scale ventures with small individual investment and limited risk and is evidence of rising overhead and of the evolution of more sophisticated business practices. It may also be evidence of a more cautious outlook in the business community perhaps prompted by the incipient depression. Certainly the day of the daring individual, the gambler who took great chances for great profits, was passing. The merchants of Bruges were of medium wealth, apparently satisfied to remain that way.

Nevertheless, they were clearly motivated by a desire for gain. This was contrary to Christian principle, which had always emphasized the doctrine of the "just price," that nothing should be sold for more than its worth. Worth was determined by adding to the cost of production a sum to provide the workman a living wage. It did not include a percentage for a "middle man," and certainly none for pure profit. Usury, lending money at interest, was strictly prohibited. Commerce and banking, even on a mediocre scale, were simply not valid pursuits for good Christians. In changed social circumstances, the older ethic was bound to change. The great thirteenth century scholastics, Thomas Aquinas and Duns Scotus, argued that a businessman deserved a fair return for the risks he took and other writers went further. They even found certain cases where interest taking might not be sinful, though the question of usury remained a sticky one well into early modern times. Merchants themselves, however, were imbued from childhood with a more rigorous, old-fashioned view, and many of them sought to salve their consciences in their later years by good works and philanthropy.

INDUSTRY AND THE CRAFT GUILDS

The merchant's profession was not confined only to buying and selling in the late Middle Ages. In a few areas, notably Italy and Flanders, where the cloth industry was highly developed, merchant-industrialists manufactured the goods they sold. They bought the raw wool and the materials needed to finish it, parcelled them out to workers at home or gathered together in a factory building, and marketed the finished product. Cloth-making was particularly well-suited to this development because it was made up of many separate processes: weaving, dying, fulling, shearing, and so on. Workers specialized in each process and could be hired on a time or piece-rate basis. One such entrepreneur we know of was Jean Boine Broke, a "draper" (*drapier*) of Douai in Flanders during the second half of the thirteenth century. Boine

Broke operated a large establishment with salaried labor and also used the "putting out" system. He was a man of wealth and political power, an influential member of the guild merchant of Douai and a town councilman several times. He was the prototype of our modern captain of industry. There were others like him, especially in the city of Florence, but they constituted a relatively minor part of European industry.

The Craft Guilds

Most industry was of the handicraft type, the artisans organized into craft guilds. This period was the great age of the craft guilds, of their proliferation and their social and economic influence. We have already discussed the organization of the guild merchant and noted that the craft guild sprang from it as local manufacturing prospered under the influence of expanding commerce. The guild merchant as it matured tended to become aristocratic and exclusive, its membership restricted to the great merchants engaged in long distance trade. Usually, too, the guild merchant dominated the town government, setting political and economic policies fashioned in their own interest. The craft guilds were organized in response to this situation. They were composed of the small businessmen, the artisans and storekeepers catering to the local market. Their purpose was to secure the most favorable economic conditions for their members: monopoly of sales, and the right to fix prices and regulate entrance requirements and working conditions. They naturally came into conflict with the merchant governors, who as consumers and employers of labor preferred that the local market remain competitive. On the other hand, the town's lord, the count, the duke, or king, encouraged the formation of craft guilds to balance the political strength of the guild merchant. Usually the conflict resolved itself in compromise. The craft guilds received the privileges they wanted, and the town authorities insisted they maintain fair prices and adequate standards of quality. Paris saw the proliferation of over one hundred such guilds and the Flemish towns almost as many; the influence of the kings of France and the counts of Flanders is evident here. In England, the crown permitted guilds everywhere and regulated them strictly in the public interest.

The craft guild from its origins was an association of masters. Each master was a full member with the right to take part in determining guild policy. He was also a skilled artisan who had proven his abilities by years of training and perhaps the production of a "masterpiece." He might be a baker, a shoemaker, a saddler, or a goldsmith or armorer. Usually the nature of his craft determined his social standing; a butcher, for example was several rungs below a shoemaker, who was himself the social inferior of a physician. The guilds, however, were not like modern trade unions; rather, they were associations of independent businessmen, each of whom labored for himself with the help of one or more apprentices and perhaps a journeyman or two. Apprentices were young men, often the master's sons or nephews, entrusted to his care and instruction. They probably lived in his house as members of his family. They came to him at a very tender age, ten or twelve, and were put to work at simple tasks. It was excellent preparation and produced artisans of great skill. Journeymen (from the French *journée*, meaning "day") were salaried workers, former apprentices awaiting entrance to full guild membership.

Conditions in the workshops of the artisans were generally good. Often the artisans lived where they worked, in rooms behind the workshop and store. The latter fronted on the street, and was perhaps equipped with a large opening, covered by a wooden awning which could be raised in good weather. A shelf might be attached on which wares could be displayed. Hours, because artificial light was lacking, would be from sunup to sunset, six days a week. Prices, as we have said, were established by the guilds in collaboration with municipal authorities, as were the standards of quality. Failure to comply resulted in a fine or even expulsion from guild membership. Therefore, there was small opportunity for a craft guildsman to become rich. Instead, he had security of job and status. Moreover, he was a contributor to the common good, a functional being like a knight, a priest, or a peasant. In this respect, the craftsman much more than the merchant fulfilled the medieval social ideal.

In the early days of the craft guild, entrance to the masters' ranks was fairly simple, for there was a need for workers to satisfy the continually increasing demand for goods. Most young apprentices could hope to attain full guild membership at a reasonably early age. By the fourteenth century, however, the demand for goods had begun to fall off. At the same time the movement of peasants from the country filled the towns with potential workers. The mid-century depression turned the gradual stagnation of the market into a precipitate decline. These things confused and frightened the masters, for it upset their carefully regulated industry. They drew their guild membership about themselves like a protective cloak. A great historian has written:

The first half of the fourteenth century was the period when handicrafts reached their apogee. But as they evolved, the two essential features of their constitution—monopoly and privilege—naturally became more and more prominent. Each group of artisans racked its brains to increase, and to go on increasing, the protectionism that surrounded it like a fortress.[3]

Admission to guild membership was made more difficult. The apprenticeship period was lengthened and requirements made more rigorous. Entrance fees were introduced and in some cases made prohibitive, and standards for the masterpiece were made impossibly exacting. The masters sought refuge in corporatism, in group resistance. Naturally enough, their actions raised the ire of nonguildsmen, whether merchants, churchmen, or lowly journeymen and there were voices raised to disband the guilds. The helpless journeymen increased in numbers even as their hopes for relief dimmed; indeed in some of the more highly industrialized towns a true proletariat of wage workers appeared. The journeymen organized associations of their own, hoping to

[3] H. Pirenne, *A History of Europe,* "Anchor" edition (Doubleday: New York), p. 101.

attain in concert what they could not attain individually. We find a few examples of journeymen going on strike. But the merchants and artisans buried their own differences in the face of such danger. Everywhere journeymen's associations and striking were declared illegal.

SOCIAL UNREST AND REVOLUTION

The ingredients of conflict were at hand. And, beginning at the end of the thirteenth century, insurrections occurred sporadically in Europe as the lower classes of country and town rose up to challenge their betters. Some of these insurrections were simply mindless outbursts of anger and resentment. Others had organization, leadership, ideas, and clear aims. A few succeeded in laying waste a rural area or in controlling an urban government but only briefly. The forces of royalty, nobility, and patriciate were too strong in the long run. It was not yet the time for social equality and democracy. Each insurrection had its own immediate causes, a bad harvest, a rise in unemployment, a sudden heavy tax levy. But all originated in the profound social, economic, and political changes which were taking place in the fourteenth century. These changes created tension, fear, insecurity, and in some cases real physical hardships among the uncomprehending masses of people. They also improved the lot of some and made them want more. Rebellion was, on the one hand, a way to fight back, a way to restore the good old days when manorial life was safe and secure and town life held promise. On the other hand, rebellion was a means to secure gains won and perhaps add to them. We can only examine very briefly a few of the most typical insurrections, the *Jacquerie* of 1358 in France, the Peasants' Revolt of 1381 in England, and the urban uprisings in Flanders in the late thirteenth and fourteenth centuries.

The Jacquerie

The *Jacquerie* (a term probably derived from *jacque,* the peasant's jerkin) was an expression of a peasantry outraged and frustrated by the destruction of war. It took place in the neighborhood of Paris where French and English armies had devastated the land and where bands of unemployed mercenaries called *écorcheurs* had continued to burn and rob even after the fighting had ended. Many local landlords had made league with the marauders, and the wrath of the peasants was directed against these. The peasants, badly armed and unled, roved through the countryside, setting fire to manor houses and murdering their occupants, often with horrible brutality. This was as far as their planning went, however, and they were put down with ease by the crown. Many peasants were massacred.

The Peasants' Revolt

The English Peasants' Revolt was much more rational in its motivation. It was the culmination of many years of peasant unrest traceable to efforts by the king and Parliament, under pressure of the landlords, to protect and restore the landlords' privileges. The Black Death, as we have seen, left fewer workers with higher wages in its wake. Government legislation tried to turn back the clock by prescribing wages and working conditions at a pre-plague level. The peasants resisted: they saw an opportunity to bargain with their lord, to take advantage of his economic difficulties to achieve greater freedom and even perhaps become property owners themselves. From fairly reasonable demands, elimination of the remaining banalities, for example, they turned to an attack on the entire social system. Many of the malcontents were true levelers, who asked:

> Whanne Adam dalfe and Eve span,
> Who was thanne a gentilman?

Riots and mob action broke out in various parts of England in the summer of 1381, the spark apparently a poll tax introduced the year before. Leaders like Wat Tyler appeared. The lower classes of London lent their support, and a frightened king granted concessions in a charter of liberty. But reaction was swift, as all propertied groups joined together. The charter was repudiated, and soldiers and the courts finished the work of suppression and punishment.

Urban Revolutions

Urban revolution in these years generally took two forms. One set shopkeepers and artisans, the craft guildsmen, against merchant patricians for the prize of town government. The other set wage workers against the property-owning classes. The second is well illustrated by the *Ciompi* revolt of poor wool carders who achieved a moment of victory and political power in Florence at the end of the 1370's. The uprising in 1382 of journeymen in the cloth and metal trades at Rouen was bloody and unsuccessful. Rebellions by craft guildsmen occurred in many places, notably in Italy, where a number of guild constitutions were introduced. In Paris, in 1382, the men of lesser guilds, led by the butchers, rose against the patrician governors in protest against a sales tax. Barricades were thrown up, foreshadowing many later Parisian revolts and the city was taken over for a short time.

In the towns of Flanders where industrial progress was far advanced, the guildsmen began to contend for political rights in the first part of the thirteenth century and continued to do so for more than two hundred years. After 1300, the issues broadened to include the king of France. The guildsmen aligned themselves with the Count of Flanders, the patrician governors with the king who had annexed the county. In 1302 the proud cavalry of Philip the Fair was soundly beaten at Courtrai by a motley army of artisans and shopkeepers. The patricians' power was broken and the victorious guildsmen received a share in the government. In later Flemish revolutions the figure of Jan van Artevelde of Ghent looms large. Virtual dictator of the Flemish towns from 1337 to 1345, his seizure of power is more properly attributable to industrial troubles arising from the Hundred Years' War, specifically a threatened English embargo on export of raw wool, than to the ambitions of the craft guildsmen.

ECONOMIC REVIVAL

The revival of Europe's economy, like its earlier decline, is difficult to focus on. It was probably underway by the mid-fifteenth century in some places and the improved political situation of the next two generations accelerated it. It seems clear, however, that where economic progress had gone furthest prior to the decline, revival was slowest. In Italy, Flanders and the Hanseatic towns, a mature commerce and industry adjusted to change only with difficulty and on the whole without complete success. Italy was victim of forces beyond its control: northern economic expansion, the advance of the Turks in the Near East, and new trade routes. The old textile towns of Flanders suffered from their own shortsightedness. The protectionism with which their businessmen surrounded themselves stifled new growth, and Flemish industry moved to freer towns and into the countryside where cheaper labor, fewer legal restrictions and waterpower to run machines were available. The north German Hanse towns expanded their trading areas very little after their formal confederation in 1367. Rather, they were content to preserve what they already had. Symptomatic of Flemish and Hanseatic stagnation was the eclipse of Bruges as a commercial and financial center. A part of the reason for Bruges' decline was doubtless the silting up of the mouth of the Wien river which caused the town to lose its value as a port. But equally important was the economic condition of Flanders as a whole and the decline of the Hanse whose members stuck by Bruges to the end. As Bruges went down, Antwerp in neighboring Brabant came up. Antwerp's golden age would arrive with the discovery of new routes to the Far East when the town on the Scheldt would become Europe's spice market.

General economic growth was greatest, then, in those places which had been less well-developed in the thirteenth and early fourteenth centuries, chiefly England, Holland, and southern Germany. English growth was aided by the policies of the crown. On the lookout for sources of income, the crown encouraged business, while regulating it carefully and taxing it. England's principal trade had always been in raw wool, but it was carried on by independent merchants. In the mid-fourteenth century, the crown awarded a monopoly of export to the so-called "Company of the Staple," which all wool merchants joined. Its seat was at Calais, the English port on the French channel coast through which all wool exports passed. There, wool was graded, taxed, and shipped to manufacturers on the continent. Meanwhile, a native textile industry was making great strides, particularly in rural areas, as English manufacturers took advantage of the social and political troubles in the Flemish cities. This industry was in the hands of entrepreneurs who "put out" the raw wool to be worked up by individuals or established factories. These last were located beside streams, for English inventors had developed a means of fulling by waterpower. Many of the workers in these factories were Flemings, fleeing from prosecution or simply attracted by good jobs. By the end of the fifteenth century, England was transformed from primarily an exporter of raw wool to an exporter of finished cloth.

Holland, or more exactly the maritime provinces of the modern Netherlands, then lands of the duke of Burgundy, also began its rise to commercial eminence in these years. Beginning in local and short-distance commerce, the Dutch expanded their activities eastward, becoming serious rivals of the Hanseatic League by 1500. Their primary aim was to secure the carrying trade from the Baltic area to western Europe. They were remarkably successful, becoming within a few generations the virtual monopolists in this field. Hence they were ready to duplicate their feat when Portugal went into the spice business. They became the chief carriers of Portuguese spices from Lisbon to the Antwerp market. The Dutch were also merchants, particularly of the herring caught by their fishermen, salted in a secret way and famous throughout Europe. Finally, the textile industry began to grow in Holland about the same time as in England and for essentially the same reasons. The town of Leiden turned into one of the chief clothmaking towns of Europe.

The Fuggers
The most striking development occurred in the towns of southern Germany, especially Augsburg and Nürnberg where trade and manufacturing prospered and where the first great banking houses of northern Europe made their appearance at the close of the fifteenth century. The decisive influence in the rise of such bankers as the Welsers, Hochstetters, Imholts, and Fuggers, was the discovery of silver in the Tyrol and Hungary. This, on top of profits from regular mercantile activities, provided huge surpluses to lend. The Fuggers were greatest of all. Beginning in the textile trade, they became bankers to popes and kings, building up a capital of over five million gold gulden before their financial alliance with Spain proved their undoing. Jacob the Rich (1459-1525) was the business genius who contributed most to the Fuggers' success by first entering into the political affairs of the Habsburgs. Jacob provided the money to buy votes for the election of Charles V as Holy Roman Emperor in 1519 and to pay for Charles' later ventures. In 1560, Charles' son Philip II of Spain owed the Fuggers four million gold gulden. Spain's frequent bankruptcies eventually brought about the firm's decline. The Fuggers, however, for all their wealth, were not so advanced in their business practices as their Italian counterparts. The bank remained throughout its lifetime a closely held family enterprise, dominated by a single family member. Moreover, the Fuggers were not typical of northern businessmen, most of whom operated on a far smaller and less spectacular scale.

FURTHER READING

W. K. Ferguson, *Europe in Transition, 1300-1520* (1962), is thorough on economic matters, but does not attack satisfactorily the problem of the late medieval depression. Indeed, the character, extent, and length of the depression are far from settled; see the essays by M. M. Postan and R. Lopez in the *Cambridge Economic History*, Vol. II. Still useful, though lacking in recent scholarship, is J. W. Thompson, *Economic and Social History of the Late Middle Ages* (1931). The English economy has been most thoroughly studied; see, for example, E. E. Power and M. M. Postan, eds., *Studies in English Trade in the Fifteenth Century* (1941), and E. M. Carus-Wilson, *Medieval Merchant Adventurers* (1954). On other places, the following have value: J. Streider, *Jacob Fugger the Rich* (1932); R. de Roover, *Money, Banking, and Credit in Medieval Bruges* (1948); and H. S. Lucas, *The Low Countries and the Hundred Years War* (1929). An aspect of the fifteenth-century French economy is treated in A. B. Kerr, *Jacques Coeur* (1928). On social questions, see E. Levett and A. Bumard, *The Black Death* (1946), and P. Lindsay and R. Groves, *The Peasants' Revolt, 1381* (1950).

Advanced Reading

GENERAL WORKS

The student of history is fortunate in having available a guide to all *major* works currently in print and widely used in his profession. This is the *Guide to Historical Literature,* prepared by the American Historical Association under the direction of George F. Howe (1961). It can be supplemented by bibliographies and reviews found in current learned journals, particularly *The American Historical Review* (quarterly) and the *Journal of Modern History* (quarterly). Every major country has, in addition, historical reviews for more specialized information.

The chief guide to reference works, a kind of bibliography of bibliographies, is Constance M. Winchell, *Guide to Reference Books* (1951). Among advanced encyclopedias the *Encyclopaedia Britannica* will prove to be particularly useful. Every major country has, however, an encyclopedia and these are valuable for information about the country in question. *The Encyclopedia of the Social Sciences* is extremely helpful to the student of history who is interested in determining the forces which make men behave as they do. This work appeared between 1930 and 1935 but is currently being revised.

Every major nation has its own biographical dictionary, its own statistical yearbook, collection of parliamentary papers, and other papers, all of which are of utmost importance to the student of history.

Useful publications for keeping abreast of recent events are: *Facts on File: A Weekly World News Digest,* which has a cumulative index; *The Statesman's Yearbook: Statistical and Historical Annual of the States of the World;* and *L'Année politique.*

Of the great comprehensive histories, attention should be called to the *Propyläen Weltgeschichte,* 10 vols. (1963); Maurice Crouzet, ed., *Histoire générale des civilizations,* 7 vols. (1953–1959); *Peuples et civilisations,* 20 vols. (1926–1960); *The Cambridge Ancient History,* 8 vols. (1923–1939); *Cambridge Medieval History,* 8 vols. (1911–1936); *The Cambridge Modern History,* 16 vols. projected (1957 ff); and William L. Langer, ed., *The Rise of Modern Europe,* 20 vols. projected (1934 ff).

The following suggestions on various aspects of the past may be useful for introduction to certain fields: in archaeology, Glyn E. Daniel, *A Hundred Years of Archaeology* (1950), and V. G. Childe, *Piecing Together the Past* (1956); economic history, Shepard B. Clough, *The Economic Development of Western Civilization* (1959), and *The Cambridge Economic History,* 3 vols. and others projected (1942–1963 ff). On political thought, see George H. Sabine, *A History of Political Theory* (1955); on military affairs, B. H. Liddell Hart, *The Decisive Wars of History* (1929); J. F. C. Fuller, *A Military History of the Western World,* 3 vols. (1954–56), and Theodore Ropp, *War in the Modern World* (1962). On intellectual history, see J. H. Randall, Jr., *The Making of the Modern Mind* (1954); and on art, Helen Gardner, *Art Through the Ages* (1959).

For an introduction to anthropology see Alfred L. Kroeber, *Anthropology: Race, Language, Culture, Psychology, Pre-History* (1948); Ralph Linton, *The Study of Man* (1945); and Clyde Kluckhohn, *Mirror of Man* (1949); to sociology, John P. Gillin, ed., *For a Science of Social Man: Convergences in Anthropology, Psychology, and Sociology* (1954) and Robert K. Merton, *Social Theory and Social Structure* (1957); to psychology, Gardner Murphy, *Historical Introduction to Modern Psychology* (1949); Gordon W. Allport, *Personality: A Psychological Interpretation* (1937), and Otto Klineberg, *Tensions Affecting International Understanding* (1950).

For an understanding of the role of resources in history, see Erich W. Zimmermann, *World Resources and Industries* (1951); for demography and population, see Alexander M. Carr-Saunders, *World Population: Past Growth and Present Trends* (1936); for the history of science, George A. L. Sarton, *Introduction to the History of Science,* 3 vols. (1927–1948) and René Taton, ed., *Histoire générale des sciences,* 3 vols. (1957 ff); for the history of technology, see Charles J. Singer and others, eds., *A History of Technology,* 5 vols. (1954–1958); for medicine, Richard H. Shryock, *The Development of Modern Medicine* (1936); for agriculture, B. H. Slicher Van Bath, *The Agrarian History of Western Europe A.D. 500–1850* (1963); and for literature, Joseph T. Shipley, ed., *Dictionary of World Literature: Criticism, Forms, Techniques* (1953).

I. *THE BEGINNING OF CIVILIZATION*

1. THE APPEARANCE OF CIVILIZATION. Interesting discussions of early intellectual developments and institutions are found in H. Frankfurt, **Kingship and the Gods* (1948) and **Before Philosophy* (1949), as well as W. F. Albright, **From the Stone Age to Christianity* (1946), though the latter concentrates primarily on later developments, particularly in Palestine. For the scientific achievements of the ancient Orient, see O. Neugebauer, *The Exact Sciences in Antiquity* (1952).

L. Delaporte, *Mesopotamia* (1925), is still useful and so are A. Moret, *The Nile and Egyptian Civilization* (1928), and A. Moret and Davy, *From Tribe to Empire* (1926), in which the emergence of historical Egypt is studied in great detail. See also H. E. Winlock, *The Rise and Fall of the Middle Kingdom at Thebes* (1947).

Excellent illustrations of the art of the ancient Orient are found in J. Capart, *Egyptian Art* (1923), the Skira edition of *Egyptian Painting* (1954) by A. Mek-

---

* Books existing in paperback editions will be indicated with an asterisk.

hitarian, and particularly A. Parrot, *Sumer the Dawn of Art* (1961). An exciting if occasionally controversial analysis is given in E. B. Smith, *Egyptian Architecture as Cultural Expression* (1938).

2. THE CREATION OF EMPIRES. As in the case of the period discussed in the previous chapter, new material is continually being uncovered by excavations and published in monographs and learned journals.

A very good survey of the whole of western Asia is given by B. Hrozny, *Histoire de l'Asie Antérieure* (1947), and E. Dhorme, *Les Religions de Babylonie et d'Assyrie* (2nd ed., 1949) is very useful. For the peripheral area of Asia Minor, the best work available is G. Conteneau, *La Civilisation des Hittites et des Hurrites du Mitanni* (1934), but enormous amounts of work have been done recently by Russian scholars, most of which is still inaccessible to western readers.

Most of the important texts and inscriptions of the period have been published: S. Mercer, *The Amarna Letters*, 2 vols. (1939); A. Piankoff, **The Shrine of Tut-Ankh-Amon* (1955), with all the inscriptions; D. D. Luckenbill, *Ancient Records of Assyria and Babylonia*, 2 vols. (1926-7).

The art of the period has now been made available in a series of magnificent publications: E. Akurgal, *The Art of the Hittites* (1962); A. Parrot, *The Art of Assyria* (1961); and R. Girshman, *Persian Art* (1962).

3. THE SMALL NATIONS AND THE MEDITERRANEAN EMPIRE. For further studies on particular aspects of Semitic culture, see S. A. Cook, *The Religion of Ancient Palestine in the Light of Archaeology* (1930); R. Dussaud, *Les Religions des Hittites, des Phéniciens et des Syriens* (2nd ed., 1949) and *Les Découvertes de Ras-Shamra et l'Ancien Testament* (1937); G. Conteneau, *La Civilisation phénicienne* (1926); and R. Macalister, *The Philistines* (1913).

The fundamental work on the excavations in northern Crete remains A. Evans, *The Palace of Minos*, 6 vols. (1921-1936), though some aspects of it have recently been questioned, and Schliemann's own account of his discovery of *Mycenae* (1878) is still exciting to read. C. W. Blegen, *Troy and the Trojans* (1963), is a much needed account by a great specialist.

On the problems of Homer and of Mycenaean civilization the following work can be consulted with profit: W. Leaf, *Homer and History* (1915) and *Troy, A Study in Homeric Geography* (1912); M. P. Nilsson, *Homer and Mycenae* (1932) and *The Mycenaean Origin of Greek Mythology* (1932); also R. Carpenter, **Folk Tale, Fiction and Saga in the Homeric Epic* (1946).

Minoan and Mycenaean art are well presented in M. H. Swindler, *Ancient Painting* (1929), and S. Marinatos, *Crete and Mycenae* (1960).

II. *THE CLASSICAL WORLD*

1. ARCHAIC AND CLASSICAL GREECE. Particular aspects of Greek history are treated in A. Andrews, *The Greek Tyrants* (1956); K. Freeman, *The Work and Life of Solon* (1926); and W. S. Ferguson, *Greek Imperialism* (1913). On the

Athenian Constitution the work of C. Hignett, *The Athenian Constitution* (1952), should be consulted, and on political theory, E. Barker, *Greek Political Theory* (4th ed., 1951).

The classic work on Greek ideals, culture and education is W. Jaeger, *Paedeia,* 3 vols. (1939–1944). Particular aspects of special interest are treated in R. Carpenter, *The Esthetic Basis of Greek Art* (1959), and E. R. Dodds, *The Greeks and the Irrational* (1957). All aspects of Greek education are studied in H. Marrou, *Histoire de l'education dans l'Antiquité* (1948). Purely Athenian manifestations are described in G. M. Calhoun, *The Business Life of Ancient Athens* (1926), and A. W. Pickard-Cambridge, *The Dramatic Festivals of Athens* (1953). On Magna Graecia, the best book is still T. J. Dunbabin, *The Western Greeks* (1948).

2. THE HELLENISTIC WORLD. The fundamental work for the Hellenistic period is M. Rostovtzeff's monumental *Social and Economic History of the Hellenistic World,* 3 vols. (1941). No new studies have yet replaced E. Bevan, *The House of Seleucus* (1902) and *A History of Egypt under the Ptolemaic Dynasty* (1927), or A. Bouché-Leclercq, *Histoire des Lagides,* 4 vols. (1903–7) and *Histoire des Seleucides,* 2 vols. (1913–4), or again E. Meyer, *Blüte und Niedergang des Hellenismus in Asien* (1925). For the administration of the East, the main work is E. Bickerman, *Les Institutions des Seleucides* (1938). A more recent study of a minor Hellenistic state is E. Hansen, *The Attalids of Pergamon* (1947). S. E. Eddy, *The King is Dead* (1961), is an interesting study of the reaction against Hellenization, particularly in Palestine. The books of E. Bickerman on the period of the Macabees mentioned in Part I, Chapter 3, should also be consulted.

The clash between Rome and the Greeks in the East is treated by M. Holleaux, *Rome, la Grèce et les monarchies hellenistiques au IIIe siècle avant J.C.* (1921). Particular moments in Rome's imperial expansion are studied in H. H. Scullard, *Scipio Africanus in the Second Punic War* (1930), and F. W. Walbank, *Philip V of Macedon* (1940). T. R. S. Broughton, *The Magistrates of the Roman Republic,* 2 vols. (1951–2) is a definitive study of the subject.

Volume I of T. Frank and others, *An Economic Survey of Ancient Rome* (1933), is devoted to the republican period, and N. Lewis and M. Reinhold, *Roman Civilization I, The Republic* (1951), is an admirable collection of texts illustrating every aspect of the life of the Republic. A very useful survey of Roman historiography is also to be found at the beginning of this volume.

3. THE ROMAN EMPIRE. The main works on the economic and social structure of Roman society are M. Rostovtzeff, *Social and Economic History of the Roman Empire* (1926), and T. Frank and others' monumental *Economic Survey of Ancient Rome,* 5 vols. (1936–1940), which discusses the Empire province by province. Lewis and Reinhold's *Roman Civilization II, The Empire* (1955) has the same standard of excellence as the first volume mentioned in the preceding chapter. Of great interest also are the more specialized studies of M. P. Charlesworth, *Trade-Routes and Commerce of the Roman Empire* (2nd ed., 1926); C. Goodfellow, *Roman Citizen-*

ship (1935); A. M. Duff, *Freedmen in the Early Roman Empire* (1928); and R. M. Barrow, *Slavery in the Roman Empire* (1928).

For the military structure of the Empire, see H. Parker, *The Roman Legions* (1928); C. Starr, *The Roman Imperial Navy* (1941); and M. Durry, *Les Cohortes prétoriennes* (1938).

The main introductions to Roman literature are J. Duff's *A Literary History of Rome from the Origins to the Close of the Golden Age* (3rd ed., 1953) and *A Literary History of Rome in the Silver Age* (2nd ed., 1960). Both H. J. Wolff, *Roman Law* (1951), and H. Jolowicz, *Historical Introduction to Roman Law* (2nd ed., 1952), are very useful, and J. Beaujeu, *La Religion romaine à l'apogée de l'Empire* (1955), is a detailed study of the policies of the Antonines. The problems of city-planning and administration are studied by L. Homo, *Rome impériale et l'urbanisme dans l'antiquité* (1951). An interesting discussion of Roman contacts with the outside world is found in M. Wheeler, **Rome Beyond the Imperial Frontier* (1954). On Rome's opponent in the East the only general study is still N. Debevoise, *A Political History of Parthia* (1938).

III. *THE FORCES OF DISRUPTION*

1. THE FORCES OF DISRUPTION. An interesting recent interpretation of the decline of the Empire is R. M. Haywood's, *The Myth of Rome's Fall* (1958). Among the various explanations of this fall, see A. E. R. Boak, *Manpower Shortage and the Fall of the Roman Empire in the West* (1955), and M. Rostovtzeff, "The Decay of the Ancient World and Its Economic Explanation," *Economic History Review II* (1930). A good survey of most recent interpretations is given by N. H. Baynes, "The Decline of Roman Power in Western Europe. Some Modern Explanations," *Journal of Roman Studies XXXIII* (1943).

On the transformations of the Empire in the third and fourth centuries see L. L. Howe, *The Pretorian Prefect from Commodus to Diocletian* (1942); P. Lambrecht, *La Composition du Sénat Romain de Septime Sévère à Dioclétien* (1937); and W. Seston, *Dioclétien et la Tétrarchie* (1946). An interesting symposium on *The Age of Diocletian* was held in 1951 at the Metropolitan Museum of Art in New York and the papers subsequently published.

For the Constantinian empire and the East, the best general works are A. Piganiol, *L'Empire Chrétien* (1947), and O. Seeck, *Le Bas-Empire I, de l'état romain à l'état byzantin 284–476* (1949). See also the bibliographies for Part III, Chapter 2 and Part IV, Chapter 1.

The best work on Rome's great enemy in the East is A. Christiansen, *L'Iran sous les Sassanides* (2nd ed., 1944). L. Halphen, *Les Barbares* (5th ed., 1948), is a particularly interesting survey of early medieval history in terms of successive periods of barbarian invasions.

E. Gibbon's classic, *The Decline and Fall of the Roman Empire,* the best edition of which is that of J. B. Bury (1909–13), but of which extensive excerpts have been published in paperback, can still always be read with pleasure if circumspection.

2. CHRISTIANITY AND THE EMPIRE. A new study of Roman imperial worship has appeared in L. Cerfaux and J. Tondrieu, *Un concurrent du christianisme, le culte des souverains dans la civilisation Graeco-Romaine* (1957).

Various interpretations of the Dead Sea scrolls and of their relation to Christianity can be found in J. Allegro, **The Dead Sea Scrolls* (1956); R. K. Harrison, **The Dead Sea Scrolls: an Introduction* (1961); R. E. Murphy, **The Dead Sea Scrolls and the Bible* (1956); J. Daniélou, **The Dead Sea Scrolls and Primitive Christianity* (1962); and A. Dupont-Sommer, **Essene Writings from Qumran* (1962).

For the early church a fundamental work is F. Foakes-Jackson and K. Lake, *The Beginnings of Christianity*, 5 vols. (1920–1933). See also W. Ramsay, *The Church in the Roman Empire before 170 A.D.* (1893), and G. Bardy *La Conversion au christianisme durant les premiers siècles* (1949). Christian reactions to the imperial control of the church are discussed by K. Setton, *Christian Attitude Towards the Emperor in the Fourth Century* (1941).

The best surveys of Christian literature are P. de Labriolle, *Histoire de la littérature grecque chrétienne*, 3 vols. (1928–1930) and *Histoire de la littérature latine chrétienne* (1920). The great *History of Dogma*, 7 vols. (1896–1905) of A. Harnack should still be consulted. The best collection of Christian sources in English translation is found in P. Schaff and H. Wace, *A Select Library of the Nicene and Post-Nicene Fathers*, series I, 14 vols. (1886–1890); series II, 14 vols. (1890–1900). English translations of the following sources are also available in the *Loeb Classical Library:* St. Augustine, *The Confessions* and *The Apostolic Fathers;* Eusebius, *The Ecclesiastical History;* St. Basil, *Letters;* St. Jerome, *Select Letters,* etc.

The best short treatment of the Manichaean heresy is Ch. Puech, *Le Manichéisme* (1949), and for a recent review of studies on Constantine, see A. Pigagnol, "L'Etat actuel de la question constantinienne," *Historia I* (1950).

IV. *THE NEW SYNTHESES*

1. THE EMPIRE RECREATED. Two excellent discussions of the period of Justinian are to be found in E. Stein, *Histoire du Bas-Empire II* (1949), and B. Rubin, *Das Zeitalter Iustinians* (1961). A. A. Vasiliev, *Justin the First* (1950), argues that some of the policies attributed to Justinian should be traced back to the preceding reign.

L. Halphen, *Charlemagne et l'empire carolingien* (1947), gives a more detailed account and occasionally a different interpretation from that of Fichtenau.

The fundamental work for all the aspects of the church is A. Fliche and V. Martin, *Histoire de l'église,* of which volumes V and VI (1937–8) deal with the Gregorian and Carolingian periods. The important role played by the church in the civilization of the West is studied by G. Schnürer, *Church and Culture in the Middle Ages I* (1956).

Very interesting studies of the persistence of the imperial ideal in the Middle Ages and of the legend of Charlemagne have been made by R. Folz, *L'idée de l'empire en occident du Ve au XIVe siècle* (1953) and *Le souvenir et la légende de Charlemagne dans l'empire germanique mediéval* (1950).

2. THE NEW FORCES. A detailed and very useful bibliographical guide and study of Muslim historical literature is now available in B. Lewis and P. M. Holt, *Historians of the Middle East* (1962). Of great importance for the study of Islam are R. Blachère, *Le Problème de Mahomet* (1952); M. Gaudefroy-Demombynes, *Mahomet* (1957); and the fundamental work of I. Goldziher, *Le Dogme et la loi de l'Islam* (1958). A. Mazahéri, *La vie quotidienne des musulmans au moyen-âge* (1951), is an interesting reconstruction of the period.

For the manoeuvers of the Slavic kingdoms between East and West, see F. Dvornik's *Les Slaves, Byzance et Rome au IXe siècle* (1926).

C. M. Haskin's *Studies in Norman Institutions* (1918) is the basic work on the subject, as is F. Chalandon, *Histoire de la domination normande en Italie et en Sicile,* 2 vols. (1917). A. A. Vasiliev, *The First Russian Attack on Constantinople* (1946), is a most interesting study of the double Viking raid on Constantinople in 860–861.

Byzantine influence on Norman Sicily is studied by O. Demus, *The Mosaics of Norman Sicily* (1950), and can be observed in the publication by P. Toesca of the *Mosaïques de la Chapelle Palatine à Palerme* (1955).

3. FROM MONARCHY TO ANARCHY. The main areas of difficulty for the Byzantine empire are indicated in C. Diehl's *Les Grands problèmes de l'histoire byzantine* (1941). An outline of Byzantine philosophy is provided by B. Tatakis, *La Philosophie byzantine* (1949), and two detailed studies of the eastern church are given by J. Pargoire, *L'Eglise byzantine 527–847* (3rd ed., 1923), and G. Every, *The Byzantine Patriarchate 451–1204* (2nd ed., 1962). The classic work on the relations of Byzantium with the papacy is W. Norden, *Das Papsttum und Byzanz* (1903), and the definitive study on the schism of the ninth century is to be found in F. Dvornik, *The Photian Schism* (1948).

For particular periods of the empire which have received special studies, see J. B. Bury, *The Imperial Administration in the Ninth Century* (1911); R. Schlumberger, *L'Epopée byzantine à la fin du dixième siècle,* 3 vols. (1925); F. Chalandon, *Les Comnènes,* 3 vols. (1912); D. Geneakopoulos, *The Emperor Michael Palaeologus and the West* (1959). J. Longnon, *L'Empire Latin de Constantinople* (1949), is an excellent survey of the crusader states. On the peripheral areas of the empire, see W. Miller, *Trebizond the Last Greek Empire* (1926); D. M. Nicol, *The Despotate of Epiros* (1957); D. Zakythinos, *Le Despotat grec de Morée* (1932, 1953); and A. Gardner, *The Lascarids of Nicaea* (1912).

New studies on the Byzantine social structure are appearing rapidly, see G. Ostrogorsky's excellent, *Pour l'histoire de la féodalité byzantine* (1954), and G. Rouillard, *La Vie rurale dans l'empire byzantin* (1953). However, no collection of documents on social and economic problems in Byzantium has yet been published in western languages though such a compilation has appeared in Russian. W. Heyd, *Histoire du Commerce du Levant au Moyen Age,* 2 vols. (1923), is a detailed study of all aspects of eastern trade. A thorough study of the imperial structure in the tenth century has also been made possible by the translation and study by G. Moravczik, R. J. H. Jenkins and others of Constantine Porphyrogenitus' *De Administrando Imperio,* 2 vols. (1949, 1962), one of the main sources for our knowledge of the period. On the other hand, the translation by J. Mavrogordato of the popular epic, *Digenis Akrites* (1956), gives a glimpse of the military life of the Asia Minor frontier and of Byzantine-Muslim relations in the tenth century.

There are many splendid editions of Byzantine works of art, particularly, D. Talbot Rice, *The Art of Byzantium* (1959). For illustrations of Byzantine buildings in peripheral areas of the empire and examples of Byzantine influence beyond the borders of the Empire, see W. L. MacDonald, *Early Christian and Byzantine Architecture* (1962), and C. Stewart, *Byzantine Legacy* (1947).

The revised edition of the *Cambridge Medieval History,* volume IV which is devoted to the Byzantine empire, is expected to appear in 1964 under the supervision of J. Hussey and should become the first source of reference for the entire field.

V. *THE EMERGENCE OF EUROPE*

1. FEUDALISM AND THE RISE OF FEUDAL MONARCHY. The classic work on English common law is F. Pollock and F. W. Maitland, *The History of English Law before the Time of Edward I,* 2 vols. (2nd ed., 1898). A shorter, more recent treatment is T. F. T. Plucknett, *A Concise History of the Common Law* (5th ed., 1956). F. Olivier-Martin, *Histoire du droit français des origines à la Revolution* (1948), is a standard account for France. On political thought, see C. H. McIlwain, *The Growth of Political Thought in the West* (1932); C. C. J. Webb, *John of Salisbury* (1932); and P. Vinogradoff, *Roman Law in Medieval Europe* (2nd ed., 1929). E. H. Kantorowicz, *The King's Two Bodies: A Study in Medieval Political Theology* (1957), treats an interesting aspect of political theory. A classic, principally on Germany, is O. Gierke, **Political Theories of the Middle Age* (1900).

The standard account of the English monarchy is contained in the *Oxford History of England*: F. M. Stenton, *Anglo-Saxon England* (2nd ed., 1947), and A. L. Poole, *From Doomsday Book to Magna Carta* (2nd ed., 1955). A wider-ranging interpretive work is F. M. Powicke, *Medieval England, 1066-1485* (1948). For France, nothing compares to the relevant volumes of E. Lavisse, *Histoire de France* (1901ff.). See also the somewhat dated but still useful P. Guilhiermoz, *Essai sur les origines de la noblesse en France au moyen âge* (1902), and J. W. Thompson, *The Development of the French Monarchy under Louis VI le Gros* (1895). For Germany, one may compare the interpretations of G. Barraclough, *Medieval Germany, 2 vols.* (1938), with J. W. Thompson, *Feudal Germany* (1928). A standard work on Spain is R. B. Merriman, *The Rise of the Spanish Empire,* vol. I (1918). A brilliant work by a great American medievalist is C. H. Haskins, *The Normans in European History* (1915).

2. MEDIEVAL ECONOMY AND SOCIETY. For more specialized interests, the standard work is now J. H. Clapham, *et al.,* eds., *The Cambridge Economic History,* Vols. I–III. In considering the Pirenne Thesis, the following might be read: A. Dopsch, *The Economic and Social Foundations of European Civilization* (1937); R. Latouche, *Les origines de l'economie occidentale* (1956); F. Lot, *The End of the Ancient World* (1931); and H. St. L. B. Moss, "The Economic Consequences of

the Barbarian Invasions," *The Economic History Review*, VII (May, 1937). W. S. Davis, *Life on a Medieval Barony* (1923), and U. T. Holmes, *Daily Living in the Twelfth Century* (1952), contain material on the economy. Urban development is the subject of C. Stephenson, *Borough and Town* (1933), and J. Tait, *The Medieval English Borough* (1936), both of which are from English sources and should be used to supplement Pirenne's *Medieval Cities*. See also N. Ottokar, *Le città francesi nel medio evo* (1927); J. Lestocquoy, *Les villes de Flandre et d'Italie sous le gouvernement des patriciens* (1952); H. Planitz, *Die deutsche Stadt im Mittelalter* (1954); and H. Pirenne, *Early Democracies in the Low Countries* (1915). An important contribution to the history of economic thought and a model of scholarship is B. N. Nelson, *The Idea of Usury* (1949).

3. THE STRUGGLE FOR LEADERSHIP IN THE WEST. A very thorough treatment of the growing power of the Church after its eclipse in the tenth century is to be found in the relevant volumes of A. Fliche and V. Martin, *Histoire de l'Eglise*, vols. vii–ix (1950, 1953). See also the articles on the Investiture contest in *Studi Gregoriani* (1947—).

When complete, the most extensive history of the Crusades will be K. Setton and M. Baldwin, eds., *A History of the Crusades*, 2 vols. (1955, 1962). The best collection of sources on the Crusades is the multivolume publication of the Academie des Inscriptions et des Belles-Lettres, *Recueil des Historiens des Croisades* (1841–1906). Anna Comnena, *The Alexiad*, tr. A. S. Dawes (1928), and *The Autobiography of Ousâma*, tr. G. R. Potter (1929), give a picture of the Crusaders as seen through contemporary Byzantine and Muslim eyes. For the relations of the Crusaders with the Byzantine empire, the relevant Byzantine studies and sources listed in Part IV, Chapter 1 should also be consulted as well as J. La Monte, "To What Extent was the Byzantine Empire the Suzerain of the Latin Crusading States?" *Byzantion* VII (1936).

4. FEUDAL MONARCHY AT ITS HEIGHT. More specialized studies of England in the thirteenth century include F. M. Powicke, *The Thirteenth Century, 1216–1307* (1953); W. S. McKechnie, *Magna Carta* (1914); and D. Pasquet, *An Essay on the Origins of the House of Commons* (1925). An aspect of English social history is treated in G. C. Homans, *English Villagers of the Thirteenth Century* (1940). A most suggestive study of the changing climate of opinion in the thirteenth century is J. R. Strayer, "Laicization of French and English Society in the Thirteenth Century," *Speculum*, XV (April, 1940). For Germany in this period, see A. L. Poole, *Henry the Lion* (1912), and E. Kantorowicz, *Frederick II* (1931). Imperial constitutional development is the subject of C. C. Bayley, *The Formation of the German College of Electors* (1949). The standard treatment of medieval warfare is C. W. C. Oman, *The Art of War in the Middle Ages* (2nd rev. ed., 1953).

5. THE CHURCH AND MEDIEVAL CULTURE. Longer Church histories include D. S. Schaff, *History of the Christian Church* (1907); P. Hughes, *A History of the Church*, vols. II & III (1935–47); and K. S. Latourette, *A History of Christianity* (1953). A valuable study of an important aspect of the Church as an institution,

with documents, is W. E. Lunt, *Papal Revenues in the Middle Ages,* 2 vols. (1934). A. Luchairé, *Innocent III,* 6 vols. (1905–08) is an exhaustive biography. On the Inquisition, see C. Douais, *L'Inquisition: ses origines, sa procedure* (1906).

H. Rashdall, *The Universities of Europe in the Middle Ages,* 3 vols. (rev. ed., 1936), is the standard work. E. Gilson, *History of Christian Philosophy in the Middle Ages* (1955), is the fruit of years of study. More specialized is H. Marrou, *St. Augustine and His Influence Through the Ages* (1957). The immense research that has gone into L. Thorndike, *A History of Magic and Experimental Science,* 6 vols. (1923 ff), has made it the basic book on the subject. A. C. Crombie, *Grosseteste and the Origins of Experimental Science* (1953), is a more lively account of its subject. A recent study of medieval architecture is O. von Simpson, **The Gothic Cathedral* (1956).

VI. *THE CLOSE OF THE MIDDLE AGES*

1. POLITICS AND THE CHURCH. H. Pirenne, *et al., La fin du moyen âge* (1946), and F. Baethgen, *Europa im Spätmittelalter* (1951) are better than their counterparts in English. For England, the Oxford series now includes M. McKisack, *The Fourteenth Century, 1307–99* (1959), and E. F. Jacob, *The Fifteenth Century, 1399–1485* (1961). More specialized studies include F. Thompson, *A Short History of Parliament, 1295–1642* (1953); S. B. Chrimes, *English Constitutional Ideas in the Fifteenth Century* (1936); A. Steel, *Richard II* (1941); and E. F. Jacob, *Henry V and the Invasion* (1946). For France, the appropriate volumes of E. Lavisse, *Histoire de France* (1901 ff), are unsurpassed.

On the Church, the classic study is L. von Pastor, *History of the Popes,* vols. I–VII (1905–53). A. C. Flick, *The Decline of the Medieval Church,* 2 vols. (1930), is informative, but must be read with a critical eye. G. Mollat, *Les Papes d'Avignon* (1949), contains a complete bibliography on the activities of the Papacy at Avignon. The introductory essays in J. H. Mundy and K. M. Woody, eds., *The Council of Constance* (1961), are based on the most recent scholarship. They should be supplemented with B. Tierney, *Foundations of the Conciliar Theory* (1955). The standard work in the Conciliar Movement is now H. Jedin, *The Council of Trent,* vol. I (1957).

2. ECONOMIC AND SOCIAL DEVELOPMENTS. Among more advanced readings available, R. Koitsche, *Allgemeine Wirtschaftgeschichte des Mittelalters und der Neuzeit,* vol. I (1928), is standard. For differing views on the late medieval depression as well as other economic problems of the period, see M. Mollat, *et al.,* "L'economie europeénne aux deux derniers siècles du moyen âge," *Relazioni del X Congresso Internazionale di Scienze Storiche,* III (1957); E. Perroy, "Les crises du XIVe siècle," *Annales,* IV (1949); and the article by E. Kosminsky in *Studi in Onore di Armando Sapori,* vol. I (1957). Two other articles embodying recent research are A. R. Lewis, "The Closing of the Medieval Frontier," *Speculum,* XXXIII (1958), and H. van Werveke, "Industrial Growth in the Middle Ages: the Cloth Industry in Flanders," *The Economic History Review,* 2nd series, VI (1954). A recent work on the Hanseatic League is K. Pagel, *Die Hanse* (1943).

On social revolution see the following: for the Low Countries, H. Pirenne, *Histoire de Belgique,* vols. I & II (1903), and H. van Werweke, *Jacques van Artvelde* (1943); and for France, Y. le Tabore, *Étienne Marcel et le Paris des marchands au XIV siècle* (1927). The views of a brilliant contemporary may be found in A. T. Sheedy, *Bartolus on Social Conditions in the Fourteenth Century* (1926).

Index

Athens, 64; in Age of Pericles, 67–69; decline of *polis* in, 69–72; defeat of, 71; empire of, 70; growth of democracy in, 64–67

Attila, 121

Augustine, St., 133, 134, 174, 266

Augustus (Octavian), 91, 97–99

Avars, 156, 162, 164, 200

Averroës, 266

Avicenna, 263

Avignon, removal of Popes to, 250, 286–287

Babylon, 20, 40

Bacon, Roger, 267

Baghdad, 158, 161, 181

Banking, rise of, 302

Bannockburn, battle, 242

Barbarians: Angles, Saxons, Jutes, 120; Franks, 120, 121; Germans, 117–118; Goths, 119, 120–121; Huns, 119, 121; Vandals, 119, 120

Barons: English, 240–243; French, 280–281; in later Middle Ages, 279–280

Basil I, Byzantium, 176

Basil II, Emperor, 165

Basil, St., 133

Basileus, the title, 174

Becket, Thomas à, 197

Belisarius, 141–142

Benedict, St., 146, 212, 259

Benedict XI, Pope, 285, 286

Berber tribes, 142

Bernard of Clairvaux, St., 228–229, 230, 260

Besançon, Diet of, 231

Black Death, 292

Bonaventure, 266

Boniface VIII, Pope, 250, 284–286

Book of the Dead, 25

Book of the Prefect, 178

Bordeaux, 294

Bouvines, battle of, 239

Bracton, 192

Britain, Roman province, 120, 121. *See also* England

Broke, Jean Boine, 296–297

Bronze Age, 17–18, 36

Bruce, Robert, 242

Bruges, 295–296, 301

Bulgars, 162, 164, 165

Burgundians, 119, 121

Byzantium, 171–182; administration of, 173–174; cultural isolation of, 174; end of Empire, 179–182; iconoclasm in, 175; Macedonian Dynasty, 176–179; map, 177; opposition to West, 171–172

Caesar, Gaius Julius, 95–97, 117

Calais, in Hundred Years' War, 276–277

Calixtus II, Pope, 224

Cambridge University, 264

Cannae, Roman defeat at, 87

Canute, King, 168

Capet, Hugh, 197–198

Capetians, 197–200, 277

Cardinals, College of, 222

Carolingians, 148–153, 200; Charlemagne, 149–153; Charles Martel, 148; empire of (map), 149; Pepin the Short, 148–149

Carthage, 80, 86; Punic Wars, 86–88

Cassiodorus, 146

Catholic Church. *See* Roman Catholic Church

Causation, and the study of history, 6–7

Cave paintings, 16

Celts, 117

Central Europe: buffer between two halves of Europe, 169; Slavs in, 162

Chaeronea, 71, 72, 74

Chalcedon, Council at, 135

Chaldeans, 40

Champagne, 214, 295

Chanson de Roland, 267

Charlemagne, 149–153; administration of, 152–153; crowned emperor at Rome, 150–151; and Harun ar-Rashid, 151; the man, 153

Charles I, Emperor, *see* Charlemagne

Charles IV, Emperor, 282

Charles V, Emperor, 284, 302

Charles V (France), 277

Charles VI (France), 280

Charles VII (France), 281

Charles Martel, 148, 158

Chartres, cathedral of, 270; cathedral school, 263

Children's Crusade, 227

Chivalry, 267

Christianity: appearance of, 125–128; development of, 129–131; literature of, 133; medieval, 255–262; organization of Church, 131–133; relation to contemporary religions, 128–129; relation to Islam, 157. *See also* Church

Church: anti-papalism, 288; architecture, 269, 300; beliefs of, 255–262; feudalism and, 190–193; growth of "national" churches, 287; and heresy, 134–136, 257–259; Iconoclastic Controversy, 175; Investiture Controversy, 219, 222–224; in later Middle Ages, 275, 284; medieval administration of, 253–255; monasticism, 146–147, 212, 259–260; organization of, 131–132; papacy, 147, 202–203, 219; papal monarchy, 252–255; separation into east and west, 180; and state, 174, 191–192, 219–220, 285–286. *See also* Roman Catholic Church

Church of England, 287

Cicero, 93, 95

Cimbri, 117

Cistercians, 212, 228, 260

City of God, 133

City-states, 61–63; decline of, 69–72

Civilization: appearance of, 11, 13–27; in Asia Minor, 51; Assyrian, 39; Egyptian, 25–27; Greek, 68–69; Hellenic, 77–82; Indo-European, 35–37; imperial Rome, 102–106; Mycenaean, 54–55; Persian, 40–42; primitive Roman, 83; study of, 2

Clarendon, Constitutions of, 197

Cleisthenes, 66

Clement V, Pope, 286

Clement VII, Pope, 287

Cleopatra VII, Queen of Egypt, 97

Clermont, Council of, 225

Clovis, 121, 148

Cluniac reform movement, 212, 221, 259

Cluny, 269

Cologne, 295

Commerce: medieval, 294–296; Roman, 104

Common law, 196; in England, 241, 243; in France, 246–247

Commons, House of, 244, 279

Communication: Assyrian, 39; lack of, under Charlemagne, 152; Persian, 41; Roman, 104

Conciliarism, 289

Confessions, St. Augustine, 133

Conrad I (Germany), 200

Conrad II (Holy Roman Empire), 203

Conrad III (Germany), 229, 236

Constance, Council of, 288, 289

Constance, Peace of, 232

Constantine I, Emperor, 116, 120, 123, 130

Constantine VII, Emperor, 179

Constantinople, 123, 143; attacked by Northmen, 166; center of culture, 171; in the Crusades, 229; fall of, 172, 182

Constantinople, University of, 178

Crécy, battle of, 276

Crete, 49–52; excavations in, 49; Minoan civilization, 51–52; Thalassocracy, 50; sources, 49

Croesus, 48

Cro-Magnon man, 15

Crusades, 162, 214, 225–230; Children's, 227; First, 227–228; Fourth, 229, 253; later, 228–230; People's, 227; significance of, 228

Culture: study of, 2; under feudalism, 267; and the universities, 262–267. *See also* Civilization

Cuneiform writing, 22, 37

Currency, first coined, 48

Cyril, St., 163, 177

Cyrus the Achaemenid, 40

Cyrus the Great, 45

Danelaw, 167–168

Darius the Great, 40, 66

David, King, 45

Dead Sea Scrolls, 127

Delian League, 67, 68, 70

Democracy, in Greece, 64–66, 68

Dictators, Roman, 95, 96

Digenis Akrites, 179

Diocletian, Emperor, 111, 130; persecution of Christians, 130; reforms of, 114–116

Dionysius, 126

Domesday Book, 196

Dominican Order, 260, 262

Dorians, 59

Draconian laws, 64

Duns Scotus, 266, 296

Gregorian chant, 270
Gregory the Great, Pope, 147
Gregory VII, Pope, 204, 253, 259
Gregory IX, Pope, 258
Gregory XI, Pope, 287
Gregory Nazianzenus, St., 133
Guelfs and Ghibellines, 230, 236
Guilds: craft, 296–299; guild merchant, 216–217, 297
Guti, 20

Habsburgs, 281, 283–284
Hadrian, Emperor, 101–102, 127
Haghia Sophia, 179
Hammurabi, 20; Code of, 22
Hannibal Barca, 87
Hanseatic League, 295, 301
Harold, King of England, 195
Harun ar-Rashid, 151, 161
Hastings, battle of, 168, 195
Hatshepsut, Queen, 30
Hebrews, 43–46
Heidelberg man, 15
Hellenes, 54. *See also* Greece
Hellenic League, 74
Hellenistic civilization, 77–80
Henry I (England), 196
Henry II (England), 196–197, 200, 238
Henry II (France), 203
Henry III (England), 239, 241–242
Henry III (Germany), 203, 221
Henry IV (England), 280
Henry IV (Germany), 223
Henry V (England), Prince Hal, 280–281
Henry V (Germany), 224, 236
Henry VI (England), 281
Henry VI (Germany), 232, 237
Henry VII (Germany), 281–282
Heresy, Christian, 134–136; Arianism, 135; Gnosticism, 134–135; medieval, 257–259; Nestorianism, 135
Herodotus, 60, 69
Hesiod, 60–61
Hildebrand (Gregory VII, Pope), 222–224
History: and archaeology, 14–16; beginnings of, 13–14; medieval writing of, 268; problems of, 6–8; Roman writing of, 105; study of, 1–2

Hittites, 31, 34, 36, 37, 45, 54
Holland, *see* Netherlands
Holy Roman Empire: at end of 11th century (map), 201; after death of Frederick II (map), 238; under Charles IV, 282–283; relation to papacy, 223–224
Homer, 52
Horace, 99
Hortensian Law, 85
Hospitallers, 228
House of Lords, 244
Hundred Years' War, 200, 275–281
Hungary, settled by Magyars, 165, 200
Huns, 119, 121, 164
Hurrite Kingdom, 37
Hus, Jan, 288
Hyksos, 23, 27

Iberian Peninsula, *see* Spain
Iconoclastic Controversy, 175
Iliad, 52
Indo-Europeans, 35, 59
Indulgences, theory and sale of, 254, 256–257
Industry: craft guilds, 296–299; revival of, in Middle Ages, 213–216; Roman, 104
Innocent III, Pope, 219, 232–233, 239–240, 241, 252, 261; and Albigensians, 258; Fourth Lateran Council, 253, 255
Inquisition, 258–259
Inventions: chariot, 27; early, 17–18; mounted troops, 118; of writing, 21–22
Investiture Controversy, 219, 222–224
Ionia, 60
Iron, first use of, 36
Irrigation, Egyptian, 24, 26
Isis, cult of, 126
Islam, 145, 157; Crusades and, 225–230; effects of conquest, 160–162; empire of the Caliphs (map), 159; expansion of, 158–162
Israel, ancient, 45
Issus, 74, 78
Italy: Etruscans, 82; Greek colonies in, 81–82; Roman history, 82–89, 97–102; trade in Middle Ages, 214, and late Middle Ages, 294–296

213; feudalism vs. monarchy in, 234–251; learning in, 262–267; literature of, 267–268; manors, 206–208, (plan of) 207; principal towns of (map), 215; revival of urban life in, 213–216; rural life in, 209–211; town government, 216–217

Medina, 157

Mediterranean Sea, 57; controlled by Arabs, 161; recovered by West, 213–214; Western, 80–89

Megiddo, 37

Menander, 78

Menes, 23

Merovingians, 148

Mesopotamia, 18–23

Metals, age of, 15, 17–18

Methodius, 163, 177

Michael I Paleologue, 181

Middle Ages, early: architecture, 269–271; art, 268–271; Church, 190–193; literature, 267–268; manorialism, 206–208; music, 270–271; rural life, 209–211; universities, 262–267. *See also* Feudalism, Medieval Europe, Middle Ages (close)

Middle Ages, close of: breakdown of manorialism, 293–294; Church, 275, 284–289; commerce, 294–296; economic decline, 292; economic revival, 301–302; fall in population, 291–292; monarchy, 277–284; social unrest, 299–300

Middle class, under feudalism, 193, 198

Milan, 231

Milan, Edict of, 130

Minoan civilization, 49–52

Minos, King, 49

Mitanni, 37

Mithra, worship of, 126

Mithridates, 94

Monarchy: conflict in feudalism, 234–235; in France, 245–251; growth of in England, 238–245; in later Middle Ages, 277–284

Monasteries: in medieval Europe, 212; reform of, 259–262

Monasticism, 146–147

Mongols, 162, 164

Monte Cassino, 146

Montfort, Simon de, 242, 244

Muhammed, 157

Music, medieval church, 270–271

Muslims, Mohammedans, *see* Islam

Mycenae, 53–55

Mystery cults, Roman, 126

Naram Sin, 20

Nebuchadrezzar II, 40, 45

Nefertiti, 31

Neolithic Age, 15–17

Neolithic Revolution, 15, 16–17

Neo-Platonists, 126

Nero, 99, 100

Nestorius, 135

Netherlands, the, medieval commerce, 301–302

Nicaea, Council of, 132, 135, 175

Nicholas I, Pope, 220

Nile River, 24

Nineveh, 38–39

Nominalism, 265

Normans, 156, 168–169

Northmen, 165–169; expansion of (map), 167; fragmentation of Europe by, 169

Octavian, *see Augustus*

Odyssey, 52

Old Stone Age, 15

Ostrogoths, 119, 121, 135, 142

Otto I, German Emperor, 165, 201–203, 220

Otto II, German Emperor, 203

Otto III, German Emperor, 203, 220

Otto IV, German Emperor, 237, 253

Ottomans, 179

Oxford, Provisions of, 241–242

Oxford University, 264

Paleolithic Age, 15

Palestine, 40, 126–127, 228. *See also* Israel

Panhellenism, 62–63

Papacy: administration by, 253–254; and the Crusades, 225–230; decline of, 220, 284–289; Fourth Lateran Council, 253; Frederick Barbarossa and, 230–233; French monarchy and, 250–251; growth of anti-papalism, 288; on heresies, 287–289; and Holy Roman Empire, 202–203, 223–224; Investiture Controversy, 219, 222–224; in later Middle Ages, 284; mon-